The Mediterranean Kitchen

JOYCE GOLDSTEIN

Drawings by Rachel Goldstein

Wine Recommendations by Evan Goldstein

WILLIAM MORROW AND COMPANY, INC., NEW YORK

Library of Congress Cataloging-in-Publication Data

Goldstein, Joyce Esersky.
    The Mediterranean kitchen / Joyce Goldstein : wine notes by Evan Goldstein.
        p. cm.
    Includes index.
    ISBN 0-688-07283-6
    1. Cookery, Mediterranean.   I. Title.
TX725.G655   1989   89-34478
641.592833—dc20   CIP

Printed in the United States of America

First Edition

        4 5 6 7 8 9 10

BOOK DESIGN BY JOEL AVIROM

The Mediterranean Kitchen
CONTENTS

ACKNOWLEDGMENTS
7

A PERSONAL NOTE
9

INTRODUCTION
13

APPETIZERS
17

ANTIPASTO AND OTHER MIXED PLATES
37

MEDITERRANEAN-INSPIRED SALADS
55

SOUPS
81

PASTA
107

BEANS, RICE, AND OTHER GRAINS
149

FISH AND SHELLFISH
165

POULTRY
199

MEATS
233

VEGETABLES
301

DESSERTS
317

EVAN'S WINE RECOMMENDATIONS
359

INDEX
397

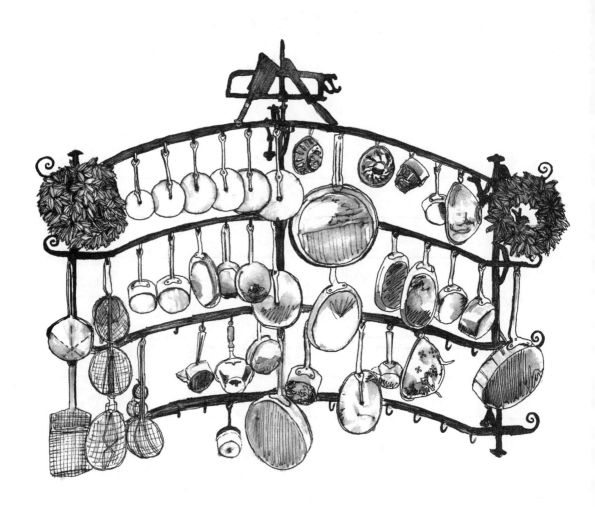

The Mediterranean Kitchen
ACKNOWLEDGMENTS

I always wondered why, on record albums, there were hundreds of lines, set in tiny type, thanking everyone who ever knew the recording artist, down to his grade school teacher, his dentist, and the person who made the grilled cheese sandwiches for the recording sessions. Well, as someone who has just finished a cookbook, I realize that without a cast of hundreds, this book might not be here, either. So I must say thank you to the following people, who contributed their time, energy, love, support, and ideas, and tastebuds.

To my beloved Danny, for being there through the chaos of restaurant life.

To Evan, my son the sommelier, for his wine knowledge and his wine advice, and for making me proud.

To Paul Buscemi, for supervising the kitchen, cooking some of the best damned food in the world, and helping to create some of the signature dishes that are known as Square One, and for his sense of humor and special perspective.

To Ron Chez, for helping me to get Square One off the ground and helping me to keep it aloft; also for sacrificing himself by tasting all the desserts.

To Alice Waters, for giving me my break in show business.

To M.F.K. Fisher, for reminding me that food is more than cooking.

To Rachel, for her artistic soul and her beautiful illustrations.

To Karen, for helping to remind me that even if I am a chef, I am always a mother.

To Ann Bramson, for editorial expertise and a simpatico spirit.

To Maureen and Eric Lasher, for believing in the project and returning my phone calls.

To Bob Simmons, for making me computer literate.

To Barbara Ottenoff, for asking all the right questions.

To Carol Field, for her friendship, her great bread recipes that helped Square One get its rep for the best bread in town, and for bringing me all of those cookbooks from Italy.

To Craig Sutter and Diane Dexter, for helping to get the pastry department on its feet and setting a collective sweet tooth for our restaurant clientele. To Jennifer Millar, Cameron Ryan, and Jerry Tewell, who continue the tradition. To Dan Glazier and David Nussbaum for the bread.

To Suzanne MacDowell and Albert Stachelsky, for helping to transcribe the recipes, and to Gary Woo, Gerald Gass, and Michael Perlov for reading and correcting errant recipes. To our kitchen staff over the years—Wendy and Wendy, Jimmy B., Julia, Tim, Gerald, Ricardo, Ceci, Douglas, Marta, Nora, Michael, and all the rest who tested recipes and tasted and tasted again.

To Vivian Rodriguez, Lesley Hoelper, and Susana Munoz for helping to run the restaurant so smoothly. To our fabulous floor staff, who tasted the food and served it with warmth and enthusiasm. And of course many thanks to our regular Square One customers for their feedback, affection, loyalty, and support.

A PERSONAL NOTE

When I was young I was known as the family's "problem eater." What no one seemed to notice was how well I ate when we went out to restaurants. I would devour huge bowls of steamed clams and a large lobster with no difficulty. I had favorite dishes at the local Chinese restaurants and soon started to travel on the subway to investigate restaurants that served food from France, Italy, India, and the Middle East. All cuisines interested me.

I didn't approach a stove until I was in graduate school at Yale, studying painting with Josef Albers. There I discovered that cooking, my new "hobby," was much like painting, my "career." You combined textures, colors, and "tastes," and the whole, when it worked, was more than the sum of its parts. The palette and the palate were related. And if artists communicated with the public via exhibitions, cooks could communicate in a more direct manner. Cooking brought people together; it was art and it was social. As a shy person, it allowed me to be with people in a relaxed way, because the atmosphere was under my control. I could work and play at the same time.

After the birth of my third child, I realized that I didn't have much time to paint. For me, it was was not something that I could toss off in a half-hour-here, half-hour-there manner. It requires many hours of uninterrupted time. But cooking is flexible. I found that I could accomplish a lot in a short while. A stew can simmer while you take the kids to the park, but a painting cannot.

As my children got older, I had a little more free time. Friends asked me to teach them how to cook. In 1965 I started cooking classes at home, after dinner, when the children were in bed or upstairs playing before bedtime. When they went to school I added day classes that ended at lunchtime so I could be free when the children got home. It was a career that adapted well to the demands of my family life.

As orderly as my life was, I was still the obsessive. I was Mom by day, food maniac by night. I read cookbooks voraciously. Cooking for friends became the testing ground for new recipes, new classes. If I was "into a little Persian cooking" on Monday, they were eating it on Saturday night. My classes expanded. As they became more popular, they began to intrude on my home life. I started to run out of refrigerator space. The children were older and didn't want to stay upstairs while I was teaching. So in 1971 I opened the California Street Cooking School in an old storefront building a few blocks from my home. I was cooking for fifty people a day, doing all of the marketing, the preparation, the recipe development, the teaching, and the cooking, dining with the students and discussing the food. I did the bookkeeping, the mailers, and press releases. My former students remind me that in those days when they asked me if I was going to open a restaurant I replied, "I'm not ready." I see now that I was, in fact, running a small restaurant, but calling it a school.

Timing, of course, is a very important element in life. When I first started teaching, all that people wanted to learn was "gourmet French." I was interested in offering courses in cuisines from around the world. It took time to build trust, but eventually I was able to fill classes in Italian, then Continental, Middle Eastern, and Oriental cooking. I continued my classes for a few more years until I began to burn out and decided that I wanted a new line of work that didn't involve cooking. I began to teach a class in kitchen design at the University of California architecture school.

Then something funny happened, one of those serendipitous events that changes everything. One day, my son, Evan, who was working at Alice Waters's new café at Chez Panisse (today he is a Master Sommelier), called and said, "Mom, come and do Alice a favor. Fill in for the baker for six weeks." I was pretty nervous because I had never worked in a restaurant before.

What happened, of course, is the result of taking an addict to the source of her addiction. What began as a part-time fill-in became my full-time job. I stayed at Chez Panisse for three years, ultimately running the café, planning the menus, developing the recipes, hiring and training the kitchen staff, cooking, ordering food, and talking with the customers. I was having such a good time that one of the partners actually had to remind me to ask for a raise. My experience at Chez Panisse was wonderful. I had the best ingredients at my disposal, and an eager and adventurous food audience. Alice gave me lots of freedom and the opportunity to see what I was capable of doing. Gradually I realized that it was inevitable that I would have to run my own restaurant, and I set out to find the perfect San Francisco location for Square One. After a year of research and planning, I finally located the restaurant's present site.

Timing has finally worked in my favor. For the first time I am in the right place and the right profession at the right time. People today are truly interested in food from around the world. I consider myself blessed because I have a career that I love. I enjoy the food of many countries, but I find that I am happiest when I am cooking the full-flavored, sensual foods of the Mediterranean. At Square One I continue to refine my voice, my style, my culinary point of view. The restaurant is a focus for my food obsession. It provides me with an opportunity to explore the possibilities, with an open mouth and an open mind. It is a work in progress, ever evolving and alive with creative challenges and the joys of cooking for others who share my table and my excitement about good food.

INTRODUCTION

*I*n talking about her first visit to France, M.F.K. Fisher said that there are places where "we feel more at ease in our skin." That was how I felt when I went to study in Italy. I was "home." I enjoyed the leisurely meal, the extended coffee hours, the gossip at the market and wine shops. Sitting in village squares in Greece, Turkey, Spain, France, surrounded by the architecture of the past and present, I felt I always would belong in the Mediterranean, where art and life were inseparable.

To say that Mediterranean food is the food of Spain, Portugal, Italy, France, Greece, Turkey, North Africa, and the Middle East is to play geography and list the names of nations on a map. It doesn't tell you much about the tastes and aromas of the place. The Mediterranean is more than a place on the map. It is a state of mind.

When I say Mediterranean, I see warm earth colors. I feel the sun. I am aware of time passing slowly, of history marking a landscape of incredible beauty: ancient ruins next to modern buildings; a continuity that affects art, architecture, agriculture,

and cuisine. It's all so rich, so layered, so mysterious yet unaffected.

What are the tastes of the Mediterranean? Simple and unpretentious foods such as grains, pasta, and beans that may be enriched by the pungent and earthy flavors of garlic, onions, tomatoes, eggplants, peppers, and artichokes. The perfume of olives, toasted nuts, lemons, oranges, figs, dates, and wild berries. Fish, just hours old, grilled with freshly picked herbs, a plate of sliced tomatoes still warm from the sun and anointed with olive oil from a neighboring olive orchard. Nowhere is yogurt so thick and rich as in Greece; spread with local honey, its creamy texture and the tart but not sour taste are unforgettable, especially after a plate of dolmas, olives, feta cheese, and bread strewn with sesame seeds. This is food with a sense of place: the peppery kebabs you ate at a roadside restaurant in Turkey; the smell of garlic cooking in a small hut on the site of the Etruscan tombs in Cerveteri; the first time you tasted all six varieties of goat cheese, after lunch at a perfect little country restaurant in France; the overwhelming smell of orange blossoms as you drove along the coast of Sicily, the whole island enveloped in their perfume.

In the Mediterranean, food is tied to nature, to seasons, to ripeness. Simple food, simply prepared, with the best fresh ingredients, food that reflects the environment of sun-earth-sea, a regional cuisine and not overly refined by too much analysis and made frivolous by fussiness of presentation.

One of the reasons that I am drawn to Mediterranean food is that it is simple, unpretentious food, not elaborate restaurant cuisine. It is satisfying to eat and not too complicated to prepare. Most of the cooking techniques and implements are basic and most of the ingredients are available at the average market. Now, you may wonder about the authenticity and quality of our American ingredients. Can we cook the foods of the Mediterranean accurately? Our soil is not the same. We don't cultivate things the same way. Our spinach doesn't taste like the spinach in Italy. Our tomatoes don't either. Our chickens, free range or not, bear a pale resemblance to the *poularde de Bresse*. Should we accept defeat and say, "Well, no Italian or Spanish food for me because

I'm not Italian or Spanish, and I'm not there"? Of course not. We'll cook this food with the best ingredients available. It will be in the spirit of the Mediterranean and it will taste wonderful.

Are Square One's recipes completely authentic? Are we faithful to the letter? No, not really. We are faithful to the spirit, to the soul of the dish. We respect the culture. We stay within the country's idiom and we accentuate and heighten those key flavors of the idiom. We want to educate palates with the tastes of a country, but we won't get locked into a recipe just because it's "authentic."

When I develop a recipe for the restaurant, I do a few things to get my imagination flowing. Let's say we decide to cook a lamb stew. If we wanted to give it the taste of Greece, we might add marjoram, garlic, cinnamon, and olive oil. For the flavor of southern Italy we'd add oregano, hot pepper, lots of garlic, and some tomato. For Morocco we'd add cumin, cayenne, paprika, cinnamon, lemon, perhaps cilantro. The use of spices and herbs is the signature of the different cuisines. Try to get the ingredients that are as close as possible to those in the original recipe. Be sensitive in your substitutions and additions. If the dish is too oily, cut back on the fat. If you like one spice more than another, accent it a bit. While you can't take too many liberties with the recipe and still keep it in character, you can put your own personal stamp on it that says this is your version of the food.

Taste, taste, taste, and taste again. Nibble on the garlic; if it's "hot," cook it longer to soften its bite. Chew on the basil; if it's bitter, use another fresh herb in its place, one that might be sweeter that day.

Sometimes when I am cooking I can be transported to the Mediterranean simply by a whiff of garlic, warm fruity olive oil, a branch of fresh rosemary, the perfume of honey melting in a pan on the stove. I want my cooking to merge with that sensation, where the meal is a moment of true relaxation and respite from daily routine. At Square One and in *The Mediterranean Kitchen* I want to share those feelings of sensual pleasure, well-being, and timelessness, of sun-earth-sea, the sense of place that is my Mediterranean, tastes remembered, tastes imagined, tastes created with the Mediterranean spirit and vocabulary in mind.

APPETIZERS

In this and the following two chapters, you will find many of my very favorite dishes. Days can go by without my eating a "main course," as I am often happier eating assorted salads and what we call (and rightly so) appetizers. I can't imagine life without tasty tidbits spread on good bread, and the pleasure of eating with my fingers. I am not grazing—I am dining. What I love best about these foods are the contrasts: tart and sweet, crunch and creaminess, spicy and cool.

In the Mediterranean, people do not eat their meals in set courses. There are times when all you may feel like eating is a large salad, or decide to make a salad and a cheese dish your entire meal. There is no need to stay tied to the American three-course meal when we are in the Mediterranean mode!

You will notice some recipes in this chapter for goat cheese. I know it is on every menu and in every cookbook these days, but it is a very flavorful and tangy cheese. Since 1957, when I first went to France and discovered cheese, chèvre has been one of my favorites. We are fortunate that some brave folks in our country have

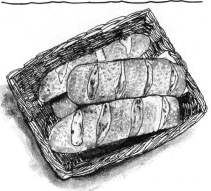

embarked on the process of making American goat cheese. Encourage them by trying the product. We want to inspire an American cheese revolution, and I don't mean Velveeta.

Of course, chèvre is not the only cheese for appetizers. I love rich Fontina when it is melting and creamy, and moist chewy fresh mozzarella melted or marinated. Shavings of Parmesan and pecorino can enliven even the stodgiest of greens. And Gorgonzola *dolce latte* (sweet rather than sharp) or a good creamy blue crumbled into a vinaigrette adds another dimension of texture and flavor to delight the palate.

I have included some recipes for *crostini* and croutons and things that go well with bread, toasted or plain. Try to find crusty real bread and not American balloon bread. Encourage your local bakers to try some whole-grain peasant breads. These taste great and, of course, are better for you. Remember that a slice of great bread can make the meal. It's not just filler.

Most of the filo dough at our markets has been frozen. Occasionally it has been thawed in shipping and then, alas, refrozen, leaving you with potential grief and frustration, as you struggle to separate the layers. Do not despair. Just try another brand or market. If filo is made fresh in your area, you will be delighted with its ease of handling and its flaky texture. Remember to cover the filo sheets with a damp cloth or sheet of plastic while you are working with it so it doesn't dry out.

Bocconcini

MARINATED FRESH
MOZZARELLA

*1 cup extra virgin olive
    oil*

*1 teaspoon dried red
    pepper flakes*

*1 teaspoon freshly ground
    black pepper*

*1 teaspoon finely minced
    garlic*

*1½ teaspoons dried
    oregano*

Pinch salt

*1 pound fresh mozzarella,
    cut into 1½-inch
    chunks*

In Italy fresh mozzarella comes in a variety of sizes. The smallest are called *bocconcini* or little mouthfuls, and they are addictive. When I was living in Rome, these were my favorite midmorning snack. Our local mozzarella producers will not make these little mozzarellas as they are very time consuming, but they do make a fine one-pound fresh mozzarella, which I cut into chunks about 1½ inches square. I marinate them for a few hours and serve them atop a salad of assorted greens dressed with a simple vinaigrette. They can be eaten plain, of course, without the salad accompaniment or become part of an antipasto platter. ♦ *Serves 4*

Warm the olive oil slightly in a small saucepan over low heat. Add the red and black peppers, garlic, and oregano. Let it infuse for a few minutes over low heat, then allow it to cool. Add the salt. Pour the seasoned oil over the cheese in a dish and toss the pieces well in the marinade. Marinate at room temperature for several hours, then serve.

Baked Goat Cheese in Filo

FOR EACH SERVING

1 sheet filo dough, about
   15 by 11 inches
2 tablespoons unsalted
   butter, melted
1 thick slice mild goat
   cheese (about 3 inches
   in diameter and 1 inch
   thick, 2½ to 3 ounces)

This appetizer is in the tradition of the Greek and Turkish borek, which is a seasoned cheese mixture wrapped in filo dough. We serve the filo-wrapped goat cheese with a variety of seasonal accompaniments. In the dead of winter we serve it with a salad of arugula and strips of sun-dried tomatoes or with a salad of Belgian endive, apple or pear slices, and walnuts. But in the summer we love to serve this with slices of melon, quartered fresh figs, and small clusters of grapes. It is a tasty first course, but with fruit it makes a wonderful dessert.

Preheat the oven to 400° to 450°.

Place the sheet of filo on a clean surface and brush with melted butter. Fold the sheet crosswise in half and brush with butter; fold in half again the opposite way and brush again with butter. Place the slice of goat cheese in the center of the folded filo dough. Fold the long sides over the cheese and brush with butter, then fold the short sides over like an envelope, and brush with butter again. (The filo package can be refrigerated a day or two before baking. Place the filo package on a baking sheet lined with bakers' parchment and cover loosely with a foil tent or bakers' parchment.)

Place the filo package on a small baking sheet and brush the top with melted butter. Bake until the filo is golden brown, about 6 minutes. Serve at once.

Tomini Elettrici in Salsa Rossa

GOAT CHEESE IN SPICY
TOMATO VINAIGRETTE

½ cup olive oil

1 tablespoon dried red
   pepper flakes (see
   Note)

Pinch cayenne pepper, if
   needed

1½ cups pureed drained
   canned plum tomatoes

½ cup canned tomato
   puree

⅓ cup red wine vinegar

2 cloves garlic, finely
   minced (optional)

½ teaspoon salt

¼ teaspoon freshly
   ground pepper

1½ pounds mild goat
   cheese, cut into 6 slices

This recipe is from Piemonte in northern Italy. The spicy and *elettrico* salsa is not to be confused with that river of red sauce that runs through many of America's Italian restaurants. It is *piccante* and rich and makes a wonderful contrast to the creamy *tomini,* or goat cheese. ♦ *Serves 6*

Warm the olive oil slightly in a small saucepan over low heat. Add the red pepper flakes and let it infuse a few minutes over low heat. Taste for the heat of the red pepper. If it is not very hot, add a pinch of cayenne. Let cool to room temperature, then combine with the remaining ingredients except the cheese. This is the *salsa rossa.*

Arrange the goat cheese in a single layer in a dish. Pour the tomato vinaigrette over the cheese, cover the dish, and marinate in the refrigerator 2 to 4 days, basting occasionally. Let warm to room temperature before serving. Serve the goat cheese with some of the vinaigrette and croutons. A small green or arugula salad makes a fine accompaniment.

NOTE: Red pepper flakes vary considerably in degrees of heat. We like this sauce to be slightly hot, but you may adjust the temperature to suit your palate.

Tomini al Pesto

GOAT CHEESE IN PESTO VINAIGRETTE

1 ½ cups Pesto (recipe
    follows)
3 tablespoons red wine
    vinegar
¼ cup fruity olive oil
¼ cup mild olive oil
½ teaspoon salt
¼ teaspoon freshly
    ground pepper
8 round slices mild goat
    cheese, about 2 ½ to 3
    ounces each

Pesto

2 cups (tightly packed)
    basil leaves
2 teaspoons finely
    chopped garlic
2 tablespoons pine nuts or
    walnuts, toasted
½ to 1 teaspoon salt
½ teaspoon freshly
    ground pepper
1 cup mild olive oil
½ cup freshly grated
    Parmesan cheese

Traditionally pesto is a sauce for pasta, often with Parmesan cheese added. We prefer to leave the cheese out until we know what we are going to do with it. If it is to be used as a sauce for pasta, we will add the cheese to each dish. But if we decide to use the pesto as a sauce for grilled swordfish or tuna, we don't want any cheese in the puree. In fact, we have found that the pesto keeps infinitely better if the cheese is omitted.

This pesto vinaigrette is excellent for a rice salad or as a salad dressing for boiled potatoes and green beans or sliced tomatoes and fresh mozzarella. ◆ *Serves 8*

Whisk together all the ingredients except goat cheese, then taste and adjust the seasoning. Arrange the goat cheese in a single layer in a shallow dish. Pour the pesto vinaigrette over the cheese and marinate in the refrigerator overnight. Let warm to room temperature and serve with croutons or roasted little potatoes, spreading the pesto vinaigrette and cheese on the warm potatoes. Yum.

Fresh basil varies from week to week and from batch to batch. Sometimes, ironically enough, hothouse basil is sweeter than field basil. In very hot weather, basil grown outdoors can be bitter and metallic in flavor. Taste a leaf before you buy it. You don't want to put up a big batch of pesto with inferior basil. ◆ *Makes about 3 cups*

Place all the ingredients except the olive oil and cheese in a food processor or blender and process until combined. If you are adding cheese later, use just ½ teaspoon salt and season to taste after the cheese is added. Add about half the oil and quickly puree, then add the remaining oil and process to a thick puree. Don't overprocess the pesto; you should be able to see tiny pieces of basil rather than a green homogenous paste. To store the pesto, pour it into a jar and film the top with a little olive oil to keep its bright green color. The pesto will keep this way in the refrigerator for weeks. If you want to freeze it, you might be better off just processing the basil with the oil and adding the seasonings when you use it.

If the pesto will be used immediately for pasta, add the cheese and process until blended.

Bruschetta

GRILLED GARLIC BREAD

Amounts, proportions, and measurements are unimportant in this recipe. What is important is that the bread be crusty, flavorful, and hearty, the olive oil fruity, the garlic pungent but not bitter, and the grill or broiler hot enough to mark the bread evenly.

Slice the bread about ½ inch thick and brush both sides with virgin olive oil. Grill or broil the bread until it is marked on both sides and somewhat crisp. Immediately rub the bread with a cut clove of garlic and eat.

As a variation you may rub the garlic bread with a cut tomato or cover it with finely chopped tomato and sprinkle with freshly ground pepper. This is a little messier to eat, but it is really delicious and worth the risk of a few specks of tomato on your shirt.

Crostini di Fegatini alla Fiorentina

CHICKEN LIVER
CROUTONS

*4 tablespoons unsalted
    butter*

*4 tablespoons olive oil,
    plus additional for the
    bread*

*1 pound chicken livers,
    well trimmed*

1 cup diced onions

6 fresh sage leaves

*¼ cup (or to taste) dry
    Marsala*

*Salt and freshly ground
    pepper*

Lemon juice, if needed

*12 thick slices (½ inch)
    peasant bread, cut
    crosswise in half*

An ideal appetizer and a perfect part of an antipasto selection. This Florentine classic is offered as a nibble to start the meal in many trattorie. ✦ *Makes 24*

Melt half the butter and oil in each of 2 sauté pans or skillets over medium heat. Add the livers to one pan and the onions and sage to the other. Cook, stirring frequently, until the livers are cooked through but still pink in the center and the onions are tender and translucent, 5 to 8 minutes. Add the Marsala to the livers and cook a few minutes. Using a slotted spoon, transfer half the livers and half the onion mixture to a food processor. Process with pulses until coarsely chopped (not pureed) and transfer to a mixing bowl. Repeat with the remaining livers and onion mixture. Stir the pan juices into the liver mixture and season to taste with salt and pepper. You may want to add a little lemon juice or more Marsala to round out the flavor.

Brush both sides of the bread slices with olive oil, then grill or broil the slices until golden and toasted on both sides. Spread the bread with the warm liver mixture and serve warm or at room temperature.

Capriata

GRILLED BREAD WITH
WHITE BEAN PUREE AND
WILTED GREENS

1 cup dried white beans

*8 tablespoons fruity olive
oil, plus additional for
the bread*

*2 to 4 large cloves garlic,
very finely minced*

*Salt and freshly ground
pepper*

*6 cups greens, such as
escarole, Swiss chard,
dandelion, or broccoli
rabe, rinsed well*

*2 tablespoons red wine
vinegar*

*6 thick slices peasant
bread*

1 clove garlic, halved

You may wonder how anything that sounds like mashed beans and wilted greens on bread can be good, but it is better than good—it is wonderful. This dish originates in Apulia, in the south of Italy, and is a peasant snack that feeds your soul as well as your tummy. I use it as a centerpiece in a simple antipasto plate accompanied by a few slices of *coppa,* strips of pecorino *fresco,* peperonata, olives, and some slices of tomato, or in winter sun-dried tomatoes.
♦ *Serves 6*

Soak the white beans in water overnight. Drain and rinse. Cover the beans with fresh water and cook until very soft. Drain if necessary. Puree the beans in the food processor or mash well with a fork. Add 6 tablespoons olive oil and the minced garlic (see Note). Season to taste with salt and pepper.

Heat 2 tablespoons olive oil in a large sauté pan or skillet (not cast iron) over medium heat. Add the greens and cook, stirring constantly, a few minutes. Sprinkle with the vinegar and continue to cook until wilted. Drain the greens in a colander, then chop fine but not to a mush. Season with salt and pepper. The beans and greens can be served warm or at room temperature.

Brush both sides of the bread slices with olive oil, then grill or broil the slices until golden and toasted on both sides. Rub the hot bread with the cut garlic, spread with the bean puree, and top with the wilted chopped greens.

NOTE: If you are terrified of raw garlic and feel that it will wreak havoc with your system and your social life, you may cook the garlic in some of the olive oil for a minute or two, but do not let it brown or you will have miserable heartburn and a terrible-tasting bean puree.

Fegato alle Uova Sode

CHICKEN LIVER PÂTÉ,
ITALIAN STYLE

8 tablespoons (or as
needed) chicken or
duck fat or olive oil

2 to 3 medium onions,
finely chopped

1 pound chicken, duck, or
goose livers, well
trimmed

⅓ cup dry white wine

6 to 8 hard-cooked large
eggs

Salt and freshly ground
pepper

This is pretty close to the quintessential chopped chicken liver pâté but with an Italian touch. I found variations of this Jewish recipe in a book about Italian Renaissance cuisine from Padua. And here you thought that this was a New York deli item!

Melt half the fat in each of 2 sauté pans or skillets over medium heat. Add the onions to one pan and cook, stirring frequently, until dark golden brown. Add the livers to the other pan and sauté until pink in the center but not quivery. Add the white wine in the last few minutes of cooking and let most of it evaporate. Coarsely chop the livers and eggs separately. If you chop these in a food processor, just pulse them very quickly and in very small batches. You don't want to lose the chunky texture.

Combine the livers, eggs, browned onions, and pan juices in a bowl while all the ingredients are still warm. Season to taste with salt and pepper. If the mixture seems a little dry, add more oil or fat. Serve with crackers, matzoh, toast, or rye bread. *Buon appetito* and enjoy already!

Gorgonzola Brandy Butter

6 tablespoons Gorgonzola
dolce latte (see Note)

3 tablespoons unsalted
butter, softened

1 tablespoon brandy

Freshly ground pepper to
taste

This butter is very versatile. It makes a wonderful stuffing for celery topped with chopped toasted walnuts or pine nuts and a fine spread for croutons. When paired with sliced apple and watercress on walnut bread, it makes a fine sandwich spread. It is excellent on grilled steaks as well.
◆ *Makes about ⅔ cup, enough for 8 ribs celery*

Process all ingredients in a food processor until blended or mush them together with your hands.

NOTE: *Dolce latte* is the milder sweeter Gorgonzola. If you cannot find it and must use the stronger variety, increase the butter.

Duck Liver Mousse

½ cup plus 2 tablespoons
  unsalted butter,
  softened

2 tablespoons olive oil

1 medium onion, diced

1 small apple or ½
  medium apple, peeled,
  cored, and diced

1 pound duck livers,
  sinew and green spots
  trimmed

⅓ cup (or to taste)
  Calvados or Armagnac

¼ cup heavy cream

Salt and freshly ground
  pepper

¼ cup clarified butter
  (see Note)

This mousse is so rich and voluptuous, you will find that a little goes a very long way. It is not the world's healthiest recipe in terms of cholesterol content, but you could make it for a large party or serve a single crouton as part of an assorted appetizer platter. ♦ *Serves 12 to 24*

Melt 1 tablespoon butter with half the olive oil in a large sauté pan or skillet over medium heat. Add the onion and apple and cook, stirring frequently, until very tender. Transfer to a blender or food processor.

Add the remaining oil and another tablespoon butter to the pan and heat over high heat. Add the livers and sauté quickly until very pink in the center but not rare. Using a slotted spoon, add the livers to the onion mixture. Pour the Calvados into the pan, simmer a minute or two, scraping loose the browned bits, and add to the livers. Cut the remaining ½ cup butter into slivers and add it with the cream to the livers. Process until very smooth. If there are any lumps, press the puree through a strainer. Season to taste with salt and pepper and add more Calvados if desired.

Line the bottom of a 9 by 5-inch glass loaf pan with baker's parchment and butter the paper and sides of the pan. Pour in the mousse and spread evenly. Pour the clarified butter over the top. Cover with plastic wrap and refrigerate overnight or up to 2 days. (The mousse can also be made in buttered ramekins. Occasionally this pâté refuses to set up enough to unmold, so that ramekins are the most foolproof means of serving.)

To serve, dip the bottom of the pan in hot water, then invert the mousse onto a platter. Cut into slices and serve with croutons, apple slices, and some greens tossed with a little Walnut Vinaigrette (page 61), or simply with toast or croutons.

NOTE: To clarify butter, melt ½ cup butter in a small saucepan over low heat. Skim the foam from the top and let the milk solids settle to the bottom. Spoon the clear yellow liquid (clarified butter) into a clean container.

Suppli al Telefono

ROMAN RICE
CROQUETTES

1 cup water
½ cup Chicken Stock
   (page 103) or
   additional water
1 cup Arborio rice
1 large egg
4 tablespoons unsalted
   butter
⅓ cup freshly grated
   Parmesan cheese

FILLING

2 tablespoons dried
   porcini mushrooms
⅓ cup hot water
2 tablespoons olive oil
½ cup finely chopped
   onion
1 teaspoon finely minced
   garlic
¼ cup diced prosciutto
¼ cup tomato puree or
   sauce
Salt and freshly ground
   pepper
12 cubes (1 inch) fresh
   mozzarella

¾ cup dry bread crumbs
Peanut oil for deep frying

Suppli come by their name because when you bite into the croquette the mozzarella forms strings that resemble telephone wires. The *suppli* can be made ahead of time and refrigerated (and probably frozen, although we have never tried it). *Suppli* are great with cocktails or for lunch with a small salad. ✦ *Makes about 1 dozen*

Heat the water and chicken stock in a medium saucepan to boiling. Add the rice and reduce the heat. Simmer, partially covered, until most of the liquid is absorbed, 15 to 20 minutes. Stir in the egg, butter, and cheese. Spoon the rice into a bowl or on a baking sheet and refrigerate.

For the filling, soak the porcini in the hot water for an hour. Drain, reserving the liquid, and finely chop the mushrooms. Strain the soaking liquid.

Heat the olive oil in a sauté pan or skillet over medium heat. Add the onion and cook, stirring occasionally, until translucent, about 10 minutes. Stir in the garlic and cook a few minutes. Add the porcini and the soaking liquid, the prosciutto, and tomato puree; simmer until thickened, 15 to 20 minutes. Season to taste, then cool.

To assemble the *suppli,* take a few tablespoons rice in your hand and make a pocket in the center with your finger, cupping the rice in your hand. The rice layer should be about ½ inch thick. Put a spoonful of filling and a piece of cheese in the pocket. Mold the rice over the filling and add a little more rice to cover. Roll into a football-shaped cylinder, about 3 to 4 inches long, depending upon how nimble your fingers are. Drop it into a bowl of bread crumbs and roll it around until well coated. Place on a baking sheet lined with baker's parchment. Repeat with the remaining rice and filling.

About 15 minutes before serving, heat peanut oil in a deep fryer to about 350°. Add several croquettes and fry 3 minutes. Remove and let rest a minute or two, then return to the hot oil and fry until golden, about 3 more minutes. (This allows the mozzarella to melt.) Drain on paper towels and repeat with the remaining croquettes. Serve hot.

Spuma di Tonno

FRESH TUNA PÂTÉ

½ pound cooked fresh
tuna fillet, preferably
yellowfin
½ cup (or as needed)
unsalted butter,
softened
2 tablespoons (or to taste)
fresh lemon juice
Salt and freshly ground
pepper
Capers for garnish, rinsed

This recipe is deliciously simple and a wonderful hors d'oeuvre to serve with drinks. Most Italians would use canned light tuna packed in virgin olive oil. However we prefer to make this pâté with grilled or broiled fresh tuna, which is easily available to us from Hawaii, because we like the slightly smoky flavor grilling gives to the fish. We grill it lightly over low heat so that it doesn't develop any hard crust, but you could sauté the tuna gently in butter and get the same texture, although the smokiness would be lost. Whatever technique you decide to use, just get a beautiful piece of tuna and don't overcook it. If it is too hard and dry, it will not make a smooth puree. Cool the fish before making the pâté. ◆ *Serves 4 to 6*

Puree the tuna and butter in the food processor. Add lemon juice and salt and pepper to taste. If the fish seems excessively "fishy," add more butter to taste. Process just until blended. Spread on crackers or toast and sprinkle with capers.

Tapenade and Tapenade Butter

1 cup pitted niçoise olives
2 tablespoons chopped
rinsed capers
1 tablespoon minced
garlic
2 teaspoons chopped
anchovies
½ teaspoon freshly
ground pepper
2 tablespoons Armagnac
(optional)
1 tablesoon grated orange
zest (optional)
4 to 6 tablespoons
extra-virgin olive oil
½ to 1 cup unsalted
butter, at room
temperature (optional)

Tapenade is a Provençal olive paste that is served on croutons and as a dip for vegetables and hard-cooked eggs. We sometimes spread a thin layer on our pizza crust before adding tomatoes or cheese. It can be thinned with olive oil and a little lemon juice for a sauce or vinaigrette, but is is pretty intense. We find most people like it mixed with butter. We pipe the Tapenade Butter under the skin of chicken and roast or broil it, and spread it over grilled steak and fish. Niçoise olives are best for Tapenade. I bop them with a meat pounder to loosen the flesh, then pick out the pits. ◆ *Makes 1 cup.*

Place all ingredients except butter in the food processor and puree. Taste and adjust the seasoning, adding more anchovy, Armagnac, garlic, pepper or orange zest if you like. If you find the Tapenade too intense, add the butter and process until blended. The Tapenade and Tapenade Butter will keep in the refrigerator for days. Use recklessly!

*B*riouats

SPICED POTATO-FILLED
FILO PASTRIES

2 large baking potatoes
   (about 6 ounces each)
2 tablespoons unsalted
   butter
1 small onion, finely
   chopped
3 cloves garlic, finely
   minced
1 teaspoon ground cumin
1 teaspoon salt
½ teaspoon freshly
   ground black pepper
1 hard-cooked large egg,
   finely chopped
1 large egg
¼ cup chopped fresh
   parsley
2 tablespoons chopped
   fresh mint (optional)
½ pound filo dough
½ cup unsalted butter,
   melted
Peanut oil for deep frying

Serve these North African filo pastries as part of a Middle Eastern *mezze* assortment or on their own as an appetizer. Shaped like a strudel, they would be a great accompaniment for grilled fish or roasted lamb with Moroccan or Middle Eastern spices. These can be assembled far in advance and may be refrigerated or frozen unbaked.
♦ *Makes about 18*

Preheat the oven to 400°. Bake the potatoes until they are soft and mashable, about 1 hour. Remove the potatoes from the oven and let stand until cool enough to handle. Cut each potato in half and scoop out the pulp. Either mash the pulp or press it through a ricer.

Heat 2 tablespoons butter in a small sauté pan or skillet over medium heat. Add the onion and cook, stirring occasionally, until tender, 7 to 10 minutes. Add the garlic, cumin, salt, and pepper; cook 3 minutes more.

Combine the potatoes, onion mixture, both eggs, the parsley, and mint. Taste and adjust the seasoning.

Cut the filo into strips about 12 by 3 inches. Keep the strips covered with a damp cloth or plastic wrap.

To assemble, brush a strip of filo with melted butter. Top it with another strip and brush it with butter. Place a tablespoon of the filling about 2 inches from the top of the strips and fold the top corner of the dough over the filling and to the opposite edge so that it looks like a triangle. Continue folding the dough like a flag until the entire strip is folded. Or place the filling at the top of the strips, tuck in the sides, and roll up into a cylinder. Repeat with the remaining filo and filling.

Deep fry the pastries, a few at a time, in peanut oil in a deep fryer heated to 350° until golden. Or bake on baking sheets in a 375° oven until puffed and golden, about 7 minutes. Serve hot.

*T*iropetes

GREEK CHEESE-FILLED
FILO PASTRIES

¾ *pound feta cheese,*
crumbled

¾ *pound Monterey Jack*
cheese, grated

3 *large eggs*

¼ *cup minced fresh*
parsley

1 *tablespoon chopped*
fresh dill

½ *teaspoon grated*
nutmeg

¼ *teaspoon freshly*
ground pepper

¾ *pound unsalted butter*

1 *pound filo dough*

This is a favorite Greek and Turkish hors d'oeuvre or *mezze*. The Turks roll these into *cigari*, or cigar-shaped cylinders, and deep fry them. The Greeks fold them into little triangles, hence the name. The first time I ever tasted these was not in Europe but in a Turkish restaurant in New York about thirty years ago. What struck me then was the mixture of cheeses, some salty, some smooth and runny. It's an effect I chose to recreate by adding Monterey Jack to the traditional recipe. The creamy melting Jack cheese balances the saltiness and dryness of the feta. ✦ *Makes about 2 dozen*

Combine the cheeses, eggs, parsley, dill, nutmeg, and pepper. Melt the butter. Cut the filo lengthwise into strips about 3 inches wide. Keep these covered with a damp cloth or plastic wrap while you are working with the dough or it will dry up and fly around the room.

To assemble, brush a strip of filo with melted butter. Top it with another strip and brush it with butter. Then add a third strip and brush it as well. Place a rounded teaspoon of cheese filling about 2 inches from the top of the strips and fold the top corner of the dough over the filling and to the opposite edge so that it looks like a triangle. Continue folding the dough like a flag until the entire strip is folded. Place the completed pastry on a baking sheet lined with baker's parchment. Repeat with the remaining filo and cheese filling.

At this point, the *tiropetes* can be stored in the refrigerator for a day. Cover loosely with foil or parchment but do not press down on the completed pastries or you may tear them. If you remember, it is best to bring these to room temperature before baking; if not, they will just take a little longer to bake.

About 20 minutes before serving, preheat the oven to 450°. Brush the top of the *tiropetes* with melted butter, then bake the *tiropetes* on baking sheets until golden brown, 7 to 10 minutes. Serve hot.

VARIATION

To make *Borek,* bake the filling and filo dough as a single pastry. Cut the filo to fit a baking dish about 11 by 9 inches. Butter 10 sheets, one at a time, and place them in the pan. Add the cheese filling and spread evenly, then cover with another 10 sheets, buttering each one. Refrigerate until firm and the butter sets. Just before baking, cut into diamonds or squares with a very sharp knife. Bake at 350° until golden, about 45 minutes. You may have to recut the pieces again after baking, but it is important to cut the pieces before baking so that you do not tear the baked filo and serve shabby pastries.

Shellfish Briouats

FILO PASTRIES WITH
SHRIMP OR CRABMEAT

*2 pounds shelled shrimp
or crabmeat*

*3 tablespoons unsalted
butter*

2 cloves garlic, minced

*½ teaspoon ground
cumin*

*¾ to 1 teaspoon cayenne
pepper*

1 tablespoon paprika

*4 teaspoons all-purpose
flour*

*1 cup heavy cream or
half-and-half*

*2 tablespoons each
chopped fresh parsley
and mint or cilantro*

*1 tablespoon grated
lemon zest*

*Salt and freshly ground
pepper*

20 sheets filo dough

*8 tablespoons unsalted
butter, melted*

Peanut oil for deep frying

These are wonderful as an appetizer and can be assembled a few hours ahead of time. I served these at a Leap Year dinner at the James Beard House, where they leaped right off the plates. You may want to try these with a little added grated fresh ginger and/or green onions or ground ginger and no onions. ✦ *Makes 30*

Poach the prawns in dry white wine or fish stock until just cooked through, 3 to 5 minutes, then drain and coarsely chop. If using crabmeat, pick over the meat removing any shell or cartilage and break the meat into chunks.

Melt 3 tablespoons butter in a medium saucepan over low heat. Add the garlic and spices and cook 1 to 2 minutes. Add the flour and stir well. Cook another minute, then stir in the cream and cook until thickened (see Note). Remove from the heat and stir in the shellfish, fresh herbs, lemon zest, and salt and pepper to taste. Let cool for about 15 minutes.

Cut the filo into strips about 12 by 3 inches. Keep the strips covered with a damp cloth or plastic wrap.

To assemble, brush a strip of filo with melted butter. Top it with another strip and brush it with butter. Place a tablespoon of the filling about 2 inches from the top of the strips and fold the top corner of the dough over the filling and to the opposite edge so that it looks like a triangle. Continue folding the dough like a flag until the entire strip is folded. Or place the filling at the top of the strips, tuck in the sides, and roll up into a cylinder. Repeat with the remaining filo and filling.

Deep fry the pastries, a few at a time, in peanut oil heated to 350° until golden. Or bake on baking sheets in a 375° oven until puffed and golden, about 7 minutes. Serve hot.

NOTE: These can be made without the flour and cream to bind the filling; it will more crumbly to eat but still delicious.

DOLMAS
TWO VERSIONS OF STUFFED GRAPE LEAVES

Making dolmas is somewhat time-consuming, but, if you get organized, it won't take too long. Assemble the filling, then clear a large tabletop and lay out as many leaves as will fit. Place a bit of filling on each leaf and then roll them all up. Repeat until all of the grape leaves are stuffed. Dolmas can be made days ahead of time and served at room temperature or reheated and served warm. We prepare these two ways, with meat and without. Grape leaves come packed in brine, usually in jars. They are packed very tightly; reach in gently and pull slowly but firmly to extricate them.

Lamb Dolmas

1 cup long-grain rice, preferably basmati

4 tablespoons unsalted butter

2 medium onions, chopped (about 1½ cups)

3 cloves garlic, minced

1 teaspoon ground allspice

1 teaspoon freshly ground pepper

1 teaspoon cinnamon

1 pound ground lamb

½ cup pine nuts, toasted

½ cup dried currants, soaked in hot water and drained

2 tablespoons chopped fresh parsley

1 tablespoon salt

About 60 grape leaves, rinsed well and patted dry

1½ cups olive oil

Juice of 4 lemons (about ½ cup)

Lemon wedges and yogurt for serving

✦ *Makes about 60*

Soak the rice in cool water to cover for about 30 minutes. Drain.

While the rice is soaking, melt the butter in a medium sauté pan or skillet over low heat. Add the onions and cook, stirring occasionally, until translucent and tender, about 10 minutes. Add the garlic and spices and cook a few minutes more. Let cool about 10 minutes. Combine the onion mixture, rice, ground lamb, pine nuts, currants, parsley, and salt in a bowl.

Snip the stems off the grape leaves and place smooth side down on a table. With your hands shape about 2 teaspoons of the lamb filling into a cylinder and place near the stem end of a leaf. Repeat with the remaining filling. Fold the sides of each leaf over the filling, then roll into a cylinder. The rice expands as it cooks so do not roll too tightly.

Arrange seam side down and close together in a single layer in 2 pans. Pour half the olive oil and lemon juice over the *dolmas* in each pan, then add hot water to just cover. Weight with plates to keep them from unrolling.

Heat the liquid to boiling and cover the pans. Reduce the heat and simmer about 30 minutes. Uncover the *dolmas* so that they can cool quickly. As soon as they can be handled, remove the *dolmas* with a spatula and arrange on platters (see Note). Serve warm with lemon wedges and yogurt.

NOTE: These can be made ahead up to 2 days. Let cool completely, then refrigerate in covered containers. To reheat, arrange in a single layer in pans, add a little water, and weight with plates. Simmer covered about 7 minutes.

Vegetable Dolmas

1 cup long-grain rice, preferably basmati

3 tablespoons unsalted butter

2 medium onions, chopped (about 1½ cups)

3 cloves garlic, minced

⅔ cup diced seeded canned or peeled fresh tomatoes

½ cup pine nuts, toasted

½ cup dried currants, soaked in hot water and drained

2 tablespoons finely chopped fresh parsley

2 tablespoons chopped fresh mint (optional)

2 teaspoons salt

1 teaspoon freshly ground pepper

36 to 40 grape leaves (see Note), rinsed well, drained, and patted dry

3 ripe tomatoes, sliced ¼ inch thick (use only if in season)

1 cup olive oil

Juice of 2 lemons (about ¼ cup)

Lemon wedges and yogurt for serving

◆ *Makes 36 to 40*

Soak the rice in cool water to cover for about 30 minutes. Drain.

While the rice is soaking, melt the butter in a medium sauté pan or skillet over low heat. Add the onions and cook, stirring occasionally, until translucent and tender, about 10 minutes. Add the garlic and cook a few minutes more. Add the rice, diced tomatoes, pine nuts, currants, parsley, mint, salt, and pepper and combine well.

Snip the stems off the grape leaves and place smooth side down on a table. Place a teaspoon or so of the rice filling near the stem end of each leaf. Fold the sides of each leaf over the filling, then roll into a cylinder. The rice expands as it cooks so do not roll too tightly.

If tomatoes are in season, line a pan large enough to fit the *dolmas* in a single layer with the tomato slices. Arrange the *dolmas* seam side down and close together on the tomato slices or on the bottom of the pan. Pour the olive oil and lemon juice over top and add enough hot water to just cover the *dolmas.* Weight them with a plate to keep them from unrolling.

Heat the liquid to boiling and cover the pan. Reduce the heat and simmer 35 to 40 minutes. Uncover the dolmas so that they can cool quickly. As soon as they can be handled, remove the *dolmas* with a spatula and arrange on a platter (see Note). Serve warm or at room temperature with lemon wedges and yogurt.

NOTE: The *dolmas* can be made ahead up to 3 days. Let cool completely, then refrigerate in covered containers. Let warm to room temperature or reheat before serving. To reheat the *dolmas*, arrange them in a single layer in a pan, add a little water, and weight them again with a plate. Simmer covered about 5 minutes.

Bresaola

SPICED BEEF FILET

1 beef filet (5 to 6
    pounds), trimmed of all
    fat and sinews (about
    3 pounds after
    trimming)
2 ½ tablespoons brown
    sugar
1 tablespoon freshly
    ground pepper
½ teaspoon dried thyme
½ teaspoon ground
    ginger
½ teaspoon ground
    allspice
½ teaspoon ground mace
    or nutmeg
½ teaspoon coriander
    seeds, toasted and
    ground
¼ teaspoon ground cloves
3 cardamom seeds (from
    inside 1 cardamom
    pod), finely crushed
1 tablespoon plus 1
    teaspoon salt

Horseradish Cream

2 tablespoons finely
    minced white onion
5 to 6 tablespoons grated
    or chopped horseradish
3 to 4 tablespoons white
    vinegar
1 ½ cups sour cream
½ cup heavy cream
1 teaspoon salt
½ teaspoon freshly
    ground pepper
3 tablespoons chopped
    fresh dill (optional)

This is our version of *bresaola*, Italian air-dried beef. The curing process takes about ten days and is worth the wait. We like to slice this thin and serve it as an appetizer with slices of ricotta *salata*, a slightly salty sheep's milk cheese, and/or slices of sautéed artichokes on a bed of arugula or winter greens. You could also serve the sliced beef as an hors d'oeuvre without the accompaniments but with a ginger or horseradish aioli for a dipping sauce. Finally, you could cure the beef for a shorter time, cut it into individual steaks, and grill them. We like to serve these hot with Horseradish Cream (recipe follows) and Potato Strudel (page 303). ✦ *Serves 10 as a first course*

Rub the filet with the sugar and all the spices except the salt. Place it in a noncorrosive dish and cover with foil. Refrigerate for 2 days, turning the meat once a day. Then rub the filet with the salt and refrigerate for 8 more days, again turning the meat once a day.

Sear the filet evenly on all sides on the grill, under the broiler, or in a heavy skillet or griddle on top of the stove until a meat thermometer inserted in the center registers 90°. Let the meat cool and slice thin.

To serve the beef as an entrée, cure the filet for only 3 days, salting the meat for the last day. Cut it into 6 individual filets. Brush with oil and grill, preferably rare of course.

✦ *Makes 2 cups*

Puree the horseradish with the vinegar in a food processor. Transfer to a mixing bowl, add the remaining ingredients, and stir until blended. Use more horseradish if you like a fairly zingy sauce. This should make enough sauce for 2 pounds smoked trout, 6 beef filets, or 6 servings of roast beef.

ANTIPASTO AND OTHER MIXED PLATES

T here are times when we want to offer a spectacular first course, or put together a great picnic, summer buffet, or appetizers for a cocktail party. I usually prefer to go with an ethnic theme because it sets a definite mood and makes the selection of wines or appropriate special drinks easy. I have divided these assortments into four basic groups, hors d'oeuvres for France, *mezze* for the Middle East, tapas for Spain, and antipasto for Italy.

Many of these dishes can stand on their own, but they are so simple that they may leave you underwhelmed. However put them together with a few other salads and you create a really interesting plate. On their own, most of these recipes will serve four, but in combination they are that much more wonderful, and of course
can serve many more. If the hors d'oeuvres, *mezze*, antipasto, or tapas are to be the main part of the meal, accompanied by bread and cheese, you should prepare as many as time and money will permit.

There are no hard and fast rules about what combinations work best. I like to go with a few salads that are sharp and tart in flavor, such as those with citrus-based vinaigrettes; some that are rich and filling, like a bean salad or a dish with a mayonnaise-based sauce; and one spicy dish with a hot pepper or black pepper vinaigrette. If time permits, I will add something stuffed, such as a *dolma*, or an artichoke or zucchini filled with onions, garlic, mint, and toasted breadcrumbs, or even a simple rib of celery with Gorgonzola Brandy Butter. If the appetizers are to be a meal, by themselves, you might want to add a fish or meat appetizer, or both, instead of all vegetables and cheeses. Although one can dine very nicely on just vegetables.

I love the abundance of a table arrayed with many plates of different colors and shapes: red and golden beets, green broccoli or beans, orange carrots, brown mushrooms, pale green celery or fennel, multicolored peppers. Texture is also a consideration. Some dishes should be crunchy, some soft, some creamy.

Serve these assorted dishes at room temperature. There is nothing more jarring than biting into an ice cold salad or appetizer. Refrigeration suppresses much flavor and many nuances; it flattens out the complexities, and a cold vinaigrette has a unpleasant viscous texture.

On the other hand, a hot appetizer provides a nice counterpoint: a crisp *tiropete*, a slice of *bastilla*, a grilled sausage with hot mustard or onion marmalade, a miniature brochette, a crunchy *suppli*, a warmed slice of *focaccia*.

Please don't think of bread as just bulk. There are more and more interesting breads available at local bakeries to enrich the meal. Pita bread, *lavosh*, Italian whole-grain bread, bread sticks, *focaccia*, French baguettes and *levain* bread, Portuguese *broa* corn bread, Greek sesame seed bread all add another dimention of taste and texture to the meal.

What follows are a few ideas for antipasti, tapas, *mezze*, and hors d'oeuvres combinations. You'll probably come up with many great ideas of your own. That's part of the fun of Mediterranean cooking and dining.

FOR AN INTERESTING PLATE OF HORS D'OEUVRES,
CHOOSE AN ASSORTMENT FROM THE FOLLOWING:

Duck Liver Mousse (page 26)

Green beans or asparagus with Walnut or Hazelnut Vinaigrette (page 61)

Beets with Citrus Vinaigrette (page 63)

Roasted peppers with Anchovy Garlic Vinaigrette (page 64)

Artichokes à la grecque (Note, page 267)

Lentil Salad (page 51)

Grilled Tuna with Basic Vinaigrette or Basic Vinaigrette with Garlic (page 65)

Grilled bread

Herbed goat cheese on croutons

Radishes and sweet butter

Croutons with Tapenade (page 28)

Hard-cooked eggs with Tapenade (page 28)

Aioli (page 193) and cooked vegetables or fish

OF COURSE, THERE'S WONDERFUL ITALIAN ANTIPASTO:

Bruschetta (page 23)

Italian Eggplant Crouton (page 41)

Artichokes with Tomato or Mint Vinaigrette (page 48 or 53)

Spuma di Tonno (Fresh Tuna Pâté, page 28)

Chicken Liver Croutons (page 23)

Cauliflower with Red Pepper Vinaigrette (page 49)

Bresaola (page 35)

Bocconcini (page 19)

Goat Cheese Marinated in Spicy Tomato Vinaigrette (page 21) or in Pesto Vinaigrette
  (page 22)

Capriata (page 24)

Roasted peppers with Oregano Garlic Vinaigrette (page 67)

Vegetables with Salsa Verde (page 253)

Chick-pea salad with Basic Vinaigrette (page 65), chopped red onions, sage, and (optional)
  chopped prosciutto (see White Bean Salad, page 51)

Italian Lentil Salad (page 51)

Broccoli with olives and Basic Vinaigrette (page 65)

Broccoli or cauliflower with Toasted Bread Crumbs (page 73) and Anchovy Garlic Vinaigrette
  (page 64)

Carrots and fennel or celery with Black Pepper Vinaigrette (page 79)

Beets with Citrus or Mint Vinaigrette (page 63 or 53)

Peperonata

Suppli al Telefono (page 27)

Rice Salad with Grilled Tuna (page 75)

Tomatoes with Pesto Vinaigrette (page 22)
Grilled sausage with onion marmalade (page 295)

IF THE MOOD IS SPANISH, TRY SOME OF THESE TAPAS:

Escalivada (page 44)
Croutons with Gorgonzola Brandy Butter (page 25)
Beets with Anise Vinaigrette (page 45)
Mushrooms with Sherry or Toasted Cumin Vinaigrette (page 49 or 68) and toasted almonds
Artichokes à la grecque (page 266, Note)
Roasted peppers with Oregano Garlic Vinaigrette (page 67)
Carrots and celery with Toasted Cumin Vinaigrette (page 68)
Chick-pea Salad with Basic Vinaigrette (page 65), chopped red onions, mint, and (optional)
    tomatoes (see White Bean Salad, page 50)
Cauliflower with Red Pepper Vinaigrette (page 49)
Romescu (page 193) with cooked potatoes, beets, green beans
Leeks with Hazelnut Vinaigrette (page 61) and chopped mint
White Bean Salad (page 50)
Grilled Chorizo (page 297)

MIDDLE EASTERN MEZZE MAKE SOME OF THE BEST LITTLE MEALS:

Dolmas (pages 33–34)
Tiropetes (page 30)
Briouats or Shellfish Briouats (page 29 or 32)
Bastilla (page 218)
Moroccan Carrot Salad (page 45)
Baba Ghanouj (page 42)
Moroccan Eggplant Salad (page 43)
Cucumber Salad with Yogurt, Mint, and Raisins (page 46)
Hummus
Tarator (page 196) with cooked vegetables
Middle Eastern Lentil Salad (page 51)
Beets with Sesame Vinaigrette (page 45)
Beets with feta cheese and Walnut Vinaigrette (page 61)
Turkish Artichokes (page 47)
Zucchini Salad with Walnuts and Dill (page 46)
Grilled Tuna with Charmoula Vinaigrette (page 76)
Grilled Tuna Salad with a Moroccan Salsa (page 78)

Crostini de Melanzane Arroste

ITALIAN EGGPLANT
CROUTON

3 large or 4 medium
   eggplants

1 cup (or as needed)
   olive oil

3 cloves garlic, finely
   minced

¼ cup red wine vinegar

2 tablespoons capers,
   rinsed

Salt and freshly ground
   pepper

12 to 18 slices grilled or
   toasted croutons

Chopped fresh parsley for
   garnish

The eggplant is the quintessential Mediterranean vegetable. It is served baked, grilled, sautéed, stuffed, and stewed in hundreds of ways. When broiled or grilled, the eggplant acquires a wonderful roasted and smoky taste. If you find this smokiness too intense, you may bake half of the eggplants in the oven. Remember to prick the eggplant before baking so that it doesn't explode, although it's not necessary if you broil it.

This and the following recipe for eggplant spread are two of my very favorites. We serve them as part of a salad assortment but each is fine on its own. ✦ *Makes about 3 cups puree*

Preheat the oven to 450° and heat the broiler or grill.

Broil 1 large or 2 medium eggplants, turning several times, until soft all the way through, about 15 minutes. Prick the other eggplants with a fork and bake, turning once, until they're very soft to the touch, about 50 minutes. Let stand until cool enough to handle.

Meanwhile, heat 2 tablespoons olive oil in a small skillet over low heat. Add the garlic and cook for a minute or two to remove its bite. Do not let it brown!

Cut the eggplants in half and carefully scoop out the pulp. You should have about 3 cups. Discard the skins. Coarsely puree the eggplant in a food processor or with a knife by hand. Place it in a bowl and stir in the remaining oil, the garlic, and vinegar. Fold in the capers and season to taste with salt and pepper. If the eggplant tastes too smoky or bitter, stir in a little more olive oil. Spread the puree on the croutons and garnish with parsley.

Baba Ghanouj

MIDDLE EASTERN
EGGPLANT PUREE WITH
TAHINI

2 large or 3 medium
   eggplants
2 to 4 tablespoons olive
   oil
3 cloves garlic, very finely
   minced
¼ cup sesame tahini,
   stirred well
¼ cup (or to taste) fresh
   lemon juice
Salt
2 to 3 tablespoons cold
   water if needed
¼ cup pine nuts, toasted
2 tablespoons chopped
   fresh parsley for
   garnish
Pita breads (see Note) or
   cucumber strips,
   radishes, green onions,
   and carrot strips for
   serving

This Middle Eastern puree is voluptuous and silky in texture because of the tahini. To borrow a wine term from my son the sommelier, it has "mouth feel." While you can make a meal of this slathered on warm pita bread, for a little snack try baba ghanouj with crisp fresh vegetables; they are a good contrast to its smoky richness. ✦ *Makes about 2½ cups puree*

Preheat the broiler or heat a heavy griddle over medium heat.

Broil the eggplants or grill on the griddle, turning frequently, until charred all over and very soft, about 20 minutes under the broiler or 10 to 15 minutes on the griddle. Let stand until cool enough to handle. Carefully remove the skin, making sure none of the charred skin gets into the eggplant pulp, and drain them in a strainer.

Meanwhile, heat 2 tablespoons olive oil in a small skillet over low heat. Add the garlic and cook for a minute or two to remove its bite. Do not let it brown!

Coarsely puree the eggplants in a food processor or chop with a knife. Add the tahini, lemon juice, and garlic and process just until blended, or beat into the eggplant puree with a whisk or electric mixer. Season to taste with salt. If it's too thick, whisk in a little water and/or olive oil. Add more lemon juice if needed.

Pour the baba ghanouj into a shallow bowl and sprinkle with the pine nuts and parsley. Serve with the pita or cut raw vegetables.

NOTE: Wrap the pita breads tightly in foil and heat over steaming water to soften them, then cut into quarters.

Moroccan Eggplant Salad

2 large or 3 medium
  eggplants
1 small onion, chopped
  (about ¼ cup)
3 cloves garlic, finely
  minced
1 tablespoon ground
  cumin
2 teaspoons paprika
½ teaspoon or less
  cayenne pepper
¼ cup (or to taste) fresh
  lemon juice
¾ cup fruity olive oil
3 ripe large tomatoes,
  peeled if desired, cut
  into ½-inch dice
¼ cup chopped fresh
  parsley
Salt and freshly ground
  pepper

When tomatoes are in season, this North African "rata-touille" salad is always part of our Middle Eastern *mezze* assortment. If you want, add roasted red pepper strips to the salad. ◆ *Serves 6 to 8*

Preheat the oven to 450°.

Prick each eggplant in a few places with a fork. Roast on a baking sheet until tender but not mushy, about 45 minutes. Let stand until cool enough to handle, then peel and cut into 1½-inch cubes. Place in a colander to drain, then transfer to a large bowl.

Place the onion, garlic, spices, and lemon juice in a food processor or blender and process until completely liquefied. Pour over the eggplant.

Add the olive oil, tomatoes, and parsley; mix gently with your hands so that the eggplant doesn't break down. Season to taste with salt and pepper. Taste and add more lemon juice and spices if needed.

Escalivada

SPANISH EGGPLANT
SALAD WITH ONIONS
AND PEPPERS

2 medium red onions

1 cup olive oil, plus
    additional for the
    onions

3 medium eggplants

2 red bell peppers

3 medium tomatoes
    (optional)

½ cup fresh lemon juice

3 cloves garlic, minced

Salt and freshly ground
    pepper

1 teaspoon ground cumin,
    optional

Chopped fresh parsley for
    garnish

This salad is similar to the Moroccan salad, but it has roasted onions, roasted peppers, and, if you want, roasted tomatoes, too. It makes a wonderful sauce for sautéed chicken or a Spanish-inspired pasta. Although it is not authentic, we like to add some cumin to this salad occasionally. The Spanish do use cumin in many salads, and, besides, we like the taste combination. ◆ *Serves 6 to 8*

Preheat the oven to 400°.

Put the onions in a baking pan and rub them with a little olive oil. Roast until tender, at least 1 hour. Let stand until cool enough to handle, then peel and slice ½ inch thick.

Prick the eggplants in several places with a fork and place them in a baking pan. Roast until soft but not mushy, about 45 minutes. Let cool, then peel and cut into 1½-inch cubes. Place in a colander to drain. *Escalivar* (in Catalan) means to grill, so, if you like the smoky flavor, you may grill the eggplant instead of roasting it in the oven.

Char the peppers over an open flame or under the broiler until blackened on all sides. Transfer to a plastic container with a lid or a paper or plastic bag. Cover the container or close the bag and let the peppers steam for about 15 minutes. Peel the skins from the peppers; then cut in half, remove the stems, and scrape out the seeds. Cut the flesh into strips.

Roast the tomatoes over the flame with the peppers or in the oven for about 15 minutes. Peel and cut them into cubes.

Combine the onions, eggplants, peppers, and tomatoes in a large mixing bowl.

Whisk the olive oil, lemon juice, and garlic together, then season to taste with salt, pepper, and optional cumin. Pour over the eggplant mixture and gently toss to coat. Taste and adjust the seasoning and sprinkle with the parsley.

Beets with Sesame Vinaigrette

1 pound beets (after cooking there should be about 2 cups)

6 tablespoons mild olive oil

2 teaspoons Oriental sesame oil

2 tablespoons fresh lemon juice

2 teaspoons sesame seeds, plus additional for garnish, toasted

Salt and freshly ground pepper to taste

We try to find small beets for this salad—red or yellow or the new variegated chioggia beets which are a pale pink. For *Beets with Anise Vinaigrette*, omit the sesame oil and substitute toasted anise seeds for the sesame seeds.
◆ *Serves 4*

Trim the tops from the beets, leaving about 1/2 inch of the stem attached so that they do not bleed too much. Put the beets in a pot and cover with cold water. Heat to boiling, then reduce the heat and simmer uncovered until tender. Pour off most of the hot water and add cold water to the pot. Peel the beets while they are still warm. Or you may rub the beets with a little oil and bake them in a covered pan at 350° until tender. If the beets are large, cut them into 1/4-inch slices. If they are small, cut them into 4 or 8 wedges each. Place the beets in a large mixing bowl.

Whisk the remaining ingredients together, pour over the still warm beets, and toss to coat. Sprinkle with more sesame seeds if you like and serve.

Moroccan Carrot Salad

6–8 medium carrots

2 teaspoons paprika

1/2 teaspoon cinnamon

1/4 teaspoon cayenne pepper

1 teaspoon ground cumin

2 tablespoons fresh lemon juice

1 tablespoon sugar

1/3 cup mild olive oil

Salt

We like to serve this as part of a *mezze* platter, a Middle Eastern antipasto. If the spices in the vinaigrette aren't completely emulsified and the carrots aren't dressed while they are still warm, the vinaigrette will be gritty. ◆ *Serves 6 to 8*

Peel the carrots and thinly slice or cut into julienne strips. A mandoline will make this job easy, if you have one. If not, just try to cut the carrots in uniform pieces, because you want them all to be cooked at the same time. You should have about 2 cups.

Place the spices, lemon juice, and sugar in a mortar and grind with a pestle to emulsify. Gradually work in the olive oil. Season to taste with salt and adjust the seasoning.

Heat a medium pot of water to boiling. Salt the water, drop in the carrots, and cook until tender but still somewhat crisp. This will take just a minute or two. Quickly drain the carrots, put them in a mixing bowl, and toss them immediately with the vinaigrette. If the carrots seem gritty, add a tablespoon of cold water to smooth out the dressing.

Cucumber Salad with Yogurt, Mint, and Raisins

¼ cup raisins

1 tablespoon minced garlic

2 tablespoons olive oil

3 cups diced (½ inch) cucumbers, preferably English or Japanese (see Note)

¾ cup yogurt

3 tablespoons chopped fresh mint

¼ cup chopped toasted walnuts

Salt and freshly ground pepper

This is a wonderful addition to the Middle Eastern *mezze* platter, but we also love to serve it with shish kabobs. You could thin this with more yogurt and some ice water and serve it as a summer soup as well. ✦ *Serves 6*

Plump the raisins in hot water to cover about 15 minutes. Drain well, reserving the soaking liquid.

Heat the garlic in the olive oil for a minute or two just to remove the bite. Let cool.

Combine the raisins, garlic with oil, cucumbers, yogurt, mint, and walnuts in a mixing bowl. Season to taste with salt and pepper. Add the raisin soaking liquid to taste for a pleasing balance of sweet and tart. Serve at room temperature or slightly chilled.

NOTE: If you are using English cucumbers, it won't be necessary to peel them but do remove the seeds. Japanese cucumbers are much smaller so they will not have to be peeled or seeded. If you must use "regular" cucumbers, peel and seed them.

Zucchini Salad with Walnuts and Dill

Salt

2 cups diced (¾ inch) zucchini

¼ cup walnuts, toasted and coarsely chopped

¼ cup olive oil

1 tablespoon fresh lemon juice

2 teaspoons (or to taste) chopped fresh dill

Freshly ground pepper

Another fast and easy salad for the Middle Eastern *mezze* platter. The walnuts add a nice crunch. If fresh dill is unavailable, you could use mint instead. ✦ *Serves 4*

Heat a medium pot of water to boiling. Salt the water, add the zucchini, and cook until crisp-tender, 1 to 2 minutes. Quickly drain and refresh in cold water to stop the cooking. Place the zucchini in a mixing bowl.

Whisk together the walnuts, olive oil, lemon juice, dill, and salt and pepper to taste. Pour over the zucchini and toss to coat.

Turkish Artichokes

6 large artichokes, stems,
  tough leaves, and top 1
  inch of cone trimmed

¼ cup fresh lemon juice

¼ cup fresh orange juice
  (optional)

¾ cup olive oil

2 teaspoons red pepper
  flakes

6 thick slices (½ inch)
  orange (with peel)

12 thick slices (½ inch)
  yellow or white onions

Salt to taste

I first read this recipe in Helen Hecht's *Cuisine for All Seasons*. We have modified it only slightly, removing the sugar and increasing the orange and hot pepper. I include it here to share it with you and spread the word. These artichokes make a wonderful first course or an enticing addition to a *mezze* platter with Moroccan carrots, lentil salad with mint, and hummus or baba ghanouj. Cut into eighths and heated in a skillet, they're terrific on baked fish, such as rockfish, snapper, sea bass, and flounder. They can even be baked in the same dish. ◆ *Serves 6*

Arrange the artichokes upright in a pan just wide enough to hold them. Add the lemon and orange juices, oil, and enough water to come halfway up the sides. Sprinkle with the pepper flakes, then top with the orange and onion slices. Cover the pan and simmer until the bottoms are pierced easily with a sharp knife, about 45 minutes.

Remove the artichokes and orange and onion slices from the pan. Taste the pan juices and season with salt to taste. If you want a thicker sauce, boil the pan juices to reduce them a bit. Let cool completely.

Cut the artichokes in half and remove the fuzzy chokes with a spoon. Put the artichokes in a bowl, top with the orange and onion slices, and pour the pan juices over the top.

Artichokes with Tomato Vinaigrette

These are good as part of an antipasto assortment. We make a court bouillon to cook the artichokes and use some of the poaching liquid as a base for the tomato vinaigrette. These are best if cooked the day before and allowed to marinate overnight. ◆ *Serves 6 to 8*

COURT BOUILLON

1 cup water
½ cup dry white wine
3 tablespoons olive oil
3 thin slices lemon
2 cloves garlic, smashed and peeled
2 thyme sprigs
2 small bay leaves
1 teaspoon salt
12 black peppercorns, bruised with meat pounder
6 whole coriander seeds

12 to 16 baby or small artichokes

TOMATO VINAIGRETTE

½ cup reserved court bouillon
2 tablespoons fresh lemon juice
2 tablespoons tomato puree
2 cloves garlic, finely minced
¼ cup fruity olive oil
2 to 3 tablespoons mild olive oil
½ cup diced seeded peeled fresh tomatoes or canned plum tomatoes
Salt and freshly ground pepper

Combine all the ingredients for the court bouillon in a wide saucepan and heat to boiling.

Meanwhile, trim the artichokes: Snap off the outside dark green leaves, trim the stems, and pare the outside of the base around the stem. Cut off the top ½ inch of the cone. Drop the artichokes immediately into the simmering bouillon (see Note). Reduce the heat, cover the pan, and simmer until tender, 10 to 15 minutes. The point of a knife should penetrate the base easily. Drain, reserving ½ cup of the bouillon. If the artichokes are small and not tiny, cut them in half and scrape out the choke with a small spoon. Place the artichokes in a large mixing bowl.

To make the Tomato Vinaigrette, whisk the reserved bouillon, the lemon juice, tomato puree, and garlic together in a mixing bowl. Whisk in both oils and fold in the tomatoes. Season to taste with salt and pepper. Pour the vinaigrette over the artichokes and toss well. Refrigerate at least 4 hours or overnight. Let warm to room temperature before serving.

NOTE: You can trim the artichokes ahead of time if you keep them covered with cold water acidulated with lemon juice.

VARIATION

Add a little honey to the vinaigrette for a sweet-and-sour, or *agro-dolce,* marinade. You may also make this without the chopped tomatoes if you increase the puree a bit.

Cauliflower with Red Pepper Vinaigrette

Salt

2 small heads cauliflower, broken into florets (3 to 4 cups)

1 strip lemon zest

1 cup olive oil

2 tablespoons dried red pepper flakes

Pinch paprika (optional)

¼ cup red wine vinegar

3 cloves garlic, finely minced

2 tablespoons capers, rinsed

Another salad for an antipasto platter. For a Spanish variation of this salad, tone down the red pepper flakes and use 2 tablespoons paprika. ◆ *Serves 6 to 8*

Heat a large pot of water to boiling. Lightly salt the water, add the cauliflower and lemon zest, and cook until the cauliflower is crisp-tender, 4 to 5 minutes. Drain. Refresh in cold water and drain again. Transfer to a large mixing bowl.

Heat, but do not boil, the olive oil in a small saucepan. Remove the pan from the heat, drop in the pepper flakes, and let steep until the oil is red, about 15 minutes. Strain the oil, discarding the flakes. You may add a little paprika to heighten the color, if you want. Let the oil cool completely.

Combine the vinegar and garlic in a mixing bowl. Gradually whisk in the red pepper oil, then stir in the capers. Season to taste with salt. Pour the vinaigrette over the cauliflower and toss to coat. Let marinate at room temperature a few hours.

Mushrooms with Sherry Vinaigrette

3 cups fresh white mushrooms, cut into quarters

½ cup mild olive oil

2 tablespoons sherry vinegar

½ cup sliced almonds, toasted

½ teaspoon salt

Pinch freshly ground pepper

When you first assemble this salad all you taste are the separate components—mushrooms, almonds, and sherry vinegar. But after this salad marinates for an hour or two, all of the disparate flavors meld. We like to serve this as part of a tapas assortment platter. ◆ *Serves 6*

Toss all ingredients together and let marinate for an hour or two.

White Bean Salad

1 cup dried Great
Northern or cannellini
beans, soaked overnight
and rinsed

6 cups lightly salted
water

⅓ cup plus ½ cup virgin
olive oil

2 tablespoons (or to taste)
red wine vinegar

1 teaspoon (or to taste)
salt

½ teaspoon (or to taste)
freshly ground pepper

1 cup finely diced red
onion

1 cup diced (½ inch)
tomatoes (optional)

2 tablespoons chopped
fresh herb, such as
mint, sage, or parsley
(optional)

This is a generic bean salad that can be dressed up with chopped tomatoes and fresh herbs, such as mint, sage, basil, chives, or green onions. Whether you use the smaller Great Northerns or the larger cannellini, you will enjoy the balance of creamy richness coupled with the bite of the onions and vinegar. You could make this with chick-peas (garbanzo beans) as well, although the texture of the chick-peas is drier and crunchier. Unless you really love bean salads, you will want to serve this with other lighter salads, such as broccoli with olives and garlic vinaigrette, little cooked artichokes, carrots with a zesty citrus vinaigrette, or with grilled or canned tuna with chopped green onions.
✦ *Serves 4 to 6*

Cook the beans in the lightly salted water until tender but not soft. You should have about 3 cups. Drain and transfer to a mixing bowl. Add ⅓ cup olive oil, the vinegar, salt, and pepper; toss to coat. Let cool. Add the remaining oil, the onion, tomatoes, and herb; combine well. Taste and adjust the seasoning. You may want to add a bit more vinegar too.

Lentil Salad

1 cup green or brown
    lentils

¾ cup (or as needed)
    olive oil

1 cup diced onions

1 teaspoon minced garlic

Salt and freshly ground
    pepper

MIDDLE EASTERN SALAD

2 teaspoons ground cumin

2 tablespoons lemon juice

¼ cup chopped fresh
    mint and/or ½ cup
    crumbled feta cheese

FRENCH SALAD

⅓ cup diced carrots

¼ cup diced celery

2 tablespoons red wine
    vinegar

2 tablespoons chopped
    fresh chives

½ cup crumbled mild
    goat cheese

ITALIAN SALAD

⅓ cup diced carrots

¼ cup diced celery

1 tablespoon minced
    garlic (in addition to 1
    teaspoon)

2 tablespoons red wine
    vinegar

2 tablespoons chopped
    fresh parsley

I love the French green lentils that you can buy in a gourmet grocery or specialty store, but I realize not everyone can find them easily. They are best for salads and most cooked lentil dishes for they hold their shape and don't get mushy if you turn your back for a minute to answer the phone. The plain everyday brown lentils are ideal for soup because they cook quickly and soften fast. Obviously the brown lentils can only be used for salad if you hover over them and test them every few minutes. Brown lentils cook in ten to twelve minutes; the green, in about twenty minutes. ◆ *Serves 4*

The Middle Eastern Salad is delicious with Turkish Artichokes, Moroccan Carrot Salad, and Baba Ghanouj (pages 47, 45, and 42). Accompany the French Salad with beet salad, with chives and leeks, with mustard vinaigrette, or sliced tomatoes with basil. With the Italian Salad serve Italian Eggplant Crouton or Bruschetta topped with fresh mozzarella and sun-dried tomatoes (pages 41 or 23). Rinse the lentils, place them in a saucepan, and cover with fresh water. Gently simmer covered over low heat until *al dente*. Pay attention! Drain if necessary, transfer to a mixing bowl, and toss immediately with some of the olive oil.

Heat 3 tablespoons olive oil in a sauté pan or skillet over medium heat. Add the onion, and carrots and celery if using, and cook until tender. Add the garlic, and cumin if using, and cook a minute or two longer. Let cool, then add to the lentils and toss to combine.

Dress the salad with lemon juice or vinegar, additional oil if needed, and salt and pepper to taste. Stir in the herb and sprinkle cheese, if using, over top.

PORTUGUESE-INSPIRED SALADS

Although each of these salads could stand on its own, we prefer to serve these in a trio for a Portuguese-inspired antipasto plate. None are wholly authentic, but they capture the basic flavors of the country and make a very pretty and tasty combination.

*B*lack Beans with Eggs and Prosciutto

1½ cups dried black
  beans, soaked overnight
  and rinsed
1 cup olive oil
⅔ cup diced red onion
½ cup red wine vinegar
Salt and freshly ground
  pepper
3 ounces sliced (⅛ inch)
  prosciutto, cut into 1
  by ¼-inch strips
3 hard-cooked eggs,
  coarsely chopped
Chopped fresh parsley
  and ripe tomato
  wedges for garnish

♦ *Serves 6*

Cook the beans in fresh cold water to cover over low heat until tender but not mushy, about 45 minutes. The beans tend to firm up a bit after cooking, so cook them to the soft side of tender rather than the firmer side. Drain the beans and transfer to a large mixing bowl. Toss with enough olive oil to coat, then chill.

Add the remaining oil, the onion, and vinegar to the beans and toss to coat and combine. Season to taste with salt and pepper. I like these a bit peppery. Sprinkle with the prosciutto and eggs. Garnish with parsley and tomato wedges if you like.

NOTE: You could make this salad with white beans, black-eyed peas, or fresh fava beans, too.

Peppers with Cayenne and Cilantro

3 large red peppers
3 large green peppers
½ cup plus 6 tablespoons
    olive oil
½ teaspoon cayenne
    pepper
¼ cup red wine vinegar
Salt and ground pepper
3 tablespoons chopped
    cilantro
Several olives for garnish

♦ *Serves 6*

Cut the peppers into strips about ½ inch wide. Heat 3 tablespoons olive oil in a large sauté pan or skillet over medium heat. Add the peppers and cook until crisp-tender. Remove from the heat and set aside.

Dissolve the cayenne in some of the vinegar, then mix with the remaining oil and remaining vinegar. Season to taste with salt and pepper. Pour the vinaigrette over the peppers and toss to coat. Sprinkle with the cilantro and garnish with olives.

Carrot Salad with Mint

12 medium carrots
Salt
1½ cups Mint
    Vinaigrette

MINT VINAIGRETTE

¼ cup fresh lemon juice
¼ cup chopped fresh
    mint
1¼ cups mild olive oil
¼ cup red wine vinegar
2 tablespoons fresh lemon
    juice
½ cup (firmly packed)
    chopped fresh mint
1 teaspoon sugar
½ teaspoon salt

♦ *Serves 6*

Peel the carrots and cut into julienne strips or thin slices on a mandoline or by hand (about 4 cups). Heat a large pot of water to boiling. Lightly salt the water, add the carrots, and boil until crisp-tender, 1 to 2 minutes. Drain and refresh in ice water. Drain again and pat dry with a towel. Transfer to a large mixing bowl, add the vinaigrette, and toss to coat.

The vinaigrette is also excellent on spinach salad with feta cheese, thinly sliced red onions, and Kalamata olives, as well as Rice Salad with Grilled Tuna (page 75). ♦ *Makes about 1¾ cups, enough for 6 salads*

For the infusion, combine the lemon juice and mint in a small saucepan. Heat to boiling and remove from the heat. Let steep about 10 minutes. Strain the infusion into a mixing bowl; there should be about ¼ cup.

Add the remaining ingredients and whisk together.

MEDITERRANEAN-INSPIRED SALADS

ost Mediterranean salads are simple affairs, spontaneously put together from bits and pieces of things found in the refrigerator or larder. They may combine a few slices of ripe pear, some nuts and cheese and a leftover boiled potato. One day the classic Piemontese salad of roasted peppers with anchovy-garlic vinaigrette might be extended with slivers of fennel, slices of fontina cheese, possibly artichoke hearts, on a bed of arugula or greens. Another time it might be with slices of cooked potato or eggplant, or cooked tuna. Sometimes a little leftover gazpacho might be used as a dressing for avocado or a few cooked shrimp. Yesterday's bread might be become the basis of today's salad, tossed with a few flavorful vegetables and herbs, as in *fattoush* or *panzanella*. And occasionally cooked vegetables may be tossed with a sprightly vinaigrette and topped with toasted breadcrumbs. The variety is as infinite as your imagination and the resources of your refrigerator.

Many of my salad recipes are written in single portions because I believe that most salads are made for as many as are dining, be it one or twenty, but I wrote the recipes for the vinaigrettes to serve four or six. They can easily be multiplied to serve more, and any left over will keep perfectly in a container in the refrigerator. Just bring them to room temperature and revive them with a quick shake. These versatile dressings make great marinades for grilled or baked fish, poultry and meats, and make a wonderful non-mayonnaise–based dressing to drizzle on bread for sandwiches.

You will notice that I refer to two kinds of olive oil. By mild, I mean light in flavor and hue, such as Sasso or Bertolli olive oil. By fruity, I mean virgin or extra virgin olive oil, with its nutty or fruity flavor and rich green or deep golden color. These oils usually come from Italy, but there are several comparable oils from France, Spain, Greece, and other countries of the Mediterranean, as well as California. Hazelnut and walnut oils are very rich in flavor and add another quality to salads. However they have a short shelf life and can go rancid quickly. It is best to buy the smallest amounts possible and store them in the refrigerator. For the very same reasons, I recommend keeping all nuts in the refrigerator or in the freezer in an airtight container. Before using, spread the nuts on a baking sheet and toast in a moderate oven to bring out the flavor and revive the texture.

As for vinegar, I encourage you to taste a few for they all have distinctive personalities. Some red wine vinegars have a nice acidity; others are so caustic and unpleasant that they will ruin any salad dressed with them. I also like to use sherry vinegar, balsamic vinegar, Champagne vinegar, Japanese rice vinegar, and occasionally a drop or two of plain old white vinegar for a certain kind of sharp tartness in a pickle or sauce. I especially like to use balsamic or sherry vinegar with nut oil as their rich flavor plays off the sweetness of the oil and adds acidity without being sour.

As for the greens, all lettuces should be washed with care, spun dry, layered on towels, and refrigerated for crispness. Use a variety of greens for texture and taste contrasts. There is more to life than romaine and butter (Boston) lettuce. While not everyone is able to have his own garden or buy the great variety of esoteric and wonderful lettuces we find so easily in California, there are alternatives at your produce market. Keep an eye out for dandelion greens, *frisée* (curly endive), sweet young spinach, peppery watercress, tart sorrel, and spicy arugula. Small lettuces are best because there is less waste and the leaves will be more tender. If you are lucky, your market may occasionally offer a salad assortment called *mesclun,* the traditional mix of young leaves sold in France. Large leaves of basil and mint are also welcome in a salad, providing both surprise and contrast.

Herbs should be fresh whenever possible (except oregano, which has its own personality as a dried herb). Dried basil has an unpleasant bitterness that doesn't taste at all like basil. Dried sage is musty tasting. Dried tarragon has an unpleasant sweetness and intensity. Dried mint can be used in a pinch, but it lacks the crisp fresh punch of the real thing. As a rule for all cooking, fresh herbs will have the aroma and intensity of flavor to add a distinctive note to your food. Happily, more and more markets are carrying an assortment of fresh herbs.

Use tomatoes only when they are in season and avoid those gassed pink horrors that are available all year round. Tomatoes are the reward of summer.

Anchovies are called for in a few of these salads, and I realize many people are wary of them. They envisage those salty little coiled snakes embracing a caper and covered with poor olive oil or the forlorn and wizened strip atop a slice of pizza. That's not what I am thinking of when I say anchovy. Anchovies come packed in either salt or oil. The salted anchovies are packed in cans and come from Sicily. They're easy to clean: Just pull apart the fillets, discard the bones, and rinse well. Cover the cleaned fillets with fragrant olive oil and store in the refrigerator. Let warm to room temperature before using. The next best thing to salt packed are the flat anchovy fillets packed in good olive oil. These come in small cans or jars from Spain, Italy, or Portugal. Once you have tried these you will come to love them for the wonderful subtle flavor they impart to a vinaigrette or marinade. Anchovies are so much more than salt. It's always nice to have an assortment of good olives on hand to add sparkle and texture to your salads. I can't imagine being without the little Niçoises, the rich Kalamatas, the meaty Moroccan olives, the briny Gaetas from Sicily, and the wrinkled black beauties from the south of Italy.

Most of us love garlic, but sometimes the garlic that is available is not of the best quality, particularly in the winter when it may have sprouted in the center. Please remove those sprouts or the garlic will be unpleasantly bitter. When in doubt, sauté the garlic lightly just to remove any bite, but do not brown the garlic or it will be bitter. I suspect that people who object to garlic have had it with the bite and bitterness in full force. It is a wonderful component whose flavor is essential to many Mediterranean dishes, so learn to handle it with the respect your palate deserves.

Pairing wine with so many foods that have pungent vinaigrettes is a challenge but not an impossibility. Evan, my son the sommelier, suggests as a white a sauvignon blanc, either from California or France's Loire Valley, or one from the Friuli region of Italy. Sauvignon blanc's vegetal qualities mesh with the flavors of the foods and its high acidity enables it to hold its own with the tartness of the dressings. If you want a red wine he suggests a light and flavorful pinot noir from California or Oregon, a light French burgundy such as a Mercurey or a Givry, a Spanish rioja or an Italian valpolicella or lambrusco. These are light, tasty, easily accessible wines, not the great heavies of the wine world.

Pear, Celery, Potato, and Watercress Salad

Sweet, crunchy, smooth, creamy, and slightly piquant, this salad is complex in flavor but very simple to make. We prefer Gorgonzola *dolce latte* for its creamy texture, but you could substitute a Roquefort or blue cheese. The watercress may be augmented with Belgian endive for a tart contrast to the peppery taste of the cress. If pears are not in season, substitute blanched carrot slices, and you may replace the celery with fennel.

FOR EACH SERVING

½ cup watercress, stems trimmed

¼ cup sliced (¼ inch) boiled small potato

¼ cup thinly sliced celery, cut on the diagonal

⅓ cup Gorgonzola Cream Vinaigrette (recipe follows)

7 thin slices ripe Bartlett or Comice pear (with peel)

6 walnut halves, toasted and coarsely chopped

1 tablespoon crumbled Gorgonzola dolce latte (optional)

GORGONZOLA CREAM VINAIGRETTE

½ cup mild olive oil

¼ cup finely crumbled Gorgonzola dolce latte

¼ cup heavy cream

1 tablespoon fresh lemon juice

¼ teaspoon salt

Pinch freshly ground pepper

Make a bed of the watercress on a salad plate. Toss the potato and celery with a little of the vinaigrette and place on the watercress. Strew the pear slices over top. Drizzle with the rest of the vinaigrette and sprinkle with the walnuts. You may add a few chunks of crumbled Gorgonzola as well.

To make Gorgonzola Cream Vinaigrette, place all the ingredients in a food processor and pulse quickly just until combined. Do not overprocess. ◆ *Makes about 1 cup, enough for 3 salads*

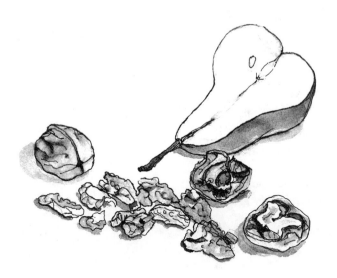

Pear, Provolone, and Arugula Salad

This salad has sparkle from mint, basil, pears, and, of course, the Champagne.

Toss the arugula and herbs with 2 to 3 tablespoons of the vinaigrette and place on a salad plate. Top with the pear slices and cheese strips, then drizzle with the remaining vinaigrette

To make Champagne Vinaigrette, whisk the oil, vinegar, and Champagne together. Season to taste with salt and pepper and add the sugar if needed to round out the flavor. ◆ *Makes 1½ cups, enough for 6 to 8 salads*

FOR EACH SERVING

1 large handful arugula
   (about 1½ cups
   loosely packed)
2 tablespoons or 2 good
   pinches chopped fresh
   mint
2 tablespoons or 2 good
   pinches chopped fresh
   basil
¼ cup Champagne
   Vinaigrette (recipe
   follows)
6 to 8 thin slices Comice
   pear (with peel)
7 or 8 strips provolone
   cheese, about 2 by ½
   inch and ⅛ inch thick

CHAMPAGNE
VINAIGRETTE

1 cup mild olive oil
¼ cup Champagne
   vinegar
½ cup Champagne
Salt and freshly ground
   pepper
Pinch sugar, if needed

Endive, Apple, and Walnut Salad

FOR EACH SERVING

2 tablespoons walnuts, toasted and coarsely chopped

¼ cup Walnut Vinaigrette (recipe follows)

1 medium Belgian endive, leaves separated

½ small Pippin or Granny Smith, cored and thinly sliced crosswise into half rounds

WALNUT VINAIGRETTE

7 tablespoons walnut oil

2 tablespoons mild olive oil

2 tablespoons balsamic vinegar

1 tablespoon sherry vinegar

Salt and freshly ground pepper

A perfect accompaniment for this salad is Baked Goat Cheese in Filo (page 20) or goat cheese that has been dipped in toasted bread crumbs and baked until warmed through.

Toss the walnuts with just enough vinaigrette to coat. Toss the endive with most of the remaining vinaigrette and arrange the leaves on a salad plate. Top with the apple slices and drizzle with a little vinaigrette. Sprinkle with the walnuts and serve at once.

To make Walnut Vinaigrette, whisk the oils and vinegars together, then season to taste with salt and pepper. This vinaigrette is also excellent with a salad of beets, oranges, onions, and watercress, a salad of romaine, butter lettuce, and Gruyère or Gorgonzola cheese, and on grilled leeks.
♦ *Makes 1½ cups, enough for 4 or 5 salads*

VARIATION

For *Hazelnut Vinaigrette,* substitute hazelnut oil for the walnut oil, and toasted hazelnuts for the walnuts.

Mushrooms, Gruyère, and Prosciutto

FOR EACH SERVING

1 large handful arugula (2 cups loosely packed)

½ Belgian endive, leaves separated (optional; if using, use less arugula)

¼ cup Lemon Cream or Balsamic Vinaigrette

2 perfect white mushrooms, sliced ⅛ inch thick

6 thin slices fennel (optional)

8 strips prosciutto, about 2 by ½ inch and ⅛ inch thick

8 strips Gruyère or Emmenthaler cheese, same size as the prosciutto

LEMON CREAM VINAIGRETTE

1 cup mild olive oil

¼ cup fresh lemon juice

¼ cup heavy cream

1 teaspoon grated lemon zest (optional)

Salt and freshly ground pepper

BALSAMIC VINAIGRETTE

½ cup mild olive oil

¼ cup fruity olive oil

¼ cup balsamic vinegar

Salt and freshly ground pepper

This salad can be dressed two ways. It takes very nicely to a rich lemon cream, especially if you add some tart Belgian endive to contrast with the nutty bite of the arugula. And it is exciting (I know that's an extreme word for a salad, but I mean exciting to the palate) with a balsamic vinaigrette.

Toss the greens with half the vinaigrette and place on a salad plate. Toss the mushrooms and fennel with enough vinaigrette to coat and arrange on the greens. Lay the strips of prosciutto and cheese on top and drizzle lightly with the remaining vinaigrette.

To make Lemon Cream Vinaigrette, whisk the oil, lemon juice, cream, and lemon zest together, then season to taste with salt and pepper. ◆ *Makes 1 ½ cups, enough for 6 salads*

To make Balsamic Vinaigrette, whisk the oils and vinegar together, then season to taste with salt and pepper. ◆ *Makes 1 cup, enough for 4 salads*

Black Radish, Carrot, and Fennel Salad with Pecorino Cheese

FOR EACH SERVING

1 small handful arugula (about ¾ cup loosely packed)

¼ cup Citrus Vinaigrette (recipe follows) or Black Pepper Vinaigrette (page 79)

3 large paper-thin slices black radish

6 thin diagonal slices carrot (about 2 inches long), blanched

6 thin slices fennel

6 to 8 long thin curls pecorino or Parmesan cheese

CITRUS VINAIGRETTE

1¼ cups mild olive oil

6 to 8 tablespoons fresh lemon juice

1 tablespoon grated lemon zest

Salt and freshly ground pepper to taste

This salad does what a salad should do—perk up the palate and stimulate the appetite. It is light, piquant, and very pretty. We slice the radishes on a slicer or mandoline and hold them in ice water where they curl up a bit. The fennel needs no blanching (you could use celery), but do cook the carrots in boiling water for a minute or two and refresh them in cold water. They should be thin but not as thin as the radish. The choice of vinaigrette is up to you. I like the citrus for most occasions, but the black pepper vinaigrette can be a wonderful "hit." If you cannot find the black radishes, you may use daikon, but it will not have that elegant black trim. You may also make this salad without the radish, in which case, please use the black pepper vinaigrette for accent. To make cheese curls, shave the piece of cheese with a sharp vegetable peeler.

Toss the arugula with enough of the vinaigrette to coat and place on a salad plate. Arrange the radish slices on top, then the carrot and fennel. Drizzle with the remaining vinaigrette and top with the curls of cheese.

To make Citrus Vinaigrette, whisk all ingredients together.
+ *Makes about 1½ cups, enough for 4 to 6 salads*

Roast Pepper, Fontina, and Arugula Salad

3 large red bell peppers

⅓ cup virgin olive oil

6 cups loosely packed arugula, trimmed

2 small bulbs fennel, trimmed, cored, and thinly sliced (optional)

Anchovy Garlic Vinaigrette (recipe follows)

4 ounces Fontina cheese, thinly sliced and cut into 3 by ½-inch strips

Freshly ground pepper (optional)

ANCHOVY GARLIC VINAIGRETTE

¾ cup mild olive oil

½ cup fruity olive oil

½ cup red wine vinegar

3 cloves garlic, finely minced

2 heaping tablespoons finely minced or pureed anchovies

Freshly ground pepper to taste

So where has arugula been hiding all this time? All at once it seems to be on everyone's menu, but for years it was growing in Italian family backyards. For those who took the time to cultivate it and knew of its special properties it was always there, but it was not easily available to the rest of us. Finally, in our current produce revolution, the word is out about what a delicious salad green it is—peppery, nutty, spicy, and crisp. It contrasts perfectly with fleshy red peppers and creamy Fontina, but remember arugula is best when the leaves are small. ✦ *Serves 6*

Char the peppers on an open flame or under the broiler until blackened on all sides. Transfer to a plastic container with a lid, or a paper or plastic bag. Cover the container or close the bag and let the peppers steam for about 15 minutes. Peel the skins from the peppers; then cut in half, remove the stems, and scrape out the seeds. Don't rinse the peppers under water to remove the skins because they lose too much flavor. You can scrape the excess char off with a knife. Cut the peppers into ½-inch-wide strips. Place them in a small bowl and cover with the olive oil.

Toss the arugula and fennel, if using, separately with most of the vinaigrette. Divide the arugula among 6 salad plates and top with the fennel. Arrange the red pepper and cheese strips over top and drizzle with the remaining vinaigrette. Grind pepper over the salads if desired and serve at once.

To make Anchovy Garlic Vinaigrette, whisk all ingredients together. This vinaigrette is excellent with a simple salad of just roasted peppers and arugula with or without thin slices of Fontina cheese, on Caponata di Verdure (page 72), and as a marinade for tuna or swordfish. ✦ *Makes 1¾ cups, enough for 4 to 6 salads*

Panzanella

ITALIAN BREAD SALAD

FOR EACH SERVING

1 cup 1-inch bread cubes (see Note)

6 tablespoons Basic Vinaigrette without mustard (recipe follows)

½ cup diced (½ inch) tomato

½ cup diced (½ inch) cucumbers (peeled and seeded if necessary)

2 tablespoons finely diced red onion

2 tablespoons slivered fresh basil

BASIC VINAIGRETTE

⅓ cup fruity olive oil

⅔ cup mild olive oil

3 tablespoons red wine vinegar

1 tablespoon balsamic vinegar

1 teaspoon Dijon mustard

Salt and freshly ground pepper to taste

The Italian *fattoush!* Or how to make a satisfying meal out of almost nothing.

Toss the bread cubes with 2 tablespoons vinaigrette and let stand about 30 minutes. Add the remaining ingredients including the remaining vinaigrette and quickly toss together. Garnish with a little more slivered basil if you want.

To make Basic Vinaigrette, whisk all ingredients together or process in a blender until combined. This is the house vinaigrette we use to dress our mixed green salads. You can add fresh herbs if you like and some minced garlic too.

✦ *Makes about 1¼ cups, enough for 5 or 6 salads*

NOTE: The bread for this salad should be Italian or French and trimmed of hard crusts. It can be a day old. Supermarket white bread will completely dissolve in this salad.

VARIATION

For *Basic Vinaigrette with Garlic*, add 1 teaspoon finely minced garlic.

Fattoush

LEBANESE TOASTED
PITA BREAD SALAD

FOR EACH SERVING

1 pita bread
1 cup (loosely packed)
   romaine lettuce strips,
   1½ inches wide
6 tablespoons Citrus
   Vinaigrette (page 63)
½ cup diced (½ inch)
   tomato
½ cup diced (½ inch)
   cucumber (peeled and
   seeded if necessary)
2 tablespoons very finely
   diced red onion
2 tablespoons finely
   chopped green onions
2 tablespoons chopped
   fresh mint
1 tablespoon chopped
   fresh parsley
Salt and freshly ground
   pepper

During the long winter months when there are no tomatoes, we dream about *fattoush,* a variation of tabouleh made with toasted pita bread instead of cracked wheat. It is our favorite summer salad. Some versions of this recipe call for the addition of powdered sumac or chopped purslane. These are somewhat esoteric, but, if you have them, add a pinch of one or the other to the salad.

Toast the pita bread until semicrisp, then break it into pieces about 2 inches long and wide. Do not crumble them or make them too small; bigger is better in this instance.

Toss the romaine with a little vinaigrette and place it on a salad plate. Toss the vegetables, herbs, and pita with the remaining vinaigrette and season to taste with salt and pepper. Mound this mixture on top of the romaine.

Greek Salad

FOR EACH SERVING

6 *paper-thin slices red onion*

4 *tablespoons Oregano Garlic Vinaigrette (recipe follows)*

12 *thin slices (⅛ inch) cucumber*

2 *slices (¼ inch) each red and yellow tomato or 4 slices red*

2 *rings (¼ inch thick) each green and red bell pepper*

2 *ounces feta cheese, coarsely crumbled*

6 *Kalamata olives, pitted if desired*

OREGANO GARLIC
VINAIGRETTE

3 *tablespoons dried oregano*

1¼ *cups mild olive oil*

½ *cup red wine vinegar*

2 *cloves garlic, very finely minced*

Salt and freshly ground pepper to taste

I know there are many Greek salads out there, but we think ours is particularly pretty and the vinaigrette especially tasty. We often make sandwiches of these ingredients with sesame seed bread. You may want to try that as well.

Toss the onion slices with 1 tablespoon vinaigrette and let marinate about 20 minutes to soften the onions and take away some of the bite.

Arrange the cucumbers on a salad plate and top with the onions. Add the tomato slices and then the pepper slices, alternating colors if possible. Top with the feta and olives. Drizzle with the remaining vinaigrette.

To make Oregano Garlic Vinaigrette, rub the oregano with your hands to warm it and release its oils or toast it in a dry skillet for a minute or two. Whisk all the ingredients together. ◆ *Makes about 1¾ cups, enough for 6 salads*

Israeli Avocado Salad

FOR EACH SERVING

½ cup mixed salad
   greens or watercress
   (optional)
5 tablespoons Toasted
   Cumin Vinaigrette
   (recipe follows)
½ avocado, cut into
   1-inch chunks
¼ cup walnuts, toasted,
   very coarsely chopped
⅓ cup diced (½ inch)
   celery
⅓ cup diced (½ inch)
   seeded cucumber
2 tablespoons finely
   chopped red onion

TOASTED CUMIN VINAIGRETTE

3 to 4 tablespoons cumin
   seeds
⅔ cup mild olive oil
⅓ cup fruity olive oil
⅓ cup fresh lemon juice
Salt and freshly ground
   pepper to taste

This salad is a delight of contrasting textures: creamy avocado, crunchy walnuts, celery, and cucumbers, and the tang of toasted cumin vinaigrette.

Lightly dress the greens with some of the vinaigrette and place on a salad plate. Toss the remaining ingredients with the remaining vinaigrette and mound on the greens.

To make Toasted Cumin Vinaigrette, toast the cumin seeds in a small skillet over low heat, stirring occasionally, until fragrant; it will take just a minute or two. Grind the cumin in a spice mill, then whisk together with the remaining ingredients. ◆ *Makes 1⅓ cups, enough for 5 or 6 salads*

Grilled Leeks with Walnut Cream Vinaigrette

24 small leeks

WALNUT CREAM VINAIGRETTE

½ *cup walnut oil*
¼ *cup mild olive oil*
½ *cup heavy cream*
2 *tablespoons balsamic vinegar*
Salt and freshly ground pepper

½ *cup walnuts, toasted and chopped*
2 *tablespoons chopped fresh parsley or mint for garnish*

As a cook I find that poached leeks with a simple vinaigrette makes a very satisfying first course, but for many of our customers they are just not glamorous. We have found a way to sex them up (the leeks, not the customers). We poach the leeks and then grill them to give them a slightly smoky flavor. Then we dress the grilled leeks with a walnut cream and top them with chopped walnuts. You may add chopped parsley or mint as a garnish and color accent.
• *Serves 4*

Cut the most of the green tops from the leeks and trim the root ends but leave them intact. Split each one down the middle almost to the root end. Rinse them thoroughly by sloshing them around in a sink full of cold water.

Heat a large pot of water to simmering. Add the leeks and simmer gently until tender. Test by pinching the root end of the leek with your fingers; if it cracks slightly, it is done. Test each one, because they differ in thickness, and refresh them in ice water to stop the cooking and set the color. Drain well.

Heat the grill or broiler. Grill or broil the leeks just a few minutes to char the outside. Arrange 6 leeks on each of 4 salad plates. They can be served warm or at room temperature.

Just before serving, make the vinaigrette: Whisk the oils, cream, vinegar, and salt and pepper to taste together in a mixing bowl or process in a blender or food processor. Spoon the vinaigrette over the leeks, then sprinkle with the walnuts and fresh parsley.

Gazpacho Vinaigrette for Avocado

5 ripe garden tomatoes,
red and yellow if
possible, peeled,
seeded, and cut into
large chunks (about 2
cups)

1 small white onion, cut
into chunks

2 cloves garlic, peeled
and halved

3 small Japanese
cucumbers or 1 English
cucumber, cut into
chunks (see Note)

½ cup finely diced red
and green bell peppers

3 tablespoons finely diced
red onion

½ cup fruity olive oil

5 tablespoons red wine
vinegar or combination
sherry and red wine
vinegars

Salt and freshly ground
pepper

20 medium shrimp,
shelled and deveined
(optional)

Dry white wine and/or
water to cook the
shrimp

2 cups torn mixed salad
greens

2 avocados

When tomatoes are in season we look for every excuse to use them. We make pasta sauces and add them to tagines and ragouts, soups, and a variety of salads. This recipe came about because we had a little gazpacho left that was so tasty we wanted to use it in some way. As we had often served avocado with a tomato basil vinaigrette, a gazpacho vinaigrette seemed logical. While this vinaigrette is excellent with just avocado, it is especially nice with shellfish. Of course, lobster would be great (and expensive) but shrimp would do nicely too. ✦ *Serves 4*

Puree about one-third of the tomatoes in a food processor (see Note) and pour into a mixing bowl. Pulse the remaining tomatoes so that they are chunky. If you're using both red and yellow tomatoes, puree just the red for color and use chunks of yellow and red for accent. Add the tomato chunks to the puree.

Add the white onion and garlic to the processor and process until completely liquefied, adding a little of the vinegar if necessary. Add to the tomatoes.

Pulse the cucumbers in the processor until finely chopped and add to the tomato mixture.

Add the bell peppers, red onion, olive oil, and vinegar. Stir well with a spoon but do not mix with a whisk or the vegetables will lose their texture. Season to taste with salt and pepper. (Some people like their gazpacho fairly spicy, but I only add heat if the tomatoes are not really sweet. If you want to heat this up, add a dash of hot red pepper sauce or Worcestershire sauce.) Refrigerate the vinaigrette at least 1 hour. In fact, you may make this the day before you serve it.

If you decide to serve this with shrimp, heat just enough white wine to cover the shrimp in a sauté pan to simmering. Add the shrimp, cover, and gently simmer until cooked through. This may take 2 to 4 minutes, depending on the size of the shrimp. Remove the shrimp to a plate and chill them.

To serve, make a bed of the greens on each of 4 salad plates. Pit and peel the avocados and cut into chunks. Add the avocados and shrimp to the greens. Ladle a generous amount of the gazpacho vinaigrette over each salad and serve at once.

NOTE: You may use other cucumbers but peel and seed them if you do.

If you do not have a food processor, you can chop the ingredients by hand. It will be well worth the effort.

Caponata di Verdure

CAULIFLOWER, CELERY,
CUCUMBER, SPINACH,
AND CURLY ENDIVE
SALAD

1 medium head
 cauliflower, cut into
 florets (about 2 cups)
4 artichokes (optional)
⅓ cup olive oil
 (optional)
2 tablespoons fresh lemon
 juice (optional)
Salt and freshly ground
 pepper (optional)
4 cups spinach leaves
4 cups torn curly endive
Anchovy Garlic
 Vinaigrette (page 64)
1 cup sliced (¼ inch)
 celery
1 cup diced (½ inch)
 cucumbers, preferably
 Japanese or English
 cucumbers (seeded and
 peeled if not)
1½ cups Toasted Bread
 Crumbs (recipe
 follows)

We have come to think of caponata as a Sicilian eggplant stew with celery, onions, tomatoes, capers, and pine nuts, usually served in an antipasto assortment. Doing some research on Sicilian food, I ran across a dish called caponata *di verdure*, which was described as a combination of cooked vegetables, such as cauliflower, celery, spinach, curly endive, chicory, spinach, and cardoons, dressed with olive oil and red wine vinegar, garnished with lemon slices, capers, strips of anchovy, and fried bread crumbs, and served at room temperature.

The dish sounded interesting, but I have noticed that Americans don't take readily to a room temperature dish of cooked vegetables dressed with a vinaigrette and covered with anchovy strips, even if it is delicious. They prefer vegetables hot and salads cold. Nevertheless I was intrigued by the concept so I turned it into a salad dressed with a garlic and anchovy vinaigrette, and topped it with toasted bread crumbs. Sort of an Italian Caesar salad. Our diners have really taken to this. Of course, you may add Belgian endive or dandelion greens to this salad. You might even chop a few capers and add them to the vinaigrette or replace some of the vinegar with lemon juice. And you might to go all the way with the "Caesar" idea and sprinkle it with grated Parmesan cheese. ✦ *Serves 4*

Cook the cauliflower in boiling salted water until it is a little past *al dente*. Refresh in cold water.

If you are using artichokes, remove all of the leaves, pare the hearts, scoop out the fuzzy chokes, and cut into about 8 slices each. Cook the slices in the olive oil, stirring often, until tender. Drizzle with the lemon juice and season with salt and pepper to taste.

Toss the spinach and endive with half the vinaigrette and arrange in a bed on each of 4 salad plates. Toss the cauliflower, artichokes, celery, and cucumbers with the remaining vinaigrette and strew these over the greens. Sprinkle generously with the toasted bread crumbs.

Toasted Bread Crumbs

2 cups fresh Italian or French bread chunks without crusts

1 teaspoon salt

1 teaspoon freshly ground pepper

½ cup unsalted butter, melted, or olive oil if cholesterol conscious

These crumbs are essential in Caponata *di Verdure* but make a wonderful addition to any tossed salad. We like to sprinkle them on blanched broccoli that has been sautéed with garlic in olive oil. We also love to toss them into pasta. Two of my favorites are *orecchiette* with broccoli, onions, garlic, and toasted bread crumbs, and *orecchiette* with steamed clams, garlic, onions, greens, and toasted bread crumbs. ◆ *Makes 2 cups*

Preheat the oven to 350°.

Process the bread with pulses in a food processor to coarse crumbs. Spread the crumbs on a baking sheet. Stir the salt and pepper into the butter or oil and drizzle it over the bread. Bake, stirring occasionally for even browning, until golden, about 20 minutes.

Avocado Catalan

1 cup mild olive oil

¼ cup sherry vinegar

¼ cup (or to taste) fresh orange juice

¾ cup sliced almonds, toasted and coarsely chopped

2 tablespoons capers, drained, rinsed, and chopped medium fine

2 tablespoons grated orange zest

1 tablespoon pureed or finely chopped anchovies

Salt and freshly ground pepper to taste

2 ripe avocados

1 small head lettuce or 2 small bunches watercress, large stems trimmed

The flavors of southern Spain permeate this dish. The sauce is thick, crunchy, and aromatic. You can use anchovies that are packed in olive oil and chop them very fine, to a paste. If you use the salt-packed anchovies be sure to fillet them and rinse well. The almonds do not have to be blanched; in fact, sliced natural almonds are ideal. Just toast them in a 350° oven until golden, about 7 minutes. ◆ *Serves 4*

Whisk all the ingredients except the avocados and lettuce together.

Divide the lettuce among 4 salad plates. Cut the avocados in half, remove the pits and peels, then cut into slices or chunks. Place the avocados on the lettuce and spoon the vinaigrette over top.

SEAFOOD SALADS

Scapece

ITALIAN SEAFOOD
SALAD

¾ cup thinly sliced red
onions

¾ cup Hot Pepper
Vinaigrette (recipe
follows)

2 bunches watercress,
large stems trimmed
(about 2 cups loosely
packed)

12 medium shrimp,
shelled, deveined, and
poached in white wine
or water just until
cooked through, about
4 minutes
or

½ pound crabmeat,
picked over for shell
and cartilage
or

1 smoked trout, skinned,
boned, and broken into
strips about 2 inches
long

2 small oranges, peel and
all white pith removed,
sliced crosswise and
seeds removed, or 1
large navel orange,
peel and pith removed,
cut into segments

Hot pepper vinaigrette is the ideal accent for this southern Italian seafood salad. When fresh crabmeat or shrimp are available, we like to to use them. Smoked trout is a rich and interesting alternative; just be sure to remove all of the bones. ◆ *Serves 2*

Toss the onions with ¼ cup of the vinaigrette and let marinate to soften them a bit.

Toss the watercress with enough vinaigrette to lightly coat and arrange in a bed on each of 2 salad plates. Top with the marinated onions. Toss the shellfish with most of the remaining vinaigrette and add to the salads. Arrange the orange slices on top and drizzle with the last of the vinaigrette. If you are using smoked trout, put the strips of trout and the orange segments atop the onions and watercress and drizzle well with vinaigrette.

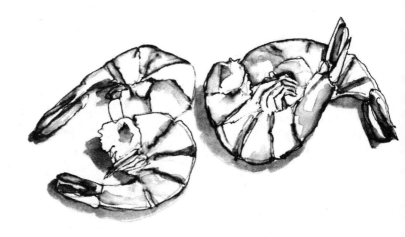

**HOT PEPPER
VINAIGRETTE**

1 cup mild olive oil

3 tablespoons dried red
  pepper flakes

⅓ cup fresh lemon juice
  or ¼ cup red wine
  vinegar

½ teaspoon minced
  garlic

Salt and freshly ground
  pepper

To make Hot Pepper Vinaigrette, heat the olive oil in a small saucepan until quite hot but not boiling. Drop in a pepper flake; if the flake skips on top of the oil and doesn't burn or sink, add the rest of the pepper flakes and remove from the heat. Let the pepper flakes steep in the oil about 30 minutes, then strain and let cool. This is called *olio santo,* or hot pepper oil.

Whisk the hot pepper oil and lemon juice together in a mixing bowl. Whisk in the garlic and season to taste with salt and pepper. You may need to add a little more olive oil if the hot oil is too hot. Pepper flakes vary wildly in degrees of hotness and so do people's capacities to take the heat. ◆ *Makes about 1⅓ cups, enough for 4 salads*

Rice Salad with Grilled Tuna

1 cup basmati rice

1½ cups water

1 teaspoon salt

1½ pounds tuna fillet,
  preferably yellowfin or
  bigeye (see Note)

Olive oil

Salt and freshly ground
  pepper

½ cup finely diced red
  onion

Mint Vinaigrette (page
  53)

This salad would be nice as part of a Portuguese, Spanish, or Italian antipasto assortment, but it also makes a good lunch or light supper. You could use cooked shellfish instead of tuna or a combination of both. You could also use Basic Vinaigrette, Anchovy Garlic Vinaigrette, or Oregano Garlic Vinaigrette (pages 65, 64, or 67). Capers may be added and lots of chopped parsley as well. ◆ *Serves 4*

Heat the rice, water, and 1 teaspoon salt in a medium saucepan to boiling. Reduce the heat and simmer covered until the water is absorbed, 15 to 20 minutes.

Meanwhile, preheat the broiler. Brush the tuna with olive oil and sprinkle lightly with salt and pepper. Broil, turning once, about 6 minutes for medium-rare to medium. Let cool.

Transfer the hot rice to a mixing bowl. Add the onion and most of the vinaigrette and toss to coat. Break the tuna into large chunks with your fingers and toss with the remaining vinaigrette. Spoon a mound of rice on each of 4 salad plates and top with the dressed tuna.

NOTE: Albacore tuna is acceptable in this recipe, but it has a tendency to dry out quickly. Canned tuna packed in good olive oil, *ventresca di tonno all'olio,* would be fine, too.

Grilled Tuna with Charmoula Vinaigrette

4 small red potatoes
Olive oil
Salt and freshly ground pepper
1 each green and red pepper
8 ounces tuna fillet, preferably yellowfin or bigeye
2 Japanese eggplants
¾ cup Charmoula Vinaigrette (recipe follows)
2 tablespoons each chopped fresh parsley and cilantro for garnish
2 lemon wedges

CHARMOULA VINAIGRETTE

½ cup (or to taste) fresh lemon juice, or ¼ cup each lemon juice and red wine vinegar
6 cloves garlic, very finely minced
1 teaspoon paprika
½ teaspoon cayenne pepper
2 teaspoons ground cumin
½ cup chopped fresh parsley
½ cup chopped cilantro
1¼ cups (or as needed) olive oil
Salt and freshly ground pepper

This is one of those food ideas that was staring me in the face conceptually but I couldn't see it. For years we have been serving grilled tuna or baked rockfish and sturgeon with Moroccan *charmoula*. One day, when I was analyzing the sluggish response to our classic salade Niçoise, I thought, I want to find another way to entice people with grilled tuna salads. The tuna and white bean salad is always a winner, but Niçoise just doesn't interest them. Maybe it is too familiar. Maybe anchovy scares them. What will they love? And the word *charmoula* entered my mind. So here is our now most popular tuna salad. (Incidentally this vinaigrette also works very well with sliced grilled or roasted chicken tossed with sliced peppers and onions.)

♦ *Serves 2*

Preheat the oven to 350°.

Rub the red potatoes with a little olive oil and salt and pepper. Bake in a baking pan until tender, 35 to 45 minutes. Let stand until cool enough to handle.

Meanwhile, heat a medium pan of water to boiling. Remove the stems and seeds from the peppers and cut into 1½-inch-wide strips. Drop the peppers into the boiling water and cook for about 3 minutes. Drain and refresh in ice water. Dry the peppers well and then thread them onto skewers for easy turning on the grill. Coat lightly with oil and sprinkle with salt and pepper.

Prepare a fire for grilling or heat a heavy skillet over high heat for the tuna and preheat the broiler for the vegetables.

Trim the tuna and cut into 1-inch-thick slices. Sprinkle with salt and pepper and brush both sides with a little olive oil. Grill quickly over high heat, turning once, until medium-rare to medium.

Cut the eggplants lengthwise in half and score the cut sides with the point of a knife. Sprinkle with salt and pepper and brush with olive oil. Grill or broil, turning once, until tender.

Grill or broil the peppers just until lightly charred on the outside. Keep all of the ingredients at room temperature.

Cut the potatoes in half. Rub with oil and sprinkle with salt and pepper. Grill or broil just before serving until marked. (You may also serve them without grilling.)

Break the tuna into large chunks and arrange the tuna and vegetables on 2 salad plates. Drizzle with *charmoula* vinaigrette, then sprinkle with chopped parsley and cilantro. Serve with lemon wedges.

To make Charmoula Vinaigrette, mix the lemon juice, garlic, paprika, cayenne, and cumin in a mixing bowl until smooth. Whisk in the parsley, cilantro, and olive oil. If necessary, add more oil so that the vinaigrette is not too thick. Taste and add more lemon juice or vinegar if needed. Season to taste with salt and pepper. ◆ *Makes about 2 cups, enough for 4 salads*

Grilled Tuna Salad with a Moroccan Salsa

½ cup peeled, white pith removed, seeded, and diced lemons

1½ cups finely diced red onions

¼ cup chopped cilantro

¼ cup chopped fresh parsley

¾ cup fresh lemon juice

¾ cup mild olive oil

¾ cup fruity olive oil

1 teaspoon salt

½ teaspoon freshly ground pepper

2 pounds tuna fillet

8 small red potatoes

2 each red and green peppers

2 large eggplants, peeled and sliced ½ inch thick

2 tablespoons chopped cilantro for garnish

An ideal dish for hot weather, this recipe is inspired by the Moroccan salad of diced lemons, onions, and parsley that often accompanies grilled fish. We thought that it most resembled a salsa. It is delicious and refreshing atop grilled tuna and grilled eggplant, peppers, and roasted potatoes. Of course, this salad is easy to prepare if the lemons are large, juicy, and not too seedy; if not, the prep time will be seemingly endless (try pushing out the seeds with a toothpick), but I promise you that it will be worth the pain! You may also serve this salsa with tuna *carpaccio*, and you can vary it by substituting fresh mint for the parsley.
✦ *Serves 8*

Whisk all the ingredients for the salsa together. Taste and adjust the seasoning.

Prepare the tuna, potatoes, peppers, and eggplant as directed for Grilled Tuna with Grilled Vegetables and Charmoula Vinaigrette (recipe precedes).

To serve, toss the tuna chunks with half the salsa and place on the plate. Arrange the vegetables near or around the tuna. Drizzle the rest of the salsa over the potatoes, peppers, and eggplants. Garnish with fresh coriander.

Scallop, Orange, and Lemon Salad

4 oranges

4 lemons or Meyer lemons

1 cup dry white wine

18 ounces bay or sea
    scallops (about 6 sea
    or 12 bay scallops per
    person)

3 large or 6 small
    bunches watercress,
    large stems trimmed

Black Pepper Vinaigrette
    (recipe follows)

BLACK PEPPER
VINAIGRETTE

1 cup mild olive oil

½ cup fresh orange juice

¼ cup fresh lemon juice

2 tablespoons coarsely
    ground pepper

Salt

We added poached scallops to the traditional Sicilian orange and lemon salad. The black pepper vinaigrette picks up the peppery quality of the watercress. ✦ *Serves 6*

Carefully cut the peel and all the white pith from the oranges and lemons. Cut crosswise into ¼-inch-thick slices and remove the seeds. There should be 24 to 30 slices of both oranges and lemons.

Heat the wine to simmering in a medium saucepan. Add the scallops and simmer gently until just barely cooked, about 1 to 2 minutes. Drain. If you want to serve the scallops warm, dress them immediately with some of the vinaigrette.

Toss the watercress in a large bowl with half the vinaigrette and arrange in a bed on each of 6 plates. Distribute the orange and lemon slices and scallops over the watercress, then drizzle with the remaining vinaigrette.

To make Black Pepper Vinaigrette, whisk all ingredients together in a small bowl. This vinaigrette is also excellent on black radish salad (page 63). For that salad, you may omit the orange juice and use all lemon juice but cut it back to just ½ cup lemon juice for 1 cup olive oil. ✦ *Makes 1¾ cups*

SOUPS

My sous chef, Paul Buscemi, and I love to make soup and fight over who will get the job for the day. Other members of the staff like to cook soup, too, but we are reluctant to give them up because they are so satisfying to make and to eat.

Too often soups are made with tired old ingredients that can't be used any other way—sort of refrigerator remnants. No wonder the result is terrible. If the ingredients are not good enough to cook for their own sake, they are not good enough for soup. Winter tomatoes won't make a tomato soup you want to eat. Bitter cucumbers, limp zucchini, starchy peas should go into the trash, not into your soup kettle.

Another reason soup can be disappointing is that it is made with poor stock. The two basic and essential ingredients for making wonderful soup are good stock (recipes are in the back of this chapter) and enough flavorful raw materials. Intensity is the key. If it's butternut squash soup you are making, use lots of butternut squash. If it's red pepper soup, use lots of red pep-

pers. You can't be chintzy if you want to produce a soup with depth of flavor.

At Square One we make two kinds of soups: purees and ones with "pieces." At first the purees sold much better than those with texture and pieces afloat, but slowly the chunky soups are becoming as popular as their smooth brothers.

In the countries of the Mediterranean, soup can often be the whole meal, and what a meal! Accompanied by good bread and, perhaps, cheese and fruit, soup can be very satisfying indeed.

Soups are versatile and chameleonlike. Change the garnish and you create a new soup. So, if you think your soup repertoire is small, think creatively about how you can transform your old boring potato soup into a fabulous Italian potato soup with a garnish of green beans, sun-dried tomatoes, and basil, or a dollop of pesto.

Most of the soup recipes serve from six to eight. You can choose to make a smaller batch or have the soup a few nights in a row. Don't wait for company! Treat yourself to a Mediterranean meal with soup, some bread, and a salad or fruit and cheese. It's not a lot of work but it is one of the great dining pleasures!

Caldo de Pimenton

RED PEPPER SOUP

6 tablespoons unsalted
butter

2 medium onions, sliced

12 pimento or red bell
peppers, stemmed,
seeded, and coarsely
chopped

4 to 5 cups Chicken Stock
(page 103)

Salt and freshly ground
pepper

This is one of my favorite soups. It is a bit deceptive, because it won't have much red pepper flavor at first. But if you refrigerate it for at least four hours, you will be amazed how vibrant the red pepper flavor will have become. I find this flavor delay in other soups, such as artichoke and cauliflower, as well. Red pepper soup is also multinational. Its country of origin changes with the garnish.

Please use the richer and fleshier pimento peppers if possible. Regular red peppers are acceptable but they will not be quite as vibrant. ◆ Serves 6 to 8

Melt the butter in a large saucepan over medium heat. Add the onions and cook slowly until translucent. Add the peppers and enough chicken stock to barely cover them. Heat to a low boil, then reduce the heat and simmer until the peppers are tender, 20 to 30 minutes.

Puree the solids in a blender or food processor. If there are too many large flecks of skin visible and they annoy you, you may pass the pureed soup through a food mill. Thin the soup with remaining stock to the desired consistency and season to taste with salt and pepper.

Refrigerate the soup at least 4 hours or overnight. You may serve this soup cold or reheat it. Taste and adjust the seasoning just before serving. Garnish as desired.

GARNISHES

- ◆ For an Italian accent, use a chiffonade of basil and a dollop of lightly whipped cream flavored with grated lemon zest or a spoonful of pesto.

- ◆ For a Spanish flavor, add roasted green pepper puree.

- ◆ For a Portuguese accent, sprinkle with chopped cilantro.

- ◆ To evoke Greece or Turkey, dollop with yogurt and sprinkle with chopped fresh marjoram.

- ◆ And for France, some crème fraîche and fresh thyme or chervil will do nicely.

NOTE: You can also vary this soup by adding a few oven-roasted or sliced fresh tomatoes. After the peppers have cooked and softened, add the tomatoes and cook them together for a few minutes. Then puree the soup and pass it through a food mill to remove the seeds and skin.

Roasted Eggplant Soup

2 small to medium
   eggplants
1 large eggplant
3 tablespoons unsalted
   butter
2 medium onions, sliced
4 to 5 cups Chicken Stock
   (page 103)
½ cup heavy cream
   (optional)
Salt and freshly ground
   pepper

I love the smoky, toasty flavor of this soup. Most people agree that it is the key to its popularity, but occasionally there is someone who says that the soup tastes burnt. Then we try to explain that we did it on purpose. If you find the smokiness too intense, add some cream to the soup or roast all the eggplants in the oven and don't put any under the broiler. ◆ *Serves 6 to 8*

Preheat the oven to 450°. Prick the 2 small to medium eggplants a few times with a fork. Bake, turning once, until very tender, about 1 hour. Transfer to a colander and let drain until cool enough to handle.

Meanwhile, preheat the broiler to low. Broil the large eggplant 4 to 6 inches from the heat, turning as needed, until charred on all sides and tender inside, about 20 minutes. You may also grill it on a heavy griddle over medium heat. This may take a little less time, but you need to have a very heavy griddle so that it cooks evenly and doesn't scorch. Transfer the grilled eggplant to a colander and let cool.

Cut the cooled eggplants in half and scoop out the flesh.

Melt the butter in a medium saucepan over medium heat. Add the onions and cook, stirring occasionally, until tender and translucent. Add 4 cups chicken stock and the eggplant pulp. Heat to boiling, then reduce the heat and simmer a few minutes. Puree the soup in a blender or food processor.

Thin the soup with chicken stock to the desired consistency. If the eggplant flavor is too smoky for your palate, add the cream. Reheat and season to taste with salt and pepper. Garnish as desired.

GARNISHES

◆ Lightly whipped cream flavored with lemon zest or pesto

◆ Chopped tomatoes and basil chiffonade

◆ Roasted pepper puree

Passato di Zucca

BUTTERNUT SQUASH
SOUP

2 large butternut or other
  yellow-fleshed sweet
  squash (even sweet
  potatoes)
6 tablespoons unsalted
  butter
2 medium onions, sliced
6 cups Chicken Stock
  (page 103)
Salt and freshly ground
  pepper
Pinch freshly grated
  nutmeg if needed
Pinch sugar if needed
2 slices French bread,
  crusts removed, cut into
  1-inch cubes
Freshly grated Parmesan
  cheese

This is the classic Italian pumpkin squash soup. Serve it with croutons and grated Parmesan or with a sage or nutmeg cream and you have a spectacular dish. But this very same soup can become the French soupe au potiron if you add some leeks in place of some of the onions and garnish it with croutons and grated Gruyère cheese.

Most recipes for pumpkin or butternut squash soup have you peel and cube the uncooked squash and then add the chunks to the pot. We have seen lots of cut fingers with this technique as the raw squashes are large, hard, and unwieldy, so we bake the squash first. It is easier on the hands, and the slightly roasted flavor adds a wonderful dimension to the soup. ◆ Serves 6 to 8

Preheat the oven to 400°. Prick each squash with the point of a knife so it won't explode when it bakes. Bake until the squash feels somewhat soft to the touch and a knife penetrates the skin easily, about 1 hour. Let stand until cool enough to handle. Cut them in half through the stem ends, remove the seeds, and scoop out the pulp.

Melt the butter in a medium saucepan over low heat. Add the onions and cook until translucent. Add the chicken stock and squash pulp. Heat to boiling, then reduce the heat and simmer for a few minutes. Puree the soup in a blender, food processor, or food mill. Season to taste with salt and pepper. If the squash is starchy rather than sweet, add some grated nutmeg and hope for the best. If this doesn't give you a proper balance, then add a pinch of sugar to help Mother Nature. Reheat the soup.

Toast or sauté the bread until golden brown and sprinkle over the soup with a little Parmesan cheese.

NOTE: You could sprinkle the soup with Gruyère cheese instead of Parmesan. Or whip about ¾ cup heavy cream and season it with chopped sage leaves or a pinch of grated nutmeg. A little dollop will do you and the soup quite nicely. For a North African soup, add a little cayenne and cumin to the soup and serve garnished with cilantro.

Potato Soup of Many Disguises

4 tablespoons unsalted
  butter
2 cups sliced onions
5 cups sliced peeled
  russet potatoes
6 cups Chicken Stock
  (page 103)
1 teaspoon salt
½ teaspoon freshly
  ground pepper
1 cup heavy cream, milk,
  or additional chicken
  stock

I don't mean to offend the lowly potato, but potato soups are boring unless the stock is spectacular or the soup garnishes are innovative. This is a basic and good soup to which you can add the garnish of your choice. ◆ *Serves 6*

Melt the butter in a heavy medium saucepan over medium heat. Add the onions, cover the pan, and sweat until translucent. Add the potatoes and stock. Heat to boiling, then reduce the heat and simmer until the potatoes are tender.

Puree the potatoes and onions with a little of the stock in a blender and stir back into the remaining stock. The soup will be thick. Thin the soup further with the cream, milk, or additional stock after you have decided what kind of soup you are going to serve. Season with salt and pepper, then reheat. Garnish as desired.

FRENCH VARIATIONS: Puree the hot soup with 4 to 6 cups chopped watercress, or add chopped watercress to the pureed soup when you reheat it. Another idea is to puree the hot soup with 3 cups chopped sorrel leaves. The heat of the soup will set the color of the sorrel so that it remains bright green and doesn't turn that sad gray-brown color. Alternatively, you can reheat the pureed soup with a chiffonade of sorrel leaves. The sorrel will turn a brownish hue but will taste good.

ITALIAN VARIATIONS: Add a chiffonade of arugula and a dice of prosciutto, or some blanched green beans, diced fresh tomatoes, and chopped cooked artichokes when you reheat the soup. Other garnish ideas are diced fresh tomatoes and some chopped fresh basil; a dollop of pesto; chopped fresh sage, majoram, or parsley and diced tomatoes; crumbled Gorgonzola cheese and a few feathery fennel tops; goat cheese, chopped walnuts and fresh basil; or chopped fresh mint and strips of Italian sun-dried tomatoes for a taste of Sardinia.

Spring Garlic and Potato Soup

2 medium or 3 small heads garlic (about 20 cloves)

¼ cup (or as needed) olive oil

1 teaspoon salt, plus additional for the garlic

½ teaspoon freshly ground pepper, plus additional for the garlic

Several sprigs fresh thyme

4 tablespoons unsalted butter

1½ cups thinly sliced onions

5 cups sliced peeled russet potatoes

6 to 7 cups Chicken Stock (page 103)

½ cup heavy cream if needed

Roasting the garlic takes away its sharpness and adds a mellow and deep flavor to the soup. If the potatoes are a little starchy, you may want to add a little cream. It will thin the soup and break up the stickiness. ◆ *Serves 6 to 8*

Preheat the oven to 300°. Cut the top off each head of garlic, exposing just a tiny bit of each clove, and place the heads in a baking pan. Drizzle with olive oil, sprinkle with salt and pepper, and add the thyme to the pan. Cover with foil and bake, basting with a little oil halfway through, until completely tender, about 1 hour. Let stand until cool enough to handle, then squeeze the garlic from the peels.

Melt the butter in a heavy medium saucepan over low heat. Add the onions and cook until tender and translucent, about 7 minutes. Add the potatoes and enough chicken stock to cover. Heat to boiling, then reduce the heat and simmer until the potatoes are very tender.

Stir the garlic into the soup and puree the soup in a blender. Thin with additional stock if necessary. Season with 1 teaspoon salt and ½ teaspoon pepper. If the soup is too garlicky, stir in the cream. Reheat and garnish. (This soup can be made a day ahead of time and reheated.)

GARNISHES

◆ Chopped fresh basil

◆ Chopped sun-dried tomatoes and fresh basil or mint

◆ Crumbled goat cheese and chopped walnuts and fresh basil

◆ Dollop of pesto

◆ Grilled or toasted croutons

◆ Chopped fresh chives

Italian Mushroom Soup with Sweet Vermouth and Tomato

One day we received a letter from one of the food magazines asking for a recipe that a customer had enjoyed at Square One. Due to a wonderful typo the soup they requested was Stallion Mushroom Soup. We wrote a fantasy recipe à la Escoffier. "Take one large stallion. Put in a large kettle with water and mushrooms. . . ." After much chuckling, we finally sent off the following recipe. ✦ *Serves 6 to 8*

6 tablespoons unsalted
   butter
2 medium onions, ¼-inch
   dice
1 pound fresh mushrooms,
   thinly sliced (see Note)
6 tablespoons rich tomato
   puree or 3 tablespoons
   tomato paste
4 cups Beef Stock or
   combination Beef and
   Chicken Stocks (pages
   104 and 103)
6 tablespoons sweet
   vermouth, such as
   Cinzano Rosso
Salt and freshly ground
   pepper
Chopped fresh parsley
Freshly grated Parmesan
   cheese

Heat 2 tablespoons butter in a heavy medium saucepan over low heat. Add the onions and cook until translucent. Melt the remaining butter in a large skillet over medium heat. Add the mushrooms and cook until they give off most of their juices and soften. Add the mushrooms with their juices to the onions. Stir in the tomato puree and stock. Heat to boiling, then reduce the heat and stir in the vermouth. Season to taste with salt and pepper. Simmer a few minutes. Serve hot, sprinkled with parsley and Parmesan cheese. You may add some toasted croutons as well.

NOTE: We have made this soup with white cultivated mushrooms, Italian brown field mushrooms, and a combination of fresh chanterelles and cultivated mushrooms. Of course the soup is more interesting and earthy with the wild mushroom flavor, however, I am sure that you will enjoy it with plain old white mushrooms too. If you do use chanterelles, reduce the vermouth to 3 tablespoons.

Mushroom and Hazelnut Soup

1 cup hazelnuts

4 tablespoons unsalted butter

6 cups sliced onions

14 cups (loosely packed) fresh white or brown mushrooms, cut in chunks (or left whole if small)

5 cups Chicken Stock (page 103)

1 teaspoon salt

1/4 teaspoon freshly ground pepper

Chopped fresh parsley for garnish

This is one of those magic combinations where the whole is more than the sum of its parts. You can taste mushrooms and you can taste hazelnuts, but the combination of the two is rich and complex, sort of a wild nutshroom flavor. The soup really needs no garnish except a little chopped parsley for color. However, if you are in a baroque mood, a sherry or Marsala cream will add another dimension to the soup and possibly your waistline. ◆ *Serves 8*

Preheat the oven to 350°. Toast the hazelnuts on a baking sheet until the skins crack a little, then rub them in a kitchen towel to remove as much of the skins as possible. Don't be disheartened if you can't get them clean for a little skin won't hurt the soup. Grind the nuts in a food processor and set aside.

Melt the butter in a large deep saucepan over medium heat. Add the onions and cook until tender and translucent, about 10 minutes. Add the mushrooms and sweat them covered about 5 minutes. Add enough chicken stock to barely cover and heat to boiling. Reduce the heat and simmer about 10 minutes.

Puree the mushrooms and onions with the nuts and a little of the hot stock in batches in a blender or food processor. Thin the soup to the desired consistency with hot stock. Season with salt and pepper. This soup can be made ahead of time and gently reheated. Thin it with chicken stock if it thickens too much.

Spinach Soup

4 tablespoons unsalted
 butter

2 medium onions, sliced
 (about 2 cups)

1 russet potato, peeled
 and thinly sliced

2 to 3 cups Chicken Stock
 (page 103)

10 to 12 cups loosely
 packed trimmed
 spinach leaves (about
 6 bunches), rinsed well
 and drained

Salt and freshly ground
 pepper

Pinch freshly grated
 nutmeg

About ¼ cup heavy
 cream if needed

This can be the best soup in the world if the spinach isn't overcooked. Use as little stock as necessary to cook the leaves, puree the soup quickly, and then thin the soup, while still hot, to the desired consistency. This way the spinach will retain its bright green color. There are many variations of spinach soup, but first let's get down to basics.
 ✦ Serves 6 to 8

Melt the butter in a large, wide heavy saucepan over medium heat. Add the onions and cook until translucent, about 7 minutes. Add the potato and 1½ cups chicken stock. Heat to boiling, then reduce the heat and simmer until the potato is very soft.

Increase the heat to high. Start adding the spinach leaves by handfuls, pushing the leaves under the hot stock, until all of the spinach is submerged. Quickly heat to boiling, then remove from the heat. Using a slotted spoon, transfer about half the solids to a blender and puree. Pour into a bowl and puree the remaining solids.

Thin the soup first with the hot stock in the pan, then with the remaining stock, also heated. Season to taste with salt, pepper, and nutmeg. If the spinach has an earthy or slightly bitter taste, add enough cream to smooth it. You may not need any cream at all if the spinach is young and sweet.

VARIATIONS

Add 2 cups fresh peas with the potatoes and a little more stock to cover. Add the spinach as directed, heat to boiling, and puree. Add a little cream, and egg yolks if you want, to smooth out the soup. Garnish with chopped fresh mint or grilled croutons.

For a Greek accent, stir 3 large egg yolks mixed with 3 tablespoons fresh lemon juice into the soup just before serving. You may add 1 cup cooked rice or orzo as well.

Stir 1 cup yogurt, at room temperature, and several tablespoons chopped fresh dill into the soup for a Turkish variation. Garnish with toasted pine nuts or chopped walnuts if you want.

Stir in 2 eggs mixed with ¼ cup freshly grated Parmesan cheese just before serving.

GARNISHES

+ Cooked polenta, cut into cubes, and freshly grated Parmesan cheese

+ Grilled croutons and freshly grated Parmesan cheese

+ One-half cup heavy cream whipped to soft peaks and flavored with grated lemon zest or nutmeg

Canja

PORTUGUESE CHICKEN
SOUP WITH RICE

5 cups reduced Chicken
   Stock (see Note)
1 cup water
1 cup long-grain or
   basmati rice
1 whole chicken breast,
   bones and skin
   removed
¼ cup fresh lemon juice
Salt and freshly ground
   pepper
6 tablespoons chopped
   fresh mint

What could be easier or simpler or more nurturing? This is Portuguese penicillin. If you start with a good rich chicken stock, you will find this soup a tonic. + *Serves 6*

Mix 1 cup chicken stock and 1 cup water in a small heavy saucepan. Heat to boiling. Stir in the rice, reduce the heat, and simmer covered until all the liquid is absorbed, about 20 minutes.

Pour the remaining stock into a medium heavy saucepan. Heat to simmering over medium heat. Meanwhile, cut the chicken breast into 1 by ½-inch strips. Add the chicken to the simmering stock, reduce the heat, and simmer very gently just until firm. Stir in the rice, lemon juice, and salt and pepper to taste. Add the mint and serve at once.

NOTE: For reduced chicken stock, boil Chicken Stock (page 103) or any other good light chicken stock until the volume is reduced by half or it tastes rich.

Sopa de Cenouras

PORTUGUESE CARROT SOUP WITH EGG AND LEMON

1 ½ pounds medium carrots (16 to 18)

4 tablespoons unsalted butter

2 medium onions, finely chopped

5 to 7 cups Chicken Stock (page 103)

Salt and freshly ground pepper

3 large egg yolks

2 tablespoons fresh lemon juice

½ cup heavy cream

2 tablespoons chopped fresh mint, cilantro, or parsley for garnish

Most carrot soups are very rich and filling, but the lemon juice adds a lightness to this soup and the mint or fresh cilantro garnish is also a refreshing touch. ♦ *Serves 8*

Peel and trim the carrots. Cut 6 carrots into thin julienne strips, about 1 ½ inches long and ⅛ inch wide. Do this on a mandoline if you have one; save all the ends and add them to the soup. Blanch the julienned carrots in a large pot of boiling water until cooked but still firm. Drain and refresh in cold water, then drain again and set aside. Cut the remaining carrots into 1-inch lengths.

Melt the butter in a heavy medium saucepan over medium heat. Add the onions and cook until tender and translucent. Add the carrot chunks and 5 cups chicken stock. Heat to boiling. Reduce the heat and simmer, partially covered, until the carrots are very soft.

Puree the soup in batches in a blender or food processor. Return the soup to the saucepan. If the carrots are very starchy and the soup is too thick, thin it with additional chicken stock. The soup should be smooth and of medium consistency. Season to taste with salt and pepper. Stir in the julienned carrots, then reheat the soup but do not boil.

Whisk the egg yolks, lemon juice, and cream together and swirl the mixture into the hot soup. Immediately ladle the soup into bowls and garnish with a chopped fresh herb.

Catalan Onion and Almond Soup

1 cup sliced almonds

1 cup heavy cream

3 strips (3 inches long
  and 1 inch wide)
  orange zest

6 tablespoons unsalted
  butter

12 cups sliced onions

2 teaspoons ground
  coriander

4 cups Chicken Stock
  (page 103)

Salt and freshly ground
  pepper

Thin curls orange zest for
  garnish

I have been struggling with this soup for years. No matter what recipe I followed, I ultimately liked the idea better than the soup itself. Most recipes call for toasting the almonds, grinding them, and cooking them up with the onions. I found that this method imparts very little almond flavor to the soup and what remains has a slightly gritty texture. Just recently the light bulb went on. Why not steal a trick from ice cream making, I thought to myself. Toast the almonds, steep them in hot cream for an hour, and then add that almond cream to the onions when pureeing the soup. Well, it works. There is a wonderful subtle almond perfume to this soup that I have been striving for all this time. I have added a little orange zest too. After all, it is Spain. ✦ *Serves 6 to 8*

Preheat the oven to 350°. Toast the almonds on a baking sheet about 7 minutes. Meanwhile, heat the cream to simmering in a small pan. Chop the almonds and add to the cream with the orange zest. Let steep about 1 hour.

Melt the butter in a large saucepan over low heat. Add the onions and cook until very tender but not brown. Add the coriander and cook a few minutes more. Add the chicken stock and heat to boiling. Reduce the heat and simmer about 5 minutes.

Using a slotted spoon, transfer the onions to a blender. Add the cream mixture (with the almonds and orange zest) and puree. Thin the soup to the desired consistency with the stock remaining in the pan. Season to taste with salt and pepper. Serve hot or cold, garnished with orange zest.

Gazpacho

COLD SPANISH TOMATO
SOUP

*9 large beefsteak
tomatoes, peeled,
seeded, and coarsely
chopped*

*1 medium-small sweet
yellow or red onion,
chopped*

*3 cloves garlic, finely
minced*

*2 medium cucumbers,
peeled, seeded, and
coarsely chopped*

*6 tablespoons (or to taste)
red wine vinegar*

*1 cup tomato juice if
needed*

*⅓ cup plus 3 tablespoons
olive oil*

*3 thick slices French
bread, crusts removed*

*2 tablespoons unsalted
butter*

*1 clove garlic, coarsely
chopped*

*1 green pepper, finely
diced*

*3 tablespoons finely
minced red onion*

This is my son Evan's favorite soup. I can make it by the gallon and he will devour it all over the course of a day. After tasting gazpacho in Spain twice a day every day for six weeks, I decided that my favorite version of this soup had a little tart edge to it, but no heat. Chile peppers and Worcestershire sauce are probably American additions. Garlic croutons are essential, at least in my bowl of soup! Please use the ripest and most flavorful tomatoes possible, for the success of the gazpacho depends on them. ◆ *Serves 8, unless one of your guests is Evan*

Cut the core from each tomato and cut a cross in the bottom. Dip each tomato first in boiling water and then ice water and peel immediately. Cut the tomatoes in half and squeeze out the seeds. Puree 3 tomatoes in a blender or food processor. If the tomatoes aren't perfectly wonderful, you will need the tomato juice for flavor. Transfer the tomato puree to a deep mixing bowl.

Puree the chopped onion and minced garlic in the blender or food processor and add to the bowl.

Coarsely mince the cucumbers with a little of the vinegar in the food processor and add to the bowl. Coarsely chop the remaining tomatoes in the food processor and add to the bowl. Add the tomato juice if needed for flavor, ⅓ cup oil, and the remaining vinegar. Stir well to combine and season to taste with salt and pepper. Refrigerate the soup until thoroughly chilled, preferably for several hours.

Cut the bread into 1-inch cubes. Heat the butter, remaining 3 tablespoons oil, and chopped garlic in a heavy sauté pan or skillet over medium heat. Add the bread and fry until golden brown.

To serve, ladle the soup into bowls and garnish each serving with diced green pepper, minced red onion, and the garlic croutons.

Tomato Soup

½ cup unsalted butter

2 large yellow onions, diced or sliced

12 large beefsteak or 18 regular very ripe tomatoes, quartered

Salt and freshly ground pepper

This is the ideal summer soup and truly vegetarian. It is one of the few soups that is not made with a meat stock, for the ripe tomatoes make their own broth. Obviously the success of this soup depends upon flavorful, really ripe tomatoes, not those pale pink imitations that you find at most supermarkets. ◆ *Serves 6 to 8*

Melt the butter in a heavy large saucepan over medium heat. Add the onions and cook until tender and translucent, 8 to 10 minutes. Stir in the tomatoes and cook, stirring occasionally to prevent scorching, over medium heat until the tomatoes are completely broken down and have released a great deal of liquid, about 20 minutes. Puree the soup in a blender or food processor, then pass it through a food mill to remove the seeds and peel. Season to taste with salt and pepper. Serve hot.

GARNISHES

◆ Chiffonade of fresh basil or mint

◆ Lightly whipped cream flavored with chopped fresh mint, grated orange zest, or pesto

◆ Grilled croutons and freshly grated Parmesan cheese

◆ Sour cream and chopped cucumbers and green onions

Zuppa di Sedano Rape e Finocchio

CELERY ROOT AND FENNEL SOUP

4 tablespoons unsalted butter

1 large or 2 medium onions, diced

2 large bulbs celery root, peeled and cut into 1-inch cubes, covered with water acidulated with lemon juice

1 large russet potato, peeled and cubed

5 to 6 cups Chicken Stock (page 103)

2 small bulbs fennel, trimmed and sliced

Salt and freshly ground pepper

Pinch (or to taste) freshly grated nutmeg

This is sort of a double celery soup. If you eliminate the fennel, it is a French-inspired soup. The fennel adds the slight hint of anise that takes this soup to Italy. ◆ *Serves 6 to 8*

Melt the butter in a medium saucepan over medium heat. Add the onion and cook until translucent. Drain the celery root and add it and the potato to the onions. Pour in enough chicken stock to cover. Heat to boiling, then reduce the heat and simmer until the celery root is very tender. Add the fennel and simmer 5 minutes more.

Puree the soup in a blender or processor and thin if necessary with hot stock. Season to taste with salt, pepper, and nutmeg.

GARNISHES

Chopped toasted hazelnuts

Lightly whipped cream flavored with grated orange zest

Grilled or toasted croutons and freshly grated Parmesan cheese

Acorda

PORTUGUESE BREAD
AND GARLIC SOUP
WITH EGG

*About 1 cup fruity olive
oil*

*12 to 18 thick (1 inch)
slices French or Italian
peasant bread (enough
to cover the bottom of
each bowl)*

*1 large clove garlic,
peeled*

*3 tablespoons finely
minced garlic*

½ teaspoon salt

*6 large eggs, at room
temperature*

*⅓ cup finely chopped
fresh parsley*

*⅓ cup finely chopped
cilantro*

*4 to 5 cups reduced
Chicken Stock (see
page 103)*

*Salt and freshly ground
pepper*

This simple peasant soup embodies what is wonderful about Mediterranean food—from a few basic and inexpensive ingredients is made a rich and delicious soup. In Spain and Italy similar garlic and bread soups are prepared but without the cilantro. Use the herbs of your choice for a personal interpretation. ✦ *Serves 6*

Film a large skillet with olive oil and heat over medium heat. Add as many slices bread as will fit without crowding and sauté, turning once, until golden on both sides. Transfer to paper towels to drain, then, while the bread is hot, rub both sides of each slice with the clove of garlic. Repeat with the remaining bread, adding more oil as needed.

Mash the minced garlic and the salt to a paste in a mortar with the pestle.

Poach the eggs until the whites are set but the yolks are still quite runny. Set them aside in a bowl of cold water. You can poach them in a pan of water with a little vinegar or in an egg poacher, which is simpler and more foolproof.

Divide the garlic paste and fresh parsley and cilantro among 6 soup bowls. Add 1 tablespoon olive oil to each bowl, then add the sautéed bread.

Heat the reduced stock to boiling. Using a slotted spoon, remove each egg from the water and gently place on the bread. Now ladle on the hot stock. Serve immediately.

Artichoke and Pea Soup

8 large artichokes

6 tablespoons unsalted butter

4 to 5 cups Chicken Stock (page 103)

3 cups diced onions

2 cups shelled fresh peas

Salt and freshly ground pepper

Lightly whipped cream flavored with grated lemon zest or chopped fresh mint for garnish

You will taste the peas immediately but the artichoke flavor is slower to develop. Wait a few hours before the final seasoning, and you will be surprised to see how much more you can taste the artichokes! ♦ *Serves 8*

Cut all the leaves from the artichokes, pare the hearts, and remove the fuzzy chokes. Cut the artichoke hearts into slices. Heat 3 tablespoons butter in a medium saucepan over medium heat. Add the artichoke hearts and 1/3 cup chicken stock; cook, partially covered, until tender, about 10 minutes.

Melt the remaining butter in another medium saucepan over medium heat. Add the onions and cook until translucent and tender. Add the remaining stock and heat to boiling. Reduce the heat and stir in the peas. Simmer about 3 minutes, then add the artichoke hearts and simmer a few minutes more.

Put the vegetables and just enough stock to process them in a blender or processor and puree. Pour into a bowl. Thin the soup to the desired consistency with the hot stock and season with salt and pepper. Refrigerate a few hours, then taste and adjust the seasoning. Reheat the soup. Ladle into bowls and dollop each serving with flavored whipped cream.

NOTE: For an avgolemono variation, whisk together 2 large eggs, the juice of 1 lemon, and 1/2 cup heavy cream until very frothy. Reheat the soup and gradually stir in the egg mixture.

Caldo Verde

PORTUGUESE SOUP
WITH POTATO,
SAUSAGE, AND GREENS

¾ pound Chorizo or
    Linguisa (page 297 or
    295)

2 tablespoons olive oil

4 cups finely diced onions

2 cloves garlic, very finely
    minced

12 scrubbed small red
    potatoes or 6 peeled
    large boiling potatoes,
    cut into ½-inch dice
    (5 to 6 cups)

8 cups Chicken Stock
    (page 103)

6 to 8 cups chiffonade of
    greens, such as Swiss
    chard, escarole, and/or
    kale

Salt and freshly ground
    pepper

This is the Portuguese national soup. You may choose to make your own sausage or buy a good commercial sausage that has a little kick to it.

Verde in the title represents the greens, traditionally kale. We have made this soup with Swiss chard, kale, and escarole. You may want to use an assortment of the three. Just be sure to cut the greens into a very, very thin chiffonade. Roll up the leaves like a cigar and slice ⅛ inch thick.

Some people like the potatoes in this soup to be falling apart, but we like them to retain a little texture. If we use small red potatoes we leave the skin on, but we do peel the larger potatoes. Traditionally this soup is made with water, but a good rich chicken stock is better. ◆ *Serves 8*

Preheat the oven to 375°. Prick the sausage in a few places with a fork and bake on a baking sheet until cooked through, about 20 minutes. Let stand until cool enough to handle, then slice about ½ inch thick.

Heat the olive oil in a medium saucepan over medium heat. Add the onions and cook until translucent, about 10 minutes. Stir in the garlic and cook 2 minutes more. Add the potatoes and chicken stock. Heat to boiling, then reduce the heat and simmer until the potatoes are tender. Add the greens and simmer 5 minutes. Add the sausage and simmer 3 minutes more. Season to taste with salt and pepper. Serve at once.

Zuppa di Ceci e Verdure

CHICK-PEA SOUP WITH GREENS AND PASTA

2 cups dried chick-peas (garbanzo beans)

14 to 16 cups water for soaking and cooking the chick-peas

About 6 tablespoons fruity olive oil

½ pound pancetta or prosciutto ends (a bone with meat left on it would be grand)

2 cloves garlic, peeled

2 large onions, diced (3½ to 4 cups)

3 cloves garlic, finely minced

3 cups chiffonade or 3 by 1-inch strips of escarole or Swiss chard, rinsed well and drained

2 to 3 cups Chicken Stock (page 103)

Salt and freshly ground pepper

½ cup small pasta shells, macaroni, or orecchiette

Grated Parmesan or pecorino cheese for serving

This is one of those meals in a bowl in the tradition of stone soup. In fact in Portugal a version of this soup is called *sopa de Pedra*, after the folktale of the same name, where something wonderful is created out of very simple and inexpensive raw materials. Put the right humble ingredients together and what have you got? A great, soul-satisfying soup. Add some sausage and eliminate the pasta and you could be in Spain or Portugal. ◆ *Serves 8*

Rinse the chick-peas and soak overnight in 6 cups water in the refrigerator. Drain and rinse.

Place half the chick-peas in a small pot and cover with 4 cups water. Heat to boiling and skim the scum from the surface. Reduce the heat and simmer covered until tender but not mushy (but not *al dente* either!), 45 to 50 minutes. Drain and toss with enough olive oil to coat them.

Place the remaining chick-peas, the pancetta, 2 whole cloves garlic, and half the onions in a larger pot. Add 4 to 6 cups water, enough to cover all ingredients. Heat to boiling and skim the surface. Reduce the heat and simmer covered until very, very soft, about an hour or more. Puree this mixture, removing the meat from the bone if using, in a blender until very smooth. If you must use a processor, puree all of the solids thoroughly, then add the cooking liquid and puree again. Remove any lumps that remain.

Heat about 4 tablespoons olive oil in a large saucepan over low heat. Add the remaining onion and cook about 5 minutes. Add the minced garlic and cook a minute or two. Add the greens and cook, stirring constantly, until wilted and somewhat tender. Add the cooked chick-peas and the chick-pea puree and stir until blended. Stir in enough chicken stock to thin the soup. Heat through and season to taste with salt and pepper. I like this soup pretty peppery. You may not need much salt because of the prosciutto. (The soup can be made ahead up to this point.)

Just before serving, cook the pasta in a medium pot of lightly salted water until *al dente*. Drain and add to the hot soup. Serve immediately, sprinkled with grated Parmesan or pecorino cheese.

Zuppa di Broccoli e Fagioli

BROCCOLI SOUP WITH WHITE BEANS

1/2 cup dried small white beans

8 cups water

1 teaspoon salt, plus additional to taste

2 to 3 tablespoons fruity olive oil

2 bunches broccoli, tough stems discarded, cut into 2-inch chunks

6 tablespoons unsalted butter or mild olive oil

2 medium onions, diced

4 to 5 cups Chicken Stock (page 103)

Freshly ground pepper

1/2 cup small shaped pasta

Grated Parmesan or pecorino cheese for serving

A classic soup from Apulia in the south of Italy. You can treat it as a broth, with chopped cooked broccoli, white beans, and pasta, or you can puree the broccoli and combine it with the pasta and beans. In any case, you're going to love it. ◆ *Serves 6 to 8*

Rinse the beans and soak overnight in 2 cups water in the refrigerator. Drain and rinse well. Place in a small pan and cover with 2 cups fresh water. Heat to boiling. Reduce the heat, add 1 teaspoon salt, and simmer until the beans are tender but not mushy, about 30 minutes. Drain and toss with toss with enough fruity olive oil to coat.

Steam the broccoli over salted boiling water until very tender. Set aside.

Melt the butter in a medium saucepan over medium heat. Add the onions and cook until translucent. Add 2 cups chicken stock and cook until the onions are very tender. Stir in the broccoli and heat through. If you want, puree the onions and broccoli in a blender and return to the pan. Thin the soup to a consistency you like with the remaining chicken stock. Season to taste with salt and pepper.

Just before serving, cook the pasta in a medium pot of lightly salted water until *al dente.* Drain well.

Heat the broccoli soup and warm the white beans slightly in a small sauté pan over low heat.

To serve, ladle the broccoli soup into bowls and add a spoonful of beans and a spoonful of pasta to each bowl. Sprinkle with grated Parmesan or pecorino cheese and serve hot.

Shellfish Acorda

About 1 cup fruity olive oil

12 to 18 thick (1 inch) slices French or Italian peasant bread (enough to cover the bottom of each bowl)

1 large clove garlic, peeled

5 tablespoons finely minced garlic

½ teaspoon salt

6 large eggs, at room temperature

5 cups Fish Fumet or Shellfish Stock (page 105)

18 large or 24 medium shrimp, shelled and deveined

2 medium onions, chopped (about 2 cups)

2 teaspoons dried red pepper flakes

12 to 18 mussels, scrubbed and bearded, or 18 Manila clams, scrubbed

⅓ cup dry white wine

¼ cup finely chopped fresh parsley

½ cup finely chopped cilantro

Technically this is not a soup as we know it but closer to a *sopa seca,* or dry soup. It's another good old Mediterranean meal in a bowl. While this is not as economical as the simple *acorda,* a little shellfish will go a long way in combination with the egg and bread and will satisfy your passion for those seafood delicacies without emptying your pocketbook. ◆ *Serves 6*

Film a large skillet with olive oil and heat over medium heat. Add as many slices bread as will fit without crowding and sauté, turning once, until golden on both sides. Transfer to paper towels to drain, then, while the bread is hot, rub both sides of each slice with the clove of garlic. Repeat with the remaining bread, adding more oil as needed.

Mash 3 tablespoons of the minced garlic and the salt to a paste in a mortar with the pestle.

Poach the eggs until the whites are set but the yolks are still quite runny. Set them aside in a bowl of cold water.

Heat the fish fumet to simmering. Add the shrimp and simmer just until cooked through, about 3 minutes. Remove with a slotted spoon and set aside.

Cook the onions in about ¼ cup olive oil in a skillet over low heat until translucent. Add the remaining 2 tablespoons minced garlic and the red pepper flakes; cook about 3 minutes, then add to the hot stock.

Just before serving, steam the mussels or clams open in the wine in a covered saucepan. Remove the mussels or clams with a slotted spoon, strain the cooking liquid, and add to the hot fish stock.

Divide the bread, fresh parsley and cilantro, and garlic paste among 6 soup bowls. Add 1 tablespoon olive oil to each bowl, then add the cooked shrimp and mussels or clams. Using a slotted spoon, remove the poached eggs from the water and very gently nestle them in with the shellfish. Now ladle on the very hot stock. Serve immediately.

STOCKS

If you cook a little or a lot, you should have a few fine stocks on hand. Years ago it was acceptable to use canned broth instead of homemade in a pinch. Sad to say, this is no longer feasible because most canned broths are loaded with salt and preservatives. A canned broth reduced for richness would be so salty it would make the dish inedible.

It is not hard work to make a good stock. After the initial assembly of ingredients, the stock can simmer untended for hours. Stocks will keep for a few days in the refrigerator, but it is best to make a large batch and freeze it in small portions.

Chicken Stock

6 pounds chicken parts,
   necks, backs, carcasses,
   thighs
2 medium onions,
   coarsely chopped
2 small carrots coarsely
   chopped
1 large rib celery,
   coarsely chopped
Green tops of 2 leeks,
   coarsely chopped
   (optional)
2 cloves garlic (optional)
Several sprigs parsley
About 6 peppercorns
1 or 2 sprigs thyme
2 small bay leaves

◆ *Makes about 4 quarts*

Rinse the chicken parts, put them in a large stockpot, and cover with cold water. Heat to boiling. Reduce the heat and skim the scum from the surface. Simmer 1 hour. Add the remaining ingredients and simmer gently uncovered 4 to 5 hours.

Remove the solids with a slotted spoon or Chinese skimmer. Pour the stock through a cheesecloth-lined strainer. Let cool, then refrigerate until cold. Remove the layer of fat from the top.

For a richer stock, gently boil the stock uncovered until reduced by half. Let cool and refrigerate or freeze.

Beef Stock

6 pounds meaty beef
   shanks, cracked

1 marrow bone, cracked

Beef trimmings from
   steaks or roasts
   (optional)

2 medium onions,
   coarsely chopped

1 leek, coarsely chopped
   (optional)

2 medium carrots,
   coarsely chopped

1 rib celery, coarsely
   chopped

2 tomatoes, halved

Mushroom stems
   (optional)

6 cloves garlic

5 sprigs parsley

8 peppercorns

3 sprigs thyme

2 small bay leaves

2 cloves

Preheat the oven to 450°. Place the beef shanks and marrow bone in a large roasting pan; roast, turning the pieces occasionally, until browned but not scorched, about 1½ hours. Put the bones in a large stockpot and cover with cold water. Add meat scraps if you have them. Heat to boiling. Reduce the heat and simmer uncovered 1 to 2 hours. Add more water as needed to keep the bones well covered and skim the scum from the surface occasionally.

Meanwhile, place the roasting pan on top of the stove and brown the onions, leek, carrots, and celery in the fat in the pan. They should be nicely caramelized; stir often so that they don't scorch. Add the vegetables to the stockpot. Pour a little water into the pan and simmer, scraping up the browned bits on the bottom. Pour the pan juices into the stock and add the remaining ingredients.

Now simmer the stock uncovered over very low heat as long as possible, preferably all day, but at least 6 to 8 hours.

Remove the solids with a slotted spoon or Chinese skimmer. Pour the stock through a strainer, then line the strainer with cheesecloth and strain the stock again. Let cool, then refrigerate until cold. Remove the layer of fat from the top.

For a richer stock, gently boil the stock uncovered until reduced by half. If you're using the stock for sauces, reduce it even more. Let cool and refrigerate or freeze.

Fish Fumet

6 to 8 pounds fish frames
(with heads and tails
but gills removed),
preferably snapper,
rockfish, halibut, and
sea bass but no
stronger-flavored fish

2 tablespoons mild olive
oil

2 quarts water or to cover

3 cups dry white wine

3 to 4 medium onions,
coarsely chopped

5 ribs celery, coarsely
chopped

4 strips lemon zest

5 sprigs parsley

2 sprigs thyme

10 peppercorns

4 whole coriander seeds

3 whole allspice

1 large bay leaf

1 walnut-sized piece fresh
ginger, peeled
(optional)

1 dried red pepper
(optional)

1 teaspoon fennel seeds
(optional)

Rinse the fish frames well. Heat the olive oil in a large stockpot over medium heat. Add the fish frames and sweat over medium heat, stirring often, until the frames give off liquid, about 10 minutes. Add the remaining ingredients and heat to the boil. Reduce the heat and simmer uncovered 30 minutes, skimming the scum from the surface often. Strain through a cheesecloth-lined strainer. Let cool to room temperature, then refrigerate or freeze.

VARIATION

For *shellfish stock*, use the shells of 6 large lobsters, chopped as fine as possible, or the shells from 3 pounds of prawns instead of the fish frames. Simmer 1 hour, then strain and reduce by half.

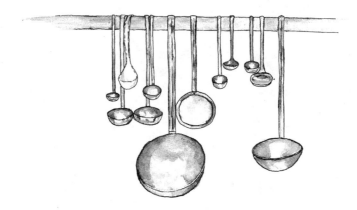

*I*t seems we've been inundated by a pasta wave both in restaurants of all persuasions and cookbooks, but none of us are complaining. Why? Because pasta is almost the perfect food. Maybe it *is* the perfect food. Pasta is a cornerstone of the Mediterranean diet. It is versatile and can be adorned simply with fruity olive oil and garlic or embellished elaborately with shellfish, meat, and other delicacies. It is great for transforming leftover tidbits into a tasty one-of-a-kind, never-to-be-repeated meal. Pasta is a most unpretentious and friendly food. Children (and fussy grown-ups) are willing to try almost any new food, even vegetables, if it is combined with pasta.

And pasta is not just Italian. You can find it in France as *nouilles* or noodles. They love ravioli on the Riviera. You can find pasta in Spain as *fideos*, in Greece as orzo and macaroni, and in the Middle East and North Africa as *reshta.* So if I take a dish from one of those countries' repertoires and turn it into a pasta, I am not really out of line. I am taking a part of the culinary tradition and giving it a twist. Instead of serving a dish with the custom-

ary rice or couscous or by itself, I serve it with pasta. When I do this, I am being economical in extending basic ingredients to feed more mouths. I am cooking healthier food, serving smaller portions of meat and fish, and combining small amounts of protein with energy-giving carbohydrates. I am not throwing culture up for grabs; I am presenting classic dishes but in a new production. That's show biz.

Although I like to be creative with pasta, I do not like bizarre combinations, ethnic hodgepodges, or innovation for its own sake. I only transform a dish when it seems to lend itself naturally to noodles, rather than being forced into the role. I believe in the power of taste memory and that classics endure because they taste good to a lot of people, not just the chef. I don't do Greco-Chinese, Thai-Italian, or Cajun-Portuguese combinations. Because of my years in Italy, my preference is for the Italian classics. I am rather stodgy about my carbonara and want it the right way with pancetta, eggs, Parmesan, and black pepper. No cream. I want my *puttanesca* to have anchovies and hot pepper, thank you. I want rigatoni alla Norma made with eggplant, not spaghetti squash, and I don't want cheese with shellfish. I like to do my homework and trace the origin of a pasta to its region and present it properly. I still believe that heavy sauces are for bigger pasta shapes and wider noodles and that lighter sauces go best on delicate pasta shapes and thinner noodles. I have respect for the Italian pasta tradition and want to keep the basic harmony of pasta and sauce in tune. But I am not so rigid and Italo-chauvinistic to believe that if a combination is not part of the Italian mainstream it must be rejected. I think pasta is for all of the people all of the time.

I have made a headstrong decision about recipe format in this chapter. I believe that there are foods people will or will not cook for themselves. Lots of fabulous dishes go by the wayside waiting for that special occasion when there are a few more people at the table. Most folks will make a stew or soup for four to six or a roast leg of lamb, but rarely for one or two. When alone, they eat more simply than if they are entertaining or cooking for a family. My experience as a cooking teacher has shown me that most people will make a salad or cook a piece of fish or chicken and, above all, find it easy and economical to cook pasta for one or two. To reflect that reality, most of the pasta recipes are written for two. You can multiply them for as many as you like. Your math is as good as mine, probably better. The pasta sauces that require special work, like making meatballs or roasting duck, I have written for four to six servings, the right amount for a pound of pasta so you can use the whole box (not that it spoils—another of its virtues!). I also have written the ravioli recipes for six because only the most fanatic pasta fan will make ravioli for just two. But don't let me stop you.

Basic Homemade Pasta

In Italy pasta is a *primo* or first course. The average Italian wants his pasta daily but in appetizer-sized portions. However we think of pasta as a main course, so we eat a larger portion (but not every day). My servings for these recipes are entrée portions. In my experience, one large egg and one cup flour makes two reasonable entree-sized portions of pasta or three to four appetizer-sized portions.

Whether you make the pasta by purist or expedient technique is up to you. Are you someone who likes to work with your hands? Does kneading dough relax you? Will you feel guilty if you "cheat" and assemble the dough in a food processor or electric mixer and knead it with the dough hook? If it's too easy will you feel like you didn't really do it? As a Jewish mother with many years of experience, I know how to make guilt work. But as your pasta "therapist" with a more modern outlook (after all, I've been living in California for over twenty-five years), I feel free to say do what feels right at the time. Of course, if you have been trained from childhood to roll out pasta by hand, you may be able to distinguish a hand-rolled noodle from one that is rolled through a machine. But I suspect that neither your guests nor family could recognize these subtle differences. So . . . if you have a spare hour and you want to assemble the dough by hand, great! But if you want fresh pasta and don't want to work at it, then use the processor or mixer to assemble the dough and the hand-cranked pasta machine to roll it out.

You will find that my recipe for fresh pasta yields a drier dough. There's a good reason for that. A drier pasta is a lighter pasta. It is easier to roll because it doesn't stick and it will be less gummy when cooked. In fact, if you associate fresh pasta with thick chewy noodles, you are in for a pleasant surprise. While dry is better, it is, of course, a little harder to work. That is where resting comes in. Not you . . . the pasta dough. A resting time of about an hour will allow the gluten in the flour to relax and make the rolling easier. If you don't have an hour, a half hour will do.

FOR 2 SERVINGS

1 cup all-purpose
   unbleached flour (see
   Note)
Pinch salt
1 large egg
2 teaspoons water, or a
   bit more if needed

FOR 4 SERVINGS

2 cups all-purpose
   unbleached flour (see
   Note)
1/4 teaspoon salt
2 large eggs
4 teaspoons water, or a
   bit more if needed

FOR 6 SERVINGS

3 cups all-purpose
   unbleached flour (see
   Note)
1/2 teaspoon salt
3 large eggs
2 tablespoons water, or a
   bit more if needed

Mix the flour and salt on a work surface and shape it into a mound. Make a well in the center and drop in the egg and water. Stir the egg and water together gradually mixing in the flour from the side of the well. Knead the dough with your hands until very smooth, 10 to 15 minutes. Or you may mix the flour and salt in a food processor or in a mixer bowl with the paddle. Add the egg and water and process or mix for a minute. The dough will be dry and crumbly. Knead it by hand about 15 minutes or with the dough hook of the mixer on low speed 8 to 10 minutes. Add a drop or two of water if necessary. Put the dough in a plastic bag and let it rest at room temperature about an hour.

When the dough is ready to be rolled, cut it in half if making pasta for 2, or quarters for 4 and so on. Flatten each piece into a rectangle about the width of the rolling bars on a hand-cranked pasta machine and thin enough to insert into the widest setting. A rolling pin may help.

Now roll the dough through the machine. Fold it in thirds and roll it through 2 times. Fold it in thirds again and roll it through once more. Now proceed through all the settings, making it thinner and thinner until you've rolled it through the thinnest setting. If you want the dough to be even thinner, let the dough rest covered for a while, then put it through the last setting again.

Cut the sheets of dough into 8- to 9-inch lengths, then cut into noodles, using the cutting bars on the machine or rolling it up like a jelly roll and cutting it by hand with a sharp knife. Toss the cut noodles with rice flour or Wondra. You may cook the noodles immediately and let them sit at room temperature for an hour or so before cooking. To store the noodles any longer, spread them on baking sheets and cover loosely with plastic wrap. They will keep in the refrigerator for a day.

To make lasagne: Roll out the dough up to (but not through) the thinnest setting. Cut into lengths the size of your pan. If you are not cooking them right away, lightly flour the noodles. Store on baking sheets lined with baker's parchment and covered loosely with plastic wrap.

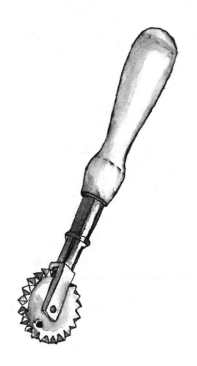

To make ravioli: Roll out the dough into sheets 15 to 18 inches long and as wide as the rolling bars, going through the thinnest setting for light fillings and through the second to the thinnest setting for dense fillings like potatoes. Fold one sheet lengthwise in half just to mark it and unfold. (Keep the other sheets covered with plastic wrap.) Place mounds of filling on the bottom half of the dough every 2 inches. Spray lightly with water, using a plant mister, and fold the top half over the bottom. Press between the mounds of filling to seal them but do not press the bottom edge. Cut into ravioli with a ravioli wheel, starting from the top and pressing the air to the bottom edge where it can escape. Press the bottom edge closed and trim it with the wheel. Pinch all the ravioli to make sure they are closed. Place the ravioli, without touching, on baking sheets lined with parchment and lightly sprinkled with rice flour or Wondra. Sprinkle the tops with flour too. These can be stored in the refrigerator for several hours, but do not cover them or they will get gummy and stick to the paper and each other. All of the ravioli recipes serve 6, so make a 3-egg batch of dough.

NOTE: Ignore all claims to the contrary and don't use semolina flour. Semolina flour is the best flour for dry extruded pasta made with commercial high-pressure machinery. It gives the pasta that wonderful chewy texture we have come to know as *al dente*, but it is too tough and coarse to roll out by hand. Fresh pasta is supposed to be tender, not chewy.

Buckwheat Pasta

FOR 2 SERVINGS

Use ⅓ cup buckwheat flour, ⅔ cup unbleached all-purpose flour, 1 large egg, pinch salt, and 1 tablespoon water, or a bit more if needed.

Whole-Wheat Pasta

FOR 2 SERVINGS

Use ½ cup whole-wheat flour, ½ cup unbleached all-purpose flour, 1 large egg, pinch salt, and 2 to 3 teaspoons water.

Red (Beet) Pasta

FOR 2 SERVINGS

1 large beet
1 large egg
1½ cups unbleached
    all-purpose flour, or as
    needed for stiff dough
Pinch salt

Cook the beet in simmering water until very tender, about 1 hour. Peel the beet, cut up, and let cool. Puree the beet and egg in a food processor. Proceed as directed in the basic recipe, adding more flour if necessary. This dough is quite electric in color, but it will cook to a less shocking shade of pink.

Rosemary Pasta

Add 1 scant tablespoon finely chopped fresh rosemary to the basic recipe.

Red Pepper Pasta

Grind dried red pepper flakes with a spice grinder or crush them with a mallet. Add 2 to 3 teaspoons to the basic recipe for a lively dough.

Black Pepper Pasta

Add 1 tablespoon freshly ground (coarse grind, please) black pepper to the basic recipe.

Saffron Pasta

Soak 1 pinch crushed saffron threads in 1 tablespoon hot water, cool, and combine the mixture with the egg. Proceed with the basic recipe, omitting the water called for in the recipe. You may want to experiment with the amount of saffron for pasta of the deepest hue without the medicinal flavor that comes from using too much saffron. A half teaspoon crushed saffron may be to your liking.

Spinach Pasta

FOR 2 SERVINGS

½ pound fresh spinach
  leaves (about 1 cup
  packed), torn into
  smaller pieces
1 large egg
1½ to 2 cups unbleached
  all-purpose flour
Pinch salt

I know that most recipes for spinach pasta call for cooked spinach, but the color—dark green—has never appealed to me. We found that if you puree fresh spinach with the egg and use the raw spinach liquid, the dough will be bright leaf green and the cooked noodles will be even brighter in color. After all, you are cooking the spinach for the first time, not the second.

So, puree the spinach and egg in a food processor or blender and proceed as directed. Add as much flour as you need for a stiff dough, as the spinach will continue to give off moisture as the dough rests. Experience is the best teacher with this particular pasta dough. I think you will love the color!

Türteln

BUCKWHEAT RAVIOLI
FILLED WITH GREENS,
RICOTTA, AND CUMIN

2 tablespoons olive oil
½ cup finely chopped
  onion
4 cups (loosely packed)
  Swiss chard or spinach
  leaves, rinsed and cut
  into chiffonade
2 cups fresh ricotta
  cheese (see Note, page
  115)
1 teaspoon ground cumin
Salt and freshly ground
  pepper
Buckwheat Pasta for 6
  (page 112)
½ cup unsalted butter,
  melted
6 tablespoons freshly
  grated Parmesan
  cheese

These ravioli are from the northern Italian province of the Trentino-Alto Adige. Traditionally they are made with rye flour and have a wonderful light brown color. We use buckwheat flour in place of the rye for the darker color and more intense flavor. The greens in the filling can be spinach, cabbage, or Swiss chard, but we prefer the chard for its texture and flavor. ◆ *Serves 6 (about 36 ravioli)*

Heat the olive oil in a wide deep sauté pan. Add the onion and cook until translucent. Add the chard and cook until completely wilted. Drain the chard mixture, then chop it fine and squeeze dry. Combine the chard mixture, ricotta, and cumin. Season to taste with salt and pepper.

Roll, fill, and cut the ravioli as directed on page 112, using 1½ tablespoons chard mixture for each piece.

Heat a large pot of salted water to boiling. Drop in the ravioli and simmer about 4 minutes. Remove them with a slotted spoon or large skimmer. Shake off the excess water and place on serving plates. Drizzle with the melted butter and sprinkle with Parmesan. Serve hot.

Cialzons di Timau

RAVIOLI FILLED WITH POTATO AND RICOTTA

4 or 5 very large russet
  potatoes
1½ cups fresh ricotta
  cheese (see Note)
2 tablespoons finely
  chopped fresh mint
2 tablespoons chopped
  fresh parsley
1 tablespoon grated
  lemon zest
½ teaspoon ground
  cinnamon
Salt and freshly ground
  pepper to taste
Basic Homemade Pasta
  for 8 (page 111)
¾ cup unsalted butter,
  melted
½ cup freshly grated
  Parmesan cheese

This filling reminds me of blintzes. It is not at all heavy, as you might expect when wrapping potato inside noodle dough. The ricotta makes the filling surprisingly light, as does the hint of lemon and mint. You may make the filling the night before and then shape and cut the ravioli a few hours before cooking them. These ravioli are from the Italian province of Friuli. ◆ *Serves 8 (about 40 ravioli)*

Preheat the oven to 400°. Bake the potatoes until tender, about 1 hour. Let stand until cool enough to handle. Cut each potato lengthwise in half and scoop out the pulp. Put the pulp through a ricer or mash it well with a fork.

Measure 3 cups potatoes and mix it with the ricotta, mint, parsley, lemon zest, cinnamon, and salt and pepper to taste. Cover and refrigerate until cold, at least 2 hours or up to 24 hours.

Roll the pasta dough up to (not through) the thinnest setting as directed on page 112. Fill and cut the ravioli, placing a generous tablespoon filling for each piece at 1½-inch intervals.

Heat a large pot of salted water to boiling. Drop in the ravioli and simmer about 5 minutes. Remove them with a slotted spoon or large skimmer. Shake off the excess water and place on serving plates. Drizzle with the melted butter and sprinkle with Parmesan. Serve hot.

NOTE: The fresh ricotta sold in Italian markets or cheese stores is much lighter in texture than the ricotta available at the supermarket. If you must use supermarket ricotta, either press it through a sieve or beat it until light.

Cassunziei Ampezzani

THREE BEET RAVIOLIS FROM THE VENETO

FILLING FOR BEET RAVIOLI ONE

2 ½ cups fresh ricotta cheese (see Note, page 115)

½ cup pureed cooked beet

2 large egg yolks

1 cup toasted bread crumbs

Salt and freshly ground pepper to taste

Basic Homemade Pasta for 6 (page 111)

½ cup unsalted butter, melted

3 tablespoons poppy seeds

FILLING FOR BEET RAVIOLI TWO

3 cups fresh ricotta cheese (see Note, page 115)

1 ½ tablespoons grated lemon zest

Salt and freshly ground pepper to taste

Beet Pasta for 6 (page 113)

½ cup unsalted butter, melted

3 tablespoons poppy seeds

Why three versions of this ravioli? Well, the first is traditional, a ravioli filled with pureed beets, ricotta, eggs, and bread crumbs, served with butter and poppy seeds. The other is a less conventional interpretation with the beets on the outside, pureed beets in the dough, a simple ricotta filling, and the butter and poppy seed sauce. This proved to be such an interesting combination and so pretty to look at that it became our Valentine's Day special. One year we went so far as to cut the ravioli into hearts, a frustrating and difficult experience. But we still liked the idea enough to come up with yet one more—beet pasta filled with greens, onions, pancetta, and toasted hazelnuts, which added crunch and contrast to the recipe. ◆ *Serves 6 (about 36 ravioli)*

Combine the filling ingredients. Roll, fill, and cut the ravioli as directed on page 112, using a heaping tablespoon of filling for each piece.

Heat a large pot of salted water to boiling. Drop in the ravioli and simmer about 4 minutes. Remove them with a slotted spoon or large skimmer. Shake off the excess water and place on serving plates. Drizzle with the melted butter and sprinkle with poppy seeds or Parmesan. Serve hot.

FILLING FOR BEET RAVIOLI THREE

8 cups (loosely packed) chopped Swiss chard or escarole or combination, rinsed well, cooked, chopped again, and squeezed as dry as possible (about 1 ½ cups)

1 cup chopped onion cooked in 3 tablespoons butter until tender

½ cup diced pancetta, rendered (see Note, page 124)

½ cup hazelnuts, toasted and chopped

¼ teaspoon grated nutmeg

Freshly ground pepper to taste

Beet Pasta for 6 (page 113)

½ cup unsalted butter, melted

6 tablespoons freshly grated Parmesan cheese

Ravioli alla Potentina

RICOTTA-FILLED
RAVIOLI WITH
PORK RAGU

RAGU

2 tablespoons olive oil

1½ pounds ground pork

2 cups finely chopped
    onions

¾ cup finely chopped
    carrots

¾ cup finely chopped
    celery

1 tablespoon finely
    chopped garlic

¾ cup dry red wine

3 cups canned crushed
    plum tomatoes

¼ cup tomato puree

¼ teaspoon grated
    nutmeg

Salt and freshly ground
    pepper

FILLING

2½ cups fresh ricotta
    (see Note, page 115)

½ cup grated pecorino
    cheese

¼ cup finely chopped
    fresh parsley

Salt and freshly ground
    pepper to taste

Basic Homemade Pasta
    for 6 (page 111)

6 tablespoons grated
    pecorino cheese

This ravioli is from the region of Basilicata, from around Potenza. ◆ *Serves 6 (about 36 ravioli)*

Prepare the ragu: Heat the olive oil in a large sauté pan over high heat. Add the pork and cook, stirring frequently, until no longer pink. Spoon off fat. Add the chopped vegetables and cook over medium heat until tender, about 20 minutes. Stir in the garlic and cook a few minutes more. Stir in the wine, crushed tomatoes, and tomato puree; simmer about 20 minutes. Season with nutmeg and salt and pepper to taste.

Combine the filling ingredients. Roll, fill, and cut the ravioli as directed on page 112, using 1 tablespoon for each piece.

Heat a large pot of salted water to boiling and, at the same time, heat the ragout. Drop the ravioli into the boiling water and simmer 4 to 5 minutes. Remove them with a slotted spoon or large skimmer. Shake off the excess water and place on serving plates. Spoon the ragu over the ravioli and sprinkle with pecorino. Serve hot.

Culingiones di Patate

SARDINIAN RAVIOLI

3 or 4 very large russet
  potatoes
1½ cups fresh ricotta
  cheese (see Note, page
  115)
⅓ cup grated pecorino
  cheese
2 tablespoons chopped
  fresh mint, plus 1
  tablespoon for garnish
½ teaspoon salt
¼ teaspoon freshly
  ground pepper
Basic Homemade Pasta
  for 6 (page 111)
2 cups Tomato Sauce
  (recipe follows)
6 tablespoons grated
  pecorino cheese

Another almost weightless potato-filled ravioli. The mint is a zippy accent and, because you can't have too much of a good thing, add a little chopped mint to the accompanying tomato sauce too. ◆ *Serves 6 (about 36 ravioli)*

Preheat the oven to 400°. Bake the potatoes until tender, about 1 hour. Let stand until cool enough to handle. Cut each potato lengthwise in half and scoop out the pulp. Put the pulp through a ricer or mash it well with a fork.

Measure 2½ cups potatoes and mix it with the ricotta, pecorino, 2 tablespoons mint, the salt, and pepper. Cover and refrigerate until cold, at least 2 hours or up to 24 hours.

Roll the pasta dough up to (not through) the thinnest setting as directed on page 112. Fill and cut the ravioli, placing a generous tablespoon filling for each piece at 1½-inch intervals.

Heat a large pot of salted water to boiling and, at the same time, heat the tomato sauce. Drop the ravioli into the boiling water and simmer about 5 minutes. Remove them with a slotted spoon or large skimmer. Shake off the excess water and place on serving plates. Drizzle with the tomato sauce and sprinkle with pecorino. Garnish with mint and serve hot.

Tomato Sauce

◆ *Makes about 3 quarts*

5 pounds canned Italian
  plum tomatoes
2 cups very rich canned
  tomato puree
6 tablespoons unsalted
  butter, cut into thin
  slivers
Salt and freshly ground
  pepper to taste

Process the plum tomatoes with their juices in a food processor until finely chopped (not pureed but not too chunky); transfer to a large heavy saucepan. Stir in the tomato puree and place the slivers of butter on top. Heat over low heat, stirring often, until the butter has melted and the sauce is slightly thickened. Season with a little salt and pepper. This sauce can be stored in the refrigerator up to 1 week or frozen.

NOTES: Italian plum tomatoes occasionally come packed in tomato puree, but the juice or water pack is acceptable because you can augment the flavor with the puree or even a little tomato paste. If you find that your tomato puree is thin, then be sure to add some tomato paste so it will thicken.

The butter may seems excessive but it does add body to the sauce and a certain unctuous quality. You may omit it and add a little virgin olive oil after cooking instead.

Ravioli Caprese

MOZZARELLA-STUFFED RAVIOLI WITH TOMATO SAUCE

1 ½ pounds fresh mozzarella cheese

Basic Homemade Pasta for 6 (page 111)

2 ½ cups Tomato Sauce (recipe precedes)

3 cups diced fresh tomatoes (optional)

6 tablespoons heavy or whipping cream

¾ cup basil chiffonade

6 tablespoons freshly grated Parmesan cheese

This is an interpretation of the classic salad Caprese. These are the easiest ravioli to make and fun to eat for the cheese melts and forms those wonderful strings *al telefono*.
✦ *Serves 6 (36 ravioli)*

Cut mozzarella into 36 pieces, about ¼ inch thick and 1 ½ inches square. Any scraps can be combined to fill a ravioli even if it's not a perfect square. Roll, fill, and cut the ravioli as directed on page 112, using 1 slice mozzarella for each piece.

Heat a large pot of salted water to boiling and, at the same time, heat the tomato sauce. Drop the ravioli into the boiling water and simmer 3 to 4 minutes. Stir the diced tomatoes into the tomato sauce, then swirl in the cream and half the basil and heat through.

Remove the ravioli with a slotted spoon or large skimmer. Shake off the excess water and place on serving plates. Spoon the tomato sauce over the ravioli, then sprinkle with the remaining basil and the Parmesan. Serve hot.

Zembi d'Arzillo

SOLE-FILLED RAVIOLI
WITH TOMATO AND
CLAM SAUCE

2 pounds sole fillets

3 tablespoons unsalted
    butter

1 cup finely chopped
    onions

4 cups spinach chiffonade

2 large eggs

½ cup (or as needed) dry
    bread crumbs

½ teaspoon grated
    nutmeg

Salt and freshly ground
    pepper

Basic Homemade Pasta
    for 6 (page 111)

4 cups Tomato Sauce
    (page 118)

36 to 48 tiny Manila
    clams, scrubbed

½ cup chopped fresh
    parsley

This Ligurian ravioli has an unusual name of Arabic origin. *Zembi* derives from *zembil,* a basket of double palm leaves, and *arzillo* is a green seaweed found on the beach with the perfume of the sea. *Arzillo* is also Ligurian slang for limpet, a small shellfish which is part of the traditional sauce for these ravioli. Lacking limpets, we have substituted Manila clams. ◆ *Serves 6 to 8 (36 to 40 ravioli)*

Steam the sole or sauté it quickly. Drain well, then finely chop.

Melt the butter in a large skillet over medium heat. Add the onions and cook until tender. Add the spinach; cook until completely wilted. Transfer to a sieve and drain well. Chop the spinach mixture and squeeze dry. Mix the sole, spinach mixture, eggs, bread crumbs, and nutmeg. Season to taste with salt and pepper. Add more bread crumbs if the mixture is wet.

Roll, fill, and cut the ravioli as directed on page 112, using 2 tablespoons filling for each piece.

Heat a large pot of salted water to boiling. Heat the tomato sauce in a wide saucepan. Drop in the clams, cover the pan, and cook until they open, 5 to 7 minutes. Keep warm.

Drop the ravioli into the boiling water and simmer 4 to 5 minutes. Remove them with a slotted spoon or large skimmer. Shake off the excess water and place on serving plates. Spoon the tomato sauce with clams over the ravioli and sprinkle with parsley. Serve hot. No cheese, please.

Ravioli Verdi al Salmone

SPINACH RAVIOLI
FILLED WITH SALMON

FILLING

3 tablespoons unsalted
  butter
1 cup finely minced
  shallots
2½ pounds salmon fillets,
  cut into ¼-pound
  pieces
1 teaspoon freshly grated
  nutmeg
Salt and freshly ground
  pepper

Spinach Pasta for 6
  (page 114)

SAUCE

3 cups heavy cream
3 tablespoons grated
  lemon zest
3 tablespoons minced
  fresh chives

We love the taste and the look of fettuccine verde with salmon, lemon, spinach chiffonnade, and cream. All that deco pink and green! However, we thought it would be an interesting twist to combine a spinach pasta with the salmon filling and nap it with the cream, lemon zest, and chives. ◆ *Serves 6 (about 36 ravioli)*

Prepare the filling: Heat the butter in a medium skillet over medium heat. Add the shallots and cook until very tender, about 10 minutes. Meanwhile, steam the salmon on a rack over simmering water until the fish flakes easily with a fork, about 6 minutes. Let cool slightly, then flake into small pieces. There should be about 4 cups loosely packed.

Place one quarter of the shallots and salmon in a food processor; process with pulses until it holds together. (You should be able to shape it into a ball in your hand.) Remove this batch to a mixing bowl and repeat with the remaining shallots and salmon. Season with nutmeg and salt and pepper to taste. (Don't be surprised if you find the salmon is taking a good deal of salt; it seems to need it.)

Roll, fill, and cut the ravioli as directed on page 112, using about 1½ tablespoons filling for each piece.

Heat a large pot of salted water to boiling. Pour the cream into a large saucepan and heat over medium heat until slightly thickened. Stir in the lemon zest, chives, and salt and pepper to taste. Simmer a minute or two and keep warm.

Drop the ravioli into the boiling water and simmer about 5 minutes. Remove them with a slotted spoon or large skimmer. Shake off the excess water and place on serving plates. Spoon the cream sauce over the ravioli and serve hot. No cheese, please.

Ravioli di Melanzane

EGGPLANT-FILLED
RAVIOLI

3 medium eggplants

1 ½ cups fresh ricotta
cheese (see Note, page
115)

10 tablespoons grated
pecorino cheese

3 tablespoons finely
chopped basil

½ teaspoon salt

¼ teaspoon freshly
ground pepper

Basic Homemade Pasta
for 6 (page 111)

2 cups Tomato Sauce
(page 118), thinned
with ¼ cup heavy
cream if desired

6 tablespoons basil
chiffonade

A delicious pasta from Basilicata/Calabria, which is in southern Italy. ✦ *Serves 6 (about 36 ravioli)*

Preheat the oven to 450°. Prick each eggplant a few times with a fork; bake on a baking sheet, turning them once, until very tender, 40 to 50 minutes. Let stand until cool enough to handle. Cut the eggplants in half and scoop the pulp into a colander. Let the pulp drain, then chop it very fine in a food processor or by hand.

Measure 2 cups eggplant and mix it with the ricotta, 4 tablespoons pecorino, the chopped basil, salt, and pepper. Refrigerate until cold, at least 2 hours or up to 24 hours.

Roll, fill, and cut the ravioli as directed on page 112, using a heaping tablespoon of filling for each piece.

Heat a large pot of salted water to boiling and, at the same time, heat the tomato sauce. Drop the ravioli into the boiling water and simmer about 5 minutes. Remove them with a slotted spoon or large skimmer. Shake off the excess water and place on serving plates. Drizzle with the tomato sauce and sprinkle with the remaining pecorino. Garnish with the basil chiffonade. Serve hot.

Ricotta-Goat Cheese

2 cups fresh ricotta
  cheese (see Note, page
  115)
1 cup goat cheese

Of course you could put this filling in a plain egg pasta, but the buckwheat adds a depth of flavor. A sauce of sun-dried tomatoes, olives, and cream is a perfect accompaniment. For sauce that is less rich, try a simple tomato sauce (page 118) with basil or thyme. ✦ *Serves 6*

Buckwheat Pasta is especially nice but you could use the basic pasta as well.

Serve with a sauce of 3 cups heavy cream, reduced slightly and combined with 6 tablespoons each of julienned sun-dried tomatoes and quartered pitted black olives.

Ricotta-Gorgonzola

1½ cups fresh ricotta
  cheese (see Note, page
  115)
1½ cups Gorgonzola
  cheese
¼ teaspoon freshly
  ground pepper

The balance of flavor depends on how intense the gorgonzola may be. You may want to play it up and serve these ravioli garnished with chopped walnuts in butter. Or you may want to play it down—increase the ricotta and add a few leaves of sage to a simple butter and parmesan sauce. Plain pasta is fine but buckwheat or whole wheat will add richness and an interesting flavor dimension. ✦ *Serves 6*

Serve with melted butter and freshly grated Parmesan cheese.

Leeks and Cheese

4 cups chopped leeks
  cooked in butter (about
  1 cup after cooking)
2 cups fresh ricotta
  cheese (see Note, page
  115)
1 cup goat cheese or
  Gorgonzola
Salt, freshly ground
  pepper, and grated
  nutmeg to taste

From the north of Italy, we bring you options: Friuli likes caraway, whereas Liguria loves walnuts. Everyone loves parmesan; whether you use gorgonzola or goat cheese is up to you. ✦ *Serves 6*

These ravioli can be made with Buckwheat, Whole-Wheat, or Basic Homemade Pasta (pages 110–113). Serve with melted butter, freshly grated Parmesan cheese, and chopped toasted walnuts or caraway seeds.

Pasta à la Barigoule

PASTA WITH ARTICHOKES

2 large or 4 small
   artichokes

1 lemon, halved

½ cup olive oil, plus 3 to
   4 tablespoons for the
   artichokes

Salt and freshly ground
   pepper

1 cup sliced (¼ inch)
   red onions

1 cup sliced (¼ inch)
   fresh mushrooms,
   white, chanterelles,
   and/or cepes

⅓ cup julienned
   prosciutto or rendered
   pancetta (see Note)

½ cup julienned zucchini
   (optional)

2 to 3 teaspoons very
   finely minced garlic

2 teaspoons chopped fresh
   thyme

6 to 8 ounces fresh
   fettuccine or dried
   penne or farfalle

2 tablespoons freshly
   grated Parmesan
   cheese

2 tablespoons chopped
   fresh parsley

We invented this pasta for a Provençal menu. Its origin is *artichauts à la barigoule,* a dish of artichokes stuffed with onions, mushrooms, and ham that is braised in the oven with mirepoix and white wine. We have served it with penne, a dry quill-shaped pasta, as well as fresh fettuccine. Both are delicious. Occasionally we substitute pancetta for ham or add a julienne of zucchini. You might like to add some fresh peas too, which is reminiscent of the pastas served in Rome in the spring when both peas and artichokes appear at the market. ◆ *Serves 2*

Break off all the large outer leaves from the artichokes. Pare the outside to expose the heart. Using a sharp spoon, remove the fuzzy chokes. Cut the artichokes into ¼-inch slices and drop them in water acidulated with lemon juice. Heat ¼ cup olive oil in a sauté pan or skillet over medium heat. Drain the artichokes and add to the pan. Squeeze a little lemon juice over the artichokes and cook covered, stirring occasionally, until crisp-tender, 5 to 7 minutes. Season with salt and pepper. (Artichokes can be prepared up to 6 hours in advance.)

Heat a large pot of salted water to boiling for the pasta.

Heat ½ cup olive oil in a large skillet over medium heat. Add the onions and cook until tender. Add the mushrooms and cook until slightly wilted. Then stir in the artichokes, prosciutto, zucchini if using, garlic, and thyme; cook until heated through. Season to taste with salt and pepper.

Meanwhile, add the pasta to the boiling water and cook until tender if using fresh pasta or *al dente* if using dried.

Drain the pasta and transfer to a pasta bowl. Add the artichoke mixture and quickly toss to combine. Sprinkle with the Parmesan and parsley. Serve hot.

NOTE: To render pancetta, cut the pancetta into ¼-inch-thick slices, then into ⅓-inch-wide strips. Put the pancetta in a large skillet with a drop or two of olive oil. Cook slowly, stirring frequently, until the pancetta releases much of its fat and softens but does not brown. Remove the pancetta with a slotted spoon. You may want to reserve the rendered fat for cooking.

Fettuccine alla Turque

PASTA WITH
ARTICHOKES, LEMON,
AND CREAM

2 large artichokes

1 lemon

*¼ cup olive oil, plus 2 to
3 tablespoons for the
artichokes*

*Salt and freshly ground
pepper*

½ cup fresh peas

*½ cup julienned carrots
(optional)*

*1 cup sliced (¼ inch)
red onion*

1¼ cups heavy cream

*2 teaspoons grated lemon
zest covered with a
little fresh lemon juice*

*2 to 4 tablespoons
chopped fresh dill*

6 ounces fresh fettuccine

*2 tablespoons freshly
grated Parmesan
cheese*

*2 tablespoons chopped
fresh parsley (optional)*

This pasta is a free interpretation of the flavors of Turkey. You might want to add a few blanched strips of carrot as well for an accent in this pale green-and-cream-colored dish. ✦ *Serves 2*

Remove all the leaves from the artichokes, then pare the hearts. Using a sharp spoon, remove the fuzzy chokes. Cut the hearts into ¼-inch slices and drop them in water acidulated with lemon juice. Heat 2 to 3 tablespoons olive oil in a sauté pan or skillet over medium heat. Drain the artichokes and add to the pan. Squeeze a little lemon juice over the artichokes and cook covered, stirring occasionally, until cooked through but not soft, 5 to 7 minutes. Season with salt and pepper. (Artichokes can be prepared up to 6 hours in advance.)

Heat a large saucepan of water to boiling. Add the peas and boil 1 minute. Remove and refresh in ice water. Add the carrot julienne, if using, to the boiling water and blanch until crisp-tender, 1 to 2 minutes. Drain and refresh in ice water.

Heat a large pot of salted water to boiling for the pasta.

Heat ¼ cup olive oil in a large skillet over medium heat. Add the onion and cook until tender. Stir in the cream, artichokes, peas, carrots, lemon zest and juice, dill, and salt and pepper to taste. Cook until the cream is slightly reduced but not thick and gluey.

Meanwhile, add the pasta to the boiling water and cook until tender, about 2 minutes if the pasta is thin.

Drain the pasta and transfer to a pasta bowl. Add the sauce and quickly toss to combine. Sprinkle with Parmesan and parsley if you like. Serve hot.

Fettuccine alla Genovese

1 ½ cups heavy cream

4 cups spinach leaves, rinsed well, drained, and cut into 1 ½-inch-wide strips

½ cup golden or dark raisins, plumped in warm water and drained

1 teaspoon (or to taste) grated lemon zest covered with 2 teaspoons fresh lemon juice (see Note)

½ cup pine nuts, toasted

Salt and freshly ground pepper

6 to 8 ounces fresh fettuccine

We were looking for an appealing vegetarian pasta and thought why not adapt the spinach sauté that accompanied many of our entrées. It is the classic *spinaci con pignoli e uvette* (spinach with pine nuts and raisins) that the Genovese, Venetians, and Romans all claim as original to them. We added grated lemon zest for accent and cream to highlight the sweetness of the raisins and pine nuts.
✦ *Serves 2*

Heat a large pot of salted water to boiling for the pasta.

Heat the cream in a large skillet over medium heat to simmering. Add the spinach and cook, stirring constantly, until just beginning to wilt. Stir in the raisins, lemon zest and juice, a few of the pine nuts, and salt and pepper to taste. Cook, stirring constantly, until slightly thickened. Be careful the sauce doesn't reduce too much.

Meanwhile, add the pasta to the boiling water and cook until tender, about 2 minutes if the pasta is thin.

Drain the pasta and transfer to a pasta bowl. Add the sauce and quickly toss to combine. Top with the remaining pine nuts. Serve hot.

NOTE: To keep the lemon zest from drying out, I cover it with lemon juice in a small bowl.

Fettuccine with Goat Cheese and Swiss Chard

Salt

2 tablespoons olive oil

5 cups Swiss chard, cut into chiffonade, rinsed well

1½ cups heavy cream

¼ pound goat cheese

¼ cup walnuts, toasted, somewhat coarsely chopped

Freshly ground pepper

½ teaspoon each grated lemon and orange zest or 1 cup diced tomatoes (optional)

6 ounces fresh fettuccine, plain, buckwheat, or whole wheat

This is a variation of the Ligurian *salsa di noci*, or walnut sauce. Some versions use ricotta and others use milk, but we like a mild goat cheese. The greens are optional.
♦ *Serves 2*

Heat a large pot of salted water to boiling for the pasta.

Heat the olive oil in a large sauté pan or skillet over high heat. Add the greens and cook, stirring constantly, until wilted. Add the cream, goat cheese, and walnuts. Reduce heat and cook, stirring constantly, until the cheese melts. Season with pepper to taste. Add the citrus zest or tomatoes if using and heat through, although it's perfectly delicious as is.

Add the pasta to the boiling water and cook until tender, about 2 minutes if the pasta is thin. Drain and transfer to a pasta bowl. Add the sauce to the pasta and quickly toss to combine. Serve hot.

VARIATION

For Fettuccine with Gorgonzola and Swiss Chard, substitute Gorgonzola for the goat cheese. Add 1 cup sliced cooked artichoke hearts and ½ teaspoon toasted caraway seeds. Omit the nuts. Or use the nuts but omit the caraway seeds.

Strascinate

FETTUCCINE WITH
PANCETTA, EGGS, AND
CREAM

4 large eggs

²/₃ cup heavy cream

2 tablespoons fresh lemon
    juice

¼ teaspoon (or to taste)
    freshly grated nutmeg

Salt

6 ounces fresh fettuccine,
    or fresh noodles cut ½
    to 1 inch wide

2 tablespoons olive oil

¼ pound partially
    rendered pancetta (see
    Note, page 124) or ½
    pound uncooked
    pancetta, cut into
    ¼-inch strips

¼ cup freshly grated
    aged pecorino or
    Parmesan cheese

This pasta is supposedly the fifteenth-century progenitor of spaghetti *alla carbonara*. It originated in the Umbrian town of Cascia and is usually prepared with a wide noodle, such as *pappardelle* or lasagne. Fresh fettuccine is more easily available, but, if you are in the mood to make your own pasta, roll away and cut the sheets by hand or with a pastry or ravioli wheel.

The verb *strascinare* means to drag or pull along the ground. In this dish the eggs are supposed to drag on the noodles. But most people overcook the eggs and end up with a scrambled mess. As a safety precaution, we have added a bit of cream and lemon to the eggs to make the dragging strands of egg a little more elegant and tender. Occasionally, we embellish this pasta with a few cooked peas. While not authentic, it is tasty. ✦ *Serves 2*

Whisk the eggs and cream together in a mixing bowl. You may add the lemon juice and nutmeg if you are planning to cook the pasta right away. If not, wait and add it later for the lemon juice thickens the cream.

Heat a large pot of salted water to boiling. Add the pasta and cook until tender, about 2 minutes if the pasta is thin.

Meanwhile, heat the olive oil in a small saute pan or skillet over medium heat. Add the pancetta and cook until golden but not crisp. Using a slotted spoon, transfer the pancetta to a slightly warmed pasta bowl. Drain the pasta and add to the bowl. Stir the lemon and nutmeg into the egg mixture if you haven't done so already and add to the noodles. Add the pecorino and quickly toss to combine. Serve at once. This pasta does not like to sit around.

Pizzoccheri

BUCKWHEAT PASTA
WITH GREENS AND
POTATOES

Salt

½ cup olive oil

*1½ cups sliced red
onions*

*2 teaspoons chopped fresh
sage*

*1 cup chunks (1 inch)
Roasted Potatoes (page
302)*

*6 cups loosely packed
Swiss chard or
escarole, cut into
chiffonade*

*⅔ cup blanched green
beans, cut into
1½-inch lengths*

*1½ tablespoons finely
minced garlic*

*Buckwheat Pasta for 2
(page 112), rolled and
cut for fettuccine or
cut by hand into
½-inch-wide noodles*

¼ cup Taleggio cheese

*¼ cup grated Fontina
cheese*

Freshly ground pepper

A hearty and robust (let's just call it filling!) pasta from the mountains in the Valtellina region of Lombardia. You can enjoy this pasta even if you haven't been tromping through the snow. ♦ *Serves 2*

Heat a large pot of salted water to boiling.

Heat the olive oil in a very large sauté pan or skillet over high heat. Add the onions and cook until tender. Stir in half the sage. If you don't mind dirtying another pan, you may brown the potatoes separately. Add the potatoes (browned or not), Swiss chard, green beans, and garlic; cook until the greens are wilted, about 3 minutes.

Meanwhile, add the pasta to the boiling water and cook until tender, about 2 minutes if the pasta is thin.

Add the remaining sage, the cheeses, and salt and pepper to taste to the greens mixture. Drain the pasta and transfer to a pasta bowl. Add the greens mixture and quickly toss to combine.

Fusilli alla Napoletana

This pasta is a surprise. The little cubes of mozzarella melt in the sauce and form strings like telephone cords (*al telefono*). It's not only tasty but also fun to eat. ◆ *Serves 2*

¼ pound pancetta, sliced ¼ inch thick and cut into ½-inch-wide strips

4 tablespoons olive oil

1 medium onion, cut into ¼-inch cubes

2 medium carrots, cut into ¼-inch cubes

1 rib celery, cut into ¼-inch cubes

Salt

2 cloves garlic, finely minced

1½ cups Tomato Sauce (page 118)

Freshly ground pepper

6 ounces fusilli

¼ pound fresh mozzarella cheese, cut into ½-inch cubes

2 tablespoons chopped fresh parsley

2 tablespoons (or more to taste) freshly grated Parmesan cheese

Sauté the pancetta in 1 tablespoon olive oil until most of the fat is rendered and the pancetta is cooked through but not browned. Remove the pancetta with a slotted spoon and discard the fat.

Add the remaining olive oil to the skillet and heat over medium heat. Add the onion, carrots, and celery; cook, stirring occasionally, until tender, about 10 minutes.

Meanwhile, heat a large pot of salted water to boiling.

Add the garlic, tomato sauce, and pancetta to the vegetables. Season to taste with salt and pepper. Heat the sauce through and keep warm.

Add the pasta to the boiling water and cook until *al dente*. Drain and transfer to a pasta bowl. Add the mozzarella to the sauce and pour it over the pasta. Quickly toss to combine. Sprinkle with the parsley and Parmesan. Serve at once.

Bigoli co l'Anara

VENETIAN
WHOLE-WHEAT PASTA
WITH DUCK SAUCE

1 ready-to-cook duck
   (about 5 pounds)
Salt and freshly ground
   pepper
3 medium carrots, finely
   diced
2 medium onions, finely
   diced
2 medium ribs celery,
   finely diced
3 cloves garlic, finely
   minced
3 cups canned Italian
   plum tomatoes, drained
   and diced, juices
   reserved
2 cups Chicken or Duck
   Stock (page 103 or
   225), reduced to 1 cup
½ cup dry red wine
1 teaspoon chopped fresh
   thyme or sage
½ teaspoon grated
   nutmeg
Whole-Wheat Pasta for 6
   (page 113), rolled and
   cut for fettuccine, or 1
   pound dried fettuccine

In the Venetian version of this pasta, the duck is boiled and served for the second course and the pasta for the first course is made with the giblets and vegetables. Since we couldn't sell boiled duck in the restaurant if our lives depended on it, we roast the duck and add the meat to the sauce. I think you'll like this pasta, even if it isn't authentic. ✦ *Serves 6*

Preheat the oven to 500°. Cut the wings from the duck. Trim all excess fat and reserve. Reserve the liver. Place the duck, breast side up, on a rack in a roasting pan and sprinkle inside and out with salt and pepper. Prick the duck all over with a fork. Roast until the juices run clear, about 1 hour. Transfer to a platter and let cool. Strain the pan drippings into a large skillet.

Add the reserved fat to the pan drippings and cook over low heat until melted. Strain the fat and measure 6 tablespoons into a cup. Reserve a little of the remaining fat for sautéing the duck liver.

Heat the fat in a large saute pan or deep skillet over medium heat. Add the carrots, onions, and celery; cook, stirring occasionally, until tender. Stir in the garlic and cook 2 minutes more. Stir in the tomatoes with their juices, the reduced stock, and wine. Simmer, stirring occasionally, 30 minutes.

Heat a large pot of salted water to boiling.

Meanwhile, remove the meat from the duck and cut it into bite-size pieces. Sauté the duck liver in a little fat in a small skillet over low heat until cooked through. Let cool slightly, then finely chop. Add the duck liver and meat to the sauce. Stir in the thyme and nutmeg; simmer about 10 minutes.

Add the pasta to the boiling water and cook until tender if using fresh pasta or *al dente* if using dried. Drain the pasta and transfer to a pasta bowl. Season the sauce with salt and pepper to taste. Add the sauce to the pasta and quickly toss to combine. Serve hot.

Rigatoni alla Norma

SICILIAN EGGPLANT
PASTA FROM CATANIA

Salt

4 Japanese eggplants or 1
  medium globe eggplant

½ cup (or as needed)
  olive oil

4 cloves garlic, finely
  minced

6 large black olives,
  pitted and quartered

12 fresh basil leaves, cut
  into chiffonade

1½ cups Tomato Sauce
  (page 118)

Freshly ground pepper

½ pound rigatoni

3 tablespoons freshly
  grated Parmesan
  cheese

Simple, tasty, and one of our most requested pastas. We prefer to make this with the sweeter Japanese eggplant, but it could be made with globe eggplant too. This pasta is named after Bellini's opera, *Norma*, and is she popular! Bellini was born in Catania. A case of local boy making good and the local opera heroine honored with a pasta named after her. ◆ *Serves 2*

Heat a large pot of salted water to boiling.

Slice the Japanese eggplants crosswise into ¼-inch slices. If you are using globe eggplant, peel and cut into 1-inch or slightly larger cubes.

Heat the olive oil in a very large skillet or 2 large skillets over high heat. Add the eggplants and sauté quickly on both sides so that the pieces brown but don't steam. Use more oil if needed. Add the garlic, olives, most of the basil, and the tomato sauce. Heat the sauce through and season with salt and pepper to taste. Keep warm.

Meanwhile, add the pasta to the boiling water and cook until *al dente*. Drain and transfer to a pasta bowl. Add the eggplant sauce and quickly toss to combine. Sprinkle with the remaining basil and the Parmesan. Serve hot.

Rigatoni with Fennel Sausage and Peppers

Salt

¼ cup olive oil

½ pound Fennel Sausage without casings (page 294)

2 medium red or yellow onions, halved through root ends and sliced crosswise ¼ inch thick (about 2 cups)

½ each green and red bell pepper, cut into strips 3 by ¼ inch (about 1 cup)

1½ cups Tomato Sauce (page 118) or ¾ cup diced fresh tomatoes

1 tablespoon finely minced garlic (optional)

½ teaspoon dried red pepper flakes (optional)

Freshly ground pepper

½ pound rigatoni

3 tablespoons freshly grated Parmesan cheese

This pasta is as good as the sausage you use. You can use a wonderful fennel sausage from your favorite Italian market and remove it from the casings, or you may make the sausage yourself, using the recipe on page 294. Sausage is very easy to make at home, for it is simply ground meat seasoned with herbs and spices and bound with a little liquid. Homemade sausage doesn't keep more than a few days, but it also isn't loaded with preservatives and nitrates. So not only will it taste better, but it will be better for you. The sausage in this recipe can be shaped into tiny meatballs or cooked loose. ✦ *Serves 2*

Heat a large pot of salted water to boiling.

Heat the olive oil in a large sauté pan over high heat. Add the sausage and cook, stirring frequently, until it starts to brown. Reduce heat. Add the onions and cook until translucent, about 5 minutes. Add the peppers and cook a few minutes more. Stir in the tomato sauce or diced tomatoes and garlic and red pepper flakes if using. Season to taste with salt and pepper. Heat the sauce through.

Meanwhile, add the pasta to the boiling water and cook until al dente.

Drain the pasta and transfer to a pasta bowl. Add the sauce and quickly toss to combine. Sprinkle with the Parmesan cheese. Serve hot.

Rigatoni with Little Herbed Meatballs

¾ pound ground beef

1 medium yellow onion, grated or pureed in a food processor

1 to 2 cloves garlic, very finely minced

3 tablespoons chopped mixed fresh herbs, such as oregano, thyme, sage, and parsley

Salt and freshly ground pepper

½ cup mild olive oil

1 pound rigatoni

3 cups Tomato Sauce (page 118)

1½ cups fresh ricotta cheese (see Note, page 115)

½ cup chopped fresh parsley

6 tablespoons (or more to taste) freshly grated Parmesan cheese

Italian-Americans rightly embarrassed by the cliché of spaghetti and meatballs claim no one in Italy eats such stuff. But there is a meatball tradition in the Abruzzi, Apulia, and south Italy, where *polpette* appear in broth, layered in lasagne, and with pasta. What you don't find are those tennis-ball-sized meatballs sitting on a bed of overcooked spaghetti dressed with tomato sauce. Anyone would be embarrassed by that mess. But wonderfully seasoned little meatballs combined with ricotta and a good tomato sauce makes a very satisfying pasta indeed. ◆ *Serves 6*

Mix the ground beef, onions, garlic, mixed herbs, and salt and pepper to taste. Shape into tiny meatballs, about 1 inch in diameter. Allow about 8 per person.

Heat the olive oil in a large skillet over high heat. Add as many meatballs as will fit without crowding and sauté until browned but still a bit rare in the center. Drain on paper towels and repeat with the remaining meatballs.

Heat a large pot of salted water to boiling. Add the pasta and cook until *al dente.*

Meanwhile, heat the tomato sauce in a large saucepan. Add the meatballs and keep warm over very low heat.

Drain the pasta and transfer to a pasta bowl. Ladle the tomato sauce with meatballs over the top and add the ricotta in dollops. Quickly toss to combine and sprinkle with the parsley and Parmesan. Serve hot.

SPAGHETTI WITH TUNA, THREE WAYS

Spaghetti with Grilled Tuna

½ to ¾ *pound tuna fillet, 1 inch thick*

¼ *cup olive oil*

Salt and freshly ground pepper

2 tablespoons finely minced garlic

2 tablespoons finely minced anchovies

1 cup Tomato Sauce (page 118)

1 cup diced (½ inch) fresh tomatoes if in season, if not increase Tomato Sauce to 1½ cups

2 teaspoons capers, rinsed well

4 to 6 Kalamata olives, pitted and quartered

3 tablespoons chopped fresh parsley

½ *pound spaghetti*

2 teaspoons grated lemon zest (optional)

While Italians use *ventresca di tonno all'olio* (canned tuna packed in olive oil) for most of their salads and pastas, we prefer fresh tuna cooked on the grill. It remains moist and doesn't need a heavy infusion of oil to replace the moisture lost in canning. The tuna closest to *ventresca* is albacore, but we use the redder fleshed yellowfin when we can get it because it stays moister. ◆ *Serves 2*

Heat the grill or broiler. Brush both sides of the tuna with a little of the olive oil and sprinkle lightly with salt and pepper. Grill or broil a few minutes on each side for medium-rare to medium doneness. Let the tuna cool, then break it into rough 1-inch chunks.

Heat a large pot of salted water to boiling.

Heat the remaining olive oil in a medium sauté pan over medium heat. Add the garlic and anchovies and cook 1 minute. Stir in the tuna, tomato sauce, tomatoes, capers, olives, and parsley; heat through.

Add the pasta to the boiling water and cook until *al dente*.

Stir the lemon zest if using into the sauce and season to taste with salt and pepper.

Drain the spaghetti and transfer to a pasta bowl. Add the sauce and quickly toss to combine. Serve hot. No cheese, please.

Spaghetti with Tuna and Dried Tomatoes

⅓ cup olive oil

1 cup thinly sliced red onion

¾ pound tuna, grilled and broken into 1-inch chunks

6 tablespoons chopped or slivered sun-dried tomatoes

6 tablespoons basil chiffonade

6 Kalamata olives, pitted and sliced

2 tablespoons (or to taste) minced garlic

½ teaspoon freshly ground pepper

Sun-dried tomatoes always add a feeling of richness to a dish, and it's not just because they are expensive. Actually, a little goes a long way. Here the combination of sun-dried tomatoes and basil plays up the meaty quality of the tuna.

✦ *Serves 2*

Heat the olive oil in a large sauté pan over high heat. Add the onion and cook until tender, about 5 minutes. Add the tuna, sun-dried tomatoes, half the basil, the olives, garlic, and pepper; heat through. Toss the tuna sauce with the cooked spaghetti and sprinkle with the remaining basil.

Spaghetti with Tuna, Lemon, and Olives

¼ cup olive oil

1 cup thinly sliced red
    onion

2 tablespoons grated
    lemon zest covered
    with a little lemon
    juice

4 teaspoons minced garlic

2 teaspoons capers, rinsed
    well

6 Kalamata olives, pitted
    and quartered

¾ pound tuna, grilled
    and broken into 1-inch
    chunks

Salt and freshly ground
    pepper

2 tablespoons chopped
    fresh parsley

This pasta tastes clean and light. The acid of the lemon and capers cuts the richness of the tuna and makes the onions seem sweet. ◆ *Serves 2*

Heat the olive oil in a medium sauté pan over high heat. Add the onions and cook, stirring frequently, until tender but not soft. Stir in the lemon zest and juice, garlic, capers, olives, and tuna. Heat through and season with salt and pepper to taste. Toss the tuna sauce with the cooked spaghetti and sprinkle with the parsley.

Pasta alla Cataplana

PASTA WITH SAUSAGE
AND CLAMS

1/4 cup olive oil

6 ounces Fennel, Chorizo,
or Linguisa Sausage
without casings (page
294, 297, or 295; or
use prepared sausage),
crumbled

2 cups (loosely packed)
sliced (1/4 inch) red
onions

1 1/3 cups Tomato Sauce
(page 118)

1 tablespoon finely
minced garlic

1 teaspoon chopped fresh
rosemary or 2
teaspoons dried
oregano or 2
tablespoons chopped
cilantro

Salt

1/2 pound dried spaghetti
or linguine

1/2 cup dry white wine

20 to 24 Manila clams,
scrubbed

2 tablespoons chopped
fresh parsley

Inevitably one day I looked at the classic Portuguese dish *ameijoas na cataplana* and wanted to turn it into a pasta. Sausage, steamed clams, wine, tomatoes, and herbs make it a natural. You can vary the ethnic flavors by changing the sausage and herbs. For Italy use fennel sausage and rosemary. For Spain, chorizo and oregano. And for Portugal, *linguisa* and cilantro. You may augment the sauce with a pinch of hot pepper flakes and any extra garlic is up to you. ✦ *Serves 2*

Heat a large pot of salted water to boiling.

Heat the olive oil in a large sauté pan over high heat. Add the sausage and cook, stirring constantly, until browned. Add the onions and cook until tender. Stir in the tomato sauce, garlic, and herb; heat through.

Add the pasta to the boiling water and cook until *al dente*.

Meanwhile, if you want perfect control and don't mind dirtying another pan, put the clams and wine in a second sauté pan, steam them open, and stir into the sauce. Or live dangerously and stir the wine into the tomato sauce, add the clams, and steam them open in the sauce.

Drain the pasta and transfer to a pasta bowl. Add the sauce and quickly toss to combine, lifting most of the clams to the top. Sprinkle with the parsley. Serve hot. No cheese.

*P*asta in Zimino

PASTA WITH SEAFOOD
AND GREENS

Salt

1 to 1¼ cups olive oil

2 pounds bay or sea
    scallops, tough foot
    removed, or deveined
    shelled shrimp, or
    cleaned squid, cut into
    ½-inch rings, tentacles
    halved if large, or
    combination of 2 or all
    3 (5 to 6 ounces
    cleaned shellfish or
    squid per person)

Freshly ground pepper

2 tablespoons minced
    garlic

1 tablespoon (or to taste)
    dried red pepper flakes

2 pounds Swiss chard,
    beet greens, escarole, or
    spinach, cut into 3 by
    ½-inch strips, rinsed
    well (about 12 large
    handfuls)

2 cups diced (½ inch)
    fresh tomatoes or 2
    cups Tomato Sauce
    (page 118) (optional)

1 pound spaghetti,
    linguine, or orecchiette
    (see Note)

In zimino is a style of cooking fish and squid with hot peppers and garlic, with variations that include tomatoes or greens or anchovies. Although Claudia Roden describes it as a Sephardic tomato and anchovy sauce for fried fish, it is more often associated with Tuscany and seems to have an old connection with fast or Lenten days. An even bigger mystery than the dish's origin is the meaning of zimino. One theory is that it derives from the Arab word zamin, which denotes a sauce of green herbs. Perhaps it's dialect for tegamino, a shallow frying pan.

What we do know is that the dish is a classic for good reason. The spiciness of peppers and garlic combines well with the sweetness of seafood and the textural contrast of greens. We usually prepare this as a seafood sauce for pasta, but it could stand alone as a sauté or pan ragout. On occasion we add tomato sauce and sometimes just throw in a handful of diced fresh tomatoes. If your budget doesn't allow for shellfish and if you don't feel like cleaning squid, just add chopped anchovy to the garlic, hot pepper, and greens for a tasty pasta. Tomatoes are optional. ✦ *Serves 6*

Heat a large pot of salted water to boiling.

Heat ½ cup olive oil in 1 very large or 2 large sauté pans over high heat. Season the scallops and/or shrimp with salt and pepper and add to the oil. Sauté very briefly until seared but barely cooked; remove with a slotted spoon. Add the remaining oil to the pan and heat. Add the garlic and hot pepper flakes; cook 1 minute. Drop in the greens, a handful at a time, and stir them in the hot oil until they wilt. Return the sautéed shellfish to the pan. Add the squid and tomatoes or tomato sauce if using. Season with salt and pepper to taste. Heat the sauce through.

Meanwhile, add the pasta to the boiling water and cook until *al dente*. Drain the pasta and transfer to a pasta bowl. Add the sauce and quickly toss to combine. Serve hot. No cheese, please.

NOTE: If you have small scallops or shrimp, they would be wonderful with the *orecchiette*, the little ear-shaped pasta that is popular in the south of Italy.

Spaghetti with Scallops, Roasted Red Peppers, and Pine Nuts

Salt

6 to 8 ounces dried spaghetti or linguine

½ cup olive oil

¾ pound sea or bay scallops (see Notes), tough foot removed

6 ounces roasted red peppers (see Notes), cut into 3 by ¼-inch strips (about 2 peppers)

2 teaspoons fresh lemon juice

½ cup pine nuts, toasted

Freshly ground pepper to taste

2 teaspoons chopped fresh chives or 2 tablespoons parsley

This pasta has three kinds of sweetness: the sweetness of the sea scallops, the roasted sweetness of red peppers, and the nutty sweetness of the pine nuts. All blend to make it a memorable pasta. ◆ *Serves 2*

Heat a large pot of salted water to boiling. Add the pasta and cook until *al dente*.

Meanwhile, heat the olive oil in a large sauté pan or skillet over high heat. Add the scallops and sear about a minute on each side. Add the roasted peppers with some of the oil they marinated in and the lemon juice. Warm through quickly and season to taste with salt and pepper.

Drain the pasta and transfer to a pasta bowl. Add the scallop mixture and pine nuts; quickly toss to combine. Sprinkle with the chives. Serve hot.

NOTES: If the scallops are large, cut them into halves or quarters. If they are also wide in diameter, cut them vertically in half as well.

To roast the peppers, char them over an open flame or under the broiler until blackened on all sides. Transfer to a plastic container with a lid or a paper or plastic bag. Cover the container or close the bag and let the peppers steam 15 to 20 minutes. Peel the skins from the peppers; then cut the peppers in half, remove the stems, and scrape out the seeds. Cut into strips and let marinate in a few tablespoons virgin olive oil several hours or overnight.

Linguine with Squid and Clams

½ cup dry white wine

30 Manila clams or 20 hard-shell clams, scrubbed

2 tablespoons dry white wine or water

½ teaspoon saffron threads

¼ cup unsalted butter

1 cup sliced (¼ inch) onion

Salt

6 to 8 ounces dried linguine

2 tablespoons olive oil

1 teaspoon (or more to taste) grated fresh ginger

1 teaspoon finely minced garlic

2 cleaned squid, cut into ½-inch rings, tentacles halved if large, or 10 deveined shelled medium shrimp

1 cup diced (½ inch) fresh tomatoes

1 tablespoon chopped cilantro

I know this pasta will look like some strange hybrid, but it does have legitimate forbears, although not as a pasta. When we were presenting a series of Moroccan meals, I wanted to add a pasta, even though Moroccans are not big on noodles, for some of my customers who always want their pasta. So I took a couple of Moroccan recipes for shellfish tagines and turned them into a linguine. We were delighted with the results. The combination is vaguely Oriental, and the ginger is a wonderful foil for the seafood.
✦ *Serves 2*

Heat ½ cup wine in a large sauté pan over high heat. Add the clams, cover, and steam until opened, shaking the pan a few times. Remove the clams with a slotted spoon and let stand until cool enough to handle. Strain the cooking liquid through cheesecloth. Remove the clams from their shells, place in a bowl, and cover with the strained liquid.

Heat a large pot of salted water to boiling.

Heat 2 tablespoons wine or water in a small pan, add the saffron, and let steep. Heat the butter in a large saucepan over medium heat. Add the onion and cook until translucent. Stir in the saffron infusion and cook for a minute or two until the onions take on the saffron flavor and hue.

Add the pasta to the boiling water and cook until *al dente*.

Meanwhile, heat the olive oil in a medium sauté pan over medium heat. Add the ginger and garlic and cook a minute or two. Stir in the squid, clams with their liquid, onion, and tomatoes. Cook, stirring constantly, until the squid is cooked through. Stir in the cilantro.

Drain the pasta and transfer to a pasta bowl. Add the sauce and quickly toss to combine. Serve hot.

Fettuccine al Barese

FETTUCCINE WITH SHRIMP AND GARLIC

Salt

¾ pound medium shrimp (about 20), shelled and deveined

Freshly ground pepper

¼ cup olive oil

4 teaspoons finely minced garlic

1 teaspoon (or more to taste) dried red pepper flakes

¼ cup dry white wine

6 ounces fresh fettuccine or tagliarini

2 tablespoons fresh lemon juice

6 tablespoons unsalted butter, softened

This simple pasta from Bari, a seaport in Apulia in southern Italy, is the *aglio-olio* classic with the added kick of hot peppers and crunch of shrimp. Bryan Miller of *The New York Times* claimed this was his favorite dish in San Francisco. Although dried pasta is traditional for the region, we prefer fresh. We think it is a better vehicle for the sauce and provides a nicer contrast to the shrimp. ◆ *Serves 2*

Heat a large pot of salted water to boiling.

Season the shrimp lightly with salt and pepper. Heat half the olive oil in a large sauté pan or skillet over high heat. Add the shrimp and sear about a minute on each side. Remove with a slotted spoon.

Add the remaining oil to the pan and heat over medium heat. Add the garlic and red pepper flakes; cook, stirring constantly, about 1 minute. Pour in the wine and boil over high heat, stirring and scraping the bottom of the pan, until reduced by half. If it flames up, reduce the heat a bit.

Add the pasta to the boiling water and cook until tender.

Meanwhile, return the shrimp to the pan and add the lemon juice and butter. Swirl the pan over very low heat until the butter melts and the sauce thickens. Season to taste with salt and pepper.

Drain the pasta and transfer to a pasta bowl. Add the shrimp mixture and quickly toss to combine. Serve hot.

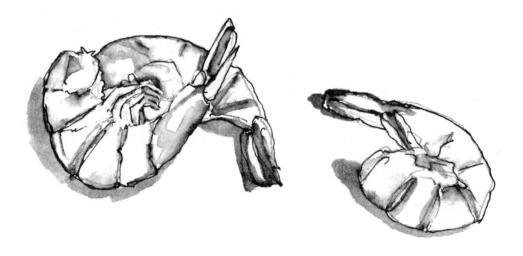

Fettuccine à la Grecque

Salt

6 ounces fresh fettuccine
   or dried linguine

4 tablespoons olive oil

¾ pound medium shrimp,
   shelled and deveined

Pizzaiola Sauce (recipe
   follows)

Freshly ground pepper

6 ounces feta cheese, cut
   into walnut-sized
   chunks

3 tablespoons chopped
   fresh parsley (optional)

We originally made this classic Greek dish in a ramekin with the prawns tossed in a garlic- and oregano-infused tomato sauce, topped with chunks of feta, and baked or glazed under the broiler. To fill out the meal, we served it with pasta. It didn't take long to go from with pasta to a pasta. ◆ *Serves 2*

Heat a large pot of salted water to boiling. Add the pasta and cook until *al dente*.

Meanwhile, heat the olive oil in a large sauté pan or skillet over high heat. Add the shrimp and sear about a minute on each side. Remove the shrimp with a slotted spoon. Add the pizzaiola sauce to the pan and simmer a minute or two. Stir the shrimp into the sauce and season to taste with pepper. Drop in the chunks of feta.

Drain the pasta and transfer to a pasta bowl. Add the shrimp mixture and quickly toss to combine. Sprinkle with parsley if using. Serve hot.

Pizzaiola Sauce

2 tablespoons extra virgin
   olive oil

2 teaspoons (or more to
   taste) minced garlic

2 teaspoons dried oregano

1½ cups Tomato Sauce
   (page 118)

Salt and freshly ground
   pepper to taste

This is an all-purpose sauce not only for pizza (hence the name) and pasta but for steaks, lamb chops, veal scaloppine, and grilled fish too. Because garlic and oregano vary from batch to batch, it would be wise to add them gradually to the sauce rather than trusting the written word.
◆ *Makes about 1½ cup*

Heat the olive oil in a medium sauté pan or skillet over medium heat. Add the garlic and oregano and cook about 2 minutes. Stir in the tomato sauce and simmer 5 minutes. Season to taste with salt and pepper.

Spaghetti alla Puttanesca

Salt

2 tablespoons olive oil

1 to 2 teaspoons minced
   garlic

1 tablespoon anchovy
   puree

2 teaspoons (or to taste)
   dried red pepper flakes

½ cup basil chiffonade
   or 2 teaspoons dried
   oregano

2 cups Tomato Sauce
   (page 118)

1 tablespoon capers,
   rinsed and finely
   chopped

20 Gaeta or Kalamata
   olives, pitted and
   quartered or sliced

Freshly ground pepper

12 ounces spaghetti

Everyone has probably heard different stories of the origin of this sauce's name. *Puttana* is Italian slang for whore, and this sauce is reportedly as hot and spicy as a lady of the evening. It is quick to assemble and quick to eat, perhaps a dish prepared between appointments. While it is best known as the classic Neapolitan sauce for spaghetti, we have discovered it is a knockout on grilled or baked swordfish, tuna, sea bass, and cod as well. This recipe will sauce six servings of fish. ◆ *Makes 4 servings*

Heat a large pot of salted water to boiling.

Heat the olive oil in a medium sauté pan over low heat. Add the garlic and anchovy and heat about 3 minutes. Add the pepper flakes and oregano if using and heat 2 minutes. Stir in the tomato sauce and simmer about 5 minutes. Add half the basil and capers if using and all the olives. Simmer about 5 minutes more. Season to taste with salt and pepper; add more red pepper if you want the sauce hotter.

Meanwhile, add the pasta to the boiling water and cook until *al dente*. Drain the pasta and transfer to a pasta bowl. Add the sauce and quickly toss to combine. Serve hot. Usually no cheese is served with this pasta because of the anchovy.

Borlenghi ai Quattro Formaggi

ROSEMARY CREPES
FILLED WITH FOUR
CHEESES

CRÊPES

1 cup water

1 cup milk

4 large eggs

2 cups all-purpose flour

½ teaspoon salt

¼ cup melted unsalted
butter, plus additional
for the pan

1 tablespoon finely
chopped fresh rosemary

FILLING

6 ounces Fontina cheese,
shredded

6 ounces mozzarella
cheese, shredded

6 ounces Gruyère cheese,
shredded

10 ounces fresh ricotta
cheese (see Note, page
115)

2 teaspoons freshly
ground pepper

2 cups medium-thick
Béchamel (page 311;
double recipe)

3 cups Tomato Sauce
(page 118)

½ freshly grated
Parmesan cheese

Crêpes can be a wonderful alternative to cannelloni. They are usually lighter in texture and require merely a seasoned crêpe pan or a nonstick skillet to roll them off your home assembly line. The batter and filling can be prepared well ahead of time, and the crêpes can be assembled a day or so before, covered and refrigerated, and then heated in the oven when you need them. This particular recipe is inspired by some from the Italian province of Emilia-Romagna. The original recipes called for either frying the batter or baking the dough in a wood-burning oven. While the Romagnoli fill them with cheese and maybe a little sausage and fold them in quarters, we roll them like blintzes around the filling and cover them with tomato sauce and a little béchamel. These are the most popular crêpes we serve at Square One. ◆ *Serves 6*

For the crêpes, place the water, milk, eggs, flour, salt, ¼ cup butter, and the rosemary in a blender or food processor and blend well. Cover and refrigerate several hours. Thin the batter with water if necessary; it should be the consistency of very heavy cream.

Heat a crêpe pan over medium-high heat. Brush the pan with melted butter and let it warm about a minute. Add a scant ¼ cup batter and swirl it around in the hot pan. The crêpe should be thin and set up almost immediately. Cook 1 minute, then flip it over either by turning it with your fingers or by flipping it into a second warm pan of slightly larger dimension. Cook the second side a moment, then turn the crêpe out onto a towel. Brush the pan lightly with butter and make another crêpe. As the crêpes cool, you may stack them. There should be enough batter for 18 crêpes. They can be held at room temperature for several hours before filling them; do not refrigerate.

Combine all the filling ingredients. Spoon about 3 tablespoons filling in the center of each crêpe and roll up, tucking in the sides. Place on baking sheets lined with baker's parchment. These can be covered and refrigerated up to 2 days. If you think of it, let the crêpes warm to room temperature before baking.

Preheat the oven to 400°. Warm the béchamel and tomato sauces.

(continued)

Butter 2 large baking dishes or individual gratin dishes. Spoon a layer of tomato sauce in the large dishes or about 3 tablespoons in each gratin dish. Place the filled crêpes in rows in the large dishes or place 3 in each gratin dish. Spread the crêpes with a layer of béchamel, then drizzle with a little more tomato sauce. Bake covered until hot, about 7 minutes. If the tops dry out, spoon a little more warm sauce over the crepes before serving. Sprinkle with Parmesan if using. Serve at once.

Gnocchi, Ristorante Archimede

POTATO GNOCCHILIKE
CLOUDS

**6 large baking potatoes
   (about 2½ pounds)**
Salt
**2 cups (or more if
   needed) all-purpose
   flour**

This is not a fairy tale. Once upon a time, many years ago, I sat down to lunch in a restaurant in Rome and ordered potato gnocchi. The gnocchi I had eaten before had been rather heavy dumplings, but, since hope springs eternal in a cook's imagination, I was curious to try yet another version. A steaming bowl was placed in front of me. These were the tiniest gnocchi I had ever seen. One bite and I was transported. They were gnocchi like clouds!

Then began the quest. I asked around and learned of a Florentine woman living in San Francisco who taught cooking in her home. Word was that she was an accomplished gnocchi maker and hers were light. Naturally I joined the class to discover some of these trade secrets. I did learn that if you baked the potatoes instead of boiling them, the gnocchi had a better chance of being light. But the demonstrated gnocchi turned out to be the same substantial dumplings I had eaten before.

Unable to return to Rome, I embarked on a course of gnocchi making at home. Two or three times a week for many weeks, my children and I made gnocchi. One day we decided to leave out the eggs and discovered that the gnocchi were infinitely lighter. The next week we tested to see just how little flour was needed to make the dough. At the last stage of this course, we made smaller and smaller gnocchi until they fairly levitated above the plate. This is it, success! ◆ *Serves 6*

Preheat the oven to 450°. Bake the potatoes until very tender, 1 hour or longer. While they are still hot, scoop the pulp out of the shells and put it through a ricer. You should have about 6 cups loosely packed. Season to taste with salt. Knead in as little flour as possible to form a dough that holds together and isn't sticky. Sprinkle flour over a work surface and roll the dough into long thin ropes, about ½ inch in diameter. Cut the ropes into ¾-inch pieces. If you want the characteristic grooves on them, press each one with a small cocktail fork; the extra step will take more time but it is worth the effort. The gnocchi can be placed in a single layer on baking sheets lined with baker's parchment, dusted with rice flour or Wondra, and held at room temperature several hours or refrigerated, uncovered, overnight.

To cook, heat a very large (6-quart) pot of salted water to boiling. Add the gnocchi and cook until they float to the top, 3 to 5 minutes. Test one to see that it tastes cooked. Using a slotted spoon, transfer the gnocchi to a warm serving bowl. Sauce with either melted butter and grated Parmesan cheese or a light tomato sauce enriched with a little cream and a sprinkling of fresh basil.

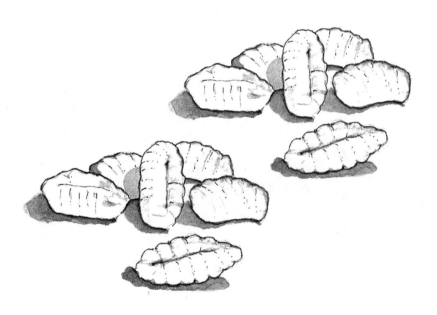

These recipes are the essential but often unsung heroes in a great plate. What would grilled veal chops and *sugo di porcini* be without polenta, Moroccan spiced lamb without couscous, Turkish chicken brochette without rice, or roast duck without braised lentils?

Although rice is primarily an ensemble player, it occasionally sings solo as risotto. In Italy, risotto is a first course, or *prima,* like pasta, but in America we will probably make a meal of it. And what a wonderful and comforting meal it is.

I will give you two techniques for making risotto: the classic stir-for-twenty-minutes version and the restaurant risotto *interruptus,* where the rice is cooked about halfway and finished just before serving. I know traditionalists will scoff and say that it can't possibly work. But after twenty years of teaching cooking, I can report the first question asked is how far ahead can it be made. If the answer is it can't, the response is "But I don't want to be in the kitchen for twenty minutes, I want to be with my guests!" For those people, risotto *interruptus* solves that dilemma and makes a pretty succulent risotto as well.

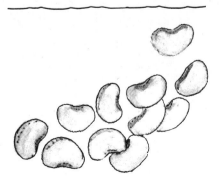

Fagioli all'Uccelletto

WHITE BEAN RAGOUT

1 cup dried white beans
3 tablespoons olive oil
1 large onion, chopped
4 cloves garlic, finely
  minced
2 cups diced fresh or
  canned tomatoes with
  1 cup juices
Salt and freshly ground
  pepper

This ragout is the ideal accompaniment for leg of lamb, lamb chops, and broiled chicken; it could even be a meal in itself if you add sausage and pancetta. If you thin the mixture with some broth, you will have a wonderful bean soup. Add some cooked pasta shells and you have *pasta e fagioli.* ✦ *Serves 4*

Soak the beans overnight in cold water and drain. Cover the beans with fresh cold water in a medium saucepan. Simmer covered until tender but not mushy, 45 to 60 minutes. Drain, reserving the cooking liquid. (Do not cook them *al dente,* but it is better to err on the side of too firm than too soft as they will cook a little longer in the ragout.)

Heat the oil in a medium sauté pan over medium heat. Add the onion and cook covered until translucent, 7 to 10 minutes. Add the garlic and cook 1 to 2 minutes more. Add the beans and the reserved cooking liquid and the tomatoes with their juices. Simmer covered until the beans are tender and the flavors blend, 10 to 20 minutes. Season to taste with salt and pepper. If the mixture is dry, add chicken stock, water, or more tomato juice.

VARIATION

For White Bean Ragout with Sausage and Pancetta, cook ½ pound prepared or homemade fennel sausage (without casings) or ¼ pound diced pancetta in a large sauté pan until the sausage is no longer pink. Add the cooked meat with the beans and tomatoes to the onion.

Lenticchie con Pancetta e Verdure

BRAISED LENTILS WITH
PANCETTA AND
AROMATIC VEGETABLES

2 cups lentils, preferably
the French green
variety

4½ cups water

¼ cup unsalted butter or
chicken or duck fat

2 medium onions, cut into
¼-inch dice

2 carrots, cut into ¼-inch
dice

1 rib celery, cut into
¼-inch dice

6 to 8 ounces pancetta,
sliced ⅛ inch thick
and cut into
¼-inch-wide strips

¾ cup Chicken Stock
(page 103)

4 cloves garlic, minced

3 tablespoons minced
fresh parsley

1 tablespoon minced fresh
thyme

Salt and freshly ground
pepper

I like to serve these lentils with a simple roast duck, leg of lamb, or as the base for a simple lamb ragout. However, they are so satisfying and seductive, you may want to eat them as is. I know that duck fat is not good for you, but it can really make this dish sublime. ✦ *Serves 6*

Combine the lentils and the water in a large saucepan. Heat to boiling. Reduce the heat to very low and simmer covered until tender but still firm to the bite, about 25 minutes for green lentils or 10 to 40 minutes for brown lentils depending on their age.

Heat the butter or fat in a large sauté pan over low heat. Add the vegetables and pancetta and cook, stirring occasionally, until tender, about 15 minutes. Stir in the lentils with their cooking liquid, the stock, garlic, parsley, and thyme; simmer covered until the flavors blend, 5 to 7 minutes more. Season to taste with salt and pepper.

Square One Rice

4 quarts water

2 tablespoons salt, plus additional to taste

2 cups basmati rice

6 tablespoons unsalted butter, melted

Freshly ground pepper

The only rice we use at the restaurant (other than Arborio for risotto) is basmati, a nutty-tasting long-grain rice preferred by Indians and Persians because it is the only rice that can be held for a while after cooking without becoming gummy or mushy. We have a special technique for preparing the rice that I think will work perfectly for you at home. ✦ *Serves 4 to 6*

Preheat the oven to 350°.

Heat the water in a large pot to boiling. Add the salt and drop in the rice. Cook quickly over medium heat until a kernel just tests done when you bite it, about 10 minutes. It should be almost completely cooked. Immediately drain the rice and rinse with warm water.

Coat a shallow baking pan with some of the melted butter. Spread the rice in the pan. Season the remaining butter with salt and pepper to taste and drizzle over the rice. Cover the pan with foil and bake 25 minutes. Serve now or hold in a warm oven up to 15 minutes.

Crocchette di Riso

RICE CROQUETTES

1½ cups water

½ cup Chicken Stock (page 103)

1 cup Arborio rice

1 large egg

5 tablespoons freshly grated Parmesan cheese

Salt and freshly ground pepper to taste

Grated nutmeg to taste (optional)

¾ cup dry bread crumbs

Peanut oil for deep frying

These are a nice addition to a good *fritto misto,* but I also like to serve them as an accompaniment for meat or chicken. They can be stuffed with a little cube of mozzarella or embellished with toasted pine nuts or chopped fresh herbs. ✦ *Makes about 12*

Heat the water and stock to boiling in a medium saucepan. Add the rice and cook covered over very low heat until all the liquid is absorbed, 15 to 20 minutes. The rice should be a little wet and sticky. Stir in the egg and Parmesan. Season to taste with salt, pepper, and nutmeg. Spread the mixture on a baking sheet and cool in the refrigerator.

Roll the rice mixture into 1½- to 2-inch balls and coat them with bread crumbs. The rice balls can be refrigerated on a baking sheet lined with parchment paper up to 1 day.

Shortly before serving, heat peanut oil in a deep fryer or wok to 350°. Drop in as many croquettes as will fit without crowding and fry until golden brown. Remove with a slotted spoon and drain on paper towels. Keep warm in a low oven up to 10 minutes if necessary. Repeat with the remaining croquettes. Serve hot.

Middle Eastern or Persian-Style Rice

4 quarts water

2 tablespoons salt, plus additional to taste

2 cups basmati rice

2 large egg yolks

6 tablespoons unsalted butter, melted

1 tablespoon hot water

Freshly ground pepper

This is not the most authentic, old-fashioned method for cooking true Persian rice because we finish this rice in the oven and not on top of the stove. But it is easier and therefore more foolproof. This rice is our usual accompaniment for shish kabobs and chicken brochettes. ✦ *Serves 4 to 6*

Preheat the oven to 350°.

Heat the water in a large pot to boiling. Add the salt and drop in the rice. Cook quickly over medium heat until a kernel just tests done when you bite it, about 10 minutes. Immediately drain the rice and rinse with warm water.

Coat a shallow baking pan, such as a lasagne pan, with some of the melted butter. Mix 1 cup of the cooked rice with the egg yolks, 2 tablespoons melted butter, and 1 tablespoon hot water. Spoon it into the baking pan and press it down with your fingers. Spread the rest of the rice in a layer on top. Season the remaining butter with salt and pepper to taste and drizzle over the rice. Cover the pan with foil and bake 25 to 30 minutes.

Spoon the layer of loose rice into another baking pan. Cover with foil and hold in a warm oven or over hot water. Return the baking pan with the bottom layer of rice (it should be ¼ inch thick) to the oven and bake until pale golden brown and chewy but not hard. Let stand on a cool surface 5 minutes; it should be easy to remove with a spatula. Break the browned rice crust into pieces and serve on top of the loose rice.

Risotto

6 cups Chicken Stock
  (page 103)
6 tablespoons unsalted
  butter
1 tablespoon olive oil
½ cup finely minced
  onion
2 cups Arborio rice
Salt and freshly ground
  pepper

Risotto is one of those dishes that makes people feel taken care of and satisfied. If the Italians hadn't come up with it, an eccentric Jewish mother might have by chance by adding too much rice to the chicken soup. Although most recipes for risotto are written for six (Italians have large families), remember that it is worth making for just you alone. It is such a comforting and wonderful food.

Arborio rice is the Italian short-grain rice from the Po delta that is used exclusively for risotto. I wish I could tell you that another short-grain rice is acceptable but I cannot. If you are unable to find this rice, forget risotto. ◆ *Serves 6*

Heat the chicken stock to boiling in a saucepan, then reduce the heat and hold at a simmer.

Heat the butter and oil in a wide heavy saucepan over low heat. Add the onion and cook until tender and pale golden. Add the rice and cook, stirring to coat with butter, until opaque, 3 to 5 minutes.

Add ½ cup hot stock and cook, stirring constantly, until the stock is absorbed. Continue adding the stock, ½ cup at a time, and stirring until the rice is creamy on the outside and *al dente* or firm in the center. You should be able to bite through it easily. The whole cooking process should take 18 to 25 minutes. You may find that you don't need all the broth, but leave the risotto a little soupier than you think is right for the rice will continue to absorb liquid in the serving bowl. Season with salt and pepper to taste and serve at once.

NOTE: For Risotto for one, use 1 cup Chicken Stock, 1 tablespoon unsalted butter, ½ teaspoon olive oil, 1 to 2 tablespoons finely minced onion, ⅓ cup Arborio rice, and salt and freshly ground pepper. (Multiply ingredients for two, three, or however many servings you like.)

VARIATION

Restaurant Risotto

With risotto the home cook has the advantage over the restaurant cook because risotto should be prepared to order and it requires twenty minutes of constant stirring and loving attention. Yet I have always wanted to cook risotto at Square One. I knew that a busy line cook could not be stirring risotto to order for twenty minutes while cooking all the other dishes. I also knew we only had so many burners that could be tied up. If risotto were to be popular, I would soon be out of stove space. Reason said forget it! Ah, but desire and some ingenuity got a succulent, creamy, and *al dente* risotto on the menu. I am happy to tell you how we licked the problem but with one caveat. It will be easier for the home cook to make the risotto from start to stop without interruption for it's impossible to describe what three-quarters-cooked rice feels like and how long it must be cooked for completion. But if you are willing to take a trial-and-error approach and fool with the timing, you too can make risotto ahead of time and revive it just before serving.

Now the procedure. Make the risotto as directed until the rice is about half to three-quarters cooked. It's a crucial decision. Is it at least past halfway cooked? Then stop the cooking. Immediately turn the rice out onto a baking sheet, spread it, and put it in the refrigerator. Turn off the stock. The rice can be refrigerated about 2 hours maximum.

Just before serving, return the stock to a simmer and the risotto to the pan. Add half the remaining hot stock to the risotto and stir well. Place the pan over low heat and cook, stirring constantly and adding the stock bit by bit, until the risotto tests done. This should take from 5 to 8 minutes, depending on how long the rice was cooked in the first stage.

NOTE: For this method, I usually cook the onions, set them aside, and make the risotto through the first stage without the onions. If you like, you can make the basic risotto without the onions and add them later when you assemble the final dish. That way you can adjust the amount of onion to suit the flavor of the risotto.

Risotto alla Paesana

PEASANT'S RISOTTO

5 to 6 cups Chicken Stock
  (page 103)
½ cup unsalted butter
3 tablespoons olive oil
2 cups diced onions
2 cups Arborio rice
2 cups rendered diced
  pancetta (see Note,
  page 124)
2 cups julienned carrots,
  blanched
2 cups diced drained
  canned Italian plum
  tomatoes
2 cups julienned zucchini
6 tablespoons basil
  chiffonade or 2
  tablespoons chopped
  fresh marjoram
  (optional)
Salt and freshly ground
  pepper
½ to ¾ cup freshly
  grated Parmesan
  cheese

In the great tradition of peasant food, this is how you can make something wonderfully tasty out of practically nothing—just a few tiny pieces of pancetta and a few shreds of vegetables. ◆ *Serves 6*

Heat the chicken stock to boiling in a saucepan, then reduce the heat and hold at a simmer.

Heat the butter and oil in a wide heavy saucepan over low heat. Add the onions and cook until translucent, about 5 minutes. Add the rice and cook, stirring to coat with butter, until opaque, about 3 minutes.

Add ½ cup hot stock and cook, stirring constantly, until the stock is absorbed. Continue adding the stock, ½ cup at a time, and stirring until the rice is about half cooked. Add the pancetta and all the vegetables except the zucchini; cook about 5 minutes more, adding stock as needed. Add the zucchini and herbs for the last minute or two. Stop cooking when the rice is *al dente* in the center and creamy on the outside. Season with salt and pepper to taste. Leave the risotto a little soupy. Sprinkle with the Parmesan and serve at once.

Seafood Risotto with Spinach and Peas

5 to 6 cups Chicken Stock
  (page 103) or
  combination Chicken
  Stock and Fish Fumet
  (page 105)
1 cup unsalted butter
1¾ pounds crabmeat,
  picked over for
  cartilage and broken
  into large pieces; or
  sole fillets, cut into 4
  by 2-inch strips; or
  salmon fillets, cut into
  1-inch squares
Salt and freshly ground
  pepper
3 tablespoons olive oil
1½ cups diced onions
2 cups Arborio rice
9 cups combination
  spinach leaves and
  watercress or all
  spinach leaves, cut into
  chiffonade
2 tablespoons finely
  minced garlic
1 tablespoon grated
  lemon zest covered
  with 1 tablespoon
  lemon juice
1½ cups fresh peas,
  blanched
¼ cup chopped fresh
  parsley

This risotto is a study in contrasts, the sweetness of the crab or fish combined with the tartness of lemon, the bitter tang of watercress, and the additional sweetness of peas. It is very beautiful to look at, but I imagine it won't be sitting in front of you very long. ✦ *Serves 6*

Heat the chicken stock to boiling in a saucepan, then reduce the heat and hold at a simmer.

Heat the half the butter in a large sauté pan or skillet over medium heat. Sprinkle the fish with salt and pepper, add it to the pan, and sauté it quickly. If you are using crabmeat, just warm it in a little butter for a minute. If you don't have a very large pan, cook it in batches.

Heat the remaining butter and the oil in a wide heavy saucepan over low heat. Add the onions and cook until translucent, about 5 minutes. Add the rice and cook, stirring to coat with butter, until opaque, about 3 minutes.

Add ½ cup hot stock and cook, stirring constantly, until the stock is absorbed. Continue adding the stock, ½ cup at a time, and stirring until the rice is almost completely cooked. Add the greens, garlic, and lemon zest with juice; cook, stirring constantly, until the greens are wilted. Add the fish or crab, peas, and parsley; cook just 2 to 3 minutes more. Season with salt and pepper to taste. No cheese, please.

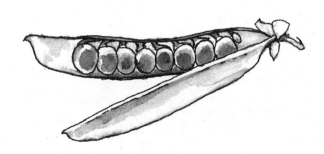

Seafood Risotto with Tomatoes and Gremolata

5 to 6 cups Chicken Stock
  or Fish Fumet (page
  103 or 105) combined
  with juices from
  tomatoes
6 tablespoons olive oil
1¾ pounds crabmeat,
  picked over for
  cartilage and broken
  into large pieces; or
  bay or sea scallops,
  tough foot removed; or
  medium shrimp, shelled
  and deveined
Salt and freshly ground
  pepper
¾ cup unsalted butter
1½ cups diced onions
2 cups Arborio rice
3 cups diced drained
  canned Italian plum
  tomatoes, juices added
  to the stock
2 tablespoons finely
  minced garlic
3 tablespoons lemon zest
  covered with 2
  tablespoons lemon
  juice
¾ cup chopped fresh
  parsley, plus additional
  for garnish

I usually serve this combination of shellfish, tomato, and *gremolata*, that magic trio of lemon zest, garlic, and parsley, as a linguine or spaghetti dish, but I find that it also makes a very sprightly risotto. ✦ *Serves 6*

Heat the chicken stock to boiling in a saucepan, then reduce the heat and hold at a simmer.

Heat the olive oil in a large sauté pan or skillet over medium heat. Sprinkle the shellfish with salt and pepper, add it to the pan, and sauté it quickly. If you are using crabmeat, just warm it in a little butter for a minute.

Heat the butter in a wide heavy saucepan over low heat. Add the onions and cook until translucent, about 5 minutes. Add the rice and cook, stirring to coat with butter, until opaque, 3 to 5 minutes.

Add ½ cup hot stock and cook, stirring constantly, until the stock is absorbed. Continue adding the stock, ½ cup at a time, and stirring until the rice is almost completely cooked. Add the tomatoes, garlic, lemon zest, and parsley and continue to cook. A minute or two before the rice is perfectly cooked, add the shellfish. Season with salt and pepper to taste and sprinkle with a little more parsley. No cheese, please.

Risotto alla Primavera

5 or 6 cups Chicken
Stock (page 103) or
combination stock and
liquid from the
tomatoes

6 tablespoons unsalted
butter

1 tablespoon olive oil

1½ cups finely chopped
onions

2 cups Arborio rice

GREMOLATA

6 tablespoons chopped
fresh parsley

1 tablespoon minced
garlic

2 tablespoons grated
lemon zest

1½ cups diced fresh
tomatoes with juices

1 cup asparagus pieces,
1½ inches long,
blanched

1 cup fresh peas,
blanched

1 cup baby artichokes

1 cup julienned zucchini,
with blossoms if
possible

½ cup julienned carrots,
blanched

½ cup green bean pieces,
2 inches long, blanched

Salt and freshly ground
pepper

½ cup freshly grated
Parmesan cheese

I have never been a great fan of *fettuccine* or *capellini alla primavera*. Most renditions of this pasta are uninteresting versions of Chinese stir-fried vegetables and noodles. Only the stir-fry is better because it has ginger and garlic. But this risotto is a different story. The *gremolata* acts as the Chinese ginger-and-garlic flavor enhancer and brightens up the dish considerably. The tomatoes are a big plus as well. ◆ *Serves 6*

Heat the chicken stock to boiling in a saucepan, then reduce the heat and hold at a simmer.

Heat the butter and oil in a wide heavy saucepan over low heat. Add the onions and cook until translucent, about 5 minutes. Add the rice and cook, stirring to coat with butter, until opaque, about 3 minutes.

Add ½ cup hot stock and cook, stirring constantly, until the stock is absorbed. Continue adding the stock, ½ cup at a time, and stirring until the rice is *al dente* in the center and creamy on the outside. The whole cooking process should take 18 to 25 minutes. Leave the risotto a little soupy.

Combine the ingredients for *gremolata* and add to the risotto with the vegetables. Cook, stirring constantly, 2 more minutes. Season with salt and pepper to taste. Sprinkle with the Parmesan and serve at once.

RISO SUPERFINO ARBORIO
Italian Rice
Net Wt 1 lb. (16 oz.)
Product of Italy

Paella

MARINADE

3 tablespoons dried
  oregano, toasted in
  small skillet until
  fragrant

3 tablespoons finely
  minced garlic

5 tablespoons red wine
  vinegar

1 tablespoon salt

2 tablespoons coarsely
  ground pepper

½ cup olive oil

6 large chicken thighs,
  excess fat trimmed

1 pound chorizo in
  casings, prepared or
  homemade (page 297)

1 cup olive oil

6 large artichoke hearts,
  cut into 8 wedges each

Juice of 1 lemon

Salt and freshly ground
  pepper

3 live lobsters (over 1¼
  pounds each) or 3 live
  Dungeness crabs
  (about 2 pounds each)

1 pound medium or large
  shrimp, shelled and
  deveined

48 Manila clams or 36
  mussels, scrubbed

2 large yellow onions, cut
  into medium dice

2 large green peppers, cut
  into medium dice

2 tablespoons minced
  garlic

2 teaspoons ground
  coriander

2 cups diced drained
  canned plum tomatoes

4 to 6 cups Chicken Stock
  (page 103)

Paella puts people in a party mood. It is a very colorful creation and a little messy to eat, so guests seem to relax and throw themselves into the spirit of the dish. Be sure to provide nutcrackers for all, a large bowl for the empty shells, and then warm wet towels or bowls of lemon water and towels for the after-dinner cleanup.

Although it may seem complicated and time consuming, most of the work can be done well ahead of time and the dish assembled in the last ten minutes. The following recipe serves six, but you may increase it at will. The more, the merrier! ◆ *Serves 6*

First, marinate the chicken thighs: Combine the oregano, garlic, vinegar, salt, and pepper in a bowl or mortar; mash to a paste with the back of a spoon or the pestle. Whisk in the olive oil. Rub the marinade over the chicken thighs and refrigerate overnight.

Preheat the oven to 350°. Prick the chorizo with a fork and bake them on a baking sheet about 25 minutes. Let stand until cool enough to handle, then cut into 1-inch chunks. Pour the fat into a small bowl and set aside.

To cook the artichokes, heat ¼ cup oil in a medium sauté pan over medium heat. Add the artichoke hearts and sprinkle with the lemon juice. Cook, stirring occasionally, until tender but not mushy. Season to taste with salt and pepper. If you're not cooking the paella until the next day, store the artichokes in the refrigerator.

To cook the lobsters or crabs (or both if you are feeling extravagant), heat a large pot of water to boiling. Salt the water and add the lobsters or crabs. Cook the lobsters 6 minutes and the crabs 10 minutes. Immediately remove them from the water and place in an ice bath to cool.

If using lobsters, cut off the tails and cut the meat into sections keeping it in the shell. Crack the claws and reserve the legs for garnish. Store in the refrigerator.

If using crabs, remove the top shell and save the juices. Remove and discard the gills and tail pieces. Crack the claws with a mallet and cut the bodies into 4 pieces each. Rinse the bodies well. Store in the refrigerator.

Shell and devein the shrimp, keeping the tails intact if you like, and refrigerate. Scrub the clams and keep them cov-

8 quarts water

¼ cup salt

4 cups basmati rice

¼ cup dry white wine

2 teaspoons saffron
   threads

6 tablespoons unsalted
   butter

1 cup fresh peas,
   blanched (optional)

2 roasted red peppers, cut
   into strips (optional)

ered in water in the refrigerator. Beard and scrub the mussels and keep them covered with ice in the refrigerator up to 1 day.

Up to 6 hours before serving, cook the chicken: Heat ½ cup olive oil in a large heavy skillet over medium heat. Add the chicken thighs and brown well on all sides, 8 to 10 minutes.

To make the base, heat about ¼ cup olive oil and the reserved chorizo fat in a large heavy saucepan over low heat. Add the onions, peppers, garlic, and ground coriander; cook until tender, about 10 minutes. Stir in the tomatoes and 4 cups chicken stock and add the chicken thighs. Heat to boiling. Reduce the heat and simmer covered until the chicken is tender, about 20 minutes; add more stock if this mixture becomes too thick. Remove the chicken pieces and set aside. Taste the base and add more oregano, garlic, salt, and pepper if needed. The base should be lively!

Preheat the oven to 350°.

Heat the water in a large pot to boiling. Add ¼ cup salt and drop in the rice. Cook uncovered over medium heat until a kernel just tests done when you bite it, about 10 minutes. Immediately drain the rice with warm water.

Meanwhile, warm the wine in a small saucepan and add the saffron. Let stand at least 10 minutes. Melt the butter and stir in the saffron infusion. Coat a shallow baking pan, such as a lasagne pan, with some of the melted butter. Pour in the rice and drizzle with the remaining butter. Cover the pan with foil and bake 25 minutes. Keep warm.

To assemble the paella, place the clams or mussels in a large wide pan. Thin the base with more chicken stock if necessary, heat to boiling, and add half to the clams or mussels. Cover and cook over high heat until all the shells open. Combine the chicken thighs, lobsters or crabs, artichokes, chorizo, shrimp, and remaining base in a second large wide pan. Simmer covered over medium heat until heated through, 7 to 10 minutes. Add the clams or mussels and peas if using during the last 2 minutes. Garnish with the little lobster legs and the red pepper strips.

Spoon the rice into individual serving bowls or a very large platter, then spoon the chicken and seafood mixture over top. Serve at once and enjoy!

*P*olenta

7 to 8 cups cold water

*2 cups coarse cornmeal
for polenta*

¾ cup unsalted butter

*1 cup freshly grated
Parmesan cheese*

Salt

It's not that we go out of our way to be different or difficult, but we have found that the traditional method for cooking polenta is fraught with too great a potential for problems, namely lumps. Most recipes tell you to add polenta in a thin stream to boiling water while stirring constantly. And what usually happens? Lumps! So we have developed another technique. We start our polenta off in cold water and then cook it until thick and, of course, lump free. At Square One, we serve polenta soft right out of the pot (it can be held in a double boiler and kept loose with additional water or stock), or we cool it on buttered baking sheets and cut it into shapes, which we then bake, deep fry, or sauté. ✦ *Serves 6 to 8*

Stir 7 cups cold water and the polenta together in a large heavy saucepan. Cook over low heat, stirring often and scraping the bottom of the pot, until thick and it no longer feels grainy on your tongue, about 30 minutes. Add more water if the polenta thickens too much before it's cooked. Stir in the butter and Parmesan and season to taste with salt. Serve the polenta soft right out of the pot or pour it into a double boiler and keep it warm over simmering water, adding water or stock as needed.

Or spread the polenta on 1 or 2 buttered baking sheets and refrigerate until firm. Once it's cooled, cover it with plastic wrap. Cut the polenta into strips or triangles in the baking sheet.

To sauté, cook the polenta in clarified butter or olive oil in a cast-iron skillet over high heat until golden on both sides. To bake, place the pieces in buttered gratin dishes and sprinkle with Parmesan cheese. Bake at 400° until hot and crusty. To deep fry, coat the pieces first with flour, then egg, then bread crumbs. Place the pieces on a wire rack and let the coating set. Deep fry a few at a time in peanut oil heated to 350°.

Couscous

2 cups medium-grain
    couscous (we use
    Ferrero)

3 cups water

4 tablespoons unsalted
    butter

1 teaspoon salt

1 teaspoon cinnamon
    (optional)

Couscous is a hard-wheat semolina grain that is the perfect accompaniment for North African and many Middle Eastern dishes. There has been much discussion about how inferior instant (*pre-cuit*) couscous is to the long-cooking kind. But the fact of the matter is most markets only carry the instant. So let me show you how to make the best of a good thing. Ignore the instructions on the box and proceed as follows. ✦ *Serves 4 to 6*

Pour the couscous grains into a shallow baking pan or ceramic dish about 9 inches square and 2 inches high. Heat the water, butter, salt, and cinnamon to boiling. Pour over the couscous and stir once to mix. Cover the dish with foil or a lid and let stand about 10 minutes. Break up the couscous with a fork or fluff it with your fingers. You can serve it immediately, or keep it in an oven warmed by just the pilot light for several hours and heat it later over hot water in a double boiler. Fluff it again just before serving.

If you have a *couscousière,* a special double boiler with a perforated top half, place the accompanying ragout in the bottom half, and warm the couscous in the top half by the steam generated from the simmering ragout.

FISH AND SHELLFISH

*I*n the recent past, most people did not enjoy eating fish as much as they do today. Many of the fish markets were smelly and no one wanted to bring the aroma of *eau de mer* back home. Freshness was not the norm, and what little fish was bought was cooked to a certain death. Why should we have loved it?

Restaurants have changed the way Americans now think of fish. Because many restaurants offer impeccably fresh fish and prepare it with a little savoir faire, we have come to know and love the taste. Fish is satisfying but not overly filling. It offers a shot of protein and energy and now we even find out that it is good for us. As our palates are better educated, we have become more demanding of our fishmongers and many of them are trying to accommodate our newfound desires for greater variety of the freshest fish. We can get tuna and swordfish flown in daily from Hawaii, Louisiana shrimp from the Gulf, mussels from Prince Edward Island or Puget Sound, salmon from Alaska and Oregon, even Norway! Local fish is more readily available and now proudly advertised as such. No wonder we are more willing to cook fish at home.

A new style of fish cookery is emerging as well. Years ago the standard recipe directed us to cook fish until it flaked with a fork. This translated into dry fragments of anonymous pulp. Many of us have found that slightly undercooked fish is more flavorful and delicious. I don't mean that all fish should be served as if it were *sashimi*, but moist is infinitely more appealing than dry.

Because fish is in such demand, I am always looking for new and wonderful ways to serve it at the restaurant. Ironically the simplest and most traditional renditions are usually the most popular. I think that since many people are just getting to know fish, they want less art in its presentation. They want to taste it.

In the Mediterranean, fish is cooked very simply. It may be poached, grilled, sautéed, or baked with a simple sauce or vinaigrette. Sometimes it is dressed with just a splash of olive oil and an herb infusion, sometimes with white wine or a little tomato sauce. The most elaborate presentations are usually fish and shellfish ragouts. We have tried to present the best and most loved fish and shellfish recipes from our Mediterranean repertoire. Remember that freshness is essential and that timing is everything . . . in life as well as fish cookery.

Trote Ripiene Grigliate all'Iseana

GRILLED STUFFED
TROUT FROM LAKE ISEO

1 cup blanched whole
  almonds

3 or 4 slices hearty
  French or Italian
  bread, crusts removed,
  cut into 2-inch cubes
  (about 2 cups)

6 tablespoons unsalted
  butter

1 medium onion, finely
  diced

2 cloves garlic, finely
  minced

6 tablespoons finely
  minced fresh parsley

½ cup freshly grated
  Parmesan cheese

1 tablespoon grated
  lemon zest (optional)

Salt and freshly ground
  pepper

Grated nutmeg

6 boned trout with head
  and tail, about ½
  pound each

Olive oil for brushing the
  fish

Lemon wedges for serving

Fortunately this wonderful recipe for stuffed trout from Lake Iseo in Lombardy is easy for us to duplicate here because trout are readily available. The only real work is sewing the cavities closed to hold the stuffing in place. On the mornings that we prep this dish for sixty, we call ourselves the School of Trout Stitchery. I bought some carpet needles to make this group embroidery a little easier, but you may use a large sewing needle. Sewing just six trout will not take very long, and they are so delicious you will be convinced they are worth every effort. Steamed asparagus or sautéed spinach or Swiss chard makes a fine accompaniment. ◆ *Serves 6*

Preheat the oven to 400°. Toast the almonds on a baking sheet until golden, about 8 minutes. Let cool completely. Process the almonds with pulses in a food processor until crumbly but with some chunks or chop them by hand. Place in a mixing bowl. Process the bread to crumbs and combine with the almonds.

Melt the butter in a small skillet over medium heat. Add the onion and cook until almost transparent. Add the garlic for the last 2 minutes of cooking time. Stir the onion mixture into the almond mixture, then stir in the parsley, Parmesan, and lemon zest if using. Season to taste with salt, pepper, and a little nutmeg.

Spoon the stuffing mixture into the cavities of the trout and sew the openings closed with a large sewing needle and white thread.

Heat the grill or broiler. Brush each fish with olive oil and sprinkle lightly with salt and pepper. Grill or broil until just cooked through, about 4 minutes each side. (The trout can also be baked in a 375° oven about 15 minutes, or sautéed in a skillet over medium heat if you are very careful.) Serve hot with lemon wedges.

Trota allo Zenzero

TROUT WITH GINGER
AND SHALLOT BUTTER

12 tablespoons unsalted
    butter
2 tablespoons finely
    minced shallots
3 tablespoons dry
    vermouth
3 tablespoons grated fresh
    ginger
Salt and freshly ground
    pepper
6 boned trout, heads
    removed, about ½
    pound each
Olive oil for brushing the
    fish

I know ginger seems a little strange in a basic Italian vocabulary of ingredients, but dried ginger was popular in Roman cooking. It mysteriously disappeared for a few centuries and then reappeared with Marco Polo, when it played a part in the complicated and rich Renaissance dishes of Modena. Dried ginger is still used in Basilicata and Calabria, in Venetian cookery, and in some dishes of Florentine origin. But we don't have to wait for the slow boat from China for ginger. It's available fresh at nearly all our markets. Why not use it? ♦ *Serves 6*

Melt 2 tablespoons butter in a small sauté pan over medium heat. Add the shallots and cook gently several minutes. Add 2 tablespoons vermouth and simmer until the liquid is absorbed and the shallots are tender, about 3 minutes. Let cool.

Puree the ginger and remaining tablespoon vermouth in a food processor; set aside.

Process the remaining 10 tablespoons butter in the food processor until smooth. Add the shallot and ginger mixtures; process with pulses until blended. Season to taste with salt and pepper. Refrigerate until ready to serve.

Heat the grill or broiler. Brush each fish with olive oil and sprinkle lightly with salt and pepper. Grill or broil until just cooked through, about 4 minutes each side. (The trout can also be sautéed in a little butter or olive oil in a large sauté pan over medium heat about 3 minutes each side.) Spread the flavored butter over the trout and serve hot with sautéed spinach or steamed snow peas or asparagus.

NOTE: This butter would also be tasty with salmon.

Salmon Wrapped in Grape Leaves

6 salmon fillets, about 6 ounces each

12 large grape leaves, rinsed and patted dry, stems removed

¾ cup dark raisins, plumped in hot water

1 cup extra virgin olive oil, plus additional for brushing the fish

3 tablespoons (or to taste) fresh lemon juice

Salt and freshly ground pepper

½ cup pine nuts, toasted

Spain, Italy, Greece, and Turkey all have this dish as part of their cuisine. Now at Square One we consider it part of ours because our customers request it so often. ◆ *Serves 6*

Wrap each salmon fillet around the middle with 2 grape leaves (the ends will be exposed). You may secure the leaves with toothpicks, but they stick pretty well without any help.

Drain the raisins, saving the soaking liquid. Puree about ¼ cup raisins in the food processor and transfer to a mixing bowl. Add the remaining whole raisins, 1 cup olive oil, the lemon juice, and about ¼ cup of the soaking liquid. Stir well, then season to taste with salt, pepper, and lemon juice if needed.

Heat the grill or broiler. Brush the wrapped salmon with olive oil and sprinkle lightly with pepper. Grill or broil 3 to 4 minutes each side. If your grill or broiler is slow, cook a minute or two longer. The fish should be cooked through but still quite moist and juicy.

Place the fish on serving plates. Spoon the raisin mixture over top and sprinkle with the toasted pine nuts. Serve with rice pilaf and sautéed spinach or grilled or sautéed zucchini.

VARIATION

Add ¾ cup diced peeled tomatoes (canned plum tomatoes are okay) or 1 cup Tomato Sauce (page 118) to the raisin mixture.

Salmone al Giuliese

BAKED SALMON WITH
CAPERS AND TOASTED
BREAD CRUMBS

FOR EACH SERVING

1 tablespoon olive oil

1 teaspoon fresh lemon
juice

5 ounces salmon fillet

Salt and freshly ground
pepper

½ cup Toasted Bread
Crumbs (page 73)

1½ tablespoons capers,
rinsed

1 tablespoon unsalted
butter, melted

A nice simple way to dress up salmon, rockfish, snapper, or sea bass.

Preheat the oven to 450° to 500°. Mix the olive oil and lemon juice and brush it on a baking pan and both sides of the salmon. Place the salmon in the pan and sprinkle with salt and pepper. Cover the salmon with the bread crumbs, then sprinkle with the capers and drizzle with the butter. Bake until the fish is just cooked through, 5 to 7 minutes. Serve with sautéed spinach or Swiss chard or broccoli.

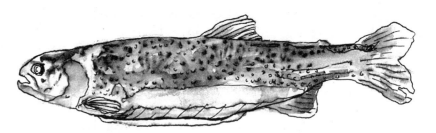

Salmonete Grelhado com Maionese Setubalense

GRILLED SALMON WITH
ORANGE AND
BLACK PEPPER AIOLI

2 tablespoons kosher salt

¼ cup sugar

2 tablespoons grated
   orange zest

1 teaspoon freshly ground
   pepper

6 salmon fillets, 6 to 7
   ounces each

AIOLI

2 large egg yolks, at room
   temperature

1 tablespoon (or more to
   taste) fresh lemon juice

2 cups olive oil

1 tablespoon pureed
   garlic (mash the garlic
   with a pinch of salt in
   a mortar with a pestle;
   it must be very smooth)

3 to 4 tablespoons fresh
   orange juice

2 tablespoons grated
   orange zest

2 teaspoons freshly
   ground pepper
   (medium grind)

Salt to taste

Olive oil

12 orange slices for
   garnish

2 tablespoons chopped
   fresh mint, cilantro, or
   parsley for garnish

This Portuguese fantasy is usually made with red mullet, but we have substituted more readily available salmon. Setubal is known for their bitter oranges. The original sauce was a wine-and-orange-flavored butter and the fish was covered with orange slices and baked. We like to rub the fish with orange zest, salt, and sugar and cure it for a few hours before grilling it. We have kept the original orange slices and added a little mint for garnish, although you could use cilantro for the Portuguese love both herbs. The first few times we served this we made the wine-and-orange butter, but then we tried it with an orange aioli seasoned with black pepper. That got the thumbs-up sign from our guests. Hope you agree. ✦ *Serves 6*

To cure the salmon, mix the salt, sugar, orange zest, and pepper; rub over both sides of the salmon fillets. Refrigerate about 3 hours.

For the aioli, whisk the egg yolks and lemon juice in a mixing bowl or process with pulses in a food processor until blended. Gradually whisk or beat in the oil. The mixture should be thick and emulsified. Whisk or beat in the garlic, 3 tablespoons orange juice, the zest, and pepper. Season to taste with salt. If the orange flavor is weak, add more orange juice; if the sauce is too sweet, add lemon juice to taste. Refrigerate until ready to serve.

Heat the grill or broiler. Brush the fish fillets with a little olive oil. Broil or grill until just cooked through, 2 to 3 minutes each side. Place on serving plates and top with dollops of the aioli. Garnish with orange slices and herb of choice.

Portuguese-Style Salmon with Curry, Lemon, and Cream

1 tablespoon curry powder

½ teaspoon ground ginger (optional)

1 tablespoon fresh lemon juice

2 cups heavy cream

½ teaspoon salt, plus additional for the fish

Pinch freshly ground pepper, plus additional for the fish

6 salmon fillets, about 6 ounces each

Olive oil for brushing the fish

What is curry doing in Portugal? Back in the fabulous fifteenth century, Vasco da Gama rounded the Cape of Good Hope and brought spices, such as cinnamon, cloves, nutmeg, pepper, and curry, back to Portugal. You can make the curry and lemon cream ahead of time and either bake, poach, or broil the salmon. Serve it with minted rice and sautéed spinach for a tasty and colorful dinner.
◆ *Serves 6*

Mix the curry powder, ginger if you like the flavor, and lemon juice, then whisk it into the cream. Season with salt and pepper. Store in the refrigerator.

Preheat the oven to 450° to 500° or heat the grill or broiler. Sprinkle the salmon with salt and pepper and place on an oiled baking sheet. Bake until just cooked through, 5 to 7 minutes. Or brush the fish with oil and sprinkle with salt and pepper. Grill or broil 3 to 4 minutes each side. (The fish can also be poached in the simmering cream sauce; it should take 5 to 7 minutes.)

Meanwhile, heat the cream in a medium saucepan to boiling, stirring occasionally. Immediately reduce the heat and simmer until reduced by a third. Spoon the sauce over the salmon and serve at once.

VARIATIONS

We have used this curry lemon cream as a pasta sauce with shrimp, scallops, or crabmeat and fettuccine. You may want to increase the ginger a little bit and add a chiffonade of spinach or chopped chives for color.

If you are feeling rich, you could add 24 poached small shrimp or ½ pound fresh crabmeat to the sauce.

Salmon with Red Onions and Red Wine

1 cup unsalted butter

6 large red onions, sliced ¼ inch thick (about 8 cups)

3 cups full-bodied red wine, such as Zinfandel or Côtes du Rhône

1 to 3 tablespoons sugar

Salt and freshly ground pepper

2 cups Fish Fumet (page 105)

6 salmon fillets, 5 to 6 ounces each

The French love to cook vegetables until they are as sweet as sugar. They call this a confit, short for confiture or jam. For this dish, we cook the red onions to the consistency of marmalade and flavor them with red wine. We poach the fish in red wine too. This combination is, as they say, formidable. ◆ *Serves 6*

Melt ½ cup plus 1 tablespoon butter in a large heavy sauté pan over medium heat. Add the onions and cook until tender but still a bit *al dente*, about 15 minutes. Add 2 cups wine and continue cooking until the onions are very tender, about 8 minutes more. Sweeten to taste with sugar and season with salt and pepper. Let stand. (You should have about 3 cups confit.)

Heat the remaining wine and the fish fumet in a wide saucepan to simmering (see Note). Add the fish and poach gently over low heat until just cooked through, about 7 minutes. Using a slotted spatula, transfer the salmon to a warm platter. Boil the poaching liquid until somewhat syrupy, then stir in the onion confit and just heat through. Swirl in the remaining 7 tablespoons butter, 1 tablespoon at a time, taking the pan on and off low heat so that the butter emulsifies before it melts. Spoon the onion sauce over the salmon.

NOTE: The salmon can also be baked. Place it in a single layer in an oiled baking dish, sprinkle with salt and pepper, and spoon the onion confit over the top. Bake at 450° until just cooked through, about 7 minutes.

Baked Fish with Preserved Lemons and Onion Confit

This recipe is a composite, sort of a cross between the Moroccan classic *m'qualli* chicken with lemon and olives and fish with *charmoula*. I liked the idea of the traditional *charmoula* marinade but wanted the sex appeal of the onions laced with lemons and those voluptuous marinated olives. It seemed the perfect sensual dish to serve at a special dinner at the James Beard House on Leap Year night. ✦ *Serves 4 to 6*

PRESERVED LEMONS

2 large lemons
½ cup sugar
1 cup water

MARINATED OLIVES

*24 Kalamata or
    Moroccan olives*
*4 tablespoons fruity
    olive oil*
*1 tablespoon grated
    orange zest*
2 cloves garlic, crushed

ONION CONFIT

*6 tablespoons unsalted
    butter or olive oil*
*6 large onions, thinly
    sliced (about 12 cups)*
4 teaspoons ground ginger
½ teaspoon turmeric
*1 teaspoon ground
    coriander*
1 teaspoon ground cumin
*2 teaspoons paprika
    (optional)*
Salt and ground pepper

The day before serving, prepare the preserved lemons and marinated olives: Rinse the lemons and wipe dry. Cut each one into 8 or 16 thin wedges. Cook in a large pot of boiling water about 5 minutes and drain. Soak in cold water to cover 1 hour, then drain.

Mix the sugar and water in a medium saucepan. Heat, stirring occasionally, over medium heat until the sugar is dissolved. Add the lemons and simmer until tender, about 20 minutes. If the syrup seems too thin, remove the lemons and reduce the syrup a bit. Let cool. Store the lemons in syrup in the refrigerator.

Crack the olives with a mallet and place in a bowl. Add the fruity olive oil, orange zest, and garlic; stir to combine. Let marinate at room temperature or in the refrigerator overnight.

The next day, make the onion confit. Melt the butter in a large skillet over medium heat. Add the onions and cook until very sweet and soft, about 20 minutes. Stir in the spices and cook a few more minutes. Season to taste with salt and pepper. Let stand at room temperature.

Rub both sides of the fish fillets with the *charmoula* and let marinate about an hour in the refrigerator.

Heat the oven to 450°.

Using a slotted spoon, remove the preserved lemons from the syrup and stir them into the onion confit. Add the syrup to taste.

2 pounds firm fish fillets,
  such as snapper,
  rockfish, or flounder
1 cup Moroccan
  Charmoula (recipe
  follows)
½ cup Fish Fumet (page
  105)
Chopped fresh parsley or
  cilantro for garnish

Oil a baking sheet and place the fish on it in a single layer. Spoon the onion mixture over the fillets and drizzle each fillet with a few drops of fish fumet. Bake until the fish is just cooked through, 7 to 10 minutes.

Meanwhile, warm the olives in their marinade in a small pan for a minute or two.

Transfer the fish to serving plates and garnish with the olives and chopped parsley or cilantro. Serve with couscous or roasted potatoes.

Moroccan Charmoula

1 cup fruity olive oil
½ cup fresh lemon juice
½ cup chopped fresh
  parsley
½ cup chopped cilantro
6 cloves garlic, finely
  minced
1 tablespoon paprika
2 teaspoons ground cumin
½ teaspoon cayenne
  pepper
Salt and freshly ground
  pepper to taste

This is the all-purpose, most loved sauce for fish. You can bake it, grill it, or poach it. Just marinate the fish in a little *charmoula*, the classic Moroccan marinade for fish, spoon a little more over the top when you serve it, and you have a winner on your plate! ✦ *Enough for 6 to 8 servings*

Place all the ingredients in a mixing bowl and whisk together lightly. Rub a little over the fish up to 3 hours before cooking and let it marinate in the refrigerator. Cook the fish and spoon some more over the top. Serve the fish with couscous.

Spiced Red Wine Butter

1 cup plus 3 tablespoons unsalted butter
1 cup finely diced onion
½ teaspoon cinnamon
¼ teaspoon ground cloves
1 cup full-bodied red wine, such as Côtes du Rhône or Zinfandel
Salt and freshly ground pepper

This compound butter is imbued with the flavors that entered Italian cooking during the Renaissance when the spice trade was flourishing. It is excellent on baked, poached, or grilled fish, such as salmon, tuna, and halibut. ◆ *Makes ¾ cup, enough for 6 servings*

Melt 3 tablespoons butter in a medium sauté pan over medium heat. Add the onion and cook until tender, about 10 minutes. Stir in the cinnamon and cloves and cook 1 minute longer. Add the red wine and cook over high heat until reduced by half and syrupy. Let cool.

Process the remaining 1 cup softened butter and the cooled wine mixture in a food processor until completely blended. Season to taste with salt and pepper.

Roll the butter into a log in plastic wrap. Refrigerate or freeze. Cut 1-inch-thick slices from the log as you need it. Let warm to room temperature before using.

Swordfish à la Turque

1 medium onion, chopped (about 1 cup)
1 tablespoon paprika
2 small bay leaves, crumbled
½ teaspoon freshly ground pepper
¼ cup fresh lemon juice
½ cup mild olive oil
¼ cup fruity olive oil
¼ teaspoon (or to taste) salt
6 pieces swordfish fillet or steaks, about 6 ounces each

Traditionally this is served as a brochette, but you can just as easily use swordfish steaks. If you can get fresh bay laurel leaves, the dish will be more pungent; you may want to cut back on them in the marinade. If you do want to cube the fish and treat it as a brochette, alternate thin lemon slices and bay leaves on the skewers with the fish. This marinade would also work with other mild and dense-textured fish, such as mahi mahi. ◆ *Serves 6*

Place the onion, paprika, bay leaves, pepper, and lemon juice in a food processor and puree. With the machine running, gradually pour in the olive oils. The sauce should be thick and emulsified. Season with salt. Place the fish in a single layer in a large shallow dish, pour the marinade over the fish, and turn to coat. Marinate several hours in the refrigerator.

Heat the grill or broiler. Grill or broil the swordfish about 3 inches from the heat until cooked through but still juicy, about 3 minutes each side. We like to serve this with rice pilaf and sautéed spinach, or roasted potatoes and grilled eggplant and zucchini.

Pescespada Ripieno alla Siciliana

SICILIAN-STYLE STUFFED SWORDFISH

4 pieces swordfish fillet,
    about 1½ inches thick
    and ½ pound each

1½ cups fresh bread
    crumbs

7 tablespoons unsalted
    butter, melted

2 tablespoons olive oil,
    plus additional for
    brushing the fish

1 medium onion, finely
    diced

½ teaspoon finely minced
    garlic

1 teaspoon fennel seeds,
    toasted and ground

¼ cup pine nuts, toasted

Salt and freshly ground
    pepper

2 cups Tomato Sauce
    (page 118)

2 tablespoons chopped
    fresh parsley for
    garnish

This dish is a specialty of Messina, but you can find it in Palermo and Catania as well. Some versions add provolone cheese to the filling, but I just don't like it that way. Others add raisins to the filling, and, while I can understand it, I don't want to do that either. I prefer to cut a pocket in the side of thick pieces of fish fillet and stuff it with filling. Some recipes have you roll pounded strips of fish around the filling, but this seems like extra work to me. Now, if you are really looking for extra work that will result in something wonderful, clean some medium-sized squid, chop the tentacles and add them to the filling, then stuff the squid too and serve them with a smaller piece of fish. With or without squid, sauce this dish with a light tomato sauce and serve it with roasted potatoes and sautéed broccoli with olives and garlic. ◆ *Serves 4*

Cut a pocket in the side of each piece of swordfish. Refrigerate.

Preheat the oven to 400°. Toss the bread crumbs with 5 tablespoons of the butter on a baking sheet. Toast in the oven, stirring occasionally, until golden, about 15 minutes. Pour the remaining butter into a small sauté pan and add 1 tablespoon olive oil. Heat over medium heat. Add the onion and cook until tender; add the garlic for the last 2 minutes of cooking time. Combine the bread crumbs, onion mixture, fennel seeds, and pine nuts. Season to taste with salt and pepper. Let cool to room temperature.

Heat the grill or broiler or preheat the oven to 450°. Warm the tomato sauce.

Stuff the swordfish with the bread crumb mixture. Brush the fish with olive oil and sprinkle with salt and pepper. Grill or broil until cooked through but still juicy, about 5 minutes each side. Or bake in a single layer in a baking dish about 10 minutes. Transfer the fish to serving plates and spoon tomato sauce over top. Sprinkle with parsley and serve at once.

Espadarte Grelhado a Lisboeta

GRILLED SWORDFISH,
LISBON STYLE

1 cup chopped seeded
    canned or fresh plum
    tomatoes
1 cup olive oil, plus
    additional for brushing
    the fish
20 Kalamata olives,
    pitted and coarsely
    chopped
3 tablespoons fresh lemon
    juice
3 tablespoons finely
    chopped fresh parsley
1 tablespoon tomato paste
    or 3 tablespoons
    tomato puree
1 tablespoon finely
    chopped anchovy
Salt and freshly ground
    pepper to taste
6 swordfish steaks, 6 to 7
    ounces each

While this simple dish could be from Sicily or other parts of Italy, it is Portuguese in origin. Tomatoes, olives, and anchovies are a terrific trio when it comes to fish.
♦ Serves 6

Combine all the ingredients except the fish.

Heat the grill or broiler. Brush the fish lightly with oil and sprinkle with salt and pepper. Grill or broil about 3 inches from the heat until cooked through but still juicy, about 4 minutes each side. Transfer to serving plates and spoon the sauce over the fish. Serve with roasted potatoes and sautéed greens or zucchini.

VARIATION

For Sephardic *Zemino* Sauce, replace the lemon juice with red wine vinegar, double the anchovy, and add 6 minced cloves of garlic.

Grilled Swordfish or Tuna with Sun-Dried Tomatoes

Although it may seem that we are drowning in a sea of sun-dried tomatoes, so hot and heavy is the trend, they are part of a real Italian tradition. Many families dry their own year's supply. I remember watching women in Ragusa Ibla in Sicily turn trays of tomatoes and tomato paste in the sun. Trendy they weren't. They were simply preparing for winter when the desire for tomatoes was there and the fresh tomatoes weren't. ◆ *Serves 6*

½ cup olive oil, plus additional for brushing the fish

¼ cup fresh lemon juice

3 tablespoons finely chopped pitted Niçoise olives

2 tablespoons very finely chopped sun-dried tomatoes (packed in oil)

3 tablespoons oil from the sun-dried tomatoes

2 teaspoons finely minced garlic

¼ cup finely chopped fresh mint

½ teaspoon freshly ground pepper, plus additional to taste

6 pieces swordfish or tuna fillet, about 7 ounces each

Salt

Combine all the ingredients except the fish and salt.

Heat the grill or broiler. Brush the fish lightly with oil and sprinkle with salt and pepper. Grill or broil about 3 inches from the heat until cooked through but still juicy, about 3 minutes each side for swordfish or a little less for tuna if you like it a bit rare in the middle.

Transfer to serving plates and spoon the sauce over the fish. Serve with roasted potatoes and sautéed Swiss chard or broiled eggplant and zucchini.

*T*onno all Griglia con Pepe Ammaccato

GRILLED TUNA WITH
CRACKED PEPPER

LEMON BUTTER

½ **cup unsalted butter,
softened**

2 **to 3 teaspoons grated
lemon zest**

2 **tablespoons fresh lemon
juice**

1 **teaspoon salt**

4 **pieces yellowfin or
bigeye tuna fillet, 6 to
7 ounces and ¾ inch
thick**

¼ **cup olive oil**

¼ **cup cracked black
peppercorns (not too
fine nor too coarse)**

1 **teaspoon dried red
pepper flakes
(optional)**

Salt

One day at the restaurant, the cooks and I were in the kitchen admiring the gorgeous tuna that had just been delivered. Someone remarked it was so red and meaty that it looked like steak. Today, I thought, let's treat it like steak—let's serve it *au poivre,* or with cracked black pepper. We felt very happy with our decision, and the tuna was truly delicious.

Weeks later I was researching a special menu for the restaurant featuring Italian Renaissance food. My son, Evan, had recently returned from Venice with a new cookbook for me called *La Cucina Veneziana* by Maffioli. In the list of fish dishes was *tonno con limone e pepe ammaccato.* Tuna with lemon and cracked black pepper! *Ammaccare* means to bruise or smash. Some novel idea. Only centuries old!
✦ *Serves 4*

For the lemon butter, place the butter, lemon zest and juice, and salt in a food processor and process until blended. Taste and add more juice or salt if needed.

Heat the grill or broiler. Coat the tuna with the olive oil. Mix the black and red peppers (if desired) on a plate and coat both sides of the fish with the mixture. Sprinkle with salt. Grill or broil about 3 inches from the heat 2 to 3 minutes each side for medium-rare. Transfer to a serving plate and top with the lemon butter. Sautéed spinach is an ideal accompaniment, and you may want to extend the steak theme a little and serve french fries too.

*T*onno in Gradela

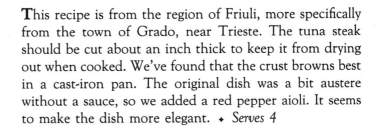

MARINATED SAUTÉED
TUNA IN A FENNEL AND
BREAD CRUMB CRUST

¾ *cup olive oil*

2 *tablespoons fresh lemon
juice*

4 *pieces yellowfin or
bigeye tuna fillet, 6 to
7 ounces each and
about 1 inch thick*

*Salt and freshly ground
pepper*

1¼ *cups dry bread
crumbs*

¼ *cup ground toasted
fennel seeds*

1 *cup Red Pepper Aioli
(page 183)*

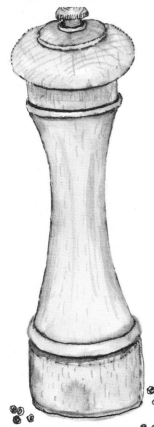

This recipe is from the region of Friuli, more specifically from the town of Grado, near Trieste. The tuna steak should be cut about an inch thick to keep it from drying out when cooked. We've found that the crust browns best in a cast-iron pan. The original dish was a bit austere without a sauce, so we added a red pepper aioli. It seems to make the dish more elegant. ✦ *Serves 4*

Mix ¼ cup olive oil and the lemon juice and brush over the tuna. Let marinate in the refrigerator at least 2 hours.

Heat the remaining ½ cup olive oil in a heavy skillet over high heat. Sprinkle the tuna with salt and pepper. Mix the bread crumbs and fennel seeds and coat the tuna with the mixture. Add the tuna to the skillet and sauté, turning once, until crusty and light brown on the outside and medium-rare in the center, 2 to 3 minutes each side. Serve with red pepper aioli and accompany with sauteed Swiss chard.

NOTES: This recipe should also work well with salmon. For a variation, add a little grated orange zest to the bread crumb mixture and a squeeze of orange juice to the marinade. You could also serve this with a butter flavored with lemon or orange zest instead of the aioli.

Incidentally, you can grill the coated fish instead of frying it.

Bolinhos de Santola

PORTUGUESE CRAB CAKES WITH MINT AND CILANTRO

¼ cup unsalted butter

2 medium onions, finely minced (about 1¼ cups)

4 ribs celery, chopped

1 tablespoon dry mustard

1 teaspoon cayenne pepper

2 pounds crabmeat, picked over for cartilage

½ cup mayonnaise, preferably homemade (see next recipe)

2 large eggs

¾ cup fresh bread crumbs

¼ cup chopped fresh mint leaves

¼ cup chopped cilantro

2 teaspoons grated lemon zest

Salt and freshly ground pepper to taste

1 cup dry bread crumbs

1 cup olive oil or as needed for frying.

Red Pepper Aioli (recipe follows)

This recipe is a compromise because the original is made with salt cod, a fish most chefs and some Italians, Spaniards, and Portuguese adore but that we cannot sell to the average American diner. Since we are in San Francisco, home of the famous crab, we substituted crabmeat for the cod. Now we cannot keep up with the demand for these cakes. ◆ *Serves 8*

Melt the butter in a medium saucepan over medium heat. Add the onions and celery; cook until translucent, 5 to 7 minutes. Add the dry mustard and cayenne; stir well and cook 3 more minutes. Let cool completely.

Add all the remaining ingredients except the dry bread crumbs, oil, and aioli to the onion mixture and combine well. Shape into 16 patties, about ½ inch thick. Coat each crab cake with dry bread crumbs. (At this point the cakes can be refrigerated on a baking sheet lined with baker's parchment or waxed paper up to 24 hours.)

Heat the olive oil in a large heavy skillet over medium-high heat. Add as many crab cakes as will fit without crowding and sauté until golden brown, about 3 minutes each side. Serve hot with red pepper aioli and sauteed Swiss chard or other greens.

Red Pepper Aioli

♦ *Makes about 2 cups*

MAYONNAISE

2 medium red peppers

2 large egg yolks, at room
*   temperature*

2 tablespoons fresh lemon
*   juice*

2 cups mild olive oil

1 tablespoon smooth
*   pureed garlic*

½ teaspoon (or to taste)
*   cayenne pepper*

Salt to taste

Char the peppers over an open flame or under the broiler until blackened on all sides. Transfer to a plastic container with a lid or a paper or plastic bag. Cover the container or close the bag and let the peppers steam for about 15 minutes. Peel the skins from the peppers; then cut the peppers in half, remove the stems, and scrape out the seeds. Puree the peppers in a blender or food processor.

To make the mayonnaise, whisk the egg yolks and half the lemon juice together in a mixing bowl or blend in a food processor. Gradually beat in the olive oil until a thick emulsion is attained. Set aside ½ cup for the Bolinhos.

Add the pepper puree, garlic, and cayenne to the remaining mayonnaise. Season to taste with salt and add enough of the remaining lemon juice to bring up the red pepper flavor.

Merluzzo all'Istriana

BAKED COD WITH
ONIONS AND MINT

6 tablespoons unsalted
  butter
3 medium onions, sliced
  ¼ inch thick
2 cloves garlic, finely
  minced
1 cup fresh mint leaves,
  finely chopped
1 cup fresh flat-leaf
  parsley, finely chopped
Salt and freshly ground
  pepper
4 cod fillets, 6 to 7
  ounces each
2 tablespoons olive oil
2 tablespoons fresh lemon
  juice
2 green onions, chopped
2 tablespoons capers,
  rinsed well
4 anchovies, rinsed, cut
  into long strips

Cod is not the glamour fish that salmon, tuna, and sword-fish have become. It hasn't received bad press; it just somehow has never caught the imagination of the dining public. It's sort of a familiar and comfortable fish, rather than a sexy, dramatic, daring number. But there are days when comfort and familiarity are just what your palate craves. Here is a simple and delicious recipe that makes tried-and-true cod a little special without much effort and with minimal expense. The recipe comes from the Italian province of Friuli. ✦ *Serves 4*

Preheat the oven to 450°. Melt the butter in a medium saucepan over medium heat. Add the onions and cook until tender. Add the garlic and cook a minute or two, then add the mint and parsley and cook a minute longer. Season to taste with salt and pepper.

Spread the onion mixture in a shallow baking pan just large enough to hold the cod. Arrange the cod fillets on top and brush them with olive oil and lemon juice. Sprinkle with salt and pepper.

Bake until cooked through but still juicy, about 10 minutes. Transfer the fish and onion mixture to serving plates. Garnish with the green onions, capers, and anchovies. Serve with roasted potatoes.

Polpettine di Pesce all'Ebrea

SALMON CROQUETTES, JEWISH STYLE

2 pounds salmon fillet

¼ cup unsalted butter or olive oil

2 cups finely diced yellow onions

1 teaspoon ground cinnamon

¼ teaspoon ground cloves

¼ teaspoon grated nutmeg

¼ cup chopped fresh parsley

1 cup fresh bread crumbs

¾ cup homemade mayonnaise (see recipe page 183)

Salt and freshly ground pepper

1 cup dry bread crumbs

1 cup clarified butter (page 26) or mild olive oil for frying

Every year around Passover I try to offer an Italian Jewish dinner as part of our regional menu series. When my son returned from a trip to Venice, he brought me a few new cookbooks to add to my collection. In them I found chapters on *la cucina ebrea,* or traditional Jewish cooking, in Venice and Padova. Many of the recipes dated from the fifteenth century. Foods that I had come to think of as Eastern European turned out to have Italian roots. For example, they served smoked sturgeon, *fegato all' uove sode* or chopped chicken livers with hard-cooked eggs (page 25), *spuma di tonno* or tuna pâté (page 28), *rotolo de verze* or stuffed cabbage, *haroseth,* the Passover condiment of dried fruits in wine, stuffed goose neck (*helzel*), a *tsimmes* or stew of yellow squash and carrots to accompany roast duck, goose, or veal, and *grigole,* or *gribenes,* those beloved but deadly deep-fried chicken cracklings. They even served meatloaf with a hard-cooked egg in the middle, a dish I always thought was a New York Jewish specialty. In amongst these treasures I found a description of *polpettine di pesce,* sort of a fish cake not unlike gefilte fish but seasoned with cinnamon and cloves. The following recipe is my interpretation of this dish. It isn't kosher but it sure is delicious. ◆ *Serves 6 to 8*

Poach or steam the salmon until flaky and cooked through but not dry. Let it cool, then break it up into small pieces with your fingers.

Heat ¼ cup butter or olive oil in a medium sauté pan over low heat. Add the onions and cook until tender but not browned. Stir in the spices and parsley and cook a minute or two longer. Combine the onion mixture, salmon, fresh bread crumbs, and mayonnaise. Season to taste with salt and pepper.

Shape the salmon mixture into 12 to 16 croquettes, about 1 inch thick. Coat on all sides with the dry bread crumbs. (At this point the croquettes can be refrigerated on a baking sheet lined with baker's parchment or waxed paper up to 6 hours.)

To cook, heat the clarified butter or olive oil in 2 large skillets over medium heat. Add the croquettes and sauté until golden on all sides, 6 to 8 minutes. Serve the croquettes with a simple lemon wedge, Orange and Black Pepper Aioli (page 171), or *Agliata* (page 197). The best accompaniment is sautéed spinach.

*T*eglia di Branzino e Granchio

GRATIN OF SEA BASS
AND CRABMEAT

1 cup Tomato Sauce
  (page 118)

1 pound sea bass, cut into
  3 by 1-inch strips

1 pound crabmeat, picked
  over for cartilage and
  bone

2 cups diced peeled fresh
  tomatoes

4 teaspoons chopped fresh
  mint

2 teaspoons chopped fresh
  tarragon

2 tablespoons chopped
  fresh parsley

¾ cup toasted bread
  crumbs (page 73)

½ cup freshly grated
  Parmesan cheese

¼ cup unsalted butter,
  melted

We didn't have enough sea bass to serve all day, and our fishmonger had just a small amount of crabmeat. But, as luck would have it, I found a wonderful recipe from the Roman province of Lazio in central Italy that combined the two. The grated Parmesan seems to me a French influence for the Italians rarely put cheese on fish, but it does add to the crunchy topping. ◆ *Serves 4*

Preheat the oven to 450° to 500°. Spoon the tomato sauce over the bottom of each of 4 individual gratin dishes, about 5 inches in diameter. Place the strips of sea bass on the sauce. Bake about 2 minutes and remove from the oven.

Combine the crabmeat, diced tomatoes, and herbs and spoon this mixture over the sea bass. Combine the bread crumbs and Parmesan cheese and sprinkle over the crabmeat mixture. Drizzle with the melted butter. Bake until heated through and the top is golden brown, 10 to 15 minutes. Serve at once.

Tiella di Cozze

GRATIN OF MUSSELS, ONIONS, AND POTATOES

8 little red potatoes

½ cup plus 2 tablespoons olive oil

Salt and freshly ground pepper

2 cups diced onions

1⅓ cups dry white wine

6 pounds mussels (about 15 per serving), scrubbed

1 cup toasted bread crumbs (page 73)

4 teaspoons finely minced garlic

½ cup chopped fresh parsley

½ cup freshly grated pecorino or Parmesan cheese

This recipe from Apulia demonstrates the ingenuity of good cooks in making something wonderful and rich in flavor out of a few inexpensive ingredients. ◆ *Serves 4*

Preheat the oven to 375°. Rub the potatoes with 2 tablespoons olive oil and sprinkle with salt and pepper. Roast in a baking dish until tender but still firm enough to slice, about 25 to 30 minutes.

Heat ¼ cup oil in a large skillet over medium heat. Add the onions and cook until tender, 5 to 7 minutes.

Pour the wine into a wide saucepan, cover, and heat to simmering. Drop in the mussels and steam covered until they open. Using a slotted spoon, transfer the mussels to a colander. Let stand until cool enough to handle. Strain the liquid through a cheesecloth-lined strainer. Carefully remove the beards from the mussels and remove them from the shells. Add the mussels to the cooking liquid and refrigerate.

Preheat the oven to 350°. Oil 4 individual gratin dishes, about 5 inches in diameter.

Slice the potatoes about ⅓ inch thick and toss with ¼ cup olive oil. Sprinkle lightly with salt and pepper. Layer them in the gratin dishes and top with the cooked onions. Add the mussels and drizzle all with about 2 tablespoons of the liquid. Combine the bread crumbs, garlic, parsley, and cheese and sprinkle over the top of the gratins.

Bake until bubbly and the tops are browned, 10 to 12 minutes.

La Triestina

SHELLFISH RAGOUT
FROM TRIESTE

2 small crabs (about 2
   pounds each) or two
   1½-pound lobsters (see
   Note)
½ cup dry red wine
1 cup Fish Fumet (page
   105)
16 mussels, scrubbed and
   bearded
16 Manila clams,
   scrubbed
16 sea scallops
16 medium shrimp,
   shelled and deveined
4 small squid, cleaned,
   bodies cut into rings,
   large tentacles halved
4 cups Triestina Sauce
   (recipe follows)

There are so many tall tales in the archives of the origin of the famous San Francisco specialty cioppino, it is hard to know which one might have a grain of truth. What I suspect is that cioppino is related to the *cacciucco* of Livorno and the fish stews of the Friuli region of Italy. These are made with a red wine base. This ragout, which we serve over soft or baked polenta, is from the Dalmatian coast. For cioppino, sprinkle the ragout with chopped parsley and serve with slices of grilled French bread rubbed well with garlic.

Obviously this dish can be expanded to serve 8. The sauce is a good, rich basic marinara with some extra heat and fennel. It will keep for a few days in the refrigerator. You may make the sauce, make two portions of ragout one night, and then, a day or so later, make spaghetti marinara with the rest. ✦ *Serves 4*

Cook the crabs in a large pot of boiling salted water about 12 minutes. Drain and chill in ice water. To clean the crabs, remove and discard top shell, gills, and tiny tail piece, but save any crab "butter" from the top shell and add to the sauce. Wash the body under cold water. Remove the claws. Cut the body into quarters. Crack the claws with a mallet for easier eating.

Heat the wine and fish fumet in a large pan over high heat. Add the crabs or lobster, mussels, and clams. Cook covered, 2 minutes. Add the scallops, shrimp and any optional fish; cook 2 minutes more, shaking the pan once or twice. Add the squid and Triestina sauce. Heat through and simmer until all is cooked, about 2 minutes more. Serve the ragout over soft or baked polenta. For cioppino, ladle into wide bowls and serve with grilled French bread rubbed well with garlic.

NOTE: Lobster can be used in place of the crab, as could any thick meaty fish, such as angler or cod. The lobster should be cooked for 7 minutes, drained and chilled, removed from the shell and cut into chunks.

Triestina Sauce

½ cup olive oil
3 cups chopped onions
1 cup chopped celery
3 tablespoons minced
  garlic
2 small bay leaves
2 sprigs fresh thyme
1 tablespoon dried red
  pepper flakes
2 teaspoons ground
  toasted fennel seeds
3½ cups canned Italian
  plum tomatoes, pulsed
  in the food processor
  with their juices, or
  drained and chopped
  (about 2½ cups) and
  combined with their
  juices (about 1 cup)
1½ cups Fish Fumet
  (page 105)
1 cup red wine
½ cup canned thick
  tomato puree
3 tablespoons red wine
  vinegar
Salt and freshly ground
  pepper

You know, you don't have to make cioppino to enjoy this sauce. It is totally satisfying on pasta, with or without clams, or spooned over simple poached or broiled fish.
◆ *Makes about 6 cups*

Heat the olive oil in a large saucepan over medium heat. Add the onions and cook until translucent, about 5 minutes. Add the celery, garlic, bay leaves, thyme, red pepper flakes, and fennel. Reduce the heat to low and cook 5 minutes more. Stir in the tomatoes, fish fumet, wine, tomato puree, and vinegar; simmer uncovered about 10 minutes. Season to taste with salt and pepper.

Fish Couscous with Charmoula

Moroccan Charmoula
(page 175)

2 ½ to 3 pounds rockfish,
grouper, sea bass,
flounder, and/or
halibut fillets, cut into
3 by 2-inch pieces

FISH SOUP BASE

¼ cup olive oil

2 large onions, diced
(about 3 cups)

5 ribs celery, diced (about
1 ½ cups)

6 cloves garlic, finely
minced

2 teaspoons dried red
pepper flakes

2 teaspoons ground cumin

1 tablespoon paprika

½ teaspoon cinnamon

Pinch ground cloves

1 ½ cups canned Italian
plum tomatoes, drained
and diced

4 cups Fish Fumet (page
105), made with 2 or 3
dried hot peppers,
several coriander seeds,
and 1 cinnamon stick

Salt and ground pepper

COUSCOUS

2 ¼ cups water

¼ cup unsalted butter

1 teaspoon cinnamon

1 teaspoon salt

1 ½ cups medium-grain
couscous (we use
Ferrero)

This much-requested Square One dish evolved from a combination of recipes. It either comes from North Africa via Sicily or the other way around. At first we called it *Cuscusu Trapanese* but realized after a while that this dish was much too spicy and North African in spirit to be a true Sicilian fish couscous. Paula Wolfert suggested a compromise—a couscous from Pantelleria, an island between Sicily and North Africa. Geography may be destiny, but our customers don't seem to care what we call this fish ragout. They just keep requesting it, and we keep cooking it because we enjoy receiving compliments.

The *cuscusu* may be presented as a brothy soup with a few pieces of fish and a generous spoonful of steamed couscous, or it may be served as a fish ragout with just enough sauce to moisten the couscous and the fish. ✦ *Serves 6 to 8*

Rub all of the *charmoula* over the fish in a shallow nonaluminum container. Let marinate 2 to 4 hours in the refrigerator.

Prepare the fish soup base: Heat the olive oil in a large saucepan over medium heat. Add the onions and celery; cook covered until translucent, about 10 minutes. Add the garlic, pepper flakes, and spices; cook a few more minutes. Stir in the tomatoes and fish fumet; simmer uncovered 10 minutes. Season to taste with salt and pepper. Reheat just before serving.

Prepare the couscous: Heat the water, butter, cinnamon, and salt in a saucepan to boiling. Pour the couscous grains into a 9-inch square baking dish. Add the hot water mixture and stir once to mix well. Cover the pan with a lid or foil and let stand about 10 minutes. Break up any lumps with a fork and fluff it with your fingers. The couscous can be kept warm over hot water for several hours; fluff it with a fork occasionally.

HARISSA

**2 tablespoons cayenne
pepper**
¼ cup ground cumin
¼ cup fresh lemon juice
½ cup olive oil
**Salt and freshly ground
pepper**

For the *harissa*, mix the cayenne and cumin in a mixing bowl. Gradually whisk in the lemon juice, then the olive oil. Season with salt and pepper. This potent condiment should be used sparingly.

To bake the fish, heat the oven to 450°. Arrange the fish on a baking sheet, sprinkle with a little fish fumet, and bake until just cooked through, about 7 minutes. To poach the fish, add it to the hot soup base and simmer very gently until just cooked through, 4 to 5 minutes.

To serve, spoon the couscous into serving bowls and add the fish and soup base. Serve hot and pass the harissa.

Rape con Grelos y Almejas

CATALAN FISH RAGOUT

¼ cup olive oil

2 medium onions, diced

3 cloves garlic, finely minced

1½ teaspoons dried red pepper flakes

1 bay leaf

4 cups Fish Fumet (page 105)

Salt and freshly ground pepper

1 to 2 tablespoons fresh lemon juice (optional)

2 pounds anglerfish (monkfish), rockfish, or sea bass, trimmed and cut into 3 by 2-inch pieces

36 Manila clams, scrubbed

1 pound Swiss chard or escarole, tough stems removed, cut into fine chiffonade, rinsed well and drained

6 slices (about ½ inch) French or Italian bread, grilled or toasted, rubbed with virgin olive oil and a cut clove garlic, each slice cut into thirds

Romescu or Aioli (recipes follow)

This is one of our favorite fish ragouts, although we had a problem when we called it rape, which means anglerfish or monkfish in Spanish, on the menu. People just couldn't bring themselves to order it. Now we call it a Catalan fish ragout with clams and greens and it sells a lot better.
♦ *Serves 4*

Heat the olive oil in a deep saucepan over medium heat. Add the onions and garlic and cook a few minutes. Stir in the pepper flakes and bay leaf; cook until the onions are translucent but do not let the garlic brown. Add the fish fumet and simmer about 15 minutes. Season to taste with salt and pepper. Add the lemon juice if you want. This base can be made hours ahead and refrigerated.

To make the ragout, heat the base to simmering in a wide saucepan with a tight-fitting lid. Add the fish, clams, and greens; simmer covered until the clams open and the fish is cooked through, about 5 minutes. Ladle the ragout into bowls and top each serving with the croutons and a good dollop of *romescu* or aioli.

Aioli

2 large egg yolks

3 to 4 tablespoons fresh
  lemon juice

2 cups mild olive oil

1 tablespoon finely
  chopped garlic, rubbed
  to a very smooth paste
  with a pinch of salt

The Mediterranean solution for what goes with every-thing—almost. Serve this all-purpose spread as is or add puréed red peppers, sun-dried tomatoes, chopped herbs, or grated lemon or orange zest and you have a sauce that makes bread, fish, meat, vegetables, or your fingers taste even better. ✦ *Makes 2 cups*

Process the egg yolks in a blender or food processor until blended. Add 3 tablespoons lemon juice and blend. With the machine running, gradually add the olive oil. The sauce should be thick and emulsified. Stir in the garlic paste and remaining lemon juice to taste. If the aioli is too thick, thin it with a little hot water.

Of course, aioli can be made by hand with a whisk. It is a satisfying experience and the texture will be a little lighter if you do.

If you leave out the garlic, you have mayonnaise.

Romescu

2 cups Aioli (recipe
  precedes)

1 cup sliced almonds,
  toasted and finely
  chopped

¾ cup finely chopped
  seeded drained canned
  Italian plum tomatoes

½ to 1 teaspoon cayenne
  pepper or to taste

3 to 4 tablespoons red
  wine vinegar

2 tablespoons tomato
  puree

Salt and freshly ground
  pepper to taste

This spicy Catalan tomato-and-almond-enriched aioli can perk up a simple plate of steamed vegetables or grilled fish or meat. But if you want to know what the cooks' favorite nosh is, try this with fried potatoes. ✦ *Makes 3 cups*

Combine all ingredients.

Ameijoas na Cataplana

PORTUGUESE STEAMED
CLAMS WITH SAUSAGE

1 pound Linguisa (page
   295) or Chorizo (page
   297), prepared or
   homemade
½ cup olive oil
3 medium red onions,
   halved and thinly
   sliced
1 tablespoon paprika
1 teaspoon dried red
   pepper flakes, crushed,
   or ½ teaspoon cayenne
   pepper
3 cups diced peeled fresh
   or canned plum
   tomatoes with their
   juices
1 cup dry white wine
½ cup julienned
   prosciutto
½ cup chopped fresh
   parsley, plus additional
   for garnish
2 tablespoons finely
   minced garlic
2 bay leaves, coarsely
   crumbled
Salt and freshly ground
   pepper to taste
60 tiny Manila clams or
   36 larger clams,
   scrubbed

This dish is a specialty of the province of Alentejo. It is named after the copper cooking vessel with a hinged lid and shaped like a clamshell called a *cataplana*. We don't have this special pan, but we've found that a covered saucepan works very well. We transfer the *"cataplana"* to a pretty terra-cotta *cazuela* and serve it with rice as a sort of Portuguese paella. ◆ *Serves 6*

If the sausage is not in casings, break it up into chunks with your fingers and fry it in oil until lightly browned. If it is in casings, prick the sausages with a fork and bake in a baking pan at 400° about 20 minutes. Cut into 1-inch chunks. Drain the sausage chunks or pieces and save the fat.

Heat the olive oil and sausage fat in a large sauté pan or skillet over medium heat. Add the onions and cook until tender, about 10 minutes. Add the paprika and pepper flakes; cook a few more minutes. Add the sausage and remaining ingredients except the salt and pepper and clams. Simmer until somewhat thickened, about 5 minutes. Season to taste with salt and pepper but be careful with the salt because the clams will be steamed in the sauce and add salt too.

Just before serving, heat the sauce to boiling. Add the clams, cover the pan, and steam over medium heat until they open. Sprinkle with a little parsley and serve with steamed rice.

Fritto Misto al Mare

MIXED FRY OF FISH OR SHELLFISH

2 large eggs

2 tablespoons cold water

2 cups all-purpose flour

1 teaspoon salt

½ teaspoon freshly
   ground pepper

16 large shrimp (about 1
   pound), shelled and
   deveined

24 mussels or littleneck
   clams, scrubbed,
   steamed open in white
   wine, and removed
   from the shells

1 pound squid, cleaned
   and cut into rings,
   large tentacles halved
   (about ½ pound after
   cleaning)

½ pound bay or sea
   scallops, tough foot
   removed

1 pound sole fillets, cut in
   3 by 1-inch strips
   (optional; cut back on
   the shellfish if using)

Peanut oil for deep frying

2 lemons, cut into wedges

Agliata or Tarator Sauce
   (recipes follow on
   pages 197 and 196)

The crispness, lightness, and sheer fun of eating it all contribute to the delight of this dish. Start with the best fish and shellfish available to you. Figure on seven to eight ounces of fish and shellfish (out of the shell) per person. We like to mix shrimp, squid, mussels or clams, scallops, and occasionally sole fillets. We serve the *fritto* on a large oval plate with two big wedges of lemon and sauteed greens. We usually offer a ramekin of *Agliata* (the Renaissance saffron walnut aioli) or *Tarator* Sauce (recipes follow) for dipping the seafood, but you might prefer Red Pepper Aioli (page 183) or *Romescu* (page 193). ◆ *Serves 4*

Whisk the eggs and cold water together in a mixing bowl. Season the flour with the salt and pepper in a second bowl. Dip the shellfish and fish in batches in the egg wash, then coat them with the seasoned flour. Transfer to a strainer and shake off the excess flour.

Heat at least 3 inches peanut oil in a deep fryer or wok to 350°. Add as many pieces shellfish and fish as will comfortably fit and fry until golden. It will take just a few minutes. Do not overcook! Remove from the oil with a strainer and drain on paper towels. Transfer to warm plates and add lemon wedges and a small ramekin of *agliata* or *tarator* sauce to each plate. Serve with sauteed greens. Enjoy!

VARIATION

For Baked Fish with *Tarator* Sauce, sprinkle fish fillets, such as flounder, snapper, sea bass, or swordfish, with salt and pepper and spread with the sauce. Bake at 450° until just cooked through, 7 to 10 minutes. Garnish with parsley or cilantro and coarsely chopped nuts. Serve with roasted potatoes and zucchini, green beans, or spinach.

Tarator Sauce

1 cup shelled walnuts,
  hazelnuts, pistachios,
  almonds, or pine nuts,
  toasted
2 cloves garlic, finely
  minced
6 tablespoons tahini
  (sesame seed paste),
  stirred well
4 to 5 tablespoons fresh
  lemon juice
¼ to ½ cup cold water
  or as needed
Olive oil (optional)
Salt and freshly ground
  pepper
Cayenne pepper
  (optional)
Chopped fresh parsley or
  cilantro for garnish

This is an all-purpose Middle Eastern sauce for fish, salads, cooked vegetables, and pita bread. The Turks prefer to use walnuts and hazelnuts. The Syrians and Lebanese use pine nuts and occasionally almonds. I like it with walnuts (even though it turns a funny shade of purple), hazelnuts, pine nuts, and the less conventional pistachios. The latter is especially good with the *fritto misto* of shellfish, especially deep-fried mussels.

Tarator can be spread on fish before baking; the tahini keeps the fish very moist. One of the biggest surprises I had when travelling in the Yucatan was to find *samak tarator* on a menu in Merida. It was baked snapper with a pine nut version of this sauce. I later learned there was a large Lebanese population in Merida that had intermarried with the local Indians. This ethnic mix certainly produced some interesting cuisine. ◆ *Makes 2 cups*

Place the nuts and garlic in a food processor and pulse until combined. Add the tahini and 4 tablespoons lemon juice and puree. Mix in cold water by tablespoons until the sauce is thinned to the consistency of sour cream. You could also thin it with a little olive oil for a more spreadable consistency. Season to taste with salt and pepper. If you would like some heat, add cayenne to taste. Garnish with parsley or cilantro.

NOTE: This sauce thickens as it sits. Add additional cold water as needed to regain spoonable texture.

Agliata
(Saffron and Walnut Aioli)

4 large egg yolks, at room
  temperature

¼ cup fresh lemon juice

3 cups mild olive oil

½ cup walnuts, toasted,
  finely ground

1 piece (2 inches) fresh
  ginger, peeled and
  grated

1 to 1½ tablespoons
  saffron infusion (see
  Note)

1½ tablespoons finely
  pureed garlic

Salt and freshly ground
  pepper to taste

While doing research for a Renaissance menu for our Wednesday series of Italian menus, I came upon this sauce in *La Cucina Padovana* by Giuseppe Maffioli. It was part of a fifteenth-century menu described by the writer called *Il Ruzzante*. We love to serve this aioli as a sauce for the seafood *fritto misto*, but it is also wonderful with cooked artichokes, asparagus, cauliflower, hard-cooked eggs, and poached fish, shrimp, and chicken. ◆ *Makes 2¼ cups*

Process the egg yolks in a blender or food processor until blended. Add the lemon juice (as in other aioli) and blend. With the machine running, gradually add the olive oil. The sauce should be thick and emulsified. Stir in the remaining ingredients.

NOTE: Crush about ½ teaspoon saffron threads in a small pan. Add 2 tablespoons dry white wine and warm over low heat for a minute or two. Remove from the heat and let steep at least 10 minutes. Add this infusion gradually to the mayonnaise because saffron varies in intensity. Too much and the sauce will taste like medicine.

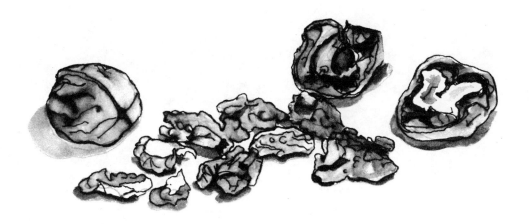

hicken can be a foil for a great variety of sauces and marinades. As a matter of fact, a mediocre chicken can be made positively brilliant by the use of a good, full-flavored marinade. Remember that most marinades should be much more intense than a sauce, for the flavor dissipates on the grill or in the sauté pan. So when you taste the marinade make sure you say "Wow! this is too strong to eat as is"; then it will be right. For chicken brochettes we prefer to use boneless thighs because they are the juiciest. We also prefer thighs for stews, ragouts, and tagines. Boneless, skinless breasts have a tendency to become dry and tough when grilled; they are best poached or sautéed.

Because chicken is so neutral in flavor, it is perhaps one of the best vehicles to convey the tastes of the Mediterranean. Chicken harmonizes well with herbs and spices, subtly absorbing the flavors conveyed by paste marinades and intense vinaigrettes. Sauces seem "clearer" with chicken because the meat is not aggressive in taste. On occasion, you might want to substitute squab just to taste the transformation of flavor as the same mari-

nades and sauces pair with the more robust and meaty squab.

A few words about duck. We serve duck the old-fashioned way, that is, cooked. We find that it tastes "duckier" that way. Rare duck is meatier in flavor, but not duckier. Most of the time we roast the whole duck and serve half per person. Squab, on the other hand, is a bird we like to serve rare or medium-rare to maximize its velvety texture. An overcooked squab is a tough little devil.

We have selected some of our favorite poultry recipes for this section. We could have included many more but then this would have been a poultry cookbook and not a rational balanced work. So here are our candidates for some of the best birds of the Mediterranean.

Grilled Chicken in an Algerian Marinade

4 cloves garlic, peeled

1 piece (2 inches) fresh ginger, peeled and sliced

2 tablespoons anise seeds, toasted and crushed

½ teaspoon saffron threads, finely chopped

2 teaspoons paprika

½ teaspoon (or to taste) cayenne pepper

⅓ cup fresh lemon juice

2 small bunches cilantro, chopped (about ⅓ cup)

6 green onions, chopped (about ⅓ cup)

1 cup mild olive oil

Freshly ground pepper

4 poussins (young chickens), about 1 pound each (see Note)

Salt

Lemon wedges for serving

The anise seeds, saffron, and cilantro make this chicken dish very aromatic. We love to serve this with couscous and Algerian Vegetable Tagine (page 313) or assorted grilled vegetables, such as eggplant, zucchini, and peppers.
♦ *Serves 4*

Process the garlic and ginger to a paste in a food processor. Add the anise, saffron, paprika, cayenne, and lemon juice and pulse to combine. Transfer the mixture to a bowl, add the chopped cilantro and green onions, and whisk in the olive oil. Season to taste with cayenne and black pepper; the marinade should be spicy!

To butterfly the poussins, insert a heavy, sharp knife at the neck cavity and carefully cut down one side of the backbone. Cut along the other side of the backbone to separate it from the body. Pull open the sides of the poussin, turn it skin side up, and press firmly on the breast with the heel of your hand to flatten it. Fold the wings back against themselves so they lie flat. Trim the excess skin at the neck end.

Place the butterflied poussins in a shallow nonaluminum container; cover with the marinade and turn the poussins to coat. Cover and refrigerate overnight.

Let the poussins warm to room temperature. Heat the grill or broiler. Remove the poussins from the marinade and reserve the marinade. Sprinkle the birds lightly with salt. Grill or broil, skin side away from the flame, about 5 minutes, basting occasionally with the marinade. Turn and continue cooking and basting until the juices run clear when the leg is pierced with a skewer and the skin is golden and slightly crisp, about 5 more minutes. Serve hot with lemon wedges.

NOTE: The marinade works equally well with half-broilers, boneless chicken thighs, and, of course, is sensational with squab. If you wish to use chicken thighs for a brochette or as part of a mixed grill, allow 3 thighs per person. If you use squab, please remember to grill them rare!

Catalan-Style Grilled Chicken

½ cup honey

¾ cup olive oil

3 tablespoons sherry vinegar

2 tablespoons cumin seeds, toasted and ground

1 tablespoon finely minced garlic

1 teaspoon freshly ground pepper

4 poussins (young chickens), about 1 pound each (see Note)

Salt

We read about this recipe for chicken marinated in honey, cumin, and vinegar in Penelope Casas's book *The Foods and Wine of Spain*. It is, of course, a classic sweet-and-sour or *agro-dolce* chicken, not dissimilar from many early Roman dishes. What makes it Spanish is the toasted cumin. Instead of brushing the sauce on the bird as it cooks, we marinate it overnight and then grill it, basting as we go. We like to serve this chicken with another Catalan-inspired dish, Baked Eggplant with Honey, Tomatoes, and Cheese (page 312), but it would be equally delicious with sautéed spinach with toasted pine nuts and raisins and little roasted or fried potatoes. ✦ *Serves 4*

Combine all ingredients except the poussins and salt in a small saucepan and warm over low heat until the honey is liquefied. Adjust the sweet-and-sour balance as brands of honey and sherry vinegar vary in intensity. Let cool.

To butterfly the poussins, insert a heavy, sharp knife at the neck cavity and carefully cut down one side of the backbone. Cut along the other side to separate it from the body. Pull open the sides of the poussin, turn it skin side up, and press firmly on the breast with the heel of your hand to flatten it. Fold the wings back against themselves so they lie flat. Trim the excess skin at the neck end.

Place the butterflied poussins in a shallow nonaluminum container; cover with the marinade and turn the poussins to coat. Cover and refrigerate overnight.

Let the poussins warm to room temperature. Heat the grill or broiler. Remove the poussins from the marinade and reserve the marinade. Sprinkle the birds lightly with salt. Broil or grill, skin side away from the flame, 5 to 6 minutes, basting occasionally with the marinade. Turn and continue cooking and basting until the juices run clear when the leg is pierced with a skewer and the skin is slightly crisp, 4 to 5 minutes longer. Do not be alarmed when the poussins turn quite dark, almost black—it is the honey caramelizing. It will taste great.

NOTE: You could use half-broilers, chicken thighs, squab, or quail, perhaps as part of a Catalan Mixed Grill (page 298).

Grilled Chicken in a Moroccan Marinade

¾ cup honey

6 tablespoons sesame seeds

1½ teaspoons cinnamon

1 teaspoon ground cumin

3 tablespoons mild olive oil

2 tablespoons fresh lemon juice

12 boneless chicken thighs, about 2½ pounds (on the bone, about 4 pounds)

Salt and freshly ground pepper

This recipe is a crossbreed. I read about it as a roast chicken basted with honey and spices and stuffed with couscous, fruits, and nuts. The toasted sesame seeds were just a garnish on top. It was delicious but we decided to try a variation for the grill. We still serve the chicken with a side dish of couscous with almonds and raisins, but the sesame seeds, honey, and spices have become ingredients in a marinade for brochettes of boneless chicken thighs. You can, of course, use this marinade for half-chickens, chicken on the bone, a butterflied whole chicken, or even squab. We have found that brochettes are the most popular. Count on three boneless thighs per person. ◆ *Serves 4*

Warm the honey in a small saucepan over medium heat until liquefied. Toast the sesame seeds in a small dry skillet over medium heat until they start to pop. Save about 2 tablespoons for garnish and grind the rest in a spice mill. Stir the ground sesame seeds, the cinnamon, cumin, oil, and lemon juice into the honey.

Place the chicken in a shallow nonaluminum container. Pour the honey mixture over the chicken and turn to coat. Cover and refrigerate overnight.

Let the chicken warm to room temperature. Heat the grill or broiler. Remove the chicken from the marinade, reserving the marinade. Thread the boneless thighs onto skewers, 3 per skewer, and sprinkle lightly with salt and pepper. Grill or broil, basting often with the marinade, until cooked through, about 4 minutes each side. Sprinkle with the reserved sesame seeds. Serve with couscous with almonds and raisins and Moroccan Carrots (page 315) or Swiss Chard Tagine (page 315).

Grilled Chicken with Piri-Piri Hot Sauce

This dish gets its name from the African hot peppers imported to Portugal during the age of exploration. This should be pretty zippy. ◆ *Serves 4*

MARINADE

1½ cups olive oil

2 tablespoons dried red pepper flakes

½ cup fresh lemon juice

4 large cloves garlic, crushed

2 teaspoons freshly ground pepper

4 poussins (young chickens), about 1 pound each (see Note)

PIRI-PIRI BUTTER

½ cup unsalted butter

1½ tablespoons finely minced garlic

¼ cup olive oil

1 tablespoon plus 2 teaspoons dried red pepper flakes

2 tablespoons (or to taste) fresh lemon juice

1 teaspoon (or to taste) salt

For the marinade, heat the oil in a small saucepan over medium heat until very hot but not boiling. Drop in a red pepper flake; if it skips to the surface of the oil and bubbles, the oil is the correct temperature. If the pepper turns brown or black, the oil is too hot and you will have to let it cool a while. If the pepper flake sinks and does not bubble, the oil is not hot enough. Keep heating and testing until you've got it right. When the oil is the correct temperature, remove it from the heat and add the remaining pepper flakes. They will sizzle and bubble on the surface of the oil a few minutes. When the action subsides and the oil turns a pale orange color, add the lemon juice, garlic, and ground pepper. Let cool completely.

To butterfly the poussins, insert a heavy, sharp knife at the neck cavity and carefully cut down one side of the backbone. Cut along the other side of the backbone to separate it from the body. Pull open the sides of the poussin, turn it skin side up and press firmly on the breast with the heel of your hand to flatten it. Fold the wings back against themselves so they lie flat. Trim the excess skin from the neck end. Place the poussins in a shallow nonaluminum container; cover with the marinade and turn the poussins to coat. Cover and refrigerate overnight.

For the butter, heat the butter with the garlic in a small saucepan over low heat until melted. Heat the olive oil until very hot (see instructions for heating in the marinade) in a small saucepan over medium heat. Remove it from the heat and add the red pepper flakes, cool for 10 minutes, then the garlic butter, then the lemon juice and salt.

Let the poussins warm to room temperature. Heat the grill or broiler. Remove the poussins from the marinade and sprinkle lightly with salt. Grill or broil skin side away from the flame 5 to 6 minutes, basting once or twice with the *piri-piri* butter. Turn and cook until the juices run clear when the leg is pierced with a skewer and the skin is golden and slightly crisp, about 5 minutes more.

Serve the poussins with the remaining butter hot in ramekins and accompany with fried potatoes and sliced tomatoes sprinkled with a little chopped mint or cilantro.

NOTE: You may also use half-broilers or chicken thighs for this dish.

*T*avuk Izgara

TURKISH-STYLE GRILLED CHICKEN WITH YOGURT AND CUMIN

2 tablespoons cumin seeds
1 small onion, coarsely chopped
4 to 6 cloves garlic, finely minced
1 tablespoon paprika
Juice of 1 lemon
1 cup plain yogurt
12 boneless chicken thighs, about 2 to 2½ pounds, or 4 half-broilers
Salt and freshly ground black pepper
Lemon wedges for serving

This is one of the easiest and tastiest grilled chicken dishes that I know. As in the Indian tandoori chicken, the yogurt in the marinade acts as a tenderizer. While you could use ground cumin, I prefer to toast the cumin seeds and grind them in a spice mill as they are more fragrant. The chicken should marinate overnight in the refrigerator or at room temperature for two to three hours. Serve with rice pilaf with pine nuts and currants and sautéed zucchini with dill and tomatoes. ◆ *Serves 4*

Toast the cumin seeds in a small sauté pan over medium heat until the seeds are fragrant and start to pop in the pan. Remove from the heat and grind in a spice mill.

Place the cumin onion, garlic, paprika, and lemon juice in a food processor or blender and pulse to liquefy. Add the yogurt and pulse just until blended.

Put the chicken thighs in a shallow nonaluminum baking dish or bowl. Pour the marinade over the chicken and toss well to coat. Let stand at room temperature at least 2 hours or cover and refrigerate overnight.

Preheat the broiler or make a charcoal fire. Thread the thighs if using on 4 skewers. Sprinkle the chicken with salt and pepper. Broil or grill until the juices run clear, about 6 minutes each side. Serve hot with lemon wedges.

NOTE: One thigh per person is ideal for a Middle Eastern mixed grill (page 299). Serve with souvlaki or a little lamb chop in a souvlaki marinade (page 272), or the pork brochette in pomegranate (page 285) or the Greek loukanika sausage (page 296).

Pollo al Pumate e Mirto

SARDINIAN-STYLE
GRILLED CHICKEN

MARINADE

2 cups olive oil

½ cup (or to taste) fresh
  lemon juice

12 bay leaves

4 large cloves garlic,
  crushed

1 tablespoon freshly
  ground pepper

20 to 24 sun-dried
  tomatoes (packed in
  oil), drained and finely
  chopped

½ cup oil from jar of
  sun-dried tomatoes

4 poussins (young
  chickens) or
  half-broilers, about 1
  pound each

8 medium or 16 small
  sun-dried tomatoes
  (packed in oil),
  drained

2 tablespoons chopped
  pitted Kalamata olives

2 tablespoons chopped
  sun-dried tomatoes
  (packed in oil)

Salt and freshly ground
  pepper

Lemon wedges for serving

This is a combination of two Sardinian chicken dishes; one, a roast chicken stuffed with giblets, sun-dried tomatoes, hard-cooked egg yolks, and cream, the other a chicken boiled with bay leaves. Both seemed a little far out for the average American (my childhood memories of boiled chicken are horrendous). So we took the sun-dried tomatoes from one recipe and the bay leaves from the other, put the chicken on the grill (most people seem to love grilled chicken), and everyone is happy. ◆ *Serves 4*

Combine all the marinade ingredients in a small saucepan and heat over medium heat until very warm; do not boil. Let cool. Reserve ½ cup for the sauce.

To butterfly the poussins, insert a heavy, sharp knife at the neck cavity and carefully cut down one side of the backbone. Cut along the other side to separate it from the body. Pull open the sides of the poussin, turn it skin side up, and press firmly on the breast with the heel of your hand to flatten it. Trim the excess skin at the neck end. Starting at the neck, gently slip your hand underneath the skin and carefully detach it from the breast meat. Slip 1 medium or 2 small tomatoes under each side of the breast skin. Fold the wings back against themselves so they lie flat.

Place the butterflied poussins in a large nonaluminum container. Pour the cooled marinade over top and turn to coat. Cover and refrigerate, turning occasionally, 2 days.

Let the poussins warm to room temperature. Heat the grill.

For the sauce, combine the reserved ½ cup marinade, the olives, and chopped sun-dried tomatoes; set aside.

Remove the poussins from the marinade, reserving the marinade, and sprinkle with salt and pepper. Grill or broil skin side away from the heat, basting often with the marinade, about 5 minutes. Turn and continue to cook until juices run clear when the thigh is pierced with a skewer and the skin is golden and slightly crispy, about 5 more minutes. Serve with the sauce and lemon wedges. Accompany with Braised Lentils with Pancetta and Aromatic Vegetables (page 151) or a dish of buckwheat ravioli filled with ricotta, goat cheese, and greens, and sauced with sun-dried tomatoes, olives, basil, and cream.

Koto Psito

GREEK-STYLE ROAST
CHICKEN

STUFFING

¾ cup dried currants
2 cups water
Salt
1 cup long-grain rice,
   preferably basmati
⅓ cup unsalted butter
1 large onion, diced
1½ teaspoons ground
   allspice
¾ cup pine nuts, toasted
2 tablespoons grated
   lemon zest (optional)
Freshly ground pepper

BASTING BUTTER

6 tablespoons unsalted
   butter
½ teaspoon ground
   allspice
2 cloves garlic, minced
3 tablespoons fresh lemon
   juice

4 Rock Cornish game
   hens, about 1½
   pounds each (see Note)

If you cook rice with sautéed onions and allspice, you have a true pilaf, but we wanted the rice to be a bit drier because this is a stuffing and the chicken gives off a lot of juice. So we cook the rice and onions separately and combine them just before stuffing the birds. ◆ *Serves 4*

For the stuffing, soak the currants in hot water to cover for 30 minutes; drain and set aside. Heat the water in a saucepan to boiling. Add 1 tablespoon salt and stir in the rice. Cover and simmer over low heat until the water has been absorbed, 15 to 20 minutes; transfer to a mixing bowl and set aside. Heat the butter in a medium sauté pan over medium heat. Add the onion and cook until tender and translucent, 8 to 10 minutes. Stir in the allspice and cook a few minutes more. Add the onion mixture, currants, pine nuts, and lemon zest if using to the cooked rice and stir to combine. Season to taste with salt and pepper. Let cool.

For the basting butter, melt the butter and stir in the allspice, garlic, and lemon juice. Season to taste with salt and pepper; set aside.

Preheat the oven to 400°. Spoon the stuffing into the cavities of the hens. Place the hens on a rack in a shallow roasting or sheet pan. Sprinkle with salt and pepper and roast, basting occasionally with the butter, until the juices run clear when the leg is pierced with a skewer, 45 to 60 minutes.

NOTE: You can also make this dish with 4 poussins or a 6-pound roasting chicken or capon.

VARIATION

Add 2 teaspoons cinnamon to the stuffing mixture and substitute almonds for the pine nuts.

Puddighinos a Pienu

SARDINIAN-STYLE
ROAST CHICKEN WITH
STUFFING

4 cups fresh bread
  crumbs
1¼ cups unsalted butter,
  melted
Salt and freshly ground
  pepper
¾ cup dry white wine
½ teaspoon saffron
  threads
¾ pound chicken
  gizzards
⅓ cup (or as needed)
  Chicken Stock
  (page 103)
2 medium onions,
  chopped
¼ cup sun-dried tomatoes
  (packed in oil),
  drained but oil
  reserved
4 Rock Cornish game
  hens, about 1½
  pounds each, or a
  6-pound roasting
  chicken or capon

We have taken to using Cornish hens for roasting instead of young poussins because we've found that the hen's skin is crisper and its meat remains moister during cooking. When roasting the birds, baste with a little of the olive oil drained from the sun-dried tomatoes. The stuffing may be made the day before. ◆ Serves 4

Preheat the oven to 400°. Toss the bread crumbs with ¾ cup melted butter and spread on a baking sheet. Toast, stirring occasionally, until lightly browned, about 20 minutes. Season with salt and pepper to taste; set aside.

Heat ¼ cup wine in a small saucepan over medium heat until warm. Remove from the heat, add the saffron, and let steep 15 minutes.

Trim the gizzards well, peeling the cartilage and tough membrane away to leave the meaty center nugget. Heat 2 tablespoons butter in a large skillet over medium heat. Add the gizzards and cook, stirring occasionally, until browned, about 8 minutes. Add the remaining ½ cup wine and the chicken stock; cover and braise over low heat until tender, about 1 hour. Remove the gizzards from the pan with a slotted spoon and coarsely chop (do not do this in a food processor); set aside. Reserve any pan juices.

Heat 6 tablespoons butter in a medium sauté pan over medium heat. Add the onions and cook until tender and translucent, 8 to 10 minutes. Add the saffron-infused wine and cook 5 minutes longer.

Preheat the oven to 400°.

Chop the tomatoes and combine in a mixing bowl with the bread crumbs, giblets and pan juices, and the onion mixture. Season the stuffing mixture to taste with salt and pepper. Let cool if necessary, then spoon the mixture into the cavities of the hens.

Place the birds on a rack in a shallow roasting or sheet pan and sprinkle with salt and pepper. Roast, basting 3 times with the oil from the sun-dried tomatoes, until the juices run clear when the thigh is pierced with a skewer, about 45 minutes. Cut the birds in half and serve with sautéed greens or green beans.

Moroccan-Style Roast Chicken Stuffed with Couscous

STUFFING

¾ cup raisins

3 tablespoons dry white wine

½ teaspoon saffron threads, chopped

1 cup instant couscous

1½ cups water

6 tablespoons unsalted butter

2 medium onions, chopped

2 teaspoons cinnamon

¾ cup sliced almonds, toasted

Salt and freshly ground pepper

1 tablespoon honey (optional)

BASTING BUTTER

⅓ cup unsalted butter

¼ cup dark honey

¾ teaspoon cinnamon

¼ teaspoon turmeric or cumin

4 Rock Cornish game hens, about 1½ pounds each, or poussins (young chickens), about 1 pound each

A flavorful and easy roast chicken. ◆ *Serves 4*

For the stuffing, soak the raisins in hot water to cover for 30 minutes; drain and set aside. Heat the wine in a small saucepan over medium heat until warm. Remove from the heat, add the saffron, and let steep 15 minutes. Put the couscous in a shallow baking dish (a 9-inch square will do fine). Heat the water and 4 tablespoons butter to boiling, then pour over the couscous and stir well. Cover with foil and let stand 15 minutes. Fluff the couscous with a fork.

Melt the remaining 2 tablespoons butter in a medium sauté pan or skillet over medium heat. Add the chopped onion and cook until tender and translucent, 8 to 10 minutes. Add the cinnamon and cook 2 minutes. Add the saffron-infused wine and cook 1 minute. Stir the onion mixture, raisins, almonds, and honey, if using, into the couscous. Season to taste with salt and pepper. Let cool.

For the basting butter, melt the butter and stir in the honey, cinnamon, and turmeric. Season to taste with salt and pepper; set aside.

Preheat the oven to 450°. Spoon the cooled stuffing into the cavities of the hens. Place the hens on a rack in a shallow roasting or sheet pan. Sprinkle with salt and pepper and roast, basting occasionally with the butter, until juices run clear when the thigh is pierced with a skewer, about 45 minutes. Serve with Swiss Chard Tagine or grilled Japanese eggplant.

Roast Chicken Stuffed with Ricotta and Pesto

We all love a roasted stuffed chicken, but another technique for stuffing that produces equally delicious results is to stuff the chicken under the skin. The bird looks plump and voluptuous and the stuffing sets up like a soufflé. It is best to use a moist "fresh" ricotta, available in cheese shops and good Italian markets, rather than supermarket ricotta, which may be heavy and compact in its container. If the latter is all that is available, sieve or whip the cheese in the processor with a little milk to lighten it. ◆ *Serves 4*

STUFFING

2 cups fresh ricotta
    cheese (see Note, page
    115)
⅓ cup Pesto (page 22)
Salt and freshly ground
    pepper

BASTING BUTTER

⅓ cup unsalted butter or
    part unsalted butter
    and part olive oil
⅓ cup Pesto (page 22)

4 Rock Cornish game
    hens, about 1½
    pounds each, or
    poussins (young
    chickens), about 1
    pound each

For the stuffing, mix the ricotta and pesto and season to taste with salt and pepper.

For the basting butter, melt the butter and stir in the pesto.

Preheat the oven to 400°. Starting at the neck end of each hen, slide your hand underneath the breast skin to loosen it, then slide your hand back to the leg and loosen the skin all the way to the drumstick. Spoon the stuffing mixture into a pastry bag fitted with a wide tip; pipe the stuffing in a ½-inch layer beneath the thigh and breast skin of the hens. If you don't have a pastry bag, you can push the stuffing in with your fingers.

Place the hens on a rack in a shallow roasting or sheet pan and sprinkle with salt and pepper. Roast, basting occasionally with the butter, until juices run clear when the leg is pierced with a skewer, about 45 minutes. (Poussin may take 35 minutes.)

VARIATION

For *Ricotta Stuffing with Prosciutto*, combine 2 cups fresh ricotta cheese, ⅓ cup diced prosciutto, 1½ teaspoons minced garlic cooked in a little olive oil, 2 tablespoons chopped fresh parsley, 1½ teaspoons chopped fresh marjoram, and salt and freshly ground pepper to taste.

Fricassee of Chicken with "Forty Cloves" of Garlic

4 heads garlic, with large
    cloves

4 to 6 thyme sprigs

2 large or 4 small bay
    leaves

Olive oil

2 large whole chicken
    breasts, split

4 chicken thighs

½ cup (or as needed)
    unsalted butter

Salt and freshly ground
    pepper

1 tablespoon chopped
    fresh sage

1 tablespoon chopped
    fresh rosemary

2 tablespoons chopped
    fresh thyme

1½ tablespoons chopped
    fresh marjoram or
    oregano

2 tablespoons chopped
    fresh parsley, plus 2
    tablespoons for garnish

1½ cups Chicken Stock
    (page 103)

Traditionally this dish is made with a whole roast chicken, baked in a sealed casserole with the garlic cloves and a bouquet garni. The chicken cooks slowly in the oven, and when the casserole is opened the wonderful aroma of the garlic permeates the air. It is really a homestyle dish and not appropriate to the busy open-line restaurant format at Square One. For years I have wanted to adapt this recipe to the constraints of the restaurant. The need for individual servings demanded that I use a poussin or chicken parts; a large roaster would result in portioning problems. But in the short time it takes to cook the little poussin, the garlic would not become sufficiently tender to spread on bread. The recipe that follows is our solution to the problem. The dish can be prepared ahead of time, in stages, and reheated at the last moment without loss of flavor or texture. ◆ *Serves 4*

Break the garlic heads into individual cloves, peel them, and put them in a small saucepan. Add the thyme sprigs, bay leaves, and enough olive oil to cover completely. Heat to a low boil. Reduce the heat to low and simmer gently until the cloves are tender but not soft, about 15 to 20 minutes. (The garlic will be cooked again with the chicken so the cloves shouldn't be too soft.)

Cut each chicken breast half crosswise in half so that there are 8 quarters. Trim the thighs of excess fat. Heat half the butter and 2 tablespoons olive oil in each of 2 large sauté pans over high heat. Sprinkle the chicken pieces with salt and pepper and brown on both sides until about halfway cooked through, about 10 minutes. Remove the chicken from the pans and pour off the fat and any badly burned bits, then return the chicken to the pans.

Remove the garlic from the oil (reserve the oil for other dishes if you like). Divide the chopped herbs and garlic between the sauté pans. Add ½ cup stock to each, cover, and cook over low heat until the chicken is tender and the garlic is meltingly soft, 15 to 20 minutes.

Remove the chicken and garlic and set aside. Combine the pan juices in one pan, add the remaining stock, and cook until slightly reduced, about 10 minutes. Season to taste

(continued)

with salt and pepper. Return the chicken and garlic to the skillet and heat through over low heat. Sprinkle with parsley and serve with lots of bread to sop up the juices and softened garlic.

NOTE: If you wish, you can refrigerate this fricassee up to 1 day. To serve, heat the sauce to simmering, add the chicken and garlic, and heat over low heat until hot.

VARIATION

Use four 1-pound poussins (young chickens) or 1½-pound Rock Cornish game hens. Brown the birds in the butter and oil in a skillet on top of the stove, then stuff with the half-cooked garlic and the herbs. Roast in a 400° oven about 30 minutes. Just before serving, quarter the birds and heat covered on top of the stove with the garlic, herbs, and chicken stock. The sauce will not have as deep a flavor as the chicken dish, but the method is less time consuming and uses less fat in the cooking. So you gain in healthfulness what you lose in complexity of flavor. You decide.

Sautéed Chicken with Moroccan Hot and Sweet Tomato Sauce

1 medium onion, chopped

2 small cloves garlic, finely minced

2 tablespoons unsalted butter

¾ teaspoon cinnamon

¼ teaspoon ground ginger

¼ teaspoon (or to taste) cayenne pepper

2 cups Tomato Sauce (page 118)

3 tablespoons dark honey

Salt and freshly ground pepper

4 whole chicken breasts, boned, skinned, and split (see Note)

3 tablespoons olive oil

Couscous (page 163)

2 tablespoons sesame seeds, toasted

2 tablespoons chopped cilantro (optional)

This is a nice variation on the old chicken and tomato sauce routine. The ingredients are familiar but there is a North African twist—the heat of cayenne and the sweetness of honey, cinnamon, and ginger. And, instead of pairing this with pasta or potatoes, we serve couscous. The sauce can be prepared ahead of time and so can the couscous. You may hold them over hot water and just sauté the chicken at the last minute. If you want to serve a vegetable accompaniment, we suggest zucchini or Swiss chard. Broiled eggplant is also harmonious with the sweet and hot flavors. ◆ *Serves 4*

Puree the onion and garlic in a food processor or blender. There should be about 1 cup.

Heat the butter in a medium saucepan over medium heat. Add the onion mixture and cook until tender, 7 to 10 minutes. Stir in the cinnamon, ginger, and cayenne; cook a few minutes more. Add the tomato sauce and honey and simmer 5 minutes. Season to taste with salt and pepper; set aside.

Sprinkle the chicken with salt and pepper. Heat the oil in 2 large sauté pans over medium heat. Add the chicken and cook until lightly browned on both sides, 6 to 8 minutes (do not overcook). Add the seasoned tomato sauce and warm over medium heat 2 to 3 minutes.

Spoon a bed of couscous on each of 4 plates. Top with 2 chicken pieces to cover the grain. Spoon the sauce over top and sprinkle with the sesame seeds and cilantro if using.

NOTE: You can also make this with thighs or bone-in breasts. Brown the chicken pieces, add about ⅓ cup stock to each pan, and cook covered until the chicken is almost done, about 10 minutes. Add the seasoned tomato sauce and simmer covered over low heat about 10 minutes longer.

*P*ollo alla Potentina

CHICKEN WITH
TOMATO SAUCE, HOT
PEPPER, AND PANCETTA

½ *cup plus 2 tablespoons
olive oil*

¾ *cup diced (½ inch)
pancetta*

4 *whole boneless, skinless
chicken breasts, split
and cut into 2-inch
pieces*

2 *cups diced onions*

2 *teaspoons (or to taste)
dried red pepper flakes*

1 *cup dry white wine*

1½ *cups Tomato Sauce
(page 118)*

½ *cup basil chiffonade*

¼ *cup finely chopped
fresh parsley*

*Salt and freshly ground
pepper*

This recipe originates in the region of Basilicata, and we can see from its name that it is very popular in Potenza. It is usually prepared with pieces of bone-in chicken, but we find that for our format it is easier and faster to cook boneless chicken breasts. So forgive us this liberty. You may cook this with chicken parts as well, but you'll have to increase the cooking time. ◆ *Serves 4*

Heat 2 tablespoons olive oil in a small sauté pan over medium heat. Add the pancetta and cook until tender but not brown and most of the fat is rendered, about 10 minutes. Remove the pancetta from the pan and reserve the fat.

Heat ½ cup oil in 2 large sauté pans over very high heat. Add the chicken pieces and cook until lightly browned on all sides but still rare in the center, about 4 minutes. Remove the chicken from the pan and set aside.

Return the pancetta fat to the pan and heat over medium heat. Add the onion and cook until nearly tender, 8 to 10 minutes. Add the pepper flakes and cook 1 minute to release their heat. Stir in the pancetta and wine; cook until the liquid is slightly reduced, about 5 minutes. Stir in the tomato sauce and add the chicken; simmer until the chicken is cooked through, 3 to 4 minutes. Add the basil and parsley for the last 2 minutes cooking time. Season with salt and pepper to taste and serve hot.

NOTE: We love to serve this with mashed potatoes, but it would be nice with pasta as well. One of my friends has requested green fettuccine, and while not authentic, it sure would be tasty!

Pollo con Carciofi

CHICKEN WITH
ARTICHOKES

8 small or 12 tiny red
    potatoes
4 cloves garlic, unpeeled
3 or 4 thyme sprigs
¾ cup olive oil
Salt and freshly ground
    pepper
4 large artichokes
Juice of 3 large lemons,
    about ⅓ cup
4 whole boneless, skinless
    chicken breasts, split
    and cut into 2-inch
    chunks
2 red onions, sliced ¼
    inch thick
½ cup julienned
    prosciutto, 2 by ¼ by
    ⅛-inch strips
½ cup Chicken Stock
    (page 103)
4 cloves garlic, minced
¼ cup Niçoise olives
¼ cup chopped fresh
    parsley

This dish from Apulia is one of our most requested recipes. Although the artichokes are a little bit of work, the results are well worth the effort. ◆ *Serves 4*

Preheat the oven to 400°.

Place the potatoes, garlic cloves, and thyme in a baking dish; rub with 2 tablespoons olive oil and sprinkle with salt and pepper. Roast until the potatoes are pierced easily with a skewer, 25 to 35 minutes. Do not overcook. Let stand until cool enough to handle, then cut them into halves or quarters, depending on the size of the potatoes.

Pull off the outside leaves of the artichokes. Using a serrated knife, cut off the top of the cone just above the choke. With a very sharp paring knife, trim off the remaining leaves. Scoop out the fuzzy chokes with a spoon, cut the hearts into sixths or eighths, and place in a bowl of cold water acidulated with 2 tablespoons lemon juice.

Heat ¼ cup olive oil in a medium sauté pan over medium heat. Dry the artichoke pieces and add to the pan. Reduce the heat and sprinkle with a tablespoon of two of lemon juice. Cook, partially covered and stirring occasionally, until tender but not mushy, 10 to 15 minutes. Season with salt and pepper.

Sprinkle the chicken pieces with salt and pepper. Heat ¼ cup olive oil in a very large sauté pan or 2 smaller pans over high heat. Add the chicken pieces and brown lightly on all sides, 3 to 4 minutes. Remove the chicken from the pan.

Heat the remaining 2 tablespoons oil in the same pan over medium heat. Add the onions and cook 5 to 7 minutes. Add the roasted potato pieces and cook, turning often, until the potatoes are browned and the onions translucent, 3 to 5 minutes. Return the chicken and artichokes to the pan and add the prosciutto, chicken stock, minced garlic, and remaining 2 tablespoons lemon juice. Cook until the liquid is slightly syrupy. Season to taste with salt and pepper and more lemon juice if you like. Sprinkle with olives and parsley. Serve hot.

VARIATION

Omit the potatoes and toss the mixture with cooked penne, rigatoni, or fettuccine.

*P*ollo con *P*umate

CHICKEN WITH
SUN-DRIED TOMATOES

¾ *cup olive oil or
combination olive oil
and oil from sun-dried
tomatoes*

⅔ *cup diced pancetta*

4 *whole boneless, skinless
chicken breasts, split
and cut into 2-inch
chunks*

*Salt and freshly ground
pepper*

2 *cups sliced (¼ inch)
red onions*

4 *heaping tablespoons
julienned sun-dried
tomatoes (packed in
oil)*

2 *tablespoons finely
minced garlic*

½ *cup Chicken Stock
(page 103)*

⅔ *cup basil chiffonade*

½ *cup Niçoise olives*

Although there is no such thing as a chicken pasta in Italy, you could turn this fast and easy sauté into a sauce for fusilli or rigatoni. Purists may serve potatoes! • *Serves 4*

Heat ¼ cup olive oil in a medium sauté pan over medium heat. Add the pancetta and cook until the fat is rendered and the pancetta is reduced in volume to ⅓ cup, 10 to 15 minutes. Remove the pancetta with a slotted spoon and set aside. Discard the fat or save it for another use.

Sprinkle the chicken with salt and pepper. Heat ¼ cup oil in a very large sauté pan over high heat. Add the chicken pieces and brown well on all sides, about 5 minutes. Remove the chicken from the pan and discard the oil.

Add the remaining ¼ cup oil to the pan and heat over medium heat. Add the onions and cook 5 minutes. Stir in the pancetta and tomatoes and cook until the onions are browned, about 4 minutes. Stir in the garlic and add the stock. Return the chicken to the pan and stir in half the basil. Cook over low heat 2 to 3 minutes, then sprinkle with the olives and remaining basil. Serve with mashed or roasted potatoes or pasta.

Kotopitta

GREEK CHICKEN PIE
WITH A FILO CRUST

12 sheets filo dough

½ cup unsalted butter,
melted

10 skinless, boneless
chicken breast halves,
about 4 ounces each

2 cups heavy cream

½ cup unsalted butter

2 medium onions, diced

4 to 6 cloves garlic,
minced

1 pound spinach, cut into
1-inch-wide chiffonade,
rinsed and drained

5 tablespoons all-purpose
flour

6 tablespoons chopped
fresh dill or 3
tablespoons dried

1 teaspoon ground
nutmeg

Salt and freshly ground
pepper

⅓ pound feta cheese,
crumbled

2 tablespoons chopped
fresh parsley or dill for
garnish

We have combined the recipe for *spanokopita* (spinach pie) and a chicken filo turnover to make a very tasty "deep-dish" chicken pie. Some versions of this recipe have you line the pie pan with filo, pour in the chicken mixture, and top with more filo. However, experience has shown us that if you assemble the pie too far ahead of time the bottom may become soggy. Therefore we assemble and bake the chicken and spinach mixture in a ramekin and bake the filo lid separately to keep it crisp. You can make this in a single unlined pie plate with a large filo lid if you don't have any individual gratin dishes. ♦ *Serves 6*

To make the filo lids, use scissors and one of six 1-cup gratin dishes as a guide to cut 24 circles (or ovals, depending on the shape of the dish) from the filo. Or make 6 large circles to fit the top of a pie dish. Brush each circle with melted butter and build 6 stacks of 4 layers each (or 1 stack of 6 large layers) on a foil- or parchment-lined baking sheet. Refrigerate until needed.

Poach the chicken breasts in a single layer in simmering water to cover until almost cooked through, about 7 minutes (or broil them 3 minutes each side). Let cool, then cut into 1-inch-wide strips.

Heat the cream to almost boiling and keep warm.

Melt ½ cup butter in a large heavy skillet over medium heat. Add the onions and sauté until translucent, 7 to 10 minutes. Add the garlic and cook 2 minutes. Add the spinach and cook, stirring often, until wilted, about 3 minutes. Add the flour and stir well to blend. Simmer 2 minutes, then add the warm cream and heat to boiling. Reduce the heat to low and stir in the dill, nutmeg, and salt and pepper to taste.

Preheat the oven to 450°. Ladle about half the spinach mixture into the 6 gratin dishes or single pie dish. Cover the mixture with chicken strips. Top with the remaining spinach mixture and sprinkle with the feta. Place the dishes or dish on a baking sheet and bake until the cheese melts and the mixture is bubbly, 5 to 7 minutes. Bake (at the same time, if you have the oven space) the filo lids or lid until golden, about 4 minutes. Top each of the dishes with a pastry lid and sprinkle with chopped parsley or dill. Serve hot.

Bastilla

MOROCCAN FILO PIE
WITH PIGEON OR
CHICKEN AND
ALMONDS

1 ½ cups slivered
blanched or sliced
almonds

2 tablespoons granulated
sugar

5 teaspoons cinnamon

2 small chickens or
squabs, about 1 ½
pounds each (see Note)

1 ¼ cups unsalted butter

1 ½ cups chopped onions

2 teaspoons ground ginger

1 teaspoon ground cumin

½ teaspoon cayenne
pepper

½ teaspoon turmeric

¼ teaspoon saffron
threads, finely
crumbled

2 tablespoons chopped
cilantro

1 tablespoon chopped
fresh parsley

1 cup water or chicken
stock

7 large eggs

Salt and freshly ground
pepper

1 pound filo dough

3 tablespoons
confectioners' sugar

I have never met anyone who didn't love *bastilla* at first bite. We have guests who ask us to call them whenever it is on the menu. Although this voluptuous pie is traditionally made with pigeon (squab), most people make it with the less expensive and more readily available chicken. If you like dark meat, by all means use the whole chicken. Most of the time we make the *bastilla* with chicken breasts which we always have on hand. The choice is yours.

The traditional pastry sheets, *ouarka,* are very time consuming to make as well as difficult, so we use filo pastry and you should too. You will also need two 14-inch pizza pans, because, although you are making only one pie, you need to turn it during baking and it is easier to turn it from one pan to another than to wrestle it from pan to baking sheet, and then hope to hit the bull's-eye when you go to turn it back into the pan. Make it easy on yourself and buy two pans—you'll use them in any case. ◆ *Serves 6 to 8 as a main course or 14 to 16 as an appetizer*

Preheat the oven to 400°. Toast the almonds on a baking sheet until golden, about 7 minutes. Coarsely chop with pulses in a food processor. Transfer to a mixing bowl and toss with the granulated sugar and 1 teaspoon cinnamon.

Cut the chickens in half down the back and breast bones. Heat ½ cup butter in a large heavy sauté pan or skillet over medium heat. Add the chickens and cook, turning often, until evenly browned, 7 to 10 minutes. Remove from the pan. Add the onions to the pan and cook over medium heat until tender and translucent. Add the ginger, cumin, cayenne, turmeric, saffron, and 2 teaspoons cinnamon; cook 5 minutes, stirring occasionally. Add the herbs and water or chicken stock, heat to boiling, and stir to blend. Return the chicken to the pan with any accumulated juices. Cover, reduce the heat to low, and simmer until the meat is tender, about 30 minutes. Transfer the chicken to a platter and let stand until cool enough to handle.

Continue to cook the onion mixture over high heat until almost dry, 15 to 20 minutes. Beat the eggs lightly and stir gradually into the hot spiced onions. Stir over very low heat until soft curds from (the mixture will resemble softly scrambled eggs). Season to taste with salt and pepper. Transfer to a bowl and let cool.

Skin and bone the birds and tear the meat into 2 by 1-inch strips. Slice the skin, if using, into strips of the same size.

Melt the remaining ¾ cup butter. Lightly butter a 14-inch pizza pan. Working with 1 sheet at a time, brush 10 sheets of filo with melted butter and arrange them in the pan, in an overlapping, circular fashion like a pinwheel, letting the edges hang over the side of the pan (butter the overhang too). Still working with 1 sheet at a time and buttering each sheet, place 2 or 3 sheets on the center. Sprinkle with half the almonds and spoon half the egg mixture over top. Distribute the meat strips evenly on the egg mixture. Spread the remaining egg mixture over the meat and sprinkle with the remaining almonds. Fold the overhanging filo over the top and brush with butter.

Now, again working with 1 filo sheet at a time and brushing each sheet with butter, arrange 12 sheets over the filling in the same pinwheel fashion. Tuck the overhanging ends under the pie. At this point you may cover the pie loosely with foil and refrigerate overnight. Do not press the foil on the buttered filo or the filo will tear when you remove the foil.

Preheat the oven to 350°. Bake the pie until pale golden in color, about 20 minutes. Carefully tilt the pan to drain the excess butter. Place a second 14-inch pizza pan over the pie and invert, turning the pie into the second pan. Return to the oven and bake until golden brown, about 25 minutes. Invert the pie again onto the original pan so that the smoother side of the filo is on top.

Mix the remaining 2 teaspoons cinnamon and the confectioner's sugar; sprinkle over the top of the pie while still warm. (You may lay a grid of paper strips over the pie to form a pattern or just sprinkle freely.)

Let the pie cool just a bit, then cut into wedges. Eat this pie Moroccan style, with your fingers, or with a fork. A salad of sliced oranges sprinkled with cinnamon-sugar is a tasty accompaniment.

NOTE: You may also use 2 whole boneless or bone-in chicken breasts, split. Cook the boneless breasts 15 minutes with the herbs and spices, bone-in breasts 30 minutes. You will need about 3 to 4 cups cooked shredded meat; exact measurements are not crucial.

Petti di Pollo Trifolati

SAUTÉED CHICKEN
BREASTS WITH PORCINI
MUSHROOMS

½ cup dried porcini
mushrooms

1 cup hot water

½ cup all-purpose flour

Salt and freshly ground
pepper

4 whole boneless, skinless
chicken breasts, split

½ cup clarified butter
(see Note, page 26)

⅓ cup cognac

2½ cups heavy cream

⅓ pound sliced (⅛ inch
thick) prosciutto, cut
into 2 by ¼-inch
julienne strips

¼ cup chopped fresh
parsley

This recipe is so easy, I wondered if anyone really needed to be told how to cook it. But often in the world of cooking, which has now achieved glamour status and a certain mystique, when things appear so simple, people look for hidden tricks and inner complexities that don't really exist. Well, there's nothing up my sleeve! Just follow the minimal directions, and you will enjoy this sautéed chicken dish which originates in the province of Umbria, land of truffles and wild mushrooms. ◆ *Serves 4*

Rinse the mushrooms well and soak in the hot water 30 to 60 minutes. Drain and chop the mushrooms. Strain and reserve the soaking liquid.

Season the flour with salt and pepper and coat the chicken breasts with the seasoned flour. Heat the butter in a large sauté pan over medium-high heat. Add the chicken and sauté until golden brown, about 3 minutes each side. Remove the chicken to a warm platter and cover with foil.

Pour the cognac into the pan and heat, scraping loose the browned bits on the bottom. Add the porcini soaking liquid and cream; cook over high heat until slightly thickened, 5 to 8 minutes. Stir in the chopped porcini and prociutto; and simmer over low heat 1 to 2 minutes. Season to taste with salt and pepper. Return the chicken to the pan and heat through, 1 to 2 minutes. Sprinkle with parsley and serve with sautéed green beans or a julienne of carrots, zucchini, and onions. This is also delicious accompanied with fresh fettuccine tossed with julienned zucchini and peas if they are in season.

NOTE: In Italy main courses are rarely if ever accompanied with a pasta side dish. Pasta is usually the first course. But we Americans are used to having a complete plate with starch, vegetables, and protein. Most of our customers love this with fettuccine; it is delicious but not authentic!

Catalan-Style Grilled Quail Stuffed with Figs

8 boneless quail

8 fresh large black or Adriatic figs, or 16 dried Black Mission figs, soaked 1 hour in ¼ cup brandy and hot water to cover

16 grape leaves, rinsed, patted dry, and stems removed

8 long thin strips pancetta (about 4 ounces)

8 to 12 small leeks

Salt

16 small red potatoes

½ cup (or as needed) olive oil

Freshly ground pepper

2 cups Romescu Sauce (page 193), chilled

8 Chorizo links (about 4 ounces each), prepared or homemade (page 297)

We serve these as part of the Catalan Mixed Grill (page 298) accompanied by grilled Chorizo (page 297) or *Linguisa* (page 295), grilled leeks, fried potatoes, and *Romescu* Sauce (page 193). If fresh figs are not available, use plumped dried Black Mission figs instead. ♦ *Serves 4*

Stuff each quail with a fresh fig or 2 dried figs. (There is no need to skewer the quail closed.) Wrap each quail in 2 grape leaves, then again in a strip of pancetta. (The quail can be stuffed and wrapped well ahead of time and refrigerated up to 1 day.)

Trim the root end and most of the green tops from the leeks, leaving the root end intact. Split the leeks down the middle but do not cut entirely through the root ends. Rinse the leeks very well in a sink full of water to remove any sand. Blanch in a large pot of simmering salted water until tender, 5 to 8 minutes. When you squeeze the root end, it should crack a bit. Refresh in cold water and drain well.

Heat the oven to 350°. Rub the potatoes with 2 to 3 tablespoons olive oil. Place them on a baking sheet and sprinkle lightly with salt and pepper. Bake until tender, about 25 to 35 minutes. Cut in half and set aside.

Let the quail and chorizo warm to room temperature. Heat the broiler or grill. Brush the wrapped quail with olive oil and sprinkle lightly with pepper.

Grill the sausages, turning occasionally, 7 to 8 minutes. Grill the quail, turning as needed, until medium rare to medium, about 5 minutes. Brush the leeks and potatoes with oil and grill until heated through and marked, about 2 minutes each side.

Divide the *romescu* among 4 ramekins. Divide the quail, sausages, and vegetables among 4 serving plates; accompany with the sauce.

Moroccan Fried Squab with Saffron and Ginger

4 squabs, about 1 pound each

MARINADE

Scant ½ teaspoon saffron threads

2 tablespoons dry white wine, warmed

1 cup mild olive oil

6 tablespoons fresh lemon juice

4 teaspoons ground ginger

2 teaspoons freshly ground pepper

The original recipe for this dish did not call for a marinade, but we find that it adds a depth of flavor to the flesh of the squab that the sauce can only add to the surface. Marinate the squab overnight, if possible. The sauce can be made ahead of time and reheated. The Moroccans partially braise the squab in the sauce, then remove the birds and deep-fry them. As this is a little messy and there is a danger of overcooking the squab, we deep-fry the squab separately and then top with the sauce. It is cleaner in technique, and the bird stays moist and properly rare. You may also grill, broil, or saute the squab. ◆ *Serves 4*

Remove the heads and feet from the squab. To butterfly, insert a sharp knife at the neck cavity of each bird and carefully cut down one side of the backbone. Cut along the other side of the backbone to separate it from the body. Remove the breastbone, central cartilage, and ribs.

For the marinade, steep the saffron in the wine about 15 minutes. Combine with the remaining marinade ingredients in a shallow nonaluminum container. Turn the squab in the marinade, cover, and refrigerate overnight.

Prepare the sauce: Steep the saffron in the wine about 15 minutes. Heat the butter in a medium sauté or sauce pan over medium heat. Add the onion and cook until tender and translucent, about 10 minutes. Add the ginger and garlic and cook 2 to 3 minutes longer. Stir in the saffron infusion, cilantro, salt, and pepper. Add the chicken stock, heat to simmering, and simmer 5 minutes. Stir in the lemon juice and taste and adjust the seasoning.

SAUCE

½ teaspoon saffron
   threads

2 tablespoons dry white
   wine, warmed

3 tablespoons unsalted
   butter

1 cup diced onion

3 tablespoons grated fresh
   ginger

1 tablespoon minced
   garlic

3 tablespoons chopped
   cilantro

½ teaspoon salt

1¼ teaspoons freshly
   ground pepper

1 cup Chicken Stock
   (page 103)

1 tablespoon fresh lemon
   juice

Peanut oil for deep-frying

1½ cups all-purpose
   flour

1 teaspoon ground ginger

Salt and freshly ground
   pepper

2 large eggs

2 tablespoons cold water

Heat enough oil to cover the squab in a deep fryer to 350°
(see Note). Mix the flour, ginger, and salt and pepper to
taste. Lightly beat the eggs with the water in a shallow
bowl. Remove the squab from the marinade; dip in the egg
wash to coat and then in the seasoned flour. Deep-fry until
golden, about 5 minutes. Serve with the sauce and saf-
fron-flavored couscous.

NOTE: You can also simply season the squab with salt and
pepper and grill or broil them 3 to 4 minutes each side.
Top with the warmed sauce and serve. Or, sauté in 2
tablespoons each butter and oil over high heat about 3
minutes each side. Add the sauce to the pan and cook over
high heat until warmed through.

Roast Duck with Honey, Lavender, and Thyme

¾ cup lavender honey
  (see Note 1)

2 cups Duck Stock
  (recipe follows; see
  Note 2)

¾ teaspoon chopped
  fresh thyme

2 teaspoons red wine
  vinegar (optional)

Salt and freshly ground
  pepper

2 ducks, about 5 pounds
  each, necks and wing
  tips removed, excess fat
  removed, and rendered
  if desired (see Note 3)

2 sprigs fresh thyme

2 sprigs fresh lavender or
  2 teaspoons dried

This recipe, inspired by Alain Senderens but with many liberties taken, is among our favorites for duck. It evolved as I was planning a special Provençal menu featuring duck and was considering the aromatic herbs of the region. That same day, as I was picking up flowers for the restaurant, I noticed that our florist had lavender blossoms for sale. They smelled so wonderful that I decided then to use lavender with the duck. ✦ *Serves 4*

Combine the honey, duck stock, and chopped thyme in a small saucepan. Heat to boiling, then reduce the heat and simmer 5 minutes. Season with the vinegar if using and salt and pepper to taste.

Preheat the oven to 500°. Place the ducks on racks in shallow roasting pans. Place 1 sprig each thyme and lavender (or replace the fresh lavender with a scant teaspoon dried) in the cavity of each duck. Sprinkle the ducks inside and out with salt and pepper. Roast until fully cooked and tender, about 1 hour, basting with the honey mixture for the last 5 minutes of roasting.

Cut the ducks into quarters and arrange 2 quarters on each of 4 serving plates (see Note 4). Warm the honey mixture and spoon over the duck. The ideal accompaniment is little potatoes roasted in the rendered duck fat and blanched carrots sautéed in butter and sprinkled with parsley.

NOTE 1: If you cannot find lavender honey, use regular honey, and make a lavender tea by steeping lavender blossoms or dried lavender in some hot duck stock. NOTE 2: Chicken stock simmered with the necks and wings of the ducks for 2 hours can be substituted for the duck stock. NOTE 3: To render duck fat, pull all the loose fat from the duck and cut it into small pieces. Put it in a saucepan and add a few tablespoons of water. Simmer over low heat about an hour, then strain and cool. Store in a covered container in the refrigerator up to 3 months or in the freezer even longer. NOTE 4: You may roast and quarter the ducks ahead of time and set them aside at room temperature for a few hours. Reheat them in a 400° oven for 5 minutes. The sauce may be set aside at room temperature or refrigerated and reheated just before serving. If you make roasted potatoes, they also may be reheated in the oven or in a sauté pan with a little duck fat.

Duck Stock

♦ *Makes about 2 quarts*

**Carcasses, necks, wings,
and feet of 4 ducks**
2 onions, chopped
2 leeks, chopped
6 cloves garlic, smashed
**12 black peppercorns,
bruised**
8 sprigs fresh parsley
3 sprigs fresh thyme
1 bay leaf

Preheat the oven to 450°. Break up the duck carcasses and place them with the necks, wings, and feet in a roasting pan. Roast until browned, about 30 minutes. Using a slotted spoon, transfer the duck parts to a stockpot, add enough cold water to cover, and heat to boiling. Skim the scum from the surface. Reduce the heat and simmer uncovered.

Meanwhile, pour off most of the fat in the roasting pan. Add the onions, leeks, and garlic to the pan and roast until browned, about 30 minutes. Add the vegetables to the pot. Pour ¼ to ½ cup water to the roasting pan, heat, scraping up the browned bits on the bottom, and add it to the pot. Add the peppercorns and herbs. Simmer uncovered 4 to 6 hours.

Strain the stock and chill, then remove the fat from the surface. Boil until reduced by about half. This stock can be stored in the refrigerator up to 1 week or in the freezer up to 6 months.

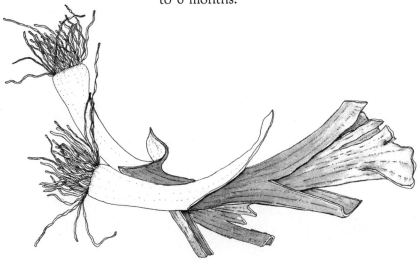

Pato con Peras

CATALAN-STYLE DUCK WITH PEARS AND ALMONDS

PEARS

1 ½ cups sugar

1 ½ cups water

1 small cinnamon stick, broken in pieces

2 cloves

4 thick slices lemon

2 French butter, D'anjou, or other pears for poaching, peeled, cored, and halved

2 tablespoons minced garlic

2 tablespoons chopped fresh thyme

2 teaspoons cinnamon

2 tablespoons brandy

2 ducks, about 5 pounds each, necks and wing tips removed, excess fat removed, and rendered if desired (see Note 3, page 224)

Salt and freshly ground pepper

This Catalan classic is usually made with goose. Some versions call for sherry instead of brandy, some use tomatoes, and others use pine nuts in the *picada* (the Catalan "final touch") instead of almonds. I have added a little lemon to the pear poaching syrup and used some of the syrup with the sliced pears in the sauce, rather than using the pears strictly as garnish as in the original recipe.
♦ *Serves 4*

Poach the pears: Combine the sugar, water, spices, and lemon slices in a saucepan. Boil 5 minutes. Add the pear halves, reduce the heat to low, and simmer until the pears are translucent and cooked through but not mushy, about 25 minutes. Remove the pears from the syrup with a slotted spoon; let cool. Reserve about ¼ cup syrup. Cut the cooled pear halves lengthwise into 4 thick slices; set aside.

Preheat the oven to 500°. Make a paste with a mortar and pestle of the garlic, thyme, cinnamon, and brandy; rub it into the cavity of each duck. Place the ducks on racks in shallow roasting pans. Sprinkle with salt and pepper inside and out and roast until tender, about 1 hour. Let stand until cool enough to handle.

SAUCE

3 tablespoons unsalted
   butter

¾ scant cup diced onion

¼ cup diced carrot

¼ cup diced celery

2 teaspoons finely minced
   garlic

1 teaspoon chopped fresh
   thyme

2 tablespoons brandy

⅔ cup Duck Stock (page
   225); see Note 2, page
   224

⅓ cup sliced almonds,
   toasted and chopped

2 tablespoons (or to taste)
   reserved pear syrup

Meanwhile, prepare the sauce: Heat the butter in a large
sauté pan or skillet over medium heat. Add the onion,
carrot, and celery; cook until tender, about 10 minutes.
Add the garlic and thyme and cook 1 minute. Add the
brandy and simmer 1 to 2 minutes. Add the stock and
almonds and simmer until slightly thickened, about 15
minutes. Stir in 2 tablespoons reserved pear syrup; taste
and add more if desired. Season to taste with salt and
pepper.

Cut the duck into quarters (or eighths if you prefer) and
warm in a 400° oven about 5 minutes. Heat the sauce to
simmering over medium heat, add the pear slices, and
simmer until heated through. Arrange 2 duck quarters on
each of 4 serving plates and spoon the sauce and pears over
top. Serve with roasted potatoes and sautéed spinach with
pine nuts and raisins.

Anitra con le Lenticchie

DUCK WITH LENTILS

2 ducks, about 5 pounds
   each, necks and wing
   tips removed, excess fat
   removed, and rendered
   if desired (see Note 3,
   page 224)

2 sprigs thyme

4 cloves garlic, finely
   minced

4 tablespoons grated
   orange zest (optional)

Salt and freshly ground
   pepper

Braised Lentils with
   Pancetta and Aromatic
   Vegetables (page 151)

2 sprigs fresh thyme,
   chopped, for garnish

One of the simplest duck recipes but one of the best. This
is from the region of Pavia. ◆ Serves 4

Preheat the oven to 450° to 500°. Place the ducks on racks
in shallow roasting pans. Place 1 sprig thyme in the cavity
of each duck. Make a paste with a mortar and pestle of the
garlic, orange zest if using, and 2 teaspoons each salt and
pepper. Rub the paste over the skin of the ducks. Roast
until tender, about 1 hour. Let stand until cool enough to
handle.

Cut the ducks into quarters and put them in a large saucepan or casserole with the lentils. Cover and heat over low
heat on top of the stove or in a 350° oven until warmed
through, about 15 minutes.

Place 2 duck quarters and a serving of lentils on each of
4 serving plates. Sprinkle with the chopped thyme and
serve hot. Follow with a simple green salad.

Anitra in Porchetta

ROAST DUCK IN THE
MANNER OF
SUCKLING PIG

2 ducks, about 5 pounds
  each, necks and wing
  tips removed, excess fat
  removed, and rendered,
  if desired (see Note 3,
  page 224)
Fresh rosemary sprigs
Fresh sage leaves
Salt and freshly ground
  pepper
2 tablespoons olive oil
1 pound fennel sausage,
  prepared or homemade
  (page 294), casings
  removed if necessary
  and crumbled
1¼ cups finely chopped
  onions
⅔ cups finely chopped
  carrots
½ cup finely chopped
  celery
3 tablespoons chopped
  fresh sage
4 to 5 tablespoons
  chopped fresh rosemary
1½ cups Beef or Duck
  Stock (page 104 or
  225)
⅓ cup sweet vermouth

This recipe came about because we were planning a menu in honor of Giuliano Bugialli and wanted to cook some of our favorite dishes inspired by his books. Given the volume and pace of our open line, we could not prepare his duck stuffed with sausage and serve it perfectly. So, as a compromise, we decided to keep the taste of the recipe by putting the sausage into a robust sauce. That way we could cook the ducks and portion them, cook the sauce separately, and we would not have to reheat the stuffing which might then dry out. To attain a looser, more saucelike consistency, we used beef stock and chose sweet vermouth because of its herbaceous quality. By the way, Giuliano liked it! ◆ *Serves 4*

Preheat the oven to 500°. Place the ducks on racks in shallow roasting pans. Place a few sprigs rosemary and a few sage leaves inside each cavity. Sprinkle the ducks inside and out with salt and pepper and roast until tender, about 1 hour. Let stand until cool enough to handle.

Meanwhile, heat the olive oil in a large sauté pan over high heat. Add the sausage and cook until well browned, about 5 minutes. Remove the sausage with a slotted spoon. Add the vegetables to the pan and cook over low heat until tender, 10 to 15 minutes. Return the sausage to the pan and add the chopped herbs; cook 5 minutes. Add the stock and vermouth and cook until the sauce is slightly thickened, about 20 minutes. Season to taste with salt and lots of black pepper (the sauce should be zippy).

Cut the ducks into quarters (or eighths if you prefer) and warm in a 400° oven for 5 minutes. Heat the sausage mixture to simmering. Place 2 duck quarters on each of 4 serving plates and spoon the sausage mixture over top.

NOTE: We usually serve the duck with an accompaniment of sautéed greens to cut the richness but also with a small portion of polenta or *farfalle*. I know, it's too much . . . but it's too good to pass up. This is not a diet plate. It is rich and voluptuous. So why cut corners now?

Duck with Port, Prunes, and Pearl Onions

1 ½ tablespoons minced garlic

2 teaspoons cinnamon

2 tablespoons fresh lemon juice

2 ducks, about 5 pounds each, necks and wing tips removed, excess fat removed, and rendered if desired (see Note 3, page 224)

Salt and freshly ground pepper

24 pearl onions

3 tablespoons butter (optional)

2 tablespoons sugar (optional)

24 pitted prunes, or more if you love them

2 cups port, preferably Ficklin or Quady

⅔ cup Duck or Chicken Stock (page 225 or 103), reduced to ⅓ cup

¼ cup fresh orange juice

1 teaspoon grated orange zest

I find the colors of this dish very pretty: the rich red of the port, the deep blackish purple of the prunes, and the golden brown of the caramelized onions remind me of autumn. Serve this with roasted potatoes and sautéed Swiss chard. ◆ *Serves 4*

Preheat the oven to 500°. Make a paste with a mortar and pestle of the garlic, cinnamon, and lemon juice; rub it in the cavities of the ducks. Place the ducks on racks in shallow roasting pans. Sprinkle inside and out with salt and pepper and roast until tender, about 1 hour. Let stand until cool enough to handle.

Meanwhile, peel the onions and trim the root ends carefully, leaving the ends intact. Cut an X in each root end so that the onions don't telescope when cooked. Simmer the onions in a large pot of salted water until tender but not mushy, 5 to 7 minutes; drain. If you like, sauté them in the butter and sugar until glazed to a rich brown color.

Put the prunes in a small saucepan, add ½ cup port, and heat to simmering over medium heat. Remove the prunes from the heat and let stand until plump, about 10 minutes.

Pour the remaining port into a small saucepan. Boil over medium heat until reduced to ½ cup. Add the reduced stock, the orange juice and zest, and remaining ¼ teaspoon cinnamon. Simmer several minutes and season to taste with salt and pepper. Stir in the prunes in port and the onions.

Cut the ducks into quarters and warm in a 400° oven about 5 minutes. Heat the sauce to simmering. Arrange 2 duck quarters on each of 4 serving plates and spoon the sauce over top.

Roast Duck with Red Wine, Orange, and Sage Sauce

2 ducks, about 5 pounds each, necks and wing tips removed, excess fat removed, and rendered, if desired (see Note 3, page 224)

2 orange halves

Fresh sage leaves

Salt and freshly ground pepper

SAUCE

1 tablespoon unsalted butter or rendered duck fat

1/3 cup diced onion

2 tablespoons (or to taste) chopped fresh sage

1 tablespoon (or to taste) grated orange zest

2 cups red wine, such as Zinfandel or Côtes du Rhône

2 cups Duck Stock (page 225); see Note 2, page 224

1/3 cup fresh orange juice

9 Kalamata olives, pitted and quartered

Pinch sugar (optional)

This recipe could be Italian, from the province of Umbria, or it could be French, from Provence. The theme of olives, wine, and herbs is a Mediterranean classic. You can choose the country of origin with the accompaniments you serve with it. ◆ *Serves 4*

Preheat the oven to 500°. Place the ducks on racks in shallow roasting pans. Place 1 orange half and a few sage leaves in the cavity of each duck. Sprinkle the ducks inside and out with salt and pepper and roast until tender, about 1 hour. Let stand until cool enough to handle.

Meanwhile, prepare the sauce: Heat the butter in a large sauté pan over low heat. Add the onion, sage, and orange zest; cook until the onion is tender, 7 to 10 minutes. Put the wine and the stock in 2 medium saucepans and reduce each by one third over medium heat. Add both to the pan with the onion mixture and simmer over medium heat until the mixture is reduced by one third, about 20 minutes. Strain into a clean saucepan. Add the orange juice, heat to simmering, and simmer 5 minutes over low heat. Add the olives and simmer 2 minutes. Taste and add more orange or sage if you like. You will probably not need more salt because of the olives, but you may want to add the pinch of sugar if the sauce is too tart.

Cut the ducks into quarters (or eighths, if you prefer) and warm in a 400° oven for 5 minutes. Heat the sauce to simmering. Arrange 2 quarters on each of 4 serving plates and spoon the sauce over top.

NOTE: For an Italian touch we serve this dish with black pepper fettucine with greens and green beans. Black pepper ravioli filled with greens would also be nice but more work. (They do serve pasta in Provence, by the way.) If you are pressed for time, you may serve this simply with sautéed greens and roasted potatoes and enjoy it too.

Grilled Quail Stuffed with Honeyed Onions

¼ cup raisins

2 tablespoons unsalted butter

2 cups diced onions

½ teaspoon plus pinch cinnamon

4 tablespoons honey

Salt and freshly ground pepper

4 boneless quail

1 tablespoon water

We usually serve one of these little stuffed quail as a part of our Moroccan Mixed Grill (page 298), which also includes *Qodban* (page 270) and *Merguez* (page 290). There is no reason, however, you couldn't make a dinner of two quail, accompanied by couscous seasoned with a little cinnamon and a vegetable tagine. ◆ *Makes 4*

Soak the raisins in hot water to cover until plump, about 30 minutes.

Melt the butter in a medium sauté pan or skillet over medium heat. Add the onions and cook until tender and sweet, 10 to 15 minutes. Add ½ teaspoon cinnamon and 2 tablespoons honey and stir over low heat 1 to 2 minutes. Drain the raisins and stir into the honey mixture. Season to taste with salt and pepper. Let cool.

Heat the grill or broiler. Spoon the onion mixture into the cavities of the quail. Skewer the neck and tail openings closed with toothpicks. Thin the remaining honey with the water and season with a pinch of cinnamon and salt and pepper to taste. Brush the quail with the honey mixture and grill or broil, basting occasionally, until medium rare to medium, about 3 minutes each side. Remove the toothpicks and serve the quail.

MEATS

The reason that the Mediterranean diet is so healthy is that meat portions are not the mammoth Paul Bunyanesque servings that we Americans have come to equate with value. A "steak as big as the plate," our typical portion for one, could feed an Italian family for a week. I remember the first time I bought two American-sized steaks from my Roman butcher; he could not believe that they were for just two people. Naturally he looked forward to the repeat business of the crazy American *signora*. To his disappointment, I gradually became converted to pasta as a *primo,* or first course, and a small meat or fish dish as a *secondo.* Upon returning to America I stuck with this moderate eating style and stayed within my household budget as well!

So, while this book offers many excellent meat recipes, the portions are not Texan. Beef, moreover, is not as popular in the Mediterranean as it is in the United States; lamb, pork, and veal are much more readily available. But the lamb is smaller than ours: little lamb rib chops are tiny, a bite per chop, and the leg is about two pounds as opposed to our five- or six-

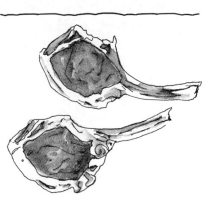

pounders. Pork is leaner and sweeter, also smaller. I have tried to walk a fine line between "normal" American appetite and habit, and what I see as the more balanced Mediterranean diet. Perhaps Americans can learn to eat meat entrées less often or in smaller portions so that we may be hungry for interesting salads and appetizers. Or maybe just eat a little meat in a pasta sauce. Every bite is more delicious and precious because there is less of it. Quality and moderation instead of overkill.

I know that we are all fanatic about trimming excess fat from meat and I agree in principle. However, a lean steak is much less flavorful than one which is well marbled with fat. And it is really hard to make a good stew with lean beef—all you get is strings. Even pork needs a little marbling so that the meat is basted from within. So, in response to the health question, why not eat meat less often and when you do eat it, eat the good stuff!

Some general pointers: We sometimes suggest pasta, polenta, potatoes, or couscous as an accompaniment. If you want to eat less meat, you might want to increase the pasta and polenta and reduce the meat serving . . . sort of a glorified pasta. Most stews benefit from being made a day ahead, so that the flavors have a chance to develop. Marinades are crucial in many of the recipes. They will elevate the dish from nice to wonderful because they act as flavor intensifiers. Years ago, due to fear of trichinosis, cookbooks recommended that pork be cooked to an internal temperature of 160°. So pork was always cooked until it was pale and dry. Fortunately, recent tests have proven that the trichina bacteria is killed at 138°, and thus we recommend cooking pork to 140°, at which point it will still be moist and juicy. So, put your fears to rest and enjoy!

VEAL

Ossobuco alla Reggiana

BRAISED VEAL SHANKS

½ cup olive oil

6 veal shanks, about 1½ pounds each, each sawed crosswise into 2 pieces

½ cup unsalted butter

3 medium onions, diced

2 pounds mushrooms, sliced ¼ inch thick

2 cups dry white wine (see Note)

2 cups dry Marsala

4 cups Beef Stock (page 104)

4 cups diced canned plum tomatoes

Salt and freshly ground pepper

The classic *ossobuco alla Milanese,* garnished with *gremolata* and served with saffron risotto, is hard to beat. But this *ossobuco* is a pleasant change of pace. The mushrooms release their juices into the sauce and the wine adds depth of flavor. ◆ *Serves* 6

Heat the oil in a large heavy sauté pan over high heat. Add as many shanks as will comfortably fit and brown on all sides. Transfer to a deep wide baking dish or roasting pan with a lid or a Dutch oven. Repeat with the remaining shanks.

Heat half the butter in another sauté pan over medium heat. Add the onions and cook until translucent, about 10 minutes; transfer to the dish with the shanks.

Heat the remaining butter in the same pan over high heat. Add the mushrooms and sauté until browned, about 3 minutes; transfer to the dish with the shanks. Add the wine, Marsala, stock, and tomatoes to the dish. Cover and braise over very low heat until the shanks are very tender, about 1½ hours (or braise in a 350° oven). Season to taste with salt and pepper and serve hot with risotto.

NOTE: You may omit the wine and substitute 2 more cups Marsala if you like.

Rolle di Vitello

BRAISED STUFFED LEG
OF VEAL

1 leg of veal, boned and
   butterflied, about 4
   pounds

6 slices prosciutto (not
   too thin)

6 slices mortadella
   (optional)

1 tablespoon chopped
   plus 3 branches fresh
   rosemary

2 teaspoons freshly grated
   nutmeg

2 to 3 medium cloves
   garlic, slivered

Salt and freshly ground
   pepper

2 tablespoons each
   unsalted butter and
   olive oil or ¼ cup
   olive oil

2 large onions, cut into
   ¼-inch dice (2½ to 3
   cups)

6 carrots, cut into ¼-inch
   dice (about ¾ cup)

4 ribs celery, cut into
   ¼-inch dice (about ¾
   cup)

1½ cups (or as needed)
   dry white wine

2 cups (or as needed)
   Chicken Stock (page
   103) or Veal Stock
   (recipe follows)

Our apartment in Rome had no refrigerator, just an ice box. As a result I marketed daily and tried to use everything as quickly as possible. Fortunately my neighborhood was wonderful for shopping. Across the street was a huge enclosed market that sold vegetables, flowers, herbs, and fish. The lamb and poultry and pork butchers were nearby, as was the formidable beef and veal butcher. Somewhat beefy himself, he stood very tall and round on a marble platform, bellowing in Roman dialect to all who entered or strolled past his shop. He taught me to plan my weekly menus in conjunction with his delivery schedule. I bought veal liver and sweetbreads on Monday when he received his delivery of two large steer and four calves. By the middle of the week we had worked our way down to the filets, steaks, and roasts, and at the end of the week there was his special leg of veal, rolled, tied and bedecked with rosemary branches, prominently displayed in the window. I first prepared his *rolle*, as he called it, as a novice cook, expecting friends on a Saturday. I asked his advice on how to cook it and went to work. No need to worry about storing leftovers—the veal was so delicious we demolished it in one sitting.

Before returning to the States I begged a demonstration from him on how to roll and stuff the leg myself. Years later, when researching some menus for the restaurant's Wednesday series on Italian regional cuisine, I discovered that this was not after all a Roman dish but a specialty of Piemonte. Yet my old butcher's personality is so firmly stamped in my memory that whenever we cook his *rolle* I think of Rome. ✦ *Serves 6 to 8*

Lay the veal leg on a cutting board, boned side up, and remove most of the gristle, tendons, and excess fat. Cover the meat with a single layer of prosciutto slices and then a second layer of mortadella slices, if using. Sprinkle with the chopped rosemary and 1½ teaspoons nutmeg. Roll the leg and tie with kitchen string. Make shallow incisions in the veal and insert the garlic slivers. Tuck the rosemary branches underneath the string in 3 places, and sprinkle with ½ teaspoon nutmeg and salt and pepper to taste.

Heat the butter and oil in a Dutch oven over high heat. Add the veal and brown on all sides, 8 to 10 minutes. Add the diced vegetables, wine, and stock to cover the roast by three-quarters. (The exact amount of liquid depends on the dimensions of your pan.) Heat to boiling, reduce the heat to low, and simmer covered until a meat thermometer inserted in the veal reads 135° to 140°, about 1 1/4 hours.

Transfer the veal to a cutting board; let rest 10 minutes. Remove the string and slice. Serve the veal with the braising juices and cooked vegetables on top of a bed of Rosemary Fettuccine (page 113). Warm any leftover slices in the leftover braising juices in a wide sauté pan over low heat.

Veal Stock

8 pounds veal shanks, bones, and any meat trimmings

1 to 2 tablespoons olive oil if needed

3 tablespoons chicken fat or butter

2 medium onions, coarsely chopped

2 carrots, coarsely chopped

1 leek, sliced (optional)

1 rib celery, coarsely chopped

5 sprigs parsley

2 small bay leaves

Several sprigs fresh thyme

2 cloves

6 peppercorns

♦ *Makes 6 to 8 quarts*

Preheat the oven to 450°. Crack the veal bones and place in a large roasting pan (see Note). Add trimmings if using with the olive oil so they don't stick. Roast until browned but not scorched. Transfer the bones and trimmings to a large stockpot. Cover with cold water and boil a few minutes. Pour off the water and scum, then cover with fresh cold water. Deglaze the roasting pan with a little water and add it to the pot. Heat to boiling, then reduce the heat and simmer uncovered about 1 hour.

Meanwhile, heat the chicken fat or butter in a sauté pan or skillet over medium-high heat. Add the vegetables and cook until tender and caramelized. Add the vegetables to the stockpot. Deglaze the pan with a little water and add it to the pot as well. Add the herbs and spices. Simmer uncovered, skimming occasionally, 6 hours.

Remove the solids from the pot with a slotted spoon or skimmer. Strain the stock through a cheesecloth-lined strainer. Let cool completely, then refrigerate until cold. Remove the layer of fat from the top of the stock. For a more intense stock, boil until reduced to the intensity you want.

NOTE: We usually make this brown veal stock at the restaurant because we prefer the intensity of flavor, but you can omit the roasting step and simply put the bones and trimmings in the stockpot.

Costata di Vitello al Sugo di Porcini

GRILLED VEAL CHOPS
WITH WILD MUSHROOM
SAUCE

2 cups dried porcini
   mushrooms
½ cup unsalted butter
2 medium onions, finely
   chopped
2 small ribs celery, very
   finely chopped
1 small carrot, very finely
   chopped
2 to 3 large cloves garlic,
   very finely minced
2 cups canned Italian
   plum tomatoes with 1
   cup of the juices
Salt and freshly ground
   pepper
3 tablespoons finely
   chopped fresh parsley
6 to 8 loin veal chops, 10
   to 12 ounces each,
   about 1 inch thick
2 tablespoons olive oil

I discovered this robust Tuscan mushroom sauce when I attended a cooking class to learn how to make the lightest possible gnocchi. Ironically, the sauce is so rich and heavy that I didn't want to serve it with gnocchi, but what a great sauce. *Grazie,* Paola! We love to serve it with a grilled veal chop and polenta.

The chopped vegetables are known as *battuto.* Traditionally they are hacked up with a curved knife called a *mezzaluna,* a knife that requires some expertise to use. You may chop everything with a cleaver or chef's knife, or you may pulse the vegetables in the food processor but be careful not to puree them. ◆ *Serves 6 to 8*

Rinse the mushrooms and soak 1 hour in hot water to cover. Drain and finely chop; set aside. Strain the soaking liquid through cheesecloth and reserve.

Melt the butter in a heavy sauté pan over medium heat. Add all the vegetables except the tomatoes and cook until tender and golden, 15 to 20 minutes. Pulse the tomatoes with their juices in a food processor until coarsely chopped and add to the pan. Add the chopped mushrooms and 1 cup of the reserved soaking liquid. Simmer uncovered over medium heat until thickened and the flavors are blended, 45 to 50 minutes. Season to taste with salt and pepper. Stir in the parsley. This sauce can be made ahead and refrigerated up to 3 days.

Heat the grill or broiler. Brush the chops with oil and lightly sprinkle with salt and pepper. Grill or broil until medium-rare, 4 to 5 minutes each side.

Reheat the sauce if necessary and spoon it over the chops. Serve with polenta.

Grilled Stuffed Loin Veal Chops

FILLING

¼ cup unsalted butter

1 large onion, cut into medium dice

1 clove garlic, finely chopped (optional)

3 bunches Swiss chard (about 1 pound), cut into chiffonade (about 6 cups)

¼ cup diced prosciutto

¼ cup mild goat cheese, such as Montrachet

¼ cup fresh ricotta cheese (see Note, page 115)

Salt and freshly ground pepper

Pinch freshly grated nutmeg (optional)

6 veal loin chops, ¾ to 1 pound each and about 1 inch thick, 2-inch-wide pocket cut in each

2 tablespoons olive oil

2 cups Tomato Sauce (page 118)

This dish has in one bite all the flavors Italians love: tender veal, leafy Swiss chard, prosciutto, sweet onions, cheese, and tomato sauce. You may make the filling the day before and stuff the chops just before you cook them. ✦ *Serves 6*

Prepare the filling: Melt the butter in a large heavy sauté pan over medium heat. Add the onion and cook until translucent, about 7 to 10 minutes. Add the garlic if using for the last 2 minutes of cooking. Add the Swiss chard and cook until wilted, 2 to 3 minutes. Drain the chard mixture and squeeze out as much moisture as possible. Then finely chop the mixture and combine with the prosciutto and cheeses in a mixing bowl. Season to taste with salt and pepper, and nutmeg if using. Refrigerate until cold and firm.

Stuff each chop with 2 to 3 tablespoons filling.

Heat the grill or broiler. Brush the chops lightly with oil and sprinkle lightly with salt and pepper. Grill or broil until the meat is medium-rare and the filling hot, 5 to 6 minutes each side.

Heat the tomato sauce to simmering. Spoon the sauce over the chops and serve with fried potatoes or baked polenta.

Costoletta del Curato

VEAL CHOPS WITH A
MUSTARD HERB SAUCE

3 cups Veal Stock or
combination Veal and
Chicken Stocks (page
237 and 103), reduced
to 1¾ cups
¼ cup Square One Hot
Mustard (recipe
follows)
2 tablespoons each
chopped fresh tarragon,
parsley, mint, and sage
Salt and freshly ground
pepper
6 veal loin chops, ¾ to 1
pound each and about
1 inch thick
2 tablespoons olive oil

This veal dish is a specialty from Orvieto, in Umbria, traditionally prepared only in May. The recipe is "secret" in that each restaurant has its own version of the sauce, which may be enlivened by as many as eighteen different herbs. Suspecting that in this case less may be more, we use only four herbs. You, however, may be as inventive as the folks in Umbria and create your own combinations. Try oregano, summer savory, thyme, or rosemary. ◆ *Serves 6*

Combine the stock, mustard, and herbs in a saucepan. Heat to simmering and simmer about 3 minutes. Season to taste with salt and pepper.

Heat the grill or broiler. Brush the chops with oil and sprinkle lightly with salt and pepper. Grill or broil until medium-rare, 4 to 5 minutes each side. Spoon the sauce over the chops and serve.

NOTE: This sauce would be tasty on veal scaloppine as well.

Square One Hot Mustard

¼ pound Colman's
mustard powder
¼ cup (or to taste)
distilled white vinegar
4 tablespoons water
2 to 4 tablespoons sugar
2 to 3 teaspoons salt
1 large egg
1 cup mild olive oil

This mustard is hot, sweet, and tart. It is a wonderful addition to sauces and vinaigrettes and will enliven the stodgiest sandwich. We make this in huge batches as it keeps for several months. If it separates or settles a bit, just stir before using. You may make this in the food processor or with an electric mixer. ◆ *Makes about 2½ cups*

Whisk the mustard, vinegar, half the water, the sugar, and salt together in a mixing bowl or food processor. Beat in the egg, then gradually beat in the oil to make an emulsion. Taste and add more vinegar, sugar, or salt to taste. Whisk in the some or all of the remaining water to thin it. Pour the mustard into a jar, cover, and refrigerate.

Sautéed Baby Veal Chops with Herbed Bread Crumbs

8 baby veal rib chops,
about 2½ pounds
total—most of it is
bone!

1 cup dry bread crumbs

4 teaspoons chopped fresh
parsley

1 teaspoon each chopped
fresh sage, rosemary,
and thyme

1 teaspoon each salt and
freshly ground pepper

½ cup all-purpose flour

2 large eggs

4 tablespoons clarified
butter (see Note, page
26) or 2 tablespoons
each unsalted butter
and olive oil

Lemon wedges for serving

If you cannot entice your butcher to special order these delicious baby chops, you may substitute veal scaloppine or boneless chicken breasts (see Note). These alternatives will not be quite as succulent as the tiny rib chops, but they still will be good. This recipe may sound mindlessly simple, but the taste and texture are rich and who says that simple can't be satisfying? We like to serve the chops with a vegetable ragout or sautéed greens with onions, peas, and a julienne of prosciutto. The chops may be breaded and refrigerated 4 to 6 hours before serving. ◆ *Serves 2*

Lightly pound the chops to flatten them slightly.

Combine the bread crumbs, herbs, and ½ teaspoon each salt and pepper in a shallow bowl. Mix the flour with the remaining salt and pepper in a second bowl and lightly beat the eggs in a third bowl. Dip the chops first in the seasoned flour, shaking off the excess, then the egg, then the herbed bread crumbs. Place the breaded chops on a rack set over a baking sheet and let stand until the breading is set, 15 to 20 minutes.

Heat the butter in a heavy sauté pan or skillet over medium-high heat. Add the chops and sauté until golden brown, about 4 minutes each side. Or brown the chops very quickly in the butter over very high heat, then put them on a baking sheet and bake 5 minutes at 350°.

Garnish with lemon wedges and serve with a sexy vegetable.

NOTE: If you are using veal scaloppine or chicken breasts, pound them lightly about ¼ inch thick and sauté in the butter over high heat until golden brown, 2 to 3 minutes each side.

Spiedini di Vitello alla Campagna

ROMAN-STYLE VEAL BROCHETTES

MARINADE

1 cup olive oil

2 cloves garlic, crushed

4 to 8 fresh sage leaves, coarsely chopped

3 tablespoons fresh lemon juice

2 strips lemon zest (½ inch wide)

2½ pounds veal head or tenderloin filet, trimmed and cut into 2-inch cubes (about 2 ounces each; see Note)

18 large slices lean prosciutto, cut lengthwise in half

18 large leaves of sage

LEMON-SAGE BUTTER

¾ cup unsalted butter

2 tablespoons (or to taste) fresh lemon juice

2 tablespoons grated lemon zest (from 1 to 2 lemons)

2 tablespoons (or to taste) chopped fresh sage (about 10 leaves)

Salt and freshly ground pepper

Lemon wedges for serving

Everyone loves food cooked on skewers, whether it be Middle Eastern shish kabobs, Moroccan *qodban*, French brochettes, or Italian *spiedini*. These *spiedini* are as popular at Square One as they are in Rome. ◆ *Serves 6*

For the marinade, heat the oil in a saucepan over medium heat until hot but not boiling, about 5 minutes. Remove from heat and add the remaining ingredients. Let steep 1 hour, until cool.

Put the veal cubes in a shallow nonaluminum container and pour the marinade over. Cover and refrigerate overnight, turning the veal occasionally.

Prepare the butter: Process the butter, lemon juice and zest, and sage in a food processor until well blended. Season to taste with salt and pepper.

Heat the grill or broiler. Drain the meat, reserving the marinade. Wrap each veal cube first with 1 sage leaf and then in a half-slice of prosciutto. Thread 3 wrapped veal cubes onto each of 6 skewers. Brush the *spiedini* with the reserved marinade and lightly sprinkle with salt and pepper. Grill or broil 4 minutes on each side for medium-rare or 5 minutes each side for medium, brushing with the marinade when turning.

Spread the *spiedini* with lemon-sage butter and garnish with lemon wedges. Serve with sautéed greens and grilled garlic bread.

NOTE: This recipe is also excellent if made with pork.

Scaloppine di Vitello con Peperoncini

SAUTÉED VEAL WITH
ROASTED RED PEPPERS

2 large red peppers
2 pounds veal tenderloin,
    cut into sixteen
    ½-inch-thick slices,
    about 2 ounces each
Salt and freshly ground
    pepper
¾ cup (or as needed)
    olive oil
8 teaspoons anchovy
    puree
4 teaspoons finely minced
    garlic
2 cups heavy cream
¼ cup preserved lemon
    zest with syrup (see
    Note)
8 tablespoons pine nuts,
    toasted, plus additional
    for garnish
8 teaspoons chopped fresh
    chives, plus additional
    for garnish

Half a pound of meat per person seems like a lot but it shrinks considerably when pounded and sautéed and just doesn't look like much. The sauce sounds very rich, but the richness is cut by lemon zest. You can increase the amount of pasta if you want to stay with a smaller meat portion. You may also omit the anchovy, but the sauce will not have that wonderful subtle flavor that only anchovy can impart. ◆ Serves 4

Char the peppers over an open flame or under the broiler until blackened on all sides. Transfer to a plastic container with a lid or a paper or plastic bag. Cover the container or close the bag and let the peppers steam about 15 minutes. Peel the skins from the peppers; then cut the peppers in half, remove the stems, and scrape out the seeds. Cut into ⅓-inch-wide strips.

Lightly pound the veal slices about ¼ inch thick between sheets of plastic wrap. Sprinkle with salt and pepper.

Heat 2 tablespoons oil in a large sauté pan over high heat. Add 4 veal slices and brown 2 minutes each side; set aside on a platter and keep warm. Repeat with the remaining veal slices, adding 1 to 2 tablespoons oil to the pans as needed for each batch. Put 2 tablespoons oil, the peppers, anchovy, and garlic in the same pan and heat 1 minute over low heat. Stir in the cream, lemon zest with syrup, and 6 tablespoons pine nuts. Heat to boiling. Reduce the heat and simmer until slightly reduced, 1 to 2 minutes. Return the veal to the pan, sprinkle with some of the chives, and warm gently 1 minute.

Place 4 slices of veal on each plate and spoon the sauce over top. Sprinkle with the remaining chives. Serve with fettuccine tossed with greens, such as Swiss chard, dandelion, or escarole, sautéed in oil with a pinch of garlic.

NOTE: To make preserved lemon zest, remove the zest of 4 lemons with a vegetable peeler and shave off any white pith. Cut the strips into fine julienne. Blanch the zest 2 minutes in boiling water to cover; drain and rinse well under cold water. Heat ½ cup water and ¼ cup sugar to boiling in a small saucepan, reduce the heat, and simmer 2 minutes. Add the zest and simmer until cooked through but not hard, about 5 minutes. Cool, then cover and refrigerate up to 1 week.

Veal Scaloppine with Eggplant and Tomatoes

2 medium eggplants, peeled and cut crosswise into eight ½-inch-thick slices each

¾ to 1 cup olive oil

Salt and freshly ground pepper

1½ to 2 pounds boneless veal loin, cut into sixteen ½-inch-thick slices

½ cup Veal, Beef, or Chicken Stock (page 237, 104, or 103)

4 teaspoons finely minced garlic

2½ cups Tomato Sauce (page 118; see Note)

20 Niçoise or Kalamata, pitted and quartered

½ cup lightly packed basil chiffonade

This is a Sicilian recipe that could pass for Neapolitan as well, with its typically southern Italian ingredients of eggplant, tomatoes, olives, and veal. What we really have here is a rigatoni alla Norma, hold the rigatoni and substitute the veal! The eggplant rounds echo the shape of the veal slices and make for a very pretty plate. You could serve this with rigatoni for a very inauthentic but satisfying dish (Italians eat pasta as a course in itself and usually do not accompany an entrée with pasta). If you wish to cut the quantity of meat (½ pound per person may seem like a lot but remember that it shrinks), try increasing the eggplant.

♦ Serves 4

Heat the grill or broiler, or preheat the oven to 400°. Brush the eggplant slices on both sides with olive oil, using about ½ cup. Sprinkle lightly with salt and pepper. Grill, broil, or bake until tender and cooked through but not mushy, about 10 minutes under the broiler or 20 minutes in the oven. Set aside and keep warm.

Lightly pound the veal slices ¼ inch thick between sheets of plastic wrap. Lightly sprinkle with salt and pepper.

Heat 2 tablespoons oil in a large sauté pan over high heat. Add 4 veal slices and brown 2 minutes each side; set aside on a platter and keep warm. Repeat with the remaining veal slices, adding 1 to 2 tablespoons oil to the pan as needed for each batch.

Add the stock to the pan and boil, scraping up browned bits on the bottom of the pan, until slightly thickened. Add the garlic and cook 1 minute over medium heat. Stir in the tomato sauce and half the olives and basil; heat through. Season to taste with salt and pepper.

Alternate slices of veal and eggplant on serving plates. Spoon the sauce over top and garnish with the remaining olives and basil. Serve hot.

NOTE: If serving with pasta on the side, increase the tomato sauce to about 3½ cups so that you have enough to sauce the noodles.

BEEF

Grilled Rib-Eye Steak with Porcini Butter

⅓ cup dried porcini mushrooms

¾ cup warm water

¾ cup plus 2 tablespoons unsalted butter, softened

½ small onion, finely minced (about 3 tablespoons)

Salt and freshly ground pepper

6 rib-eye steaks or filets, 7 ounces each

One of the most memorable tastes of my first visit to Italy was that of fresh porcini mushrooms. I saw them everywhere displayed in baskets on tables or in shop windows. I ate them thinly sliced and sautéed in the style known as *trifolati*, or grilled with garlic oil. We have them in California when mushroom hunters find them in the hills after the rains and bring them to the restaurant. Wonderful dried porcini are also available at Italian and gourmet markets.

One easy way to feast on their fabulous flavor and perfume is in a butter for steak or veal chops. The notion of a mushroom butter may seem terribly California chic and trendy, but, in fact, I stumbled upon the idea in an Italian cookbook called *I Funghi nella Cucina Veneta*, written by Giovanni Capnist and published by Franco Muzzio in Padova. The book described a sort of grilled bread sandwich with a mushroom or porcini butter that caught my attention. I thought, this is too good for just toast; why not serve it with steak or veal chops? So, yet another example of the old maxim that there is really nothing new in cooking. ◆ *Serves 6*

Rinse and soak the mushrooms 1 hour in the warm water. Drain the mushrooms; strain the liquid through cheesecloth and reserve ¼ cup.

Heat 2 tablespoons butter in a small sauté pan or skillet over low heat. Add the onion and cook until tender and translucent, about 10 minutes; cool a bit.

Pulse the mushrooms in a food processor until chopped. Add the onion, reserved mushroom soaking liquid, and remaining ¾ cup butter; process until blended. Season to taste with salt and pepper.

Heat the grill or broiler. Lightly sprinkle the steaks with salt and pepper and grill or broil 3 minutes each side for medium-rare. Place a dollop of butter on each steak and serve with fried potatoes and grilled mushrooms.

Grilled Flank Steak on a Bed of Roasted Peppers and Onions

2 flank steaks, about 3
   pounds total, trimmed
   well
8 tablespoons olive oil
3 tablespoons balsamic
   vinegar
2 teaspoons freshly
   ground pepper, plus
   additional to taste
6 large red onions
6 medium red peppers or
   combination red and
   yellow
Salt

I wish I could remember the precise origin of this recipe. It came to me as a taste memory of the full flavors of grilled beef, roasted peppers, and balsamic vinegar. The beef is marinated briefly in the vinegar with a little olive oil, and the sauce is composed of roasted peppers and onions seasoned with a bit more vinegar and olive oil. As you may know, balsamic vinegar, a specialty of Modena, has a round rich taste and is not at all sour. It is as mellow as a good wine and adds a wonderful depth of flavor to this dish. ◆ *Serves 6*

Put the steaks in a shallow nonaluminum container and sprinkle with 2 tablespoons olive oil, 1 tablespoon vinegar, and 2 teaspoons pepper. Cover and let marinate 2 hours at room temperature.

Preheat the oven to 400°. Rub the onions with 2 tablespoons oil and roast just until tender, about 1 hour. Halve and peel, then cut into 1-inch-wide slices.

Char the peppers over an open flame or under the broiler until blackened on all sides. Transfer to a plastic container with a lid or a paper or plastic bag. Cover the container or close the bag and let the peppers steam about 15 minutes. Peel the skins from the peppers; then cut the peppers in half, remove the stems, and scrape out the seeds. Cut into 1-inch-wide strips and toss with 2 tablespoons oil.

Heat the grill or broiler. Lightly sprinkle the steaks with salt and pepper and grill or broil 2 to 3 minutes each side for medium-rare.

Meanwhile, heat the sliced onions and peppers and remaining 2 tablespoons each oil and vinegar in a large sauté pan or skillet over medium heat until warmed through, about 4 minutes. Season to taste with salt and pepper.

Slice the steaks across the grain on a slight diagonal. Make a bed of pepper and onions on each serving plate and top with the steak. Serve with fried potatoes.

Bistecca al Diavolo

GRILLED STEAK WITH A
SPICY TOMATO SAUCE

2 tablespoons olive oil

1 cup diced (¼ inch)
pancetta

5 red onions, sliced about
⅓ inch thick

1 tablespoon (or to taste)
dried red pepper flakes

2 tablespoons finely
minced garlic

1 tablespoon fennel seeds,
coarsely ground

3 cups Tomato Sauce
(page 118)

1 cup Beef Stock (page
104)

¾ cup dry red wine

Salt and freshly ground
pepper

1 to 2 teaspoons sugar
(optional)

6 rib-eye steaks, about ½
pound each

Bistecca al diavolo is southern Italian in inspiration. We usually serve the *al diavolo* sauce with steak, as in this recipe, but it works equally well with pork spareribs or grilled sausage. We have also served the sauce without the pancetta on meaty fish such as grilled swordfish or tuna. You may make it as devilishly hot as you like.

This and the following three beef recipes are variations on the theme of a piquant tomato sauce with onion and spices. Although the basic ingredients are similar, the resultant flavor of each dish is quite different. ◆ *Serves 6*

Heat 2 tablespoons oil in a medium sauté pan over medium heat. Add the pancetta and cook until partially rendered, about 15 minutes. Add the onions and pepper flakes and cook until nearly tender, about 10 minutes. Add the garlic and fennel seeds and cook 2 minutes. Stir in the tomato sauce, stock, and wine. Heat to boiling, then reduce the heat and simmer until the flavors blend, 8 to 10 minutes. Season to taste with salt and pepper. If the sauce is too acidic, add the sugar.

Heat the grill or broiler. Brush the steaks with the remaining oil and sprinkle lightly with salt and pepper. Grill or broil about 3 minutes each side for medium-rare, or 4 minutes each side for medium. Spoon the sauce over and serve with polenta or mashed potatoes.

Bife Acebollado

PORTUGUESE STEAKS WITH ONIONS AND TOMATOES

MARINADE

2 to 3 tablespoons red wine vinegar

2 teaspoons finely minced garlic

1 tablespoon paprika

1 teaspoon each salt and freshly ground pepper

6 rib-eye steaks, about ½ pound each

½ cup olive oil

1 cup diced onion

2 tablespoons red wine vinegar

2 teaspoons minced garlic

2 cups canned Italian plum tomatoes, diced

¼ cup tomato puree

1 bay leaf (optional)

Salt and freshly ground pepper

3 tablespoons chopped fresh parsley

The sauce for this Portuguese steak dish is less highly spiced than the *al diavolo*. The steak itself is marinated in a piquant marinade. The Portuguese might accompany this with a hot sauce of *piri-piri* peppers served on the side. I have seen variations of the sauce with prosciutto and a little lemon juice. ◆ *Serves 6*

For the marinade, make a paste of all the ingredients and rub it over the steaks. Cover and let marinade 1 hour at room temperature.

Heat the olive oil in a large sauté pan over medium heat. Add the onion and cook until translucent, 7 to 10 minutes. Add the vinegar, garlic, tomatoes, puree, and bay leaf if using; simmer 3 to 5 minutes. Season to taste with salt and pepper. Stir in the parsley.

Heat the grill or broiler. Grill or broil the steaks 3 minutes each side for medium-rare, 4 minutes each side for medium. Spoon the sauce over the steaks and serve with fried potatoes.

Gulyas Triestina

BEEF RAGOUT FROM
TRIESTE

*3 pounds beef chuck roast
or brisket, trimmed
well and cut into
2-inch cubes*

*¼ cup plus 2 tablespoons
(or to taste) paprika*

*¾ cup (or as needed)
olive oil*

*¾ pound pancetta, cut
into medium dice*

*4 large onions, cut into
medium dice (about 6
cups)*

*2 tablespoons finely
minced garlic*

*1 teaspoon (or to taste)
cayenne pepper*

1 cup dry red wine

*3 cups diced canned
Italian plum tomatoes
with 1½ cups of the
juices*

*Salt and freshly ground
pepper*

Gulyas Triestina is a cross between an Italian stew and a Hungarian goulash; this is not surprising, as Trieste is in Friuli, very near to Austria and Yugoslavia. We like to serve this with noodles sprinkled with poppy seeds or soft polenta flavored with poppy seeds. ◆ *Serves 6 to 8*

Rub the meat cubes with 2 tablespoons paprika and ½ cup olive oil. Cover and refrigerate overnight, if possible, or let marinate 2 hours at room temperature.

Heat 2 tablespoons oil in a large sauté pan over medium heat. Add the pancetta and cook until rendered and half-cooked, 10 to 15 minutes; transfer to a large casserole with a slotted spoon. Add as many beef cubes to the sauté pan as will comfortably fit (overcrowding will cause the beef to steam, rather than brown) and brown on all sides over high heat; transfer to the casserole with the pancetta. Repeat with the remaining beef cubes, adding 1 to 2 tablespoons oil to the pan as needed for each batch. Add the onions to the sauté pan and cook over medium heat until translucent, 7 to 10 minutes. Add the garlic, cayenne, and the remaining ¼ cup paprika and cook 5 minutes longer. Transfer to the casserole with the beef.

Add the wine and diced tomatoes with juices to the casserole and heat to boiling. Reduce the heat and simmer covered until the beef is tender, about 2 hours. Season to taste with salt and pepper, and more cayenne and paprika if you like. Serve with *pappardelle,* mashed potatoes, or polenta.

Stracotto di Manzo "Peposo"

PEPPERY TUSCAN
BEEF STEW

1½ cups (or as needed)
    mild olive oil
3 tablespoons freshly
    ground pepper
3 pounds beef chuck or
    brisket, trimmed well
    and cut into 2-inch
    cubes
2 cups dry red wine
½ pound pancetta, cut
    into ¼-inch dice
3 large onions, cut into
    medium dice (4 to 5
    cups)
6 cloves garlic, finely
    minced
2 cups canned Italian
    plum tomatoes with ¾
    cup of the juices
1 cup Beef Stock (page
    104)
Salt

This tongue-tingling beef ragout is a specialty of the little hill town of L'Impruneta. The tomatoes are less prominent than in the preceding three dishes because the wine and black pepper provide strong competition. While it is often accompanied by boiled potatoes, I like to serve the stew with slices of grilled or toasted country bread, the better to sop up all the wonderfully rich, peppery sauce. ◆ *Serves 6 to 8*

Combine ¾ cup olive oil and 1 tablespoon pepper in a shallow nonaluminum container. Add the beef cubes and turn in the marinade to coat. Cover and refrigerate overnight.

Let the meat warm to room temperature. Heat 2 tablespoons oil in a large heavy sauté pan over high heat. Add as many beef cubes to the pan as will comfortably fit (overcrowding will cause the beef to steam, rather than brown) and brown on all sides; transfer to a large casserole. Repeat with the remaining beef cubes, adding 1 to 2 tablespoons oil to the pan as needed for each batch. Pour the wine into the pan and boil, scraping up the browned bits on the bottom, 1 to 2 minutes; add wine to the casserole with the beef.

Add 2 tablespoons oil to the pan and heat over medium heat. Add the pancetta and sauté until the fat is rendered, about 15 minutes. Add the onions and cook until the onions are translucent and the pancetta is cooked through but not crisp, about 10 minutes. Add the garlic and remaining 2 tablespoons pepper and cook 2 minutes. Add the onion mixture to the casserole with the beef.

Pulse the tomatoes with their juices in a food processor until coarsely chopped. Add the tomatoes to the casserole along with the stock. Heat to boiling, then reduce the heat and simmer covered until the meat is almost cooked through, about 2 hours. Remove the cover and increase the heat. Gently boil until the stewing liquids have thickened, about 15 minutes. Taste and adjust the seasoning; the sauce should be quite robust and peppery. Serve with potatoes or grilled bread.

Farsu Magru

SICILIAN BRAISED
ROLLED STEAK

3 pounds top sirloin or
 round steak in one
 piece if possible (see
 Note)

STUFFING

¾ pound ground beef

2 large eggs

2 slices bread, coarsely
 crumbled

2 tablespoons freshly
 grated Parmesan
 cheese

2 tablespoons chopped
 fresh parsley

1 teaspoon salt

½ teaspoon freshly
 ground pepper

¼ pound mortadella,
 sliced paper thin

¼ pound thinly sliced
 prosciutto

3 or 4 hard-cooked eggs,
 ends trimmed

¼ pound provolone
 cheese, cut into 3 by
 ½ by ½-inch strips

6 tablespoons olive oil

2 large onions, chopped

1 tablespoon minced
 garlic

1½ to 2 cups dry red
 wine

4 cups tomato puree

Salt and freshly ground
 pepper

The first time I ate this was at the home of Francis Coppola. His mother, Italia, was in the kitchen and she is a really wonderful cook. I remember she told me that the dish can be made with beef or veal. This version is our favorite. The name literally translates "false lean," perhaps because you are making something rich out of very lean ingredients, in the sense that the meat goes a long way. Outside of Sicily this dish may be called *braciole*. By any name, it's wonderful. You may decide to make it just for the incredibly rich sauce that it provides for accompanying rigatoni. ◆ *Serves 6 to 8*

Slice the steak almost in half horizontally and open the steak like a book. Place the steak between sheets of plastic wrap and pound as thinly as possible (about ½ inch) without tearing the meat.

Place all the stuffing ingredients in a mixing bowl and mix well with your hands. Spread an even layer of stuffing over the beef. Cover the stuffing with a single layer of mortadella slices and then a second layer of prosciutto slices. Arrange the eggs lengthwise in a row down the center of the stuffing. Arrange the provolone strips along either side of the eggs. Carefully roll the steak into a log and tie with kitchen string.

Heat 3 tablespoons oil in a heavy pan large enough to hold the beef roll over high heat. Add the roll and brown on all sides, then remove it from the pan. Discard the oil.

Add 3 tablespoons fresh oil to the pan and heat over medium heat. Add the onions and cook until translucent, about 10 minutes. Add the garlic and cook 1 minute. Stir in the wine and tomato puree and simmer 1 to 2 minutes. Return the beef roll to the pan. Heat the sauce to a low boil, then reduce the heat, cover, and simmer gently over low heat until the beef is tender, 1½ to 2 hours. Season the sauce to taste with salt and pepper.

Remove the strings from the beef roll and slice ½ inch thick. Spoon some of the sauce over the slices and serve with rigatoni or wide noodles that have been tossed in the remaining sauce. Any extra sauce is great on pasta, rice, or mashed potatoes.

NOTE: If not possible, buy 2 pieces and make 2 rolls.

Bollito Misto ai Cinque Salse

BRAISED BEEF, CHICKEN, SAUSAGE, AND VEGETABLES WITH FIVE SAUCES

3 quarts Beef Stock (page 104)

5 pounds first-cut brisket, trimmed well

3 whole chicken breasts, about 1 pound each, split, or other chicken parts for 6 servings

6 garlic sausages, about 1½ pounds, prepared or homemade (page 000)

12 leeks, trimmed and rinsed well

12 carrot sticks, about 4 by 1 by ½ inch

12 to 18 small new potatoes

Square One Hot Mustard (page 240)

Horseradish Cream (page 35)

Salsa Verde (recipe follows)

Salsa Rossa (page 21)

Aioli (page 193)

This is one of those dishes that Europeans adore and Americans think is boring. Americans have little tradition or experience with fine boiled foods, while dishes such as the French *pot au feu,* Spanish *cocido madrileno,* and Italian *bollito misto* are cornerstones of Mediterranean cuisine. When prepared with care and good ingredients these uncomplicated foods are superb. While the cooking itself is simple in technique, the dish does not come cheap; the brisket should be cooked in beef stock rather than water to guarantee that the finished broth, meats, and vegetables are truly tasty. If you are willing to sacrifice about 3 quarts of your best homemade beef stock to this dish, you will have a spectacular winter dinner for six or many nights of great leftovers, soup, and sandwiches for two.

Why five sauces? We found that these are the "sex appeal" factor that sells the *bollito* to those who might not ordinarily order plain boiled beef. People get a separate plate with five little ramekins of assorted sauces and they can play mix and match: Beef with mustard or horseradish, chicken with *salsa verde* or *rossa,* vegetables with aioli or *salsa verde,* sausage with mustard or *salsa rossa.* Of course, you are not obliged to make all five sauces, although most of them keep quite well and can be used again for other dishes.

♦ *Serves 6*

Heat the stock to simmering in a large heavy saucepan or Dutch oven with a tight-fitting lid. Add the brisket. Return the stock to a simmer and cook the brisket covered over low heat until tender, 2½ to 3 hours. Remove the brisket from the broth and set aside.

Add the chicken to the broth and simmer covered until almost cooked through, 10 to 15 minutes. Remove from the broth and set aside with the brisket. Add the sausage and simmer covered until cooked through, about 7 minutes; set aside with the brisket.

Add the leeks and simmer until cooked through, 6 to 8 minutes; set aside with the brisket. Repeat with the carrots (simmer 5 to 7 minutes), then the potatoes (simmer 8 to 12 minutes).

To serve, slice 2 thick slices brisket per person (set the remainder aside for seconds, sandwiches, or a fabulous beef and vegetable soup). Heat the broth to simmering. Add the brisket slices, chicken, sausages, and vegetables; simmer until heated through. Arrange the warmed meats and vegetables on individual large plates or on a giant platter. Boil 3 cups broth until reduced by half and spoon it over all or pass it in a sauceboat. Serve with the sauces of your choice.

Salsa Verde

1 cup finely chopped
   fresh parsley
¼ cup capers, rinsed and
   coarsely chopped
4 to 6 tablespoons very
   finely chopped white
   onion
6 to 8 cloves garlic, finely
   minced
1 to 2 tablespoons finely
   chopped or pureed
   anchovy
⅓ cup (or to taste) red
   wine vinegar or fresh
   lemon juice
½ cup toasted fine bread
   crumbs
1¼ cups fruity olive oil
Salt and freshly ground
   pepper

We usually serve this all-purpose sauce on grilled swordfish or tuna or on baked sea bass and other mild white fish. It makes a great vinaigrette for cooked fish, such as tuna or cod, potatoes, green beans, carrots, beets, and hard-cooked eggs. It is also wonderful on boiled beef, tongue, and chicken. ✦ *Makes about 3 cups*

Combine all ingredients. You may want to add just part of the vinegar and add the remaining to taste because they vary so in acidity. For a slightly milder sauce, use lemon juice instead of vinegar. If you use this sauce for grilled fish, you may omit the bread crumbs.

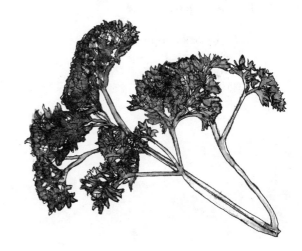

Izmir Koftesi with Hunkar Begendi

DILLED TURKISH
MEATBALLS WITH
EGGPLANT PUREE

MEATBALLS

1 ½ pounds ground beef

½ cup grated onion

2 cloves garlic, very finely
  minced

¼ cup chopped fresh dill

1 teaspoon salt

½ teaspoon finely ground
  pepper

6 tablespoons (or as
  needed) olive oil

4 cups Tomato Sauce
  (page 118)

Hunkar Begendi (page
  311)

2 tablespoons chopped
  fresh parsley for
  garnish

This dish is a "sleeper." Little did we know when we first cooked it that it would become so popular with our clientele. Even the cooks ask me to put it on the menu, and, if you want to know what the best item in a restaurant is, take a look at what the cooks are eating for dinner.
♦ *Serves 4*

For the meatballs, place all the ingredients in a mixing bowl and mix with your hands until blended. Shape into thirty-two 1 ½-inch meatballs.

Heat 3 tablespoons oil in a large skillet over high heat. Add as many meatballs as will fit without crowding and sauté until well browned on all sides and medium-rare inside, about 4 minutes. Repeat with the remaining meatballs, adding 1 to 2 tablespoons oil as needed for each batch.

Heat the sauce to simmering in a large sauté pan. Add the browned meatballs and simmer until heated through.

To serve, spoon a large mound of *hunkar begendi* on a large platter. Spoon the meatballs and sauce on and around the eggplant in a random pattern. Sprinkle with the parsley.

Kefta

MIDDLE EASTERN
"HAMBURGER"

TAHINI DRESSING

½ cup sesame tahini

½ cup fresh lemon juice

2 cloves garlic, finely
  minced

1 teaspoon (or to taste)
  salt

Water to thin

KEFTA

2 pounds ground beef

1 medium onion, grated
  (about ¾ cup)

⅓ cup chopped fresh
  parsley

2 teaspoons ground cumin

1 teaspoon salt

½ teaspoon freshly
  ground pepper

Olive oil for cooking
  kefta

6 pita breads

1½ cups chopped
  cucumber

1½ cups chopped
  tomatoes

2 tablespoons olive oil

Years ago, when I was living in Berkeley, our family used to lunch regularly at a Lebanese restaurant not too far from our house. We became addicted to a few items on their menu: a great baba ghanouj with vegetables and pita bread, a really good lamb kabob with a fine pilaf enlivened with cinnamon and vermicelli, a crunchy *falafel* sandwich and, our favorite, the *kefta*. Alas, the rest of the community did not share our passion for this food (the restaurant was located too near the campus with its greasy spoons, pizza joints, hippie vegetarian hangouts, and bad burger shops), and so, sadly, the restaurant closed. If only the students who were eating all those bad burgers had stepped inside and had a *kefta*, the restaurant might still be there. This recipe is my attempt to recreate a very special taste memory. ✦ *Serves 6*

For the dressing, place all the ingredients except the water in a blender or food processor and process until bended. Add water a few spoonfuls at a time until the dressing is the consistency of heavy cream. Taste and adjust the seasoning. If the dressing thickens too much upon standing, whisk in more water.

For the *kefta,* place all the ingredients in a mixing bowl and knead with your hands until blended. Shape into 12 oval patties.

Heat the grill or broiler. Brush the *kefta* with oil and grill or broil 3 to 4 minutes each side. Or heat 3 tablespoons oil in a cast-iron pan over high heat and sauté the *kefka* 3 minutes each side.

Meanwhile, wrap the pitas in foil and warm in a double boiler over simmering water. (The moist heat keeps the bread chewy and flexible; the heat of the oven may cause it to dry and crack.)

To serve, cut the pitas crosswise in half. Spoon 2 tablespoons each cucumber and tomato into each pita half. Spoon in some dressing, then slip in the *kefta*. Spoon over more dressing if you like. Serve with deep-fried eggplant chips (see Note).

NOTE: For Deep-Fried Eggplant Chips, cut 12 small Japanese eggplants crosswise into ¼-inch-thick slices and deep-fry in 3 to 4 inches oil until brown and crisp, about 3 minutes. Sprinkle lightly with salt and serve hot.

LIVER

Foie M'Chermel

CALVES LIVER WITH MOROCCAN SPICED ONIONS

6 tablespoons unsalted
  butter

4 medium onions, sliced
  about ¼ inch thick

5 teaspoons ground cumin

5 teaspoons paprika

¼ teaspoon (or more to
  taste) cayenne pepper

2½ tablespoons fresh
  lemon juice

3 to 4 tablespoons
  chopped fresh cilantro

Salt and freshly ground
  pepper

¾ cup all-purpose flour

1½ pounds calves liver,
  cut into eight
  ⅓-inch-thick slices

¼ cup olive oil or
  clarified butter (see
  Note, page 26)

1 cup Chicken Stock
  (page 103)

Lemon wedges for serving

I am a liver lover. Whenever we have it on the menu I am certain to have it for lunch or dinner . . . or both. This is one of my favorites, and our patrons seem to agree.
◆ *Serves 4*

Heat the butter in a large heavy sauté pan over medium heat. Add the onions and cook until translucent, 5 to 7 minutes. Add the spices and cook until the onions are tender, about 5 more minutes. Stir in the lemon juice, half the cilantro, and salt and pepper to taste. Remove from the pan and set aside.

Season the flour with salt and pepper. Dredge the liver with the seasoned flour and shake off the excess. Heat the oil in the same sauté pan over high heat. Add as many slices of liver as will comfortably fit in the pan and sear 2 minutes on each side for medium-rare; remove from the pan and keep warm. Repeat with the remaining liver. Pour off the excess oil, add the stock into the pan and boil, scraping up the browned bits on the bottom, until slightly thickened, about 2 minutes. Return the onions to the pan and heat through.

Arrange 2 slices liver on each plate and spoon the onions over top. Sprinkle with the remaining cilantro and serve with lemon wedges and roasted potatoes or couscous.

Sautéed Calves Liver with Onions, Pancetta, and Hazelnuts

A study in crunch—the toasted hazelnuts, peppery pancetta, and sweet red onions all add a wonderful texture that contrasts beautifully with the silkiness of the liver.
◆ *Serves 4*

¾ cup (or as needed)
  olive oil

4 cups thinly sliced red
  onion

¾ cup partially rendered
  diced pancetta (see
  Note, page 124)

¾ cup all-purpose flour

Salt and freshly ground
  pepper

1½ pounds calves liver,
  cut into eight
  ⅓-inch-thick slices

1 cup Chicken Stock
  (page 103)

6 tablespoons hazelnuts,
  toasted and coarsely
  chopped

Heat ¼ cup oil in a large sauté pan over medium heat. Add the onions and cook until tender, 7 to 10 minutes; remove from the pan and set aside.

Heat 2 tablespoons oil in the same pan over medium heat. Add the pancetta and cook until lightly browned and almost crunchy, about 5 minutes; remove with a slotted spoon and set aside with the onions.

Season the flour with salt and pepper. Dredge the liver with the seasoned flour and shake off the excess. Heat ¼ cup oil in the same pan over high heat. Add as many slices of liver as will comfortably fit in the pan and sear 2 minutes each side for medium-rare; remove from the pan and keep warm. Repeat with the remaining liver.

Pour off the excess oil, add the stock to the pan and boil, scraping up the browned bits on the bottom, until slightly thickened, about 2 minutes. Return the onions and pancetta to the pan and stir in the toasted hazelnuts. Season to taste with salt and pepper. Arrange 2 slices liver on each plate and spread the onion mixture over top. Serve immediately with roasted potatoes.

Fegato all'Abruzzese

SAUTEED CALVES LIVER
WITH ONIONS, ORANGE
ZEST, AND PISTACHIOS

¾ cup all-purpose flour
Salt and freshly ground
    pepper
1½ pounds calves liver,
    cut into eight
    ⅓-inch-thick slices
¾ cup (or as needed)
    olive oil
4 cups sliced red onions,
    about ¼ inch thick
1 cup Chicken Stock
    (page 103)
¼ cup grated orange zest
    covered with 2 to 3
    tablespoons fresh
    orange juice
¼ cup pistachio nuts,
    toasted and chopped,
    for garnish

The following is a loose interpretation of a recipe from the Abruzzi region of Italy that uses pork liver with these flavorings for a sausage. We find that it adapts beautifully to sautéed calves liver and would probably work with chicken livers as well. ◆ *Serves 4*

Season the flour with salt and pepper. Dredge the liver with the seasoned flour and shake off the excess.

Heat ¼ cup oil in a large sauté pan over medium heat. Add the onions and cook until nearly tender, about 5 minutes; remove from the pan and set aside.

Heat the remaining ¼ cup oil in the same pan over high heat. Add as many slices of liver as will comfortably fit in the pan, and sear 2 minutes on each side for medium-rare: Remove from the pan and keep warm. Repeat with the remaining liver.

Pour off the excess oil, add the stock to the pan and boil, scraping up the browned bits on the bottom, until slightly thickened, about 2 minutes. Return the onions to the pan, add the orange zest and juice, and cook 2 minutes. Season to taste with salt and pepper. Arrange 2 slices liver on each plate and spoon the onions over top. Garnish with the chopped pistachios and serve with fried or roasted potatoes.

Sauteed Calves Liver with Mustard Sauce

Salt

½ cup plus 6 tablespoons unsalted butter

3 cups sliced red onions, about ¼ inch thick

¼ cup olive oil or as needed

1½ pounds calves liver, cut into eight ⅓-inch-thick slices

Freshly ground pepper

1⅓ cups Chicken Stock (page 103)

½ cup Dijon and/or Square One Hot Mustard (page 240)

Black Pepper Pasta dough for 4 servings (page 113), cut for fettuccine or pappardelle

This is one of those dishes of which it is true that the whole is greater than the sum of its parts. First, the richness of the liver, then the spicy sharpness of the mustard sauce, and finally the texture of the sautéed onions. You could stop there and have a successful and tasty dish to serve with roasted or fried potatoes. But the kicker here is the addition of the black pepper fettuccine. I think you'll agree that the contrast of the mustard, liver, onion, and pepper flavors are hard to beat.

We have made this with store-bought Dijon mustard and a combination of store-bought and our own Square One Mustard. I think our mustard adds extra zip. If you use commercial mustard, try spicing it up with a few pinches dry mustard powder and a pinch of sugar dissolved in a little vinegar. ◆ *Serves 4*

Heat a large pot of salted water to boiling for pasta.

Heat ½ cup butter in a large sauté pan over medium heat. Add the onions and cook until tender, about 5 minutes; remove from the pan and set aside.

Heat ¼ cup oil in the same pan over high heat. Lightly sprinkle the liver with salt and pepper. Put as many slices as will comfortably fit in the pan and sear 2 minutes each side for medium-rare; remove from the pan and keep warm. Repeat with the remaining liver, adding more oil if needed.

Pour off the excess oil, add the stock to the pan and boil, scraping up the browned bits on the bottom, until slightly thickened, about 2 minutes. Return the onions to the pan, add the mustard, and cook, stirring constantly, 1 minute. Season to taste with salt and pepper. Return the liver to the pan and heat through.

Meanwhile, cook the pasta in the boiling salted water just until tender. Drain and toss with the remaining 6 tablespoons butter.

Arrange 2 slices of liver on each serving plate. Spoon the onion mixture over top and serve with the pasta.

NOTE: You may also make this recipe with 2 pounds duck or chicken livers, trimmed.

LAMB

TWO ITALIAN MARINADES FOR LAMB CHOPS: SCOTTADITO AND CAMOSCIO

You don't need a cookbook to tell you how to broil or grill a lamb chop, but I can tell you that the secret to tasty lamb chops is a great marinade. The advantage of a marinade is that you can do the little bit of work required a few days ahead, then casually slap the meat on the grill and wait for the compliments. Can anything this good be so easy? Yes.

The following recipes are two of the best marinades for lamb chops that I know. If you really feel like splurging, marinate and grill well-trimmed lamb loins. Serve them medium-rare, sliced across the grain.

Costolette d'Agnello Scottadito

MARINADE

1½ cups olive oil

1½ tablespoons (or to taste) dried red pepper flakes

1 cup dry white wine

18 cloves garlic, smashed

12 black peppercorns, smashed

6 tablespoons chopped fresh rosemary

1 teaspoon ground cloves

12 large lamb loin chops, about 1½ inches thick

Salt and freshly ground pepper

Scottadito literally means to burn your fingers. Does it mean the chops are hot to the touch or are they a little hot on the tongue as well? We choose to believe the latter. This version of *scottadito* could also be known as *arrabbiata,* or angry, because of the heat of the red pepper flakes. I don't think the marinade is as hot as Thai chiles or jalapeños; it has just a pleasant warmth about it. The recipe is from the Abruzzi. ◆ *Serves 6*

For the marinade, heat the olive oil and pepper flakes in a medium saucepan over medium-high heat until very hot but not boiling, 5 to 7 minutes (do not let the flakes brown). Remove from the heat and let cool 5 to 10 minutes. Stir in the remaining ingredients and let cool completely.

Pour the marinade over the chops in a shallow nonaluminum container, cover, and refrigerate 2 to 3 days.

Heat the grill or broiler and let the chops warm to room temperature.

Remove the chops from the marinade. Lightly sprinkle with salt and pepper and grill or broil chops 4 minutes each side for medium-rare. Serve with fried potatoes and artichokes or with a potato gratin with prosciutto and artichokes.

Costolette d'Agnello al Modo di Camoscio

MARINADE

1½ cups olive oil
4 bay leaves
8 large sage leaves
¾ cup dry red wine
½ cup fresh lemon juice
¼ cup red wine vinegar
1 tablespoon cinnamon
1 tablespoon juniper
  berries, coarsely ground
1 teaspoon ground cloves
1 teaspoon coarsely
  ground pepper

12 large lamb loin chops,
  about 1½ inches thick,
  or 1½ to 2 pounds
  lamb loin, well
  trimmed
2 cups Lamb Stock (page
  268)
Salt and freshly ground
  pepper to taste

So what does this mean? Literally, it is lamb chops treated as if they were game, or specifically chamois, a goatlike antelope. The recipe is from Friuli. ✦ *Serves 6*

For the marinade, heat the oil and bay and sage leaves in a medium saucepan over medium-high heat until very hot but not boiling. Remove from the heat and let cool 5 minutes. Stir in the remaining ingredients and let cool completely.

Pour the marinade over the chops in a shallow nonaluminum container, cover, and refrigerate 3 to 4 days.

Heat the grill or broiler. Let the chops warm to room temperature.

Remove the chops from the marinade. Measure 1 cup marinade into a medium saucepan, add the lamb stock, and boil until reduced by half. Skim the sauce and keep warm.

Lightly sprinkle the chops with salt and pepper and grill or broil 3 to 4 minutes each side for medium-rare. Serve with a potato gratin with wild mushrooms.

Grilled Lamb Chops with Lemon-Thyme Butter and White Bean Ragout

The combination of lamb and white beans is not exclusively French, but this particular version is from Brittany. The lemon-thyme butter will keep well in the refrigerator for 2 to 3 days. ✦ *Serves 6*

For the butter, heat 2 tablespoons butter in a small sauté pan over medium heat. Add the shallots and cook until tender. Add the thyme and cook 2 minutes more; let cool 10 minutes. Place the onion mixture, lemon juice and zest, and remaining butter in a food processor and process until blended. Season to taste with salt and pepper.

For the marinade, strip the zest from the lemons with a vegetable peeler and combine with the remaining ingredients in a nonaluminum container. Add the chops and turn to coat in the marinade. Cover and refrigerate overnight.

Heat the grill or broiler and let the chops warm to room temperature.

Remove the chops from the marinade and sprinkle lightly with salt and pepper. Grill or broil the loin chops 3 minutes each side for rare, about 2½ minutes each side for the rib chops. Spread the lemon butter over the chops and serve with the white bean ragout.

LEMON-THYME BUTTER

8 tablespoons unsalted
   butter, at room
   temperature
3 shallots, finely minced
2 tablespoons chopped
   fresh thyme (1 small
   bunch)
2 tablespoons fresh lemon
   juice
2 tablespoons grated
   lemon zest
Salt and freshly ground
   pepper

MARINADE

4 lemons
1½ cups mild olive oil
¼ cup coarsely chopped
   fresh thyme (about 2
   bunches)
3 to 4 cloves garlic,
   chopped
1 tablespoon freshly
   ground pepper

12 lamb loin chops, about
   1½ inches thick, or 18
   to 24 baby rib chops,
   about 1 inch thick
White Bean Ragout
   (Fagioli all'Uccelletto,
   page 150)

Mint and Mustard Sauce

6 tablespoons unsalted butter

¾ cup minced shallots

3 tablespoons Dijon mustard

3 tablespoons Square One Hot Mustard (page 240)

2 cups Lamb Stock (page 268)

½ cup (or to taste) chopped fresh mint

Salt and freshly ground pepper

One night at the restaurant someone asked for mint jelly for his lamb chops. We didn't have any so our guest poured crème de menthe over them and pronounced them delicious! This recipe is to spare you such a moment. In early Roman cooking mint sauces for meat and fish were made with chopped fresh mint, spices, honey, and vinegar or wine must. As cuisine evolved so did the recipes for mint sauce. It is ironic that the English mint sauce in the bottle is now so close to the early Roman recipe. However our Italo-Franchese mint sauce will serve you well on grilled chops or lamb loin or roast leg of lamb. ✦ *Makes about 2½ cups*

Heat the butter in a wide saucepan over medium heat. Add the shallots and cook until tender, 10 to 15 minutes. Add the mustards, stir well, and cook 1 minute. Add the stock and heat to simmering; simmer 10 minutes. Stir in the mint and season to taste with salt and pepper. The sauce should taste noticeably of mint; add more if the taste is too weak.

Portuguese-Style Grilled Stuffed Lamb Chops

This filling mixture resembles a Catalan *picada* except for the cilantro. Instead of using the mixture to enrich a sauce, as does a *picada,* the Portuguese use it as a stuffing. Incidentally, the stuffing is also great in a boned leg of lamb.
• *Serves 6*

STUFFING

6 tablespoons (or as needed) unsalted butter, melted

1/4 cup chopped onion

3 cloves garlic, minced

1 cup fresh bread crumbs

6 tablespoons sliced almonds, toasted and coarsely chopped

1/4 cup chopped fresh cilantro

3 tablespoons coarsely chopped pitted Kalamata olives

Salt and freshly ground pepper

LEMON-CILANTRO BUTTER

3/4 cup unsalted butter, softened

3 cloves garlic, finely minced

Juice and grated zest of 2 lemons

1/4 cup chopped fresh cilantro

12 lamb loin chops, about 1 1/2 inches thick, a generous pocket cut in each

1/4 cup olive oil

For the stuffing, heat 2 tablespoons butter in a small sauté pan over medium heat. Add the onion and cook until translucent, about 10 minutes. Add the garlic and cook 2 to 3 minutes. Remove from the heat and combine with the remaining butter, the bread crumbs, almonds, cilantro, and olives. Season to taste with salt and pepper. The stuffing should hold together when squeezed in your hand; if it is too dry add 1 to 2 more tablespoons melted butter.

For the lemon butter, place all the ingredients in a food processor and process until blended. Season to taste with salt and pepper.

Heat the grill or broiler. Stuff each chop with 2 tablespoons of the filling and brush with the oil. Lightly sprinkle with salt and pepper and grill or broil 4 minutes each side for medium-rare. Spread with the butter and serve with fried potatoes and sautéed carrots with mint.

Costoletas de Carneiro Escondidinho

GRILLED LAMB CHOPS
WITH PORT AND
MUSTARD CREAM

½ cup port, preferably Ficklin or Quady

¾ cup heavy cream

2 tablespoons Square One Hot Mustard (page 240)

1 tablespoon Dijon mustard

Salt and freshly ground pepper

12 lamb loin chops, about 1½ inches thick

2 tablespoons olive oil

This sauce also works wonderfully with grilled or sautéed loin of lamb. I'll admit that the color is a little unusual—it's pink! But the contrasting sweetness of the port, heat of the mustard, and richness of the cream makes for a flavor that will keep you dipping your spoon in for more. ◆ *Serves 6*

Heat the port in a small saucepan over high heat 1 to 2 minutes to burn off the alcohol. Reduce the cream in a second saucepan over medium-high heat to ½ cup. Add the port and mustards to the reduced cream and whisk until well blended. Season to taste with salt and pepper.

Heat the grill or broiler. Brush the chops with oil and lightly sprinkle with salt and pepper. Grill or broil 4 minutes each side for medium-rare or 5 to 6 minutes each side for medium. Heat the sauce to simmering and spoon over the chops. Serve with fried potatoes and sautéed green beans or carrots.

Fritto Misto

MIXED FRY OF LAMB
CHOPS, RICE
CROQUETTES, AND
VEGETABLES

8 baby lamb chops or
   veal chops, about 3½
   ounces each on the
   bone
3 cups water (optional)
3 tablespoons fresh lemon
   juice
¼ pound veal
   sweetbreads, cut into 4
   equal pieces (optional)
8 baby artichokes
3 tablespoons olive oil
¼ cup dry white wine
1 clove garlic, crushed
1 bay leaf
3 or 4 black peppercorns
Salt
1 small eggplant
4 medium zucchini
8 zucchini blossoms
4½ to 5 ounces fresh
   mozzarella, cut into 8
   one-inch cubes
2 teaspoons chopped fresh
   marjoram or sage

DEEP-FRY COATING

2 large eggs
3 tablespoons cold water
3 cups all-purpose flour
1 teaspoon salt
½ teaspoon freshly
   ground pepper

Peanut oil for deep frying
8 Rice Croquettes (page
   152), shaped but not
   fried
Parsley sprigs for garnish
Lemon wedges for serving

When I first arrived in Rome a friend recommended a Jewish restaurant named Piperno a Monte Cenci, located in the old ghetto. It became (and still is, thirty years later) my favorite restaurant in Rome. In the summer you can sit outside in a delightful courtyard and eat one of Piperno's specialties, the fabulously elaborate *fritto misto*. Their classic recipe has brains, sweetbreads, and assorted vegetables, plus deep-fried *bocconcini* mozzarella.

Because it is one of my favorite dishes, I have tried *fritto misto* at many other restaurants in Italy. (I have also ordered it in Italian restaurants in America, often with disastrous results.) In addition to the usual sweetbreads, brains, vegetables, and rice croquettes, I've been served chicken croquettes, baby veal chops, baby lamb chops, and even calves liver. We have tried and tried to sell this at the restaurant with innards, but to no avail. (The orders come in "*fritto misto*, hold the sweetbreads" or "hold the liver." Heaven forbid we should offer brains!) I still think that sweetbreads are the perfect touch and have included instructions on how to prepare them. Otherwise, we have made only a few minor changes in the magic Piperno formula. Because we cannot get the perfect little balls of fresh mozzarella, we stuff zucchini blossoms with fresh mozzarella and fresh marjoram. If zucchini blossoms are not available, we stuff cubes of mozzarella into the rice croquettes. You may leave out the meat entirely and serve only vegetables. You will see that the deep-fry coating is not a batter, rather just an egg wash with a dusting of seasoned flour. ◆ *Serves 4*

Trim the fat and bones from the lamb chops, then lightly pound ½ inch thick.

If using sweetbreads, heat the water and 1 tablespoon lemon juice to boiling in a medium saucepan. Add the sweetbreads, reduce the heat, and simmer until firm and cooked through but not mushy and all traces of red are gone, 5 to 10 minutes. With a slotted spoon, remove the sweetbreads to a bowl of ice water and let cool. Peel the outer membrane from the cooled sweetbreads and remove all connecting veins.

For the artichokes, trim the stems and remove all the dark green leaves down to the inner yellow leaves, then pare the bases. Soak the artichokes in a bowl of cold water to cover acidulated with 2 tablespoons lemon juice to keep them from blackening. Cut the trimmed artichokes in half and cook in the à la grecque mixture: Simmer in a medium saucepan with the oil, wine, garlic, bay leaf, peppercorns, 1 teaspoon salt, and water to cover until half cooked and the stem end is tender, about 5 minutes (see Note). Drain and set aside.

Peel and cut the eggplant into ½-inch-thick slices, then cut each slice crosswise in half. Trim and cut the zucchini lengthwise into quarters, then crosswise in half. Sprinkle the vegetables with salt and place in a colander; let stand until they have given off their water, about 30 minutes. Rinse and pat dry; set aside.

Remove the central stamen from the zucchini blossoms. Coat the cheese cubes lightly with the marjoram and place 1 cube in each blossom. Twist the ends of the blossoms to enclose; set aside.

Prepare the coating: Lightly beat the eggs with the water. Season the flour with the salt and pepper.

Heat 6 inches oil in a deep fryer or large wok to 350° over high heat. Working in batches, dip the meats, vegetables, and rice croquettes in the egg mixture and then in the seasoned flour. Shake off the excess flour and deep-fry until golden, 4 to 6 minutes. Drain on paper towels. Keep the cooked food warm while frying the remaining food. Garnish with parsley sprigs and serve at once with lemon wedges.

NOTE: For *Artichokes à la Grecque,* continue to simmer the artichokes until fully cooked, then cool completely in the liquid. Remove with a slotted spoon and serve at room temperature.

Port, Shallot, and Tarragon Sauce

This is a nice sauce to have in your repertoire. We serve it on grilled lamb chops and loin. It is a combination of French and Portuguese recipes. The sauce may be refrigerated 2 days or frozen up to a month. ◆ *Makes 2 cups, enough for 8 servings of lamb*

3 cups port, preferably Ficklin or Quady
¼ cup unsalted butter
½ cup finely chopped shallots
¼ cup finely chopped fresh tarragon
2½ cups Lamb Stock (recipe follows)
Salt and freshly ground pepper to taste

Boil the port in a saucepan over high heat until reduced to 1 cup.

Meanwhile, heat the butter in a medium sauté pan over medium heat. Add the shallots and cook until tender, 7 to 10 minutes. Add the port, tarragon, and stock and cook until reduced to 2 cups. Season with salt and pepper.

Lamb Stock

6 pounds lamb shanks and any meat trimmings
2 medium onions, coarsely chopped
3 carrots, coarsely chopped
1 rib celery, coarsely chopped
6 sprigs fresh parsley
2 sprigs fresh thyme
3 cloves garlic, smashed
2 small bay leaves
2 cloves
10 peppercorns
3 ripe tomatoes, sliced

Most people have very little use for lamb stock, but we at Square One cook so many lamb ragouts, we find this stock is essential to our larder. Occasionally it turns out not to be as flavorful as we would like, then we do a double lamb stock using the weak stock as the water with new stock ingredients. ◆ *Makes 5 to 6 quarts*

Preheat the oven to 450°. Place the bones and any trimmings in a large roasting pan and roast until browned, about 1½ hours. Transfer to a large stockpot and cover with cold water. Heat to boiling and skim the scum from the surface. Reduce the heat and simmer uncovered 1 hour, skimming frequently the first half hour.

Meanwhile, pour off most of the fat in the roasting pan. Add the onions, carrots, and celery; cook on top of the stove or in the oven until tender and browned. Add the vegetables to the stockpot. Pour a half inch or so of water into the roasting pan and boil, scraping up the browned bits on the bottom. Add to the stockpot with the remaining ingredients. Simmer uncovered 4 to 6 hours.

Remove the solids from the stock with a slotted spoon or large skimmer. Strain the stock through a cheesecloth-lined strainer and let cool to room temperature. Refrigerate until cold, then remove the fat from the top. Reduce the stock if you want a more intense lamb flavor.

Leg of Lamb Avgolemono with Asparagus

1 leg of lamb, about 5 pounds

5 cloves garlic, peeled and slivered

12 large fresh mint leaves, cut in half, or 24 small

Salt and freshly ground pepper

SAUCE

1½ pounds asparagus

4 tablespoons unsalted butter

2 medium onions, cut into medium dice

2 cloves garlic, finely minced

2 cups Lamb or Chicken Stock (page 268 or 103)

2 large eggs

¼ cup fresh lemon juice

3 tablespoons finely chopped fresh mint

This recipe is typically Mediterranean; the most well known version is undoubtedly the Greek *avgolemono*. Variations of the dish are also found in Turkey, as well as in Italy, in the region of Apulia where the Greeks had some influence on the early cuisine, in the Sephardic Jewish cooking of the Veneto, and in Tuscany. We usually prepare the dish as a ragout but tried the following version at the request of Jan Weimer when we were working on three Italian menus for *Bon Appétit* magazine. We were so pleased with the results that we decided to offer the new preparation here. Little red or white potatoes roasted in the pan along with the lamb make a very good accompaniment. ◆ *Serves 4 to 6*

Trim excess fat from the leg of lamb. Make shallow incisions in the leg and insert a garlic sliver and rolled mint leaf in each. Lightly sprinkle the leg with salt and pepper and set in a roasting pan. Cover and let stand 1 hour at room temperature.

Preheat the oven to 350°. Roast the leg until a meat thermometer registers 120° for rare, about 1 hour. Transfer to a platter, cover with foil, and let stand in a warm place.

While the lamb is roasting, trim the asparagus for the sauce and peel if the stalks are large. Heat 4 inches water to simmering in a deep sauté pan. Add the asparagus and simmer until crisp-tender, 3 to 6 minutes. Drain and refresh under cold running water. Drain again, pat dry, and cut into 2-inch-long pieces; set aside.

Heat the butter in a saucepan over low heat. Add the onions and cook until translucent. Add the garlic and cook 1 minute; set aside.

Drain the fat from the roasting pan. Add the stock and heat to boiling, scraping up the browned bits that stick to the bottom of the pan. Add the onion mixture and simmer 2 to 3 minutes. Add the asparagus and simmer until heated through. Beat the eggs with the lemon juice in a small bowl until slightly frothy and gradually whisk into the hot but not simmering sauce. Immediately remove the sauce from the heat. Stir in the mint and season to taste with salt and pepper. Slice the lamb and arrange on serving plates. Spoon the sauce over and serve.

Qodban

MOROCCAN LAMB
BROCHETTES

MARINADE

1 small onion, diced

4 cloves garlic, minced

*1 tablespoon ground
   cumin*

1 tablespoon paprika

*1/2 teaspoon ground
   ginger*

*1/2 teaspoon cayenne
   pepper*

*1 teaspoon freshly ground
   pepper*

*3 tablespoons fresh lemon
   juice*

2/3 cup olive oil

*2 tablespoons chopped
   fresh cilantro*

*2 pounds leg of lamb,
   trimmed well and cut
   into 1 1/2-inch cubes*

Salt

Harissa *(page 191)*

In this wonderful preparation, cubes of lamb are marinated in a classic *mechoui* mixture, then threaded onto skewers and grilled. We serve this kabob on its own or as part of a Moroccan mixed grill, with *Merguez* (page 290), the lamb sausage made from the trimmings of leg of lamb, and with a quail stuffed with honeyed onions and raisins (page 231) or with a chicken thigh marinated in sesame, honey, and cinnamon (page 203). Serve these brochettes with *Harissa* (page 191), a hot sauce made with cayenne and cumin. ✦ *Serves 4 to 6*

For the marinade, puree the onion, garlic, cumin, paprika, ginger, and both peppers in a food processor. Add the lemon juice and pulse a few times until blended. Stir in the oil and cilantro.

Place the lamb cubes in a shallow nonaluminum container, pour the marinade over, and toss to coat. Cover and refrigerate overnight or let stand 3 hours at cool room temperature.

Heat the grill or broiler. Let the lamb warm to room temperature if necessary. Thread the lamb onto 4 to 6 long skewers and lightly sprinkle with salt. Grill or broil 3 to 4 minutes each side for medium-rare. Serve with *harissa*, steamed couscous, and grilled eggplant and peppers that have been brushed with some of the marinade during cooking.

Roast Leg of Lamb with a Moroccan "Mechoui" Marinade

1 leg of lamb, 5 to 6
  pounds

5 cloves garlic, slivered

2 teaspoons ground cumin

2 teaspoons paprika

2 teaspoons freshly
  ground pepper

1½ teaspoons ground
  coriander

½ teaspoon cayenne
  pepper

6 tablespoons fruity olive
  oil

¼ cup fresh lemon juice

2 tablespoons finely
  minced garlic

½ cup chopped fresh
  cilantro

In Morocco, of course, this preparation implies a spit-roasted whole baby lamb. We have little occasion and space to do a classic *mechoui* but can recreate the taste with this simpler cut of meat. ◆ *Serves 4 to 6*

Trim excess fat from the leg of lamb. Make shallow incisions in the leg and insert a garlic sliver in each one. Combine the spices with the oil, lemon juice, minced garlic, and cilantro to make a paste and rub the paste over the leg. Set the leg in a roasting pan, cover, and let stand 3 to 4 hours at cool room temperature or refrigerate overnight.

Preheat the oven to 350°. Roast the leg until a meat thermometer registers 120° for rare, about 1 hour 10 minutes. Let rest 10 minutes before carving.

Slice the leg and serve with couscous with almonds and raisins, and grilled eggplant and peppers basted with Moroccan Charmoula (page 175).

NOTE: This recipe may also be made with a butterflied leg. Spread the cut side of the leg with half the paste, then roll and tie the leg. Make shallow incisions in the rolled leg and insert a garlic sliver in each one. Rub with the remaining paste and roast as directed. You could also grill the butterflied leg of lamb without rolling and trying it.

Souvlaki

GREEK LAMB
BROCHETTES

MARINADE

*1 medium onion, cut into
    chunks (about 1½
    cups)*

1⅓ cups olive oil

⅓ cup fresh lemon juice

*3 tablespoons minced
    garlic*

*3 tablespoons dried
    oregano*

*2 tablespoons freshly
    ground pepper*

*2½ to 3 pounds leg of
    lamb, trimmed well
    and cut into
    twenty-four 2-inch
    cubes*

Salt

Yet another wonderful lamb kabob. You can't have too
many in your repertoire. ✦ *Serves 6*

For the marinade, pulse the onion in a food processor until
pureed. Add the remaining ingredients and pulse just until
combined. Pour the marinade over the lamb cubes in a
shallow nonaluminum container and toss the meat to coat.
Cover and refrigerate overnight.

Heat the grill or broiler. Let the lamb warm to room temperature. Thread the cubes onto 6 skewers and lightly
sprinkle with salt. Grill or broil 3 to 4 minutes each side
until medium-rare. Remove the lamb from the skewers and
serve on top of a bed of rice pilaf, accompanied by a salad
of diced cucumbers, yogurt, and mint.

VARIATION

For *Turkish shish kabobs,* serve the lamb with pita bread,
and a sauce of diced onions that have been sautéed in
butter, with diced fresh tomatoes added just for the last
minute of cooking time, then bound with a little yogurt.

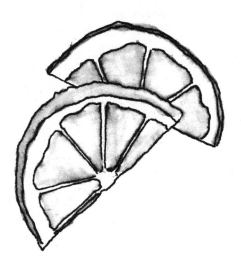

Chanfana

PORTUGUESE LAMB
RAGOUT

½ cup (or as needed)
   olive oil

3 pounds lamb shoulder,
   trimmed well and cut
   into 1½-inch cubes

2 large onions, cut into
   medium dice

3 tablespoons paprika

1 teaspoon (or to taste)
   freshly grated nutmeg

2 tablespoons finely
   minced garlic

1½ cups dry red wine

1 cup Lamb or Chicken
   Stock (page 268 or
   103)

1¼ cups slivered
   almonds

Salt and freshly ground
   pepper

6 tablespoons chopped
   fresh parsley

36 Niçoise olives

The original Portuguese recipe calls for leg of lamb, but we have adapted it for a ragout. Hot cooked rice combined with fresh mint makes a nice accompaniment.

◆ *Serves 6 to 8*

Heat ¼ cup olive oil in a heavy sauté pan over high heat. Add as many lamb cubes as will comfortably fit in the pan (overcrowding will cause the lamb to steam rather than brown) and brown on all sides; transfer to a deep casserole. Repeat with the remaining lamb cubes, adding 1 to 2 tablespoons oil to the pan as needed for each batch.

Heat the remaining ¼ cup oil in the same pan over medium heat. Add the onions and cook until tender, 7 to 10 minutes. Add the paprika and nutmeg and cook 5 minutes more. Add the garlic and cook 2 minutes. Transfer the onion mixture to the casserole with the lamb. Pour ¼ cup red wine into the sauté pan and boil a minute or two, scraping up the browned bits on the bottom; transfer to the casserole. Add the remaining wine and the stock to the casserole and heat to boiling. Reduce the heat, cover, and simmer until the meat is tender, about 1½ hours. Skim well.

Meanwhile, preheat the oven to 350°. Toast the almonds on a baking sheet until lightly browned and fragrant, about 7 minutes; chop and add to the stew for the last 30 minutes of cooking.

Season the stew to taste with salt and pepper. Add a pinch more nutmeg, if you'd like a stronger nutmeg flavor. Stir in the parsley and olives and serve.

*T*alas Borek

MIDDLE EASTERN LAMB
RAGOUT WITH A
FILO CRUST

MARINADE

½ cup olive oil

1 tablespoon cinnamon

1 teaspoon dried oregano

1 teaspoon freshly ground
   pepper

2 pounds lamb shoulder,
   trimmed well and cut
   into 1-inch cubes

¼ cup (or as needed)
   olive oil

¼ cup unsalted butter

2 large onions, chopped

6 cloves garlic, minced

2 teaspoons (or to taste)
   cinnamon

1 tablespoon (or to taste)
   dried oregano

2 cups diced canned
   Italian plum tomatoes
   with ½ cup of the
   juices

2 cups Lamb or Chicken
   Stock (page 268 or
   103)

Salt and freshly ground
   pepper

6 sheets filo dough

½ cup clarified butter
   (see Note, page 26)

¼ pound feta cheese

¼ cup chopped fresh
   parsley for garnish

Versions of this dish appear in both Greek and Turkish cuisines. The original recipes have you enclose the ragout in sheets of filo, which is not too tricky if you do it just before serving. But this is a bit hazardous if you like to get things assembled ahead of time, as the juices from the ragout will leak through the filo. As a compromise, we heat the lamb in a ramekin (you may use a single deep-dish pie or gratin mold) and bake the filo crust separately. The crust stays crisp and lamb stays juicy. ◆ *Serves 6*

For the marinade, combine all the ingredients in a shallow nonaluminum container. Add the lamb and toss to coat. Cover and refrigerate overnight.

Let the lamb warm to room temperature. Heat the oil in a large heavy skillet over high heat. Add as many lamb cubes as will comfortably fit in the pan (overcrowding will cause the lamb to steam rather than brown) and brown on all sides; transfer to a deep casserole. Repeat with the remaining lamb cubes, adding 1 to 2 tablespoons oil to the pan as needed for each batch.

Heat ¼ cup butter in the same pan over medium heat. Add the onions and cook until translucent, 7 to 10 minutes. Add the garlic, cinnamon, and oregano and cook 5 minutes; transfer to the casserole with the lamb. Add the tomatoes with their juices and the stock to the casserole and heat to boiling. Reduce the heat, cover, and simmer until the meat is tender, about 1½ hours. Skim the fat from the ragout and season to taste with salt and pepper (do not oversalt for the feta is salty). You may also want to add more cinnamon or oregano.

To make the filo lids, use scissors and one of 6 individual gratin dishes or a deep-dish pie or 1½- to 2-quart gratin mold as a guide to cut out 24 individual or 4 large rounds. Brush each with clarified butter and build 6 stacks of 4 layers each, or 1 stack of 4 large layers, on a foil- or parchment-lined baking sheet. Refrigerate until needed, up to 24 hours.

Preheat the oven to 450°. Heat the ragout to boiling and divide it among the individual gratin dishes or spoon it into the large dish. Sprinkle with crumbled feta and bake until the cheese melts, about 5 minutes. Brush the filo lids with clarified butter and bake them at the same time, if oven space allows, until golden brown, about 4 minutes. Place a lid on each ramekin or on the large dish and sprinkle with chopped parsley. Serve immediately.

Agnello al Calderotto

PUGLIESE LAMB RAGOUT WITH TOMATOES, GREENS, AND CHEESE

½ cup (or as needed) olive oil

3 pounds lamb shoulder, trimmed well and cut into 1½-inch cubes

2 large onions, cut into medium dice

⅓ cup dry white wine

3 cups diced peeled fresh or canned plum tomatoes with 1½ cups of the juices

2 tablespoons finely chopped garlic

¼ cup chopped fresh parsley

Salt and freshly ground pepper

6 cups coarsely chopped curly endive or dandelion greens

1½ cups crumbled feta or mild goat cheese

This ancient southern Italian dish takes its name from a cooking pot, the *caldaio*, in which the stew is traditionally prepared. The pot is also sometimes known as *caldariello*. But by any name, as the saying goes, the dish tastes as good. The recipe is traditionally prepared with sheep's milk; we garnish with feta or goat cheese. This rustic stew may be accompanied by grilled bread or roasted potatoes.
◆ *Serves 6 to 8*

Heat ¼ cup oil in a large sauté pan over high heat. Add as many lamb cubes as will comfortably fit in the pan (overcrowding will cause the lamb to steam rather than brown) and brown on all sides; transfer to a deep casserole. Repeat with the remaining lamb cubes, adding 1 to 2 tablespoons oil to the pan as needed for each batch.

Heat 2 tablespoons oil in the same sauté pan over medium heat. Add the onions and cook until translucent, 7 to 10 minutes; add to the casserole with the lamb. Pour the wine into the pan and boil a minute or two, scraping up the browned bits on the bottom; add to the casserole. Pulse the tomatoes with their juices in a food processor until chopped and add to the casserole along with the garlic. Heat to boiling. Reduce the heat, cover, and simmer very slowly until the meat is tender. (You will not need any stock; just let the meat and tomatoes give off their juices to make a very rich sauce.) Add the parsley for the final 10 minutes of cooking. Season to taste with salt and pepper. Skim well. (The stew may be prepared ahead up to this point.)

Just before serving, add the greens to the stew, cover, and let them wilt in the pan juices over low heat. Sprinkle with cheese and serve immediately.

Spezzatino d'Agnello con Gremolata

LAMB RAGOUT WITH GREMOLATA

8 tablespoons (or as
    needed) olive oil

3 pounds lamb shoulder,
    trimmed well and cut
    into 1½-inch cubes

2 large onions, cut into
    medium dice

2 cups diced seeded
    peeled fresh or canned
    tomatoes with 1 cup of
    the juices

1 cup Lamb or Chicken
    Stock (page 268, 103)

2 tablespoons finely
    chopped garlic

1 tablespoon grated
    orange zest

2 teaspoons chopped
    thyme

2 tablespoons grated fresh
    ginger (optional)

3 large carrots, cut into
    2-inch lengths

Salt and ground pepper

6 small zucchini, cut
    lengthwise in half, then
    into 2-inch lengths

2 cups slender green
    beans, trimmed

GREMOLATA

9 tablespoons chopped
    fresh parsley

1 tablespoon each grated
    orange and lemon zest

1 tablespoon very finely
    minced garlic

A little twist on the classic *gremolata*. The orange adds a wonderful dimension to the flavor of the lamb and the tomatoes. Try it with fresh ginger for an interesting variation. ✦ *Serves 6 to 8*

Heat 4 tablespoons oil in a large deep sauté pan or casserole over high heat. Add as many lamb cubes as will comfortably fit in the pan (overcrowding will cause the lamb to steam rather than brown) and brown on all sides; set aside. Repeat with the remaining lamb cubes, adding 1 to 2 tablespoons oil to the pan as needed for each batch.

Heat 3 more tablespoons oil in the same pan over medium heat. Add the onions and cook until translucent, 7 to 10 minutes. Return the lamb to the pan and add the tomatoes, stock, garlic, orange zest, thyme, and ginger if using. Heat to boiling. Reduce the heat to low, cover, and simmer the stew very gently until the lamb is tender, about 1½ hours. Add the carrots for the last 30 minutes of cooking. Season to taste with salt and pepper. Skim well.

Meanwhile, heat a large pot of salted water to boiling. Add the zucchini and boil until crisp-tender, about 2 minutes. Remove with a slotted spoon and refresh under cold running water. Reheat the water to boiling, add the beans, and boil until crisp-tender, about 2 minutes. Drain and refresh under cold running water.

Combine all the *gremolata* ingredients.

Stir the zucchini, beans, and *gremolata* into the finished stew and heat through. Serve with roasted potatoes or green fettuccine.

Moroccan Lamb Tagine with Lemon and Olives

This is not the real thing, but a Square One adaptation. Our customers were not wild about the briny taste of the traditional salt-preserved lemons, so we have substituted our own version, actually a quick lemon conserve that eliminates the bitterness of the lemons. ✦ *Serves 6 to 8*

MARINADE

2 teaspoons paprika

1 teaspoon ground ginger

½ teaspoon turmeric

¼ teaspoon cayenne

3 tablespoons olive oil

3 pounds lamb shoulder, trimmed well and cut into 1½-inch cubes

PRESERVED LEMONS

2 small lemons

1 cup water

¼ cup sugar

5 tablespoons (or as needed) olive oil

6 cups diced onions

8 teaspoons paprika

4 teaspoons ground ginger

1 tablespoon finely minced garlic

2½ cups Lamb or Chicken Stock (page 268 or 103) or water

18 small artichokes (about 2 inches tall), trimmed, or 6 large artichokes, trimmed, quartered, and chokes removed (optional)

18 to 24 Moroccan or Kalamata olives

2 tablespoons chopped fresh cilantro

2 tablespoons chopped fresh parsley

Salt and ground pepper

For the marinade, combine all ingredients to make a paste and rub it over the lamb cubes in a shallow nonaluminum container. Cover and let stand 3 hours at room temperature or refrigerate overnight.

For the lemons, wipe the lemons with a clean towel and cut into eighths (or sixteenths, if the lemons are large). To remove the bitterness from the peel, boil the lemons in water to cover 3 minutes, rinse under cold water, then soak in cold water 1 hour. Combine 1 cup water and the sugar in a saucepan and cook over medium heat until the sugar dissolves. Add the lemons and simmer until tender, 20 to 30 minutes (or about half that time for Meyer lemons). Remove from heat, let cool, and drain.

Heat 2 tablespoons oil in a large, deep sauté pan over high heat. Add as many lamb cubes as will comfortably fit in the pan (overcrowding will cause the lamb to steam rather than brown) and brown on all sides; set aside. Repeat with the remaining lamb cubes, adding 1 to 2 tablespoons oil to the pan as needed for each batch.

Heat the remaining oil in the same pan over medium heat. Add the onions and cook until tender, 7 to 10 minutes. Add the paprika, ginger, and garlic and cook 3 minutes more. Return the lamb to the pan, add the stock, and heat to boiling. Reduce the heat and simmer, partially covered, until the lamb is tender, about 1½ hours. Add the artichokes, if using, and simmer until almost tender, about 10 minutes. Add the lemons, olives, cilantro, and parsley; skim well and simmer 5 more minutes. Season to taste with salt and pepper (we like this peppery). Serve with couscous and *Harissa* (page 191).

Mishmishaya

MIDDLE EASTERN LAMB
RAGOUT WITH
APRICOTS

MARINADE

½ cup olive oil

1½ teaspoons ground
coriander

1½ teaspoons ground
cumin

1 teaspoon cinnamon

½ teaspoon ground
ginger

3 pounds lamb shoulder,
trimmed well and cut
into 2-inch cubes

1 teaspoon saffron threads

¼ cup hot stock or water

¾ pound dried apricots

1 cup dark or golden
raisins

½ cup unsalted butter

⅓ cup olive oil

2 large onions, diced

1½ teaspoons ground
coriander

1½ teaspoons ground
cumin

1 teaspoon cinnamon

½ teaspoon ground
ginger

3 to 4 cups Lamb or
Chicken Stock (page
268 or 103)

Salt and freshly ground
pepper

1 to 2 tablespoons honey
(optional)

2 to 3 tablespoons
chopped almonds or
sesame seeds for
garnish

The combination of meat and fruit is very popular in the cuisine of the Middle East. The Iraqi lamb and dried fruit stews, Moroccan tagines, and Persian *khoresh* are closely related. We Americans, with our predilection for sweets with our meats (witness our love of turkey with cranberry relish, roast chicken with watermelon pickle, pork chops with applesauce), should find this recipe a natural.
♦ *Serves 6 to 8*

For the marinade, combine all ingredients and rub over the lamb in a shallow nonaluminum container. Cover and refrigerate overnight.

Crush the saffron threads and steep 10 minutes in the hot stock. Soak the apricots and raisins 1 hour in hot water to cover; drain, reserving the soaking liquid.

Let the meat warm to room temperature. Heat ¼ cup butter with 2 tablespoons oil in a large heavy casserole or saucepan over high heat. Add as many lamb cubes as will comfortably fit in the pan (overcrowding will cause the lamb to steam rather than brown) and brown on all sides; set aside. Repeat with the remaining lamb cubes, adding 1 to 2 tablespoons oil to the pan as needed for each batch.

Melt the remaining ¼ cup butter in the same pan over medium heat. Add the onions and cook 7 to 10 minutes. Add the spices and cook until the onions are translucent, about 5 minutes longer. Return the meat to the pan with any accumulated juices. Add the saffron infusion and enough stock to cover. Heat to boiling. Reduce the heat and simmer covered over low heat 1 hour. Add the raisins and apricots and simmer until the meat is tender, 20 to 30 minutes. Skim well. Season to taste with salt and pepper. If the stew is too tart, add 4 to 6 tablespoons soaking liquid from the dried fruit and simmer 5 minutes. If the stew is still too tart, add the honey.

Garnish with almonds or sesame seeds if you like, and serve with rice or couscous.

PORK

Roast Pork Loin with Tarragon and Mustard Sauce

1 pork loin roast on the bone, 4 to 5 pounds

6 cloves garlic, cut into slivers

Salt and freshly ground pepper

6 tablespoons (or to taste) Dijon and/or Square One Hot Mustard (page 240)

¾ cup Chicken Stock (page 103)

1½ cups heavy cream

2 tablespoons (or to taste) chopped fresh tarragon

It is unfortunate that many people associate complexity with fine dining. They are easily impressed by elaborate presentation. Simplicity in cooking can be a virtue and is certainly not a bore! Fresh tarragon, rich cream, mustard, and a perfectly cooked piece of pork make this a wonderful and easy dinner for both the novice and accomplished cook. ✦ *Serves 6*

Preheat the oven to 400°. Cut shallow incisions between the bones of the roast (on the bone side) and insert the garlic slivers. Lightly sprinkle the pork with salt and pepper and spread with 3 to 4 tablespoons mustard. Set the pork in a roasting pan and roast until a meat thermometer registers 140°, about 1 hour. Remove the pork from the pan to a carving board, cover, and let rest.

Pour off all but 2 tablespoons fat from the roasting pan. Pour in the stock and boil, scraping up the browned bits on the bottom, until slightly thickened, about 5 minutes. Stir in the cream, remaining mustard, and the tarragon and simmer until the flavors are blended and the sauce is slightly thickened, 2 to 3 minutes. Season to taste with salt and pepper. Add more mustard or tarragon, if you like.

Slice the roast between the bones into chops. Arrange 1 or 2 chops on each serving plate and spoon the sauce over top. Serve with roasted or fried potatoes, sautéed spinach or greens, or black-pepper ravioli filled with mashed potatoes and sautéed shallots. If you like, you may garnish with apples that have been sautéed in butter with a bit of sugar; the sweetness of the apple is a nice counterpoint to the spicy sweetness of the tarragon.

NOTE: You may cook the roast and the sauce ahead of time. Slice the roast just before serving and warm it gently in the sauce.

Lomo di Cerdo Almendrado

ROAST PORK LOIN WITH ALMONDS, GARLIC, AND PARSLEY

1 pork loin roast on the
  bone, 5 to 6 pounds
3 cloves garlic, cut into
  slivers
Salt and freshly ground
  pepper

ALMOND CRUNCHIES

2 cups sliced almonds
  (not blanched)
1 cup chopped fresh
  parsley
3 tablespoons finely
  chopped garlic
¼ cup reserved pork
  drippings

SHERRY CREAM SAUCE

2 tablespoons unsalted
  butter
8 large shallots, minced
  (⅔ to ¾ cup)
1 cup Amontillado sherry
3 cups heavy cream
Pinch sugar (optional)

This is by far the most popular pork roast we serve at Square One. I suspect that people love it because it has so many interesting textures and flavors—toasted garlic, crunchy almonds, and an unctuous sherry cream sauce. We have broken down the cooking process into a series of simple steps so that you may prepare all of the components ahead of time and assemble the dish quickly at serving time. ◆ *Serves 6*

Preheat the oven to 400°. Cut shallow incisions between the bones of the roast (on the bone side) and insert the garlic slivers. Put the roast in a roasting pan and lightly sprinkle the pork with salt and pepper. Roast about 1 hour or until a meat thermometer inserted in the center registers 140°. Cover and let the roast rest up to 2 hours. Measure and reserve ¼ cup pan drippings.

For the crunchies, reduce the heat to 350°. Spread the almonds in a single layer on a baking sheet and toast until lightly browned and fragrant, 7 to 10 minutes. Let cool a few minutes, then crush them coarsely with your fingers into a small baking dish or chop them with a cleaver. Add the parsley, garlic, and reserved pork drippings and stir until blended. Bake, stirring occasionally, until golden brown, 15 to 20 minutes. Set aside up to 2 hours.

For the sauce, heat the butter in a medium saucepan over low heat. Add the shallots and cook until tender, about 7 minutes. Stir in the sherry and heat to simmering; simmer briskly 2 to 3 minutes. Add the cream and simmer until slightly reduced, about 5 minutes. Season to taste with salt and pepper. If the sauce is a bit tart, add a pinch of sugar. Set aside until serving time.

To serve, cut the roast between the bones into chops or cut the long strip of loin meat off the bones, then cut into eighteen ½-inch-thick slices. Heat the sauce to simmering in 2 wide saucepans. Add the pork and the crunchies and simmer gently until warmed through, 1 to 2 minutes for slices or about 4 minutes for chops. Taste and adjust the seasonings. Place the pork on serving plates and spoon the sauce over top. Serve with sautéed spinach or green beans and little roasted or fried potatoes.

Pork Loin Marinated in Red Wine

2 cups (or more if needed) dry red wine

3 tablespoons juniper berries, coarsely ground in a spice mill

1 tablespoon dried red pepper flakes

2 teaspoons black peppercorns, coarsely ground

8 bay leaves, crumbled

3 pork tenderloins or 1 boneless pork loin, about 2 pounds

Salt and freshly ground pepper

½ cup (or to taste) Beef, Veal, or Chicken Stock (page 104, 237, or 103)

This recipe is adapted from two Sardinian dishes: the famed *porceddu*, or roast suckling pig, and the *cinghiale alla montagnina*, or wild boar marinated in red wine. Few of us have the occasion to cook a whole pig at home—even in the restaurant, suckling pig is hardly an everyday occurrence! So we use boneless pork loin or, even better, the tenderloin, which absorbs the marinade more quickly and completely and is more tender. Remember that pork shrinks during cooking, so you must allow ½ pound per person. ◆ *Serves 4*

Combine the wine, juniper berries, pepper flakes, black pepper, and bay leaves in a shallow nonaluminum container and add the pork. If necessary, add a bit more wine just to cover the meat. Cover and refrigerate overnight for tenderloins or 2 days for the loin.

Heat the grill or broiler. Remove the pork from the marinade, reserving the marinade. Lightly sprinkle the pork with salt and pepper and grill or broil, turning occasionally, until a meat thermometer inserted in the center registers 140°, about 6 minutes for the tenderloins or 10 to 12 minutes for the loin.

Meanwhile, strain the marinade into a saucepan and boil over high heat until reduced to 1 cup. Add the stock to round out the flavor and cook until blended.

Slice the pork ½ inch thick and arrange 3 or 4 pieces on each serving plate. Spoon the sauce over top. Serve with potato gratin, roasted potatoes, or a ragout of white beans seasoned with onions, garlic, fennel, and mint. Sautéed cabbage, if you are a fan, makes a nice vegetable accompaniment to this dish. Just stir-fry it very quickly in olive oil or part oil and part pancetta fat, chicken fat, or butter; add a little lemon zest and toasted pine nuts at the end.

Costata di Maiale Ubriaco

GRILLED PORK CHOP IN A RED WINE AND SPICE MARINADE

MARINADE

2 cups dry red wine

5 bay leaves

2 tablespoons finely chopped fresh rosemary

1½ teaspoons ground coriander

½ teaspoon grated nutmeg

½ teaspoon ground cloves

6 pork loin chops, about 1½ inches thick, well trimmed

¼ cup mild olive oil

Salt and freshly ground pepper

The translation of this Florentine recipe name is drunken pork chop. The pork becomes inebriated in red wine overnight but will never get out of control. ♦ *Serves 6*

For the marinade, combine all the ingredients in a shallow nonaluminum container. Add the chops, cover, and refrigerate overnight.

Heat the grill or broiler. Let the chops warm to room temperature. Remove the chops from the marinade and pat dry, then brush with the oil and lightly sprinkle with salt and pepper. Grill or broil 4 to 5 minutes each side, until cooked through but not dry. Serve with fried or roasted potatoes and sautéed Swiss chard or red cabbage with apples and onions.

Costoletta di Maiale al Rosmarino

VENETIAN-STYLE
GRILLED PORK CHOPS
ON A BED OF
CINNAMON ONIONS

MARINADE

2 tablespoons sugar

1 tablespoon salt

6 juniper berries, bruised

2 whole allspice berries, bruised

6 whole coriander seeds

½ teaspoon white or black peppercorns

2 small bay leaves

¼ cup fresh rosemary leaves

1 teaspoon dried thyme

2¼ cups water

6 pork loin chops, about 1¼ inches thick, well trimmed

CINNAMON ONIONS

½ cup unsalted butter

12 medium onions, sliced about ¼ inch thick

1 tablespoon cinnamon

Salt and freshly ground pepper

Mild olive oil for grilling

Salt and freshly ground pepper

We find that this marinade sweetens and tenderizes American pork so that it more closely resembles Italian pork in flavor. The spiced onions are a carryover from the Renaissance. ◆ *Serves 6*

For the marinade, combine all the ingredients in a shallow nonaluminum container and stir until the sugar and salt dissolve. Add the chops, cover, and refrigerate 1 to 2 days.

For the onions, melt the butter in a large sauté pan over medium heat. Add the onions and cook very slowly until they are very soft, almost a puree, about 30 minutes. Stir in the cinnamon and salt and pepper to taste. The onions may be prepared a day ahead of time and reheated before serving.

Heat the grill or broiler. Remove the chops from the marinade and pat dry. Brush with oil and lightly sprinkle with salt and pepper. Grill or broil 4 to 6 minutes each side until cooked through but not dry. The meat will remain somewhat pink in the center due to the marinade.

To serve, spoon the warm onion mixture onto each serving plate and top with a chop. Serve with roasted or fried potatoes or Grilled Radicchio (page 307). The radicchio is a nice accompaniment as its bitterness contrasts well with the sweetness of the onions and pork.

Pork Scaloppine alla Zaragozana

1 boneless pork loin, 2 to 2½ pounds

Brine (see page 286)

⅔ cup (or as needed) mild olive oil

¾ cup Chicken Stock (page 103)

2 cups heavy cream

3 cups diced tomatoes

¾ cup julienned prosciutto (1½ by ¼ by ¼ inch strips)

Salt and freshly ground pepper

36 Niçoise olives

2 tablespoons chopped fresh parsley

This is our interpretation of a Spanish recipe for baked pork chops. As we have found that baked chops are often dry. We have adapted the recipe to pork scaloppine. We marinate the loin in a lightly spiced brine to tenderize it, then thinly slice and sauté it. This dish is best cooked in the summer when a variety of yellow and red tomatoes are available, but you may use canned tomatoes if you cook it in the winter. ✦ *Serves* 6

Add the pork to the brine in a large, deep nonaluminum container, then pour in enough cold water to just cover the pork. Cover and refrigerate overnight or up to 2 days.

Remove the pork from the brine; discard the brine. Trim all excess fat and connective tissue from the pork and cut into eighteen ½- to ¾-inch-thick slices. Pound the slices lightly between sheets of plastic wrap with a meat pounder about ¼ inch thick.

Heat the oil in 1 large sauté pan over medium heat. Add as many pork slices as will comfortably fit in each pan and cook until browned, 2 to 3 minutes each side; set aside and keep warm. Repeat with the remaining pork slices. Pour off remaining fat. Pour the stock and cream into the pan and boil, scraping loose the browned bits on the bottom, until slightly thickened, about 5 minutes. Add the tomatoes and prosciutto and boil over high heat until thickened, 2 to 3 minutes. Season to taste with salt and pepper. Arrange 3 slices of pork on each serving plate and spoon the sauce over top. Garnish with the olives and parsley. Serve with roasted or fried potatoes.

Middle Eastern Pork Brochettes with Pomegranate and Honey

The success of this easy, delicious kabob hinges on one important ingredient: Lebanese grenadine molasses, which is pomegranate juice reduced to a syrup. It can be found at stores that specialize in Middle Eastern foodstuffs. We have tried this recipe with bottled pomegranate juice from the health food store, but it is sour and thin, where the molasses is tart and thick. This kabob is the essence of sweet and tart, with a wonderful balance of flavors that accentuates the natural sweetness of the pork. ◆ *Serves 4*

⅓ cup grenadine molasses (pomegranate syrup; see Note)

1 cup (or to taste) honey

⅔ cup water

3 tablespoons freshly ground pepper

⅔ cup olive oil

2½ pounds lean pork, trimmed well and cut into 2-inch cubes

Salt and freshly ground pepper

Mild olive oil for grilling

Combine all the ingredients except the pork and pour over the pork in a shallow nonaluminum container. Cover and refrigerate overnight.

Heat the grill or broiler. Let the pork warm to room temperature. Thread the pork cubes onto skewers (you can try alternating thin slices of onion with the meat). Pat dry. Brush with oil lightly sprinkled with salt and pepper. Grill or broil, until cooked through but not dry, 5 to 6 minutes each side. Serve with cracked wheat pilaf and cucumber salad.

NOTE: If you can't get grenadine molasses but can get pomegranate juice, pour 1 cup juice into a medium saucepan and boil over medium heat until reduced to about ⅓ cup.

Lomo de Porco com Pimentos Doces

PORTUGUESE-STYLE
PORK SCALOPPINE WITH
ROASTED PEPPERS

BRINE

10 tablespoons sugar

6 tablespoons salt

½ cup warm water

6 juniper berries, crushed

8 peppercorns, white
  and/or black

3 bay leaves

2 cloves

Scant teaspoon dried
  thyme

1 boneless pork loin,
  about 2½ pounds

6 bell peppers, red, green,
  and yellow

4 to 6 tablespoons olive
  oil

3 large red onions

Salt and freshly ground
  pepper

1 cup Chicken Stock
  (page 103)

¼ cup fresh lemon juice

3 tablespoons finely
  minced garlic

½ cup chopped fresh
  cilantro

This dish, from the southern Portuguese region of the Algarve, is rich, sweet, and tart. The marinade is the same as for the Pork Scaloppine alla Zaragozana (recipe follows). ♦ Serves 6

For the brine, mix the sugar and salt in a large, deep nonaluminum container. Add the water and stir to dissolve. Add the rest of the ingredients and the pork loin, then pour in enough cold water to just cover the pork. Cover and refrigerate overnight or up to 2 days.

Char the peppers over an open flame or under the broiler until blackened on all sides. Transfer to a plastic container with a lid or a paper or plastic bag. Cover the container or close the bag and let the peppers steam for about 15 minutes. Peel the skins from the peppers; then cut the peppers in half, remove the stems, and scrape out the seeds. Cut into ½-inch-thick slices. Cover with a little oil; set aside. (These will keep 1 to 2 days in the refrigerator.)

Preheat the oven to 350°. Rub the onions with 2 tablespoons oil and bake in the oven until tender but not falling apart, about 1 hour. Cool slightly, peel, and cut into ½-inch-thick slices; set aside. Or slice the raw onions ¼ inch thick and sauté in 4 tablespoons oil over medium heat until tender.

Remove the pork from the brine; discard the brine. Trim the pork of excess fat and connective tissue. Cut it into eighteen ½-inch-thick slices and pound lightly between sheets of plastic wrap. Lightly sprinkle with salt and pepper. Heat 2 tablespoons oil in a large sauté pan over high heat. Add as many pork slices as will comfortably fit in the pan and cook 3 to 4 minutes on each side; remove from the pan and keep warm. Repeat with the remaining pork slices, adding 1 to 2 tablespoons oil as needed for each batch. Pour off excess fat. Pour the stock into the pan and boil, scraping up the browned bits on the bottom, until reduced to ½ cup. Stir in the peppers, onions, lemon juice, garlic, and ¼ cup chopped cilantro. Season to taste with salt and pepper.

Return the pork slices to the pan and simmer gently until warmed through. Place 3 pork slices on each serving plate and spoon the vegetables and sauce over top. Garnish with the remaining cilantro. Serve with fried potatoes.

NOTE: You may also make this recipe with a pork loin roast. Insert 5 cloves slivered garlic into shallow incisions cut into the pork. Rub the pork with salt, pepper, and 1 teaspoon ground cumin. Roast at 400°, until a meat thermometer inserted in the center registers 140°, about 1 hour. Let the roast rest 15 to 20 minutes, then cut the loin meat from the bones and slice 1/3 inch thick. To make the sauce, simmer the bones about 30 minutes with the stock; strain. Heat the sliced peppers and onions in 2 tablespoons olive oil over medium heat, then add the garlic, 1/4 cup cilantro, and the strained stock. Heat to simmering, add the pork slices, and warm gently 1 to 2 minutes. Garnish with the remaining cilantro and serve.

*P*olpette con Pecorino

SICILIAN MEATBALLS

1 pound ground pork
3/4 cup grated pecorino
   cheese
1 cup fresh breadcrumbs
6 tablespoons chopped
   fresh parsley
1 teaspoon salt
1 1/2 teaspoons freshly
   ground pepper
1/2 cup olive oil

These meatballs are tasty in risotto, but we like them best in this pan ragout with artichokes, peas, tomatoes, and lemon zest. The pecorino cheese adds a little crunch and salt to the mixture, but be careful when browning the meat as the cheese has a tendency to burn. ◆ *Serves 4*

Combine all the ingredients except the oil in a mixing bowl and mix with your hands until blended. Shape into thirty-two 1 1/2-inch meatballs.

Heat 1/4 cup oil in a large sauté pan over high heat. Add as many meatballs as will comfortably fit in the pan and brown on all sides until cooked through but not dry, 5 to 6 minutes. Remove from the pan with a slotted spoon. Repeat with the remaining meatballs, adding oil as needed.

Sicilian Meatball Ragout with Artichokes and Peas

2 lemons
4 artichokes
Salt
1 cup shelled green peas
½ cup olive oil
Freshly ground pepper
1½ cups medium-diced
  onions
1½ cups Tomato Sauce
  (page 118)
1 cup Beef or Chicken
  Stock (page 104 or
  103)
Sicilian Meatballs
  (Polpette con Pecorino,
  page 287)

I know it seems crazy to write a recipe that can only be made those few weeks of the year spring artichokes and little green peas are at their peak, but food fanatics are like that. This dish is one of those totally satisfying and perfect plates where all of the flavors combine to make a dish that is so simple and yet so truly taste memorable. My only caveat is that the first time you make the ragout you serve it with mashed potatoes because they complete the taste and texture composition. After that you can serve it with pasta or roasted potatoes. The meatballs alone are great in risotto or with pasta for the remaining weeks of the year.
◆ Serves 4

Grate 2 teaspoons lemon zest into a small bowl. Squeeze a few teaspoons juice over the zest; set aside. Squeeze 2 tablespoons lemon juice into a bowl of cold water for the artichokes. Squeeze an additional 2 tablespoons to season the artichokes and set aside.

Pull off the outside leaves of the artichokes. Using a serrated knife, cut parallel to the bases and across the leaves just above the chokes. With a very sharp paring knife, trim off the remaining leaves. Scoop out the fuzzy chokes with a spoon and cut the hearts into sixths. Put them in the bowl of water acidulated with lemon juice to keep them from blackening.

Heat a medium pot of salted water to boiling. Add the peas and boil just until tender, 1 to 2 minutes. Cool under cold running water; set aside.

Heat ¼ cup oil in a large sauté pan over medium heat. Add the artichokes and cook, stirring occasionally, until tender, 7 to 10 minutes. Stir in the reserved lemon juice and season to taste with salt and pepper. Remove from the pan and set aside.

Heat the remaining ¼ cup oil in the same pan over medium heat. Add the onions and cook covered until tender, 7 to 10 minutes. Stir in the tomato sauce, stock, and lemon zest with juice. Heat to simmering, add the browned meatballs, and simmer until heated through, 2 to 3 minutes. Stir in the artichokes and peas and simmer until heated through, 1 to 2 minutes. Taste and adjust the seasoning. Serve with mashed potatoes.

SAUSAGE

For years I thought sausage was very exotic and difficult to make. While it is true perfect commercial sausage with just the right emulsion and keeping power is tricky, homemade sausage is very easy. It's simply ground meat seasoned with spices with a certain proportion of fat so that it cooks up moist and juicy. You don't even have to grind the meat—your butcher can do it for you. If the meat is too lean, he can grind in some extra fat. And, since you won't be keeping sausage more than a day or two, you won't be needing the nitrates and additives that are in commercial sausage.

Not many of us have a heavy-duty mixer with a sausage stuffing attachment or a meat grinder with a sausage nozzle. If you become a sausage fanatic, you can purchase one of these machines. Then you can buy a container of hog casings packed in salt (actually, your butcher will have to order this for you) and make your sausage into links. The casings will keep in the refrigerator two to three months or you may freeze them in smaller packages. Before you use the casings, thread each one onto your sink nozzle and rinse away the salt with cold water. To fill the casing, attach the open end to your machine and push in the sausage mixture. If the mixture seems stiff, add a little water to it. You can make one long sausage link, not too tightly packed, then twist and tie into four-inch lengths.

But you don't need a special machine or hog casings to have sausage; you can make the sausage mixture and shape it into patties, or lozenges on metal skewers, or little meatballs. Although it is nice to have sausage in casings for a professional presentation, it is ultimately flavor you are after. So I urge you to try some of the sausage recipes. You won't be disappointed.

Merguez

MOROCCAN LAMB
SAUSAGE

2 pounds ground lamb,
   1/3 of the weight in fat
2 tablespoons water
1 1/2 tablespoons minced
   garlic
2 tablespoons chopped
   fresh cilantro
2 tablespoons chopped
   fresh parsley
2 tablespoons paprika
1 1/2 teaspoons ground
   cumin
1 1/2 teaspoons ground
   coriander
1 1/4 teaspoons cinnamon
3/4 teaspoon (or to taste)
   cayenne pepper
1 1/4 teaspoons (or to
   taste) salt
1/2 teaspoon (or to taste)
   freshly ground pepper
2 feet hog casing
   (optional)
Olive oil for cooking
   sausages

These spicy sausages need at least one-third fat if they are to be juicy and grill well. Count on two sausages per person. ✦ *Makes eight 4-inch sausages*

Combine all the ingredients except the casing and olive oil in a mixing bowl and mix well with your hands. Fry a small amount as a test and adjust seasonings to taste; it should be somewhat hot and the cinnamon should be balanced by the herbs.

Using the sausage attachment on a heavy-duty mixer, stuff the casings with the mixture and twist and tie to make 4-inch links. Or shape into 3-inch-long lozenges, slightly fatter in the middle, formed around metal skewers or simply into small patties.

Heat the grill or broiler. If the sausages are in casings, prick with a fork 2 to 3 times and brush with oil. Grill or broil the sausages 3 to 4 minutes each side until cooked through. For lozenges or patties, brush with a little oil and grill about 3 minutes each side or sauté the patties in a little oil over high heat.

VARIATION

Thread the sausages on skewers alternately with pieces of onion and pepper and grill. Serve atop a mound of couscous, accompanied by *Harissa* (page 191).

Umbrian Pork Sausage

½ cup raisins

2 pounds ground pork, ⅓ the weight in fat

¼ cup pine nuts, toasted

1 tablespoon grated orange zest

1 tablespoon finely minced garlic

1½ teaspoons (or to taste) salt

1½ teaspoons (or to taste) freshly ground pepper

2 feet hog casing (optional)

Olive oil for cooking sausages

This recipe came into being because we were doing a special regional menu in honor of Umbria and I was feeling sad because I couldn't get hold of any of the truffles for which Umbria is so famous. I scanned my cookbooks for inspiration and stumbled upon a recipe for *salsiccia all'uva*, or sausage with grapes, and another for *coppa* seasoned with orange peel and spices. I don't remember what possessed me to add the pine nuts, except that I suspected that the combination would taste good and sound appealing on the menu as well. We didn't have grapes, so we substituted raisins plumped in hot water. The other ingredients were added for contrast and crunch. So, true confession time, this is not a real Umbrian sausage. A composite of Umbrian tastes, the invention is pure Square One. ◆ *Makes eight 4-inch sausages*

Soak the raisins in hot water to cover 30 minutes; drain. Combine the drained raisins, pork, pine nuts, orange zest, garlic, salt, and pepper in a mixing bowl and mix well with your hands. Fry a small patty as a test and adjust seasoning to taste.

Using the sausage attachment on a heavy-duty mixer, stuff the casings with the mixture and twist and tie to make 4-inch links. Or simply shape into 4-inch patties.

Heat the grill or broiler. If the sausages are in casings, prick with a fork 2 to 3 times and brush with oil. Grill or broil the sausages 3 to 4 minutes each side until cooked through. For patties, brush with a little oil and grill about 3 minutes each side or saute in a little oil over high heat.

NOTE: We serve these sausages with Polenta (page 162) and Tomato Sauce (page 118). Serve the polenta soft or spread it ¾ inch thick on a baking sheet, cut the cooled polenta into squares, and sauté in butter or oil. Sauce the fried polenta with a little spinach chiffonade wilted in cream and spoon the tomato sauce over the sausages.

Garlic Sausage

2 pounds ground pork, ⅓ of the weight in fat

½ cup brandy or red wine

2 tablespoons chopped fresh parsley

1½ tablespoons finely minced garlic

2 teaspoons chopped fresh thyme

1½ teaspoons (or to taste) grated nutmeg

1½ teaspoons (or to taste) salt

½ teaspoon (or to taste) freshly ground pepper

2 feet hog casing (optional)

Olive oil for cooking sausages

This basic sausage is good with pasta when you don't want hot pepper or fennel flavors, and it's ideal for *Bollito Misto* (page 252). ◆ *Makes eight 4-inch sausages*

Combine all the ingredients except the casing and olive oil in a mixing bowl and mix well with your hands. Fry a small amount as a test and adjust seasonings to taste.

Using the sausage attachment on a heavy-duty mixer, stuff the casings with the mixture and twist and tie to make 4-inch links. Or simply shape into 4-inch patties (see Note).

Heat the grill or broiler. If the sausages are in casings, prick with a fork 2 to 3 times and brush with oil. Grill or broil the sausages 3 to 4 minutes each side until cooked through. For patties, brush with a little oil and grill about 3 minutes each side or sauté in a little oil over high heat.

NOTE: To poach the sausage, shape the mixture into eight 4-inch-long logs. Roll the logs in plastic wrap and tie them securely. Drop into simmering liquid and gently simmer until cooked through, about 20 minutes. You may prick them once with a thin skewer when they're almost done to let some of the fat escape. To serve, cut the strings and unwrap the sausages.

Lucanica

CALABRESE PORK AND
LAMB SAUSAGE

1 pound ground pork, 1/3
   the weight in fat
1 pound ground lamb, 1/3
   the weight in fat
3 tablespoons water
3 tablespoons chopped
   fresh parsley
2 tablespoons finely
   minced garlic
1 tablespoon dried red
   pepper flakes
1 tablespoon ground
   ginger
2 teaspoons ground fennel
   seeds
1 teaspoon (or to taste)
   salt
1 tablespoon (or to taste)
   freshly ground pepper
2 feet hog casing
   (optional)
Olive oil for cooking
   sausages

A tasty sausage from the poorest part of Italy. ◆ *Makes eight 4-inch sausages*

Combine all the ingredients except the casing and olive oil in a mixing bowl and mix well with your hands. Fry a small patty as a test and adjust seasonings to taste.

Using the sausage attachment on a heavy-duty mixer, stuff the casings with the mixture and twist and tie to make 4-inch links. Or simply shape into 4-inch patties.

Heat the grill or broiler. If the sausages are in casings, prick with a fork 2 to 3 times and brush with oil. Grill or broil the sausages 3 to 4 minutes each side until cooked through. For patties, brush with a little oil and grill about 3 minutes each side or sauté in a little oil over high heat.

Serve with Tomato Sauce (page 118) and a dish of *orecchiette* (little pasta ears) sauced with sautéed greens, onions, tomatoes, and cooked chick-peas, or serve with Onion Marmalade (page 295).

Fennel Sausage

2 pounds ground pork, ⅓ the weight in fat

¼ cup dry red wine

2 tablespoons brandy

2 tablespoons finely minced garlic

1 tablespoon ground fennel seeds

1 to 2 teaspoons dried red pepper flakes

1 ½ teaspoons dried or 1 tablespoon fresh thyme leaves

1 ½ teaspoons dried oregano

1 ½ teaspoons (or to taste) salt

2 teaspoons (or to taste) freshly ground pepper

2 feet hog casing (optional)

Olive oil for cooking sausages

This is our basic house sausage for pasta and pizza. It is excellent on its own or as a component of an Italian mixed grill. ◆ *Makes eight 4-inch links*

Combine all the ingredients except the casing and oil in a mixing bowl and mix well with your hands. Fry a small patty as a test and adjust seasonings to taste.

Using the sausage attachment on a heavy-duty mixer, stuff the casings with the mixture and twist and tie to make 4-inch links. Or simply shape into 4-inch patties.

Heat the grill or broiler. If the sausages are in casings, prick with a fork 2 to 3 times and brush with oil. Grill or broil the sausages 3 to 4 minutes each side until cooked through. For patties, brush with a little oil and grill about 3 minutes each side or sauté in a little oil over high heat.

Serve with Tomato Sauce (page 118) or with lots of fried onions. Or try it with the *diavolo* sauce (page 247) we use on steak.

VARIATION

Add 2 teaspoons cinnamon to the mixture for a Sardinian-inspired variation.

Linguisa

PORTUGUESE-STYLE
SPICY SAUSAGE

3 1/2 pounds ground pork,
   1/3 the weight in fat
3 tablespoons finely
   minced garlic
2 1/2 tablespoons ground
   cumin
2 teaspoons (or to taste)
   cayenne
1 tablespoon (or to taste)
   salt
1 1/2 teaspoons (or to
   taste) freshly ground
   black pepper
1/2 cup dry red wine
3 feet hog casing
   (optional)
Olive oil for cooking
   sausages

Another tasty sausage to add to your repertoire. Its name comes from its shape, long like a tongue. Adjust the heat by adding more cayenne if you like. ✦ *Makes twelve 4-inch links*

Combine all the ingredients except the casings and olive oil in a mixing bowl and mix well with your hands. Fry a small patty as a test and adjust seasonings to taste.

Using the sausage attachment on a heavy-duty mixer, stuff the casings with the mixture and twist and tie to make 4-inch links. Or shape into tiny meatballs.

Heat the grill or broiler. If the sausages are in casings, prick with a fork 2 to 3 times and brush with oil. Grill or broil the sausages 3 to 4 minutes each side until cooked through. For meatballs, sauté in a little oil over high heat.

Onion Marmalade

12 cups sliced (1/4 inch)
   red onions
1 tablespoon dried red
   pepper flakes
1/2 cup olive oil
3 tablespoons grated fresh
   ginger (optional)
1 tablespoon salt
2 cups brown sugar
1 1/4 cup cider or red
   wine vinegar
1 cup dry sherry or
   Marsala
2 cups raisins

This is a superb condiment for grilled sausages or even grilled hamburgers or steak. While it is not an Italian tradition to serve onion marmalade with grilled meats (it's actually sort of French), this recipe is an adaptation of a Sicilian pearl onion conserve. You can substitute pearl onions for the reds; you'll just have to cook them longer. But peeling the little onions is very time consuming, so I suspect you'll appreciate this version. The taste is the same, only the shape has changed. ✦ *Makes about 6 cups*

Heat the olive oil in a large sauté pan over medium heat. Add the onions and pepper flakes; cook covered 15 to 20 minutes. Stir in the remaining ingredients except the raisins and cook until the liquid is thickened and the onions are tender, 15 to 20 minutes. Add the raisins and simmer 2 minutes, stirring frequently. Taste and adjust the sweet, sour, and hot ratios if needed. Let cool.

Loukanika

GREEK PORK SAUSAGE

2 pounds ground pork

½ pound pork fat, finely ground

½ cup dry red wine

2 tablespoons finely minced garlic

1 tablespoon grated orange zest

1 tablespoon ground allspice

1 tablespoon ground coriander

2 teaspoons chopped fresh marjoram

1 to 1½ teaspoons salt

2 teaspoons (or to taste) freshly ground pepper

2 feet hog casing (optional)

Olive oil for cooking sausages

This sausage is not as spicy as the Calabrese *lucanica*. We like it as part of a Greek mixed grill, combined with a few pieces of souvlaki and a little piece of chicken marinated in a mixture of oregano, garlic, thyme, and lemon. ✦ *Makes eight 4-inch links*

Combine all the ingredients except the casing and oil in a mixing bowl and mix well with your hands. Fry a small patty as a test and adjust seasonings to taste.

Using the sausage attachment on a heavy-duty mixer, stuff the casings with the mixture and twist and tie to make 4-inch links. Or simply shape into 4-inch patties.

Heat the grill or broiler. If the sausages are in casings, prick with a fork 2 to 3 times and brush with oil. Grill or broil the sausages 3 to 4 minutes each side until cooked through. For patties, brush with a little oil and grill about 3 minutes each side or sauté in a little oil over high heat.

Serve with rice pilaf or roasted potatoes, a little bowl of diced cucumbers mixed with yogurt, garlic, and mint, and a roasted tomato or sautéed tomatoes with mint. If tomatoes are out of season, grill peppers and eggplant or serve zucchini sautéed with onions and toasted walnuts.

Chorizo

SPICY SPANISH
SAUSAGE

2 pounds ground pork, ⅓
   the weight in fat
¼ cup sherry vinegar
2½ tablespoons minced
   garlic
2 tablespoons paprika
1½ tablespoons dried
   oregano
1 tablespoon ground
   cumin
½ to ¾ teaspoon
   cayenne pepper
1½ teaspoons (or to
   taste) salt
1 teaspoon (or to taste)
   freshly ground pepper
2 feet hog casing
   (optional)
Olive oil for cooking
   sausages

Wonderful on the grill and essential for paella. ◆ *Makes eight 4-inch sausages*

Combine all the ingredients except the casing and olive oil in a mixing bowl and mix well with your hands. Fry a small patty as a test and adjust seasonings to taste.

Using the sausage attachment on a heavy-duty mixer, stuff the casings with the mixture and twist and tie to make 4-inch links. Or simply shape into 4-inch patties or little meatballs.

Heat the grill or broiler. If the sausages are in casings, prick with a fork 2 to 3 times and brush with oil. Grill or broil the sausages 3 to 4 minutes each side until cooked through. For patties, brush with a little oil and grill about 3 minutes each side or sauté in a little oil over high heat. Or bake the sausages or patties on a baking sheet in a 350° oven until cooked through, 15 to 20 minutes.

MIXED GRILLS

Every once in a while you may find yourself needing to go all out with an elaborate dinner presentation. The occasion might be a birthday, or your son's engagement party, or your best friend's anniversary. Or you could be feeling festive and in the mood to cook your heart out and need a few other people to help you eat the food. This is where the mixed grill dinner comes in. While it is a bit of work, most of the preparation, such as marinating the meats and preparing sauces and condiments, can be done the day before. The accompanying vegetables and grains are quick to assemble. Here are some suggested combinations:

MOROCCAN MIXED GRILL

Qodban *(page 270)*
Merguez *(page 290)*
Grilled Quail Stuffed with Honeyed Onions *(page 231)*, or
    Grilled Chicken in an Algerian *(page 201)* or Moroccan
    Marinade *(page 203)* *(serve 1 chicken thigh per person)*
Couscous *(page 163)*
Harissa *(page 191)*
Grilled peppers and eggplant or Algerian Vegetable Tagine
    (page 313)

CATALAN MIXED GRILL

Catalan-Style Grilled Quail Stuffed with Figs *(page 221)*
Catalan-Style Grilled Chicken Thighs *(page 202)*
Chorizo *(page 297)*
Grilled little lamb chops
Grilled leeks *(page 69)*
Fried Potatoes *(page 302, Variation)*
Romescu *(page 193)*

MIDDLE EASTERN MIXED GRILL

Middle Eastern Pork Brochette with Pomegranate and Honey
(page 285) or Kefta with tahini (page 255)
Souvlaki (page 272) or lamb chops in Souvlaki marinade
Turkish Style Grilled Chicken (Tavuk Izgara) (page 205)
Loukanika (page 296)
Rice pilaf
Turkish Deep-Fried Eggplant Sandwich (page 309)
Cucumber Salad with Yogurt, Mint, and Raisins (page 46)

ITALIAN MIXED GRILL

Quail with pancetta and rosemary
Roman-Style Veal Brochette (page 242)
Grilled Lamb Chops Scottadito (page 260)
Umbrian or Fennel Sausage (page 291 or 294)
Polenta or Risotto (page 162 or 154) with greens, onions,
and mushrooms, or Ravioli (page 112) filled with
mushrooms or greens

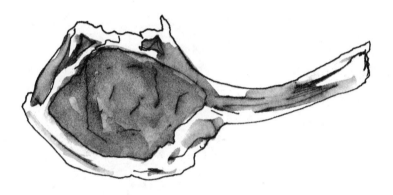

VEGETABLES

Vegetables need no introduction or sales pitch. In my mind, they really don't need many written formal recipes either. Vegetables are. They are wonderful steamed, sautéed, or broiled, and, in a sense, the less done to them the better. I live on vegetables. Little potatoes, rubbed with olive oil, salt, and pepper and roasted in the oven until they are crisp on the outside and creamy on the inside. Green beans, potatoes, beets, asparagus, broccoli, or spinach with a simple vinaigrette, or a little butter and hazelnuts. Or with garlic and toasted buttered bread crumbs. Pesto spooned over grilled eggplant or zucchini. Or a little tomato sauce. Or some grated cheese. Cherry tomatoes sauteed with a little chopped mint or basil.

Vegetables are favorites in my food stream of consciousness. I love to think about them and how they can be paired with other foods. We always try to provide each entrée with the appropriate vegetables of the country of origin. It upsets me when a client wants to eat our sweet potato strudel with grilled swordfish with puttanesca sauce. Ouch!

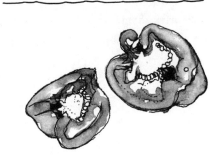

Some more complex vegetable medleys do require a recipe. However, measurements and amounts are, for me, arbitrary. What counts is the concept of the combination. An Algerian vegetable tagine or grilled vegetable ratatouille are food ideas, but the amounts and combinations of the vegetables are up to you and what is available in your market.

Remember, in the Mediterranean vegetables often make the whole meal. Picked in season at their ripest, they offer complete satisfaction.

Roasted Potatoes

16 very small new
  potatoes
2 tablespoons olive oil
Salt and freshly ground
  pepper
2 or 3 cloves garlic,
  unpeeled, lightly
  smashed
2 sprigs thyme or
  rosemary

The simplicity of this preparation allows you to taste the basic goodness of the potato. There is such a wonderful assortment available these days: *bintji,* yellow Finnish, spring creamers, ruby crescents, and fingerlings. I am happy to eat three kinds of roasted potatoes for dinner. The baking time will of course depend on the size of the potato; I have given an approximate time. ✦ *Serves 2 to 4*

Preheat the oven to 400°. Rub the potatoes with the oil and lightly sprinkle with salt and pepper. Put them in a baking dish along with the unpeeled garlic and herb and bake until tender but not mushy. Start checking after 20 minutes. Give the pan a shake from time to time to turn the potatoes.

VARIATION

To make great *Fried Potatoes*, cut the roasted potatoes into quarters and deep-fry in 4 to 6 inches oil at 350° until golden brown, about 4 minutes. You may never crave any other kind of fried potato again. Even shoestrings!

Potato Strudel

6 large russet potatoes

3 tablespoons unsalted
  butter

1 large onion, diced

½ cup diced (¼ inch)
  pancetta, thinly sliced

1 cup fresh ricotta cheese
  (see Note, page 115)

1 large egg

2 tablespoons chopped
  fresh parsley

2 teaspoons (or to taste)
  salt

1 teaspoon freshly ground
  pepper

Pinch grated nutmeg
  (optional)

12 sheets filo dough

½ cup unsalted butter,
  melted

Although this strudel is not heavy (it is lightened with ricotta cheese), it brings back memories of eating potato knishes as a kid in Brooklyn. This is an ideal accompaniment to roast beef or grilled steak. ◆ *Serves 8*

Preheat the oven to 450°. Bake the potatoes until tender, about 1 hour. Let stand until cool enough to handle, then cut lengthwise in half and scoop out the pulp. Put the pulp through a potato ricer or through the large holes of a food mill, or mash; set aside in a mixing bowl. (Do not use a blender or food processor.)

Heat 3 tablespoons butter in a large sauté pan over medium heat. Add the onion and pancetta and cook until tender and golden, about 10 minutes. Add to the potatoes along with the cheese, egg, parsley, salt, pepper, and nutmeg, if using. Mix until blended; let cool.

Lay a sheet of filo on a work surface with one long side facing you and brush with melted butter. Lay a second sheet on top of the first and brush with melted butter. Repeat with 4 more sheets to make 6 layers.

Shape about half the potato mixture into a 2-inch-thick log on one long side of the filo, leaving 2-inch borders. Fold in the sides of the filo and roll up like a jelly roll, brushing with butter as you roll. Place the strudel, seam side down, on a buttered baking sheet. Repeat with the remaining filo dough and potato mixture. The strudels may be refrigerated up to 2 days or frozen.

Preheat the oven to 400°. Bake the strudels until golden brown, 25 to 30 minutes. Let rest a few minutes, then cut into thick slices with a serrated knife. Serve with a grilled filet of beef with horseradish sauce or roast beef.

VARIATION

Use half butternut squash in the filling. Bake until tender, then put through the ricer or mash.

Potato Gratin

4 cups (or as needed)
   heavy cream
1 ½ teaspoons salt
1 teaspoon freshly ground
   pepper
¼ teaspoon (or to taste)
   freshly grated nutmeg
6 waxy new or white
   potatoes, peeled and
   sliced about ¼ inch
   thick (about 7 cups)
   (see Note)

This is a classic French potato gratin. You can make it even more French by adding sautéed leeks, roasted garlic cloves, or grated Gruyère cheese. Or, you can give it an Italian flavor by adding chopped prosciutto, sautéed artichokes, or shredded Fontina cheese. ◆ *Serves 6 to 8*

Preheat the oven to 375°. Butter a 3-quart gratin dish or large baking dish. Heat the cream to boiling in a deep saucepan. Reduce the heat, add the salt, pepper, and nutmeg to taste, and simmer 5 minutes. Layer the potatoes in the buttered dish and pour the seasoned cream over top. The cream should just cover the potatoes (if it doesn't, add more cream). Cover the dish with aluminum foil and bake 30 minutes. Remove the foil and continue baking until the potatoes are tender but still hold their shape, about 20 minutes more.

NOTE: We use waxy potatoes because they hold their shape well during cooking. If this is not a consideration, you certainly may use russets.

VARIATIONS

Cut ¼ inch from the tops of 2 heads of garlic. Rub with olive oil and place cut side up in a small baking dish. Cover with foil and bake at 350° until very tender, about 40 minutes. Squeeze the softened garlic into a bowl. Heat the garlic skins to boiling with the cream; strain. Layer the softened garlic with the potatoes in the baking dish, pour the cream over top, and bake as directed.

Layer 1 cup sautéed artichoke slices, ½ cup diced prosciutto, or 1 cup sautéed leeks or onions with the potatoes. Top with grated Gruyère cheese if you like.

Potato Pancakes

1 medium onion, finely
  diced (about 1¼ cups)

1 large egg

3 large russet potatoes,
  peeled and finely diced
  (about 4 cups)

1 teaspoon salt

½ teaspoon freshly
  ground pepper

5 to 7 tablespoons
  all-purpose flour

Vegetable shortening or
  oil for frying

Many countries boast some type of pancake in their potato repertoire. This is a generic recipe and one that you will find invaluable for its versatility. The pancakes are wonderful as an accompaniment to most fish and meat entrees, but they can also act as dinner, or as an appetizer, garnished with smoked trout or salmon and horseradish cream, or the noneconomy spread, caviar! ◆ *Makes about twelve 3-inch pancakes*

Process the onion and egg in a blender or food processor (see Note) until liquefied. Add about a third of the potatoes and process just until smooth. Add the remaining potatoes and blend quickly just to eliminate lumps but not more than a minute. Pour the puree into a bowl and season with salt and pepper. Stir in just enough flour to thicken the batter so that the pancakes are not too thin and fragile when fried. (Do a test pancake and add flour if needed.) If the batter is still wet after all the flour has been added, press a paper towel over the top to absorb the water.

Heat ½ inch shortening in a heavy sauté pan or cast-iron skillet over medium heat until very hot (about 350°). Drop as many large spoonfuls of batter into the hot fat as will comfortably fit without crowding. Fry until browned on the bottom, then turn the pancakes over and brown the second side, 2 to 3 minutes each side. Drain on paper towels and keep warm in the oven (no more than 15 minutes) while frying the remaining batter. Serve immediately.

NOTE: If you use a food processor, the mixture will have many more lumps. Do not overprocess; it's best just to pick the larger chunks out.

Potato Croquettes

4 large russet potatoes
2 large eggs, lightly
    beaten
½ teaspoon freshly grated
    nutmeg
½ cup freshly grated
    Parmesan cheese
1½ teaspoons (or to
    taste) salt
½ teaspoon freshly
    ground pepper
1 tablespoon chopped
    fresh sage or marjoram
    (optional)
½ cup pine nuts, toasted
    (optional)
1 cup toasted bread
    crumbs
Peanut or vegetable oil
    for deep frying

These can be prepared ahead of time and refrigerated for up to 24 hours before cooking them. They are a wonderful accompaniment to simple roasted or grilled meats and fish. ◆ *Makes 24 croquettes*

Preheat the oven to 450°. Bake the potatoes until tender, about 1 hour. Let stand until cool enough to handle, then cut the potatoes in half and scoop out the pulp. Put the pulp through a potato ricer or through the large holes of a food mill, or mash (do not puree in any piece of electric equipment). Measure about 3 cups.

Combine all ingredients except the bread crumbs and oil. Shape into 1½-inch balls and roll in the bread crumbs to coat.

Preheat the oven to 300°. Heat 4 to 6 inches oil in a deep fryer or heavy deep saucepan over medium-high heat to 350°. Add as many croquettes as will comfortably fit without crowding and fry, turning occasionally, until golden brown, about 5 minutes. Drain on paper towels and keep warm in the oven (no more than 15 minutes) while frying the remaining croquettes. Serve with steak, lamb, or whatever your heart desires.

Sautéed Cherry Tomatoes with Fresh Herbs

6 tablespoons unsalted
    butter
4 cups cherry tomatoes,
    cut in half
Salt and freshly ground
    pepper
4 to 6 tablespoons
    chopped fresh mint,
    chives, or basil

Ever try to stab a hot cherry tomato with a fork? Ever try to eat one? So now you know why we cut them in half before cooking. If you have no fresh herbs, the tomatoes are delicious simply sautéed. ◆ *Serves 4*

Heat the butter in a large sauté pan over medium heat. Add the tomatoes and cook, stirring constantly, until tender and warm, 1 to 2 minutes. Season to taste with salt and pepper and sprinkle with the herbs. Serve with beef, lamb, chicken, or fish.

VARIATIONS

Sauté the tomatoes in olive oil for a low-cholesterol version.

For a rich version, stir 3 tablespoons brown sugar or honey into the melted butter, add the tomatoes, and cook. Pour in 1 cup heavy cream and reduce slightly.

Grilled Radicchio

4 medium heads
  radicchio
½ cup olive oil
¼ cup (or to taste)
  balsamic vinegar
Salt and freshly ground
  pepper

Most of us are accustomed to seeing radicchio's brilliant red leaves in a salad and tasting its bitter tang tempered by vinaigrette. This is another way to pair the deep dark flavor of balsamic vinaigrette with radicchio—this time it's served hot. Be sure to cook the radicchio long enough so that the inner leaves become tender and fully cooked. To keep the radicchio from blackening, baste it with the marinade. ◆ *Serves 4*

Trim any wilted leaves from the radicchio and cut into halves or quarters. Sprinkle the pieces with the oil and vinegar and let marinate about 30 minutes.

Heat the grill or broiler. Lightly sprinkle the radicchio with salt and pepper and grill until slightly browned and cooked through, 4 to 5 minutes each side. Serve with steak, lamb, or chicken, or enjoy it by itself as a warm first course.

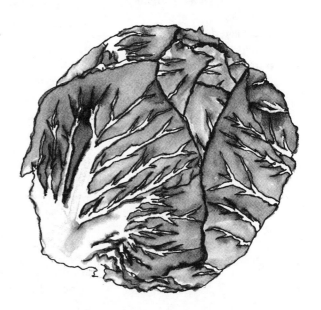

Grilled Vegetable Ratatouille

36 cloves garlic, peeled

¾ cup (or as needed) olive oil

3 sprigs thyme (optional)

6 medium zucchini, trimmed and cut lengthwise in half

2 large green bell peppers

2 large red bell peppers

3 globe eggplants, about 1 pound each, peeled and sliced 1½ inches thick

3 large red onions, peeled and sliced 1 inch thick

6 large tomatoes, cut into 1-inch dice

Salt and freshly ground pepper

½ cup fresh basil chiffonade or ¼ cup chopped fresh thyme, oregano, or marjoram

Ratatouille is a Provençal mélange of Mediterranean vegetables sautéed in olive oil, then combined and stewed or baked together. It tastes earthy and wonderful, but at the end you still have to contend with that inch of olive oil floating on the top. Grilling the vegetables reduces the oil without sacrificing flavor. I must admit that I hesitated to include this recipe in a book dedicated to the home cook; in the restaurant it is a breeze, but who is going to go to the trouble of firing up the grill at home to make a dish that one can make with much less effort on top of the stove? I offer it here not just because it tastes good (although that may be the best reason to share any dish) but because it takes a classic dish and makes it better. (There, I've said it!) And I have purposely written the recipe for a large amount because you might as well strike while the grill is hot. It keeps well, reheats beautifully, and is versatile as a filling for omelettes, as a sauce for sautéed chicken, as an accompaniment for leg of lamb, or as a filling for a tart or calzone. ◆ *Serves 12*

Put the garlic cloves in a large shallow pan and add enough oil to barely cover. Add the thyme sprigs if using. Gently simmer, partially covered, until the garlic is cooked through but not falling apart, about 20 minutes; set aside. (This is a garlic confit, or braised garlic.)

Boil the zucchini halves in a large pot of boiling salted water until cooked but still slightly firm, 2 to 3 minutes. Cool under cold running water to set the color. Skewer each half lengthwise.

Heat the grill or broiler. Brush the zucchini halves with the garlic oil and grill or broil until marked and flavorful, about 3 minutes. Let cool slightly, then cut into 1½- to 2-inch chunks; set aside.

Char the peppers over the open flame or under the broiler until blackened on all sides. Transfer to a plastic container with a lid, or a paper or plastic bag. Cover the container or close the bag and let the peppers steam for about 15 minutes. Peel the skins from the peppers; then cut the peppers in half, remove the stems, and scrape out the seeds. Cut into 1-inch wide strips and set aside.

Brush the eggplant slices on both sides with garlic oil. Grill, turning once, until cooked through but not mushy, 4 to 5 minutes. Let cool slightly, then cut into 1½-inch chunks.

Skewer the onion slices and brush both sides with garlic oil. Grill, turning occasionally, until tender, 5 to 6 minutes.

Put the garlic with ¼ cup garlic oil in a large deep saucepan or sauté pan. Add the grilled vegetables and tomatoes and heat over medium heat, stirring very gently so as not to crush the vegetables, until hot, about 6 minutes. Season to taste with salt and pepper. Just before serving, sprinkle with the basil or chopped herb. Serve hot, warm, or at room temperature.

Patlican Boregi

TURKISH DEEP-FRIED
EGGPLANT SANDWICHES

½ *cup (or as needed) olive oil*

2 large or 3 medium globe eggplants, peeled and cut into about twenty ½-inch-thick slices

Salt and freshly ground pepper

½ *pound grated Monterey Jack cheese*

½ *pound feta cheese, crumbled*

4 large eggs

3 tablespoons chopped fresh parsley

1 tablespoon chopped fresh dill (optional)

1½ cups all-purpose flour

2 cups toasted bread crumbs

Peanut or vegetable oil for deep frying

We serve these with grilled lamb chops or brochettes, but they could make a very satisfying dinner if served with tomato sauce and accompanied by rice and lentil pilaf.
✦ *Serves 6 to 8*

Preheat the oven to 400°. Brush 2 large baking sheets with olive oil. Place the eggplant slices on the baking sheets and brush both sides with oil. Lightly sprinkle with salt and pepper. Bake until almost cooked through, 15 to 20 minutes. Let cool.

Place the cheeses, 2 eggs, parsley, and dill, if using, in a mixing bowl and stir until blended. Place a few heaping tablespoons of the mixture on each of 10 eggplant slices and top with a matching slice.

Lightly beat the remaining 2 eggs in a shallow bowl. Dip the eggplant sandwiches in the flour to coat and shake off the excess. Then dip the sandwiches in the beaten egg and finally coat with the bread crumbs. Put the breaded sandwiches on a rack or baking sheet lined with baker's parchment to set at least 15 minutes or up to 1 day in the refrigerator

Heat 4 inches oil in a deep fryer or large saucepan to 325°. Add as many sandwiches as will fit without crowding and fry, turning once, until golden and the cheese is soft, 5 to 6 minutes. Drain on paper towels. Repeat with the remaining sandwiches. Cut the large sandwiches in half and serve immediately.

Eggplant, Zucchini, and Tomato Gratin

¼ cup olive oil

4 or 5 Japanese
    eggplants, trimmed (see
    Note)

4 or 5 medium zucchini,
    trimmed

Salt and freshly ground
    pepper

¼ cup Tomato Sauce
    (page 118)

4 to 6 medium tomatoes,
    thinly sliced (see Note)

¼ cup fresh basil
    chiffonade

½ pound fresh
    mozzarella, cut into 9
    or 10 slices

This vegetable gratin is an excellent accompaniment for grilled lamb chops or roast leg of lamb, or broiled or roasted chicken. It also makes a very nice lunch accompanied with some good bread and a small salad. Don't overload it with cheese—it should be light in texture. And don't worry about leftovers; the gratin is delicious reheated. ◆ *Serves 4*

Preheat the oven to 450°. Brush 2 large baking sheets with olive oil. Cut the eggplant and zucchini lengthwise into ¼-inch-thick slices. Put them on the baking sheets and brush with about 3 tablespoons oil. Lightly sprinkle with salt and pepper. Bake until almost cooked through but not browned, 10 to 15 minutes. Let stand until cool enough to handle.

Preheat the oven to 350°. To assemble the gratin, spread the tomato sauce over the bottom of a 9-inch square baking dish. Arrange half the eggplant slices on the sauce, then make a layer of half the zucchini slices, placing them at right angles to the eggplant slices. Layer half the tomatoes over the zucchini. Lightly season with salt and pepper and sprinkle with half the basil. Top with half the cheese. Repeat the layers with the remaining ingredients. Bake until the cheese melts but doesn't brown, about 15 minutes. Let cool 5 minutes and cut into 3-inch squares. Serve with meat, chicken, or fish, or simply by itself.

NOTES: You may substitute 1 globe eggplant for the Japanese eggplants. Peel and slice ¼ inch thick, then cut the slices in half.

If the tomatoes are not particularly flavorful, increase the sauce to ½ to ¾ cup and add between layers.

Hunkar Begendi

3 medium globe
   eggplants, about 1
   pound each

BÉCHAMEL SAUCE (1 CUP)

2 tablespoons unsalted
   butter

2 tablespoons all-purpose
   flour

1 cup heavy cream,
   warmed

½ teaspoon salt

¼ teaspoon freshly
   ground pepper

Pinch freshly grated
   nutmeg

½ cup freshly grated
   Parmesan cheese

This rich puree of eggplant, extra creamy and smooth with béchamel and Parmesan cheese, is a Turkish delight. We usually use it as the bed for Izmir Koftesi (page 254), little meatballs in tomato sauce. You could serve this with or without the tomato sauce as an accompaniment for a simple roast leg of lamb or grilled lamb chops. A little cumin, or allspice and dill in the tomato sauce will give the ensemble an appropriately Turkish flavor. ♦ *Serves 6*

Preheat the oven to 450°. Prick each eggplant in a few places with a fork. Put them in a roasting pan or baking dish and bake until very soft, 45 minutes to 1 hour. Turn them occasionally for even cooking. Let stand until cool enough to handle, then peel and drain the pulp in a colander for 15 minutes. Puree the pulp in a food processor (you should have 6 to 8 cups).

For the béchamel, heat the butter in a small saucepan over low heat until melted. Add the flour and cook until blended, about 4 minutes. Whisk in the cream and cook, whisking constantly, until thickened, about 4 minutes. Add the salt, pepper, and nutmeg, if using.

Combine the eggplant puree, béchamel, and Parmesan in a mixing bowl. Taste and adjust the seasoning. Keep the eggplant puree warm over hot water until ready to serve or reheat just before serving.

Catalan Baked Eggplant with Honey, Tomatoes, and Cheese

¾ cup olive oil

13 tablespoons honey

3 medium globe
  eggplants, peeled and
  sliced ½ inch thick

Salt and freshly ground
  pepper

3 cups Tomato Sauce
  (page 118)

2 cups fresh ricotta
  cheese (see Note, page
  115)

½ cup grated mozzarella
  cheese (optional)

The first recipe I read for this dish did not use tomato, but, the more I thought about it, the more I wanted to try it with the honey-sweetened tomato sauce that works so well in Moroccan cuisine (a relative of the Catalan). We have also tried this with mozzarella cheese, but I prefer ricotta. You might try a combination for a nice interplay of textures. Japanese eggplants, cut lengthwise into strips, may be used in place of the larger globe eggplants. ◆ *Serves 6 to 8*

Preheat the oven to 450°. Brush 2 large baking sheets with olive oil. Stir the oil and 3 tablespoons honey together. Place the eggplant slices on the baking sheets and brush both sides with the honey mixture. Lightly sprinkle with salt and pepper. Bake until tender but not mushy, 15 to 20 minutes; set aside.

Combine the remaining 10 tablespoons honey with the tomato sauce in a small saucepan. Heat to simmering over low heat. Season to taste with salt and pepper.

Preheat the oven to 350°. Spread about half the tomato sauce over the bottom of a 12 by 9 by 2-inch baking dish. Arrange half the eggplant slices on top and spread half the ricotta over the eggplant. Spread the remaining tomato sauce over the cheese (or save a little to drizzle over the top). Layer the remaining eggplant on top and spread with the remaining ricotta. Drizzle with a little tomato sauce if you like or sprinkle with the mozzarella. Bake until bubbly, about 25 minutes. Serve with grilled chicken or lamb.

Algerian Vegetable Tagine

6 medium artichokes

Juice of 1 lemon

1½ cups green beans

1 cup carrot chunks (1 inch)

1 cup green peas

1½ cups zucchini or summer squash chunks (1 inch; optional)

6 tablespoons (or as needed) olive oil

Salt and freshly ground pepper

2 cups diced onions

4 cloves garlic, finely minced

1 tablespoon ground coriander

2 teaspoons ground cumin

2 teaspoons freshly ground pepper

¼ to ½ teaspoon cayenne pepper

3 tablespoons chopped fresh cilantro

2 tablespoons chopped fresh mint

1 cup Tomato Sauce (page 118)

½ cup Chicken Stock (page 103) or water

Because we serve so many dishes from North Africa, we are always looking for new accompaniments to supplement the ever-present couscous and broiled eggplant and peppers. I have taken some of the Algerian spices and put together a vegetable tagine that is a wonderful accompaniment to Grilled Chicken or Squab in an Algerian Marinade (page 201). ◆ *Serves 6*

Pull off the outside leaves of the artichokes. Using a serrated knife, cut parallel to the bases and across the leaves just above the chokes. With a very sharp paring knife, trim off the remaining leaves. Scoop out the fuzzy chokes with a spoon and cut the hearts into sixths. Place in a bowl of water acidulated with half the lemon juice.

Boil the beans in a large pot of boiling water until crisp-tender, about 2 minutes. Remove with a slotted spoon and cool under running water. Add the carrots to the boiling water and cook until tender, 8 to 10 minutes. Remove with a slotted spoon and cool under running water. Repeat with the peas and zucchini, cooking each one separately for about 1 minute.

Heat 3 to 4 tablespoons oil in a large sauté pan over high heat. Add the artichoke pieces, stir a few times, and reduce the heat to low. Cook, stirring often, until tender, about 15 minutes. Sprinkle with the remaining lemon juice during the cooking. Season to taste with salt and pepper.

Heat the remaining 3 tablespoons oil in the same pan over medium heat. Add the onions and cook until tender, about 7 minutes. Stir in the garlic, coriander, cumin, 2 teaspoons pepper, and the cayenne; cook 2 minutes. Add 1 tablespoon cilantro, a pinch of mint, the tomato sauce, and stock or water; simmer 2 minutes. Add the cooked vegetables and season to taste with salt and pepper. Garnish with the remaining cilantro and mint just before serving.

Caponata de Verdure alle Sarde

SARDINIAN VEGETABLE SAUTE

2 small heads
  cauliflower, cut into
  florets (about 4 cups)
1 bunch broccoli, cut into
  florets (about 4 cups;
  optional)
½ cup olive oil
4 teaspoons (or to taste)
  finely minced garlic
4 teaspoons (or to taste)
  finely chopped anchovy
4 small bunches spinach,
  rinsed well and
  trimmed (about 8
  cups)
4 teaspoons grated lemon
  zest covered with fresh
  lemon juice
½ cup pine nuts, toasted
Salt and freshly ground
  pepper to taste
1 cup toasted bread
  crumbs

I have taken a warm vegetable medley from Sicily called *caponata di verdure* and turned it into a salad (page 72), but this Sardinian recipe is not a salad transformed into a warm vegetable dish—it is actually meant to be this way. It makes a great pasta sauce with rigatoni or penne and is a perfect vegetable dish to accompany a simple broiled chicken or fish. ◆ *Serves 4*

Cook the cauliflower in a large pot of boiling water until tender, 4 to 6 minutes. Remove from the pot and cool under cold running water. Boil the broccoli if using in the boiling water until tender, about 4 minutes. Drain and cool under cold running water.

Heat the oil in a very large sauté pan over low heat. Add the garlic and anchovy and cook 2 minutes. Add the cauliflower and broccoli; cook, stirring occasionally, until warmed through, 3 to 4 minutes. Add the spinach and lemon zest with juice; cook, stirring frequently, until the spinach is wilted, about 3 minutes. Add the pine nuts and toss well. Season to taste with salt and pepper and sprinkle with the bread crumbs.

Swiss Chard Tagine

12 cups chopped Swiss
   chard (about 3 large
   bunches)
½ cup olive oil
2 cups chopped onions
2 cloves garlic, minced
1 tablespoon paprika
1 teaspoon ground
   coriander
1 cup cooked chick-peas
   (optional)
½ cup chopped cilantro
Salt and freshly ground
   pepper
2 to 3 tablespoons fresh
   lemon juice

Great greens to serve with fish or chicken. ◆ *Serves 6*

Rinse the chard well and drain but do not dry; the water clinging to the leaves will help wilt the chard during cooking.

Heat the oil in a large sauté pan over medium heat. Add the onions and cook until translucent, about 7 minutes. Add the garlic and spices and cook 2 minutes more. Then stir in the chard and cook, partially covered and stirring occasionally, until tender and wilted, about 5 minutes. Stir in the chick-peas if using and simmer 2 minutes. Add the cilantro and salt and pepper to taste; cook 1 more minute. Stir in the lemon juice to complete the balance of flavors.

Moroccan Carrots

½ cup currants
1½ pounds carrots
   (about 18 medium)
6 tablespoons unsalted
   butter
3 tablespoons brown
   sugar
1 teaspoon cinnamon
½ teaspoon ground
   cumin
¼ teaspoon (or to taste)
   cayenne pepper
1 cup fresh orange juice
Salt and freshly ground
   pepper
2 to 3 tablespoons
   chopped fresh mint or
   parsley for garnish

A simple and excellent accompaniment to Moroccan chicken or lamb. ◆ *Serves 6*

Soak the currants in hot water to cover 30 minutes. Drain and reserve ¼ cup soaking liquid.

Thinly slice the carrots or cut into julienne strips on a mandoline. You should have about 5 cups.

Heat the butter in a large sauté pan over low heat. Add the sugar, spices, and carrots; cook, stirring constantly, 2 to 3 minutes. Stir in the orange juice and currants with reserved soaking liquid. Heat to boiling. Reduce the heat and simmer covered until tender. Season to taste with salt and pepper. Sprinkle with mint or parsley and serve hot.

DESSERTS

Dessert occupies an important position in any menu because it will be the guest's final taste of the meal, but a satisfying grand finale does not have to mean a blockbuster loaded with calories and sugar. I am an advocate of the Mediterranean custom of serving fruit for dessert and reserving the more elaborate pastries for afternoon coffee or special events. At Square One, we try to serve desserts that are not overly sweet, and we depend on the quality of our basic ingredients to make up for the reduced amount of sugar. Really ripe fruit is laden with so much natural sweetness that it does not require additional sugar. I have, of course, included a few dessert extravaganzas in this chapter, those showstoppers everyone likes to have in his or her repertoire. But, for the most part, you will see that I believe less is more than enough when it comes to really fine desserts, especially after a Mediterranean meal that is already so rich in flavor and seasoning. Our desserts look inviting without being baroque or elaborately embellished. We do not specialize in chocolate sculptures and confectionery sugar rosettes; we are interested in flavor, not frou-frou.

Eating dessert is easy, but making it is reputed to be a tricky business. Most people are semi-traumatized even before they begin. (On every phone-in talk show that I have been a part of, eighty percent of the questions come from nervous and wigged-out cooks who are having problems with baking.) I like to bake only when I have ample time and peace of mind. I don't like to rush through it. I have found that baking requires a different mental attitude than sautéing, or cooking pasta, soups, and stews. I can always improvise my way around cuisine where precision is not vital for success. But with baking you must respect the chemistry of the dish; improvisation may result in a lumpy, soggy, or dry mess.

Mediterranean food, on the whole, is home food. I imagine that most of you will be able to prepare the dessert recipes in this book with ease. They will look right (not fussed with) and will taste wonderful if you remember to get the best ingredients and leave your worries for more important things in life.

Torta di Granturco e Frutta

ITALIAN CORNMEAL
TART WITH FRUIT

CORNMEAL PASTRY

1 cup all-purpose flour

*⅔ cup sifted yellow
   cornmeal*

½ cup sugar

½ teaspoon salt

*10 tablespoons unsalted
   butter, chilled and cut
   into small bits*

2 large egg yolks

1 tablespoon honey

1 teaspoon vanilla extract

*1½ teaspoons grated
   lemon zest*

This homespun tart is made with pears or dried figs in the winter and peaches or fresh figs in the summer. We usually accompany it with an ice cream that accents the flavor of the fruit. Vanilla, of course, is always right, but cinnamon, almond, hazelnut, or lemon works well too. A zabaglione ice cream might be the perfect garnish or simply a brandy-flavored whipped cream.

One of the greatest attributes of this tart, second only to its wonderful flavor, is its rustic appearance. The top crust is molded into an artless bumpy form by the fruit underneath. So if you are not a professional baker, never fear— lumpy is good! It is the loving-hands-at-home approach that makes it so endearing.

I am indebted to Marion Cunningham, Rick O'Connell, and Carol Field for this recipe.

A few words about cornmeal crusts. They are crumbly, rich, and delicate, more cookielike than crustlike (rather like the crust of the *Crostata di Ricotta,* page 327). It is therefore wise to roll the dough out between sheets of plastic wrap so that it doesn't tear or stick. ◆ *Serves 8*

For the pastry, combine the flour, cornmeal, sugar, and salt in a mixing bowl or in the bowl of a food processor. Cut or process in the butter with short on/off pulses until the mixture resembles coarse cornmeal. Lightly beat the egg yolks, honey, vanilla, and zest together. Gradually work it into the flour mixture with your fingers, or pour it through the feed tube with the processor running and process just until the dough comes together. (Be careful to process only until the dough comes together; overprocessing will cause the dough to be tough.) Cover and let rest 10 minutes. Divide the dough in half and shape into thick disks. Wrap in plastic and refrigerate at least 1 hour or overnight.

(continued)

POACHING LIQUID

6 whole cloves

1 cinnamon stick

1 teaspoon anise or fennel seeds

6 peppercorns (optional)

Zest of 1 lemon, stripped off with vegetable peeler

4½ cups water

1½ cups sugar

4 medium Bosc or French butter pears, peeled, halved, and cored

or 5 to 7 freestone peaches, peeled (see Note), halved, and pitted

or 25 medium or 13 very large fresh purple figs, pricked with a fork

or 25 dried Black Mission figs

1 large egg yolk (optional)

1 tablespoon heavy cream (optional)

For the poaching liquid, wrap the cloves, cinnamon, anise, peppercorns if using, and zest in a square of cheesecloth and tie to enclose the spices. Place the water, sugar, and spice bouquet in a medium saucepan and boil, stirring occasionally, until the sugar is dissolved. Increase the heat and boil until slightly reduced, about 15 minutes.

Add the fruit to the syrup and reduce the heat. Simmer until the fruit is translucent, gives slightly to the touch, and is penetrated easily by a skewer, about 20 minutes for pears and dried figs, a little less time for peaches, and 5 to 7 minutes for fresh figs. With a slotted spoon, transfer the fruit to a bowl. Strain the poaching liquid into a second bowl and chill over ice, stirring occasionally. Pour the chilled syrup over the fruit and refrigerate overnight to let the flavor develop.

Freeze 1 pastry disk until very firm, 15 to 20 minutes. Remove the fruit from the syrup and let drain on paper towels. Roll out the second pastry disk into an 11-inch round, ¼ inch thick, between 2 lightly floured sheets of waxed or parchment paper. Ease into a 9-inch tart pan with a removable bottom. Or simply press the unrolled dough over the bottom and up the sides of the pan with your fingertips. Roll out the frozen dough ¼ inch thick between the sheets of waxed or parchment paper and refrigerate just until firm, about 20 minutes.

Arrange the fruit, cut side down, in the pie shell; the pears should lie with small ends facing towards the center, the peaches in concentric circles, and the figs, halved or whole, in an artistic pattern of your choice. Drape the refrigerated pastry circle over the fruit. Gently press over and around the fruit, then press the top and bottom crusts together at the edge. Trim the excess dough. Cut 3 vents in the top for steam to escape. Refrigerate 1 hour.

Preheat the oven to 375° to 400°. For a brown shiny crust, mix the egg yolk and cream together and brush over the pastry. Bake the tart 20 minutes, then reduce the heat to 300° and bake until the crust is golden brown, 12 to 15 minutes more. Serve warm with ice cream or brandied whipped cream.

NOTE: To skin peaches easily, dip in boiling water for 2 minutes, and then in ice water. The skin will slip off easily.

VARIATION

To give the poached fruit a different taste and a very pretty color, you may poach the pears or figs in a syrup made with 2 cups red wine, ½ cup sugar, 1 cinnamon stick, 3 cloves, and 3 strips lemon zest.

Plum Tart

½ recipe Pie Pastry (page 322)

½ cup hazelnuts, toasted, skinned, and finely chopped

4 teaspoons all-purpose flour

½ cup plus 2 tablespoons sugar

1 teaspoon cinnamon

2 teaspoons grated lemon zest

3 tablespoons unsalted butter

24 prune plums, halved, and pitted

½ cup plum, apple, or raspberry jelly

The first fruit tart I ever tasted in France was a plum tart. I love this one because it looks so pretty and has the added dimension of the hidden hazelnut layer. Serve with whipped cream or vanilla, cinnamon, or hazelnut ice cream for that magic marriage of pie and ice cream. ◆ *Serves 8*

Make the pastry and refrigerate as directed (you could make the full recipe and keep half in the freezer for another tart).

Roll out the pastry to an 11-inch circle on a lightly floured surface. Brush the flour from the pastry and ease it into a 9-inch tart pan with a removable bottom.

Preheat the oven to 400°. Put the nuts, flour, ½ cup sugar, the cinnamon, lemon zest, and butter in the bowl of a food processor and pulse quickly until well blended. Press this paste over the bottom of the tart shell. Arrange the plums, cut side up, in overlapping concentric circles over the paste. Sprinkle with the remaining sugar and bake 10 minutes. Reduce the heat to 350° and bake until the plums are bubbly, about 20 minutes more.

Melt the jelly and brush over the warm tart. Serve warm or at room temperature.

Craig's Tarta de Sevilla

LEMON-ALMOND PIE

PIE PASTRY

1 ½ cups all-purpose
    flour
½ teaspoon sugar
¾ cup lightly salted
    butter, frozen and cut
    into small bits
2 tablespoons solid
    vegetable shortening,
    frozen, and cut into
    small bits
2 tablespoons ice water
2 teaspoons fresh lemon
    juice

LEMON FILLING

1 cup blanched whole
    almonds
3 tablespoons cornstarch
¼ cup milk
6 large eggs
9 large egg yolks
1 cup sugar
1 ¾ cups fresh lemon
    juice (about 7 lemons)
¼ cup grated lemon zest
    (about 6 lemons)
½ cup unsalted butter
¾ cup salted butter
½ teaspoon almond
    extract
1 tablespoon amaretto
    liqueur

1 large egg yolk
1 tablespoon heavy cream
1 tablespoon sugar

This recipe came about while we were looking for a perfect citrus dessert to complement a series of Spanish menus. Craig Sutter, our pastry chef at the time, took that old favorite lemon pie and added the almonds and the flaky crust to create one of our favorite desserts.

The crust is made with a combination of butter and shortening; shortening for flakiness and butter for good flavor and a golden brown color. Salted butter is used because it has a higher water content than unsalted; water creates steam during cooking and steam makes a flaky crust. Some people have said the crust has a richer, more buttery flavor than others. ✦ *Serves 8*

For the pie pastry, combine the flour and sugar in a mixing bowl or in the bowl of a food processor. Cut or process in the butter and shortening with on/off pulses until the mixture resembles coarse cornmeal. Mix the ice water and lemon juice and gradually work it into the flour mixture with your fingers. Or pour it through the feed tube of the processor with the motor running and process just until the dough barely holds together. Do not overwork the dough or it will be tough. It should look marbled or streaky where the butter is incompletely blended with the dry ingredients; when baked, these streaky areas will create the desired flakiness. Divide the dough in half and shape into 2 thick disks. Let rest a few minutes to allow the flour to absorb the liquid. Then wrap in a damp towel or plastic wrap and refrigerate at least 30 minutes.

For the filling, preheat the oven to 350°. Spread the almonds in a single layer on a baking sheet and toast them until light gold in color, 7 to 10 minutes. Chop them medium fine and shake in a strainer to remove the almond dust, which would add an unpleasantly gritty texture to the filling.

Dissolve the cornstarch in the milk in a heavy medium saucepan. Add the eggs, egg yolks, sugar, lemon juice and zest, and butters. Bring to a boil over medium heat, stirring constantly, until the custard is thick and coats the back of a spoon, 7 to 10 minutes. Strain the filling into a bowl and stir in the chopped nuts, almond extract, and amaretto. Cool over ice water, stirring occasionally. Press a sheet of plastic wrap directly on the surface to prevent a skin from forming and refrigerate until ready to assemble the tart. (The filling can be refrigerated up to 2 days, but stir in the nuts just before assembling the tart.)

Preheat the oven to 350°. Roll out each pastry disk into a 12-inch circle on a lightly floured surface. Refrigerate 1 circle on a baking sheet. Brush the flour from the second circle and ease into a 9- or 10-inch pie pan. Pour the filling into the pie shell and brush the edge with water. Lay the second pastry circle over the filling. Let stand a few minutes to let the dough soften, then fold the edges together and flute for a decorative edge. Cut a decorative vent in the top crust with a sharp knife to allow the steam to escape.

Lightly beat the egg yolk and cream together and brush over the pastry, then sprinkle with the sugar. Bake until the crust is golden brown, 45 to 60 minutes in a Pyrex pan or about 1 hour in a metal pan. Let cool completely and serve with whipped cream if you like.

La Melissima or Torta di Mele e Noce

RUSTIC APPLE AND
WALNUT PIE

PASTRY

3 cups all-purpose flour

½ cup finely ground walnuts

¼ cup sugar

1 tablespoon grated lemon zest

½ teaspoon salt

½ cup unsalted butter, chilled and cut into small bits

4 large egg yolks

2 tablespoons water

2 tablespoons vanilla extract

APPLE FILLING

8 cups peeled apple chunks (about 1 inch), preferably Granny Smith (about 6 large apples)

1½ cups chopped walnuts

¾ cup sugar

¼ cup all-purpose flour

6 tablespoons unsalted butter, softened, and cut into bits

¼ cup dark rum

2 teaspoons vanilla extract

¾ teaspoon cinnamon

I guess I must have been pretty tired while researching the dessert specialities of Emilia-Romagna. When I read the recipe for the tart called *La Bonissima*, in my stupor I read *mele* (apples) rather than *miele* (honey). The real *La Bonissima* is a double-crusted tart filled with walnuts and honey, seasoned with a dash of rum, and glazed with chocolate or a simple sugar frosting. It is named after a medieval noblewoman who deprived herself of riches to help feed the poor. In fact, there is a statue of La Bonissima at the Palazzo Municipale in Modena. Well, the inevitable happened. Because of my garbled instructions, pastry chef Jennifer Millar baked an apple-walnut pie instead of the famous honey-walnut confection. So it seems only right that we should name it *La Melissima*. This pie has a rustic and homey look because we bake it in a springform pan instead of a shallow tart pan. It is not too sweet but can be made more elaborate with the addition of a rum- and vanilla-flavored whipped cream. ◆ *Serves 8 to 10*

For the pastry, combine the flour, walnuts, sugar, lemon zest, and salt in a mixing bowl or in the bowl of a food processor. Cut or process in the butter with pulses until the mixture resembles coarse cornmeal. Lightly beat the egg yolks, water, and vanilla together. Gradually work it into the flour mixture with your fingers, or pour it through the feed tube with the processor running and process just until the dough comes together. Divide the dough in half and shape into 2 thick disks. Wrap in plastic and refrigerate 1 hour.

For the filling, put all the ingredients into a bowl and mix with your fingers until combined.

Preheat the oven to 350°. Roll out one pastry disk into a 15-inch circle on a lightly floured work surface. Ease into a 10-inch springform pan. Spoon in the filling and spread evenly. Brush the edge of the crust with water. Roll out the second pastry disk to a 10-inch circle and lay it over the filling. Press the top and bottom crusts together to seal. Cut decorative vents in the top crust and bake until the apples are tender and the juices bubble, about 1 hour. Let cool to room temperature, then remove the side of the pan and serve.

La Bonissima

WALNUT-HONEY TART

PASTRY

2 ¾ cups all-purpose
    flour

½ cup sugar

½ pound unsalted butter,
    very cold, cut into thin
    slices

2 large egg yolks

1 tablespoon grated
    orange or lemon zest

3 tablespoons heavy
    cream

½ teaspoon vanilla
    extract

WALNUT FILLING

6 cups ground toasted
    walnuts

1 ½ cups honey

1 teaspoon cinnamon

½ cup dark rum

1 tablespoon grated
    orange or lemon zest

½ cup unsalted butter,
    softened

GLAZE

6 ounces bittersweet
    chocolate

¼ cup heavy cream

1 ½ tablespoons honey

1 tablespoon dark rum

¼ cup unsalted butter

This is the real thing—no apples. Just a dense, rich, double-crusted walnut tart with a chocolate glaze. We have defied tradition by adding a little honey to the glaze to pick up the honey in the filling. This tart is delicious served with whipped cream. ✦ *Serves 8 to 10*

For the pastry, combine the flour and sugar in a mixing bowl or in the bowl of a food processor. Cut or process in the butter with short pulses until the mixture resembles coarse cornmeal. Lightly beat the remaining ingredients together. Gradually work it into the flour mixture with your fingers, or pour it through the feed tube with the processor running and process just until the dough comes together. Divide the dough in half and shape into 2 thick disks. Cover with plastic and refrigerate about 1 hour.

For the filling, combine all ingredients except the butter in a mixing bowl.

Preheat the oven to 350°. To assemble the tart, roll out one pastry disk to an 11-inch circle on a lightly floured surface. Ease into a 9-inch tart pan. Pat the filling mixture into the tart shell and dot with the butter. Brush the edge of the crust with water. Roll out the second pastry disk to a 10-inch circle and lay it over the filling. Pinch the edges to seal and cut a vent in the top.

Bake until the crust is golden brown, about 30 minutes. Let cool to room temperature on a wire rack.

For the glaze, combine the chocolate, cream, water, and honey in the top of a double boiler and heat over simmering water until the chocolate is melted. Remove from the heat and stir in the rum and butter.

Invert the cooled tart onto a rack. Pour the glaze over the tart, smoothing it with a spatula. If the glaze is not smooth, pour a little more over it. Transfer the tart to a serving plate. Do not refrigerate.

Torta Turchesca

VENETIAN RICE
PUDDING TART

PASTRY

1 1/3 cups all-purpose
   flour

4 teaspoons sugar

3/4 teaspoon grated lemon
   zest

5 1/2 tablespoons lightly
   salted butter, very cold,
   cut into bits

5 1/2 tablespoons unsalted
   butter, very cold, cut
   into bits

4 teaspoons water

3/4 teaspoon vanilla
   extract

FILLING

1/4 cup golden raisins

2 3/4 cups milk

1/2 cup Arborio rice

1/2 cup heavy cream

1/3 cup sugar

1/4 cup chopped pitted
   dates

1/4 cup pine nuts or
   almonds, toasted and
   coarsely chopped
   (optional)

2 teaspoons grated orange
   zest

1/2 teaspoon cinnamon

4 large egg yolks

1/2 teaspoon rosewater

3/4 teaspoon vanilla
   extract

This is clearly an old recipe, probably dating from the Renaissance. Rice was introduced into Italy by Marco Polo and became very popular in the sixteenth century. The *turchesca* (turkish) tart is enriched by raisins, dates, rosewater, cinnamon, and orange. Some versions of this dish add almonds or pine nuts, and you may also if you wish. The flavors are Middle Eastern but where the Turks would serve this as a pudding, the Italians, ever opulent, bake it in a crust. • *Serves 8 to 10*

For the pastry, combine the flour, sugar, and lemon zest in a mixing bowl or in the bowl of a food processor. Cut or process in the salted butter with short pulses until the mixture resembles coarse meal. Add the unsalted butter and cut in or pulse until the dough begins to come together. Add the water and vanilla to the flour mixture; work it in with your fingers or with 2 pulses of the food processor. Gather the dough into a ball and let rest 10 minutes. Flatten the ball into a disk, wrap in plastic, and refrigerate at least 1 hour or overnight.

Preheat the oven to 425°. Roll out the dough to an 11-inch circle between lightly floured sheets of plastic wrap. Ease into a 9-inch tart pan. Roll a rolling pin over the top of the pan to trim the pastry. Line the tart shell with foil, fill with dry beans or pie weights, and bake 15 minutes. Remove the beans or pie weights with the foil and bake the shell until golden brown, about 10 minutes. Let cool on a wire rack.

For the filling, soak the raisins in hot water to cover until plump, about 30 minutes; drain. Heat 2 cups milk and the rice in a heavy medium saucepan to simmering, cover, and simmer until the rice is tender, about 15 minutes.

Preheat the oven to 350°. Stir the remaining 3/4 cup milk, the drained raisins, the cream, sugar, dates, orange zest, and cinnamon into the rice. Heat to simmering, stirring occasionally. Lightly beat the egg yolks, rosewater, and vanilla together in a small bowl. Gradually stir in about 1/2 cup of the warm rice mixture, then stir it into the remaining mixture in the pan. Stir in the nuts if using. Spoon the rice filling into the baked tart shell and smooth the top. Bake until the filling is lightly browned, about 25 minutes. Serve warm with whipped cream flavored with a little rosewater or cinnamon.

Crostata di Ricotta

ITALIAN CHEESECAKE

PASTRY

1 1/2 cups all-purpose
    flour
1/2 cup unsalted butter,
    chilled and cut into
    bits
2 tablespoons sugar
2 large egg yolks (save
    the whites for the
    filling)
1 teaspoon grated lemon
    zest
1 tablespoon dry Marsala

FILLING

3 tablespoons pine nuts
1/2 cup golden raisins
1/3 cup dry Marsala
1 pound fresh ricotta
    cheese (see Note, page
    115) or 1/2 pound each
    ricotta and cream
    cheese (see Note)
1/2 cup sugar
1 tablespoon all-purpose
    flour
4 large eggs, separated
1/2 cup sour cream or 1/4
    cup each sour cream
    and heavy cream
1 teaspoon vanilla extract
1 teaspoon grated lemon
    zest (optional)
2 large egg whites

The success of this cheesecake depends on a few important factors. First, the ricotta cheese must be fresh and creamy, and, if you're using cream cheese, it must be fresh and not stabilized with gelatin. Second, you must use a light hand folding in the egg whites. And finally, please do not refrigerate the cake or it will lose its delicate and creamy texture forever. Any leftover cake may be stored overnight at room temperature. I prefer to serve this cake warm. ◆ *Serves 8*

For the pastry, put the flour in a mixing bowl or in the bowl of a food processor. Cut or process in the butter with pulses until the mixture resembles coarse cornmeal. Mix the sugar, egg yolks, lemon zest, and Marsala and add it to the flour mixture. Gradually work it in with your fingers or pulse until well combined (the dough is too soft and rich to form a ball). Using about half the dough, press a very thin layer of dough over the bottom of a 9-inch springform pan. Snap on the side of the pan and press the remaining dough in a thin layer up the side, making sure the side and bottom are joined at the bottom edge. Refrigerate at least 1 hour or up to 24 hours.

Preheat the oven to 350°. For the filling, spread the pine nuts on a baking sheet in a single layer and toast until golden brown, about 5 minutes; set aside. Put the raisins in a small saucepan and cover with the Marsala. Heat over low heat until warm. Remove from the heat and let stand about 1/2 hour to plump.

Using the paddle on an electric mixer, beat the cheese in a mixer bowl until light and fluffy. Add the sugar and flour and beat until blended, then beat in the egg yolks, sour cream, vanilla, and lemon zest if using until fluffy. In a second mixer bowl, beat the 6 egg whites until soft peaks form. Stir a third of the whites into the cheese mixture, then fold in the remaining whites with the pine nuts and raisins with Marsala.

Pour the filling into the tart shell. Bake until the filling shimmers but is no longer liquid when jiggled, 50 to 60 minutes. Let cool in the pan 20 to 30 minutes. Remove the side of the pan and serve warm.

NOTE: You may make this cake with 1 pound cream cheese, but it will lose its Italian accent.

Cassata alla Siciliana

LAYERED SPONGECAKE
FILLED WITH RICOTTA,
CHOCOLATE, AND
ORANGE

SPONGE CAKE

6 large eggs

1 cup sugar

Pinch salt

1 cup sifted cake flour

½ teaspoon cinnamon

1 teaspoon grated orange
zest

2 teaspoons vanilla
extract

RICOTTA FILLING

1¾ pounds fresh ricotta
cheese, passed through
a medium sieve

3½ tablespoons heavy
cream

7 tablespoons sugar

5 tablespoons crème de
cacao

5 tablespoons coarsely
chopped candied
orange peel

7 tablespoons coarsely
grated semisweet
chocolate

½ teaspoon cinnamon

ICING

¾ pound semisweet
chocolate, chopped

¾ cup strong brewed
coffee

¼ cup salted butter, at
room temperature

¼ cup unsalted butter, at
room temperature

¼ cup crème de cacao

I have always found it amusing that in France basic sponge cake is called genoise, meaning in the style of Genoa, yet in Italy it is known a *pan di spagna*, or Spanish bread. Alas, we Americans are less romantic and call it sponge or sheet cake. The delicate cake and fresh ricotta filling are not overpowered by the rich chocolate frosting.

Cassata can be made several hours ahead of time, even the day before. Keep it refrigerated and let it warm to room temperature before serving. ◆ *Serves 8*

Preheat the oven to 325°. Butter and line a 15½ by 10½-inch jelly-roll pan with baker's parchment.

For the cake, whisk the eggs, sugar, and salt together in a mixer bowl and set it over very hot water. Whisk by hand until the sugar is dissolved, then beat with an electric mixer until it forms a slowly dissolving ribbon on the batter when the beater is lifted. Sift the flour and cinnamon over the batter, add the orange zest and vanilla, and gently fold until blended. Pour the batter into the prepared pan and smooth the top. Bake until a skewer inserted into the cake comes out clean and the cake pulls away from the side, 10 to 15 minutes. Let cool in the pan.

For the filling, beat the cheese, cream, sugar, and crème de cacao in a mixer bowl until light and fluffy. Add the orange peel, chocolate, and cinnamon and mix until blended.

To assemble the *cassata*, line the bottom and sides of a 9 by 5-inch loaf pan with baker's parchment and butter the paper. Turn the cake out of the pan and peel off the parchment paper. Cut crosswise into thirds and trim the strips to fit inside the pan. Brush the strips lightly with crème de cacao. Place one cake strip in the bottom of the pan, liqueur-soaked side up, and spread with half the filling. Lay a second cake strip over the filling and spread with the remaining filling. Top with the third cake strip. Cover and refrigerate at least 1 hour.

For the icing, put the chocolate and coffee in the top of a double boiler and heat over simmering water, stirring occasionally, until melted and smooth. Remove from the heat and stir in both butters. Let cool, stirring occasionally, until thickened to the consistency of frosting.

Invert the cake onto a serving platter. Whip the cooled icing until thick and fluffy, then spread over the top and sides of the cake. Cut the cake into 1-inch-thick slices and serve at room temperature.

Pan de Jerez

CHOCOLATE SHERRY TORTE

4½ ounces bittersweet chocolate

2 ounces unsweetened chocolate

11 tablespoons unsalted butter

½ cup sherry

2 tablespoons amaretto liqueur

5 large eggs, separated

¾ cup sugar

2 teaspoons vanilla extract

Pinch salt

⅓ cup sifted cake flour

Dense, moist, delicious! We add the sherry for a Spanish touch, but if you want to travel to Portugal, on the other side of the Iberian peninsula, use port instead. ✦ *Serves 8*

Place the chocolates, butter, sherry, and liqueur in the top of a double boiler. Heat over simmering water, stirring frequently, until melted and smooth. Let cool to room temperature.

Preheat the oven to 350°. Butter a 9 by 5 by 3-inch loaf pan and line the bottom with baker's parchment.

Beat the egg yolks and ½ cup sugar in a mixer bowl until it forms a slowly dissolving ribbon on the batter when the beater is lifted. In a second mixer bowl, beat the egg whites until foamy. Gradually beat in the remaining ¼ cup sugar and continue to beat to medium-soft peaks. Stir the cooled chocolate mixture, the vanilla, and salt into the egg yolk mixture. Sift the flour over the batter, add the egg whites, and fold just until combined.

Pour the batter into the prepared pan and smooth the top. Cover with plastic and place in a larger baking pan. Pour enough hot water into the larger pan to come 2 inches up the side of the loaf pan. Cover all tightly with foil. Bake just until a toothpick inserted into the cake comes out clean, 40 to 50 minutes (do not overbake). Remove the loaf pan from the water bath and let the cake cool in the pan. Run a knife around the sides of the pan and turn the cake out onto a serving platter. If the cake sticks, warm the pan slightly over very low heat on top of the stove. Cut into 1-inch slices and serve with whipped cream or custard sauce.

Zuccotto

FLORENTINE
PUMPKIN-SHAPED
PUDDING

NUT SPONGE CAKE

8 large eggs
1½ cups sugar
Pinch salt
1½ cups sifted cake flour
¼ cup finely ground
    toasted almonds or
    hazelnuts

CREAM, CHOCOLATE, AND STRAWBERRY FILLINGS

3 ounces bittersweet
    chocolate
¾ cup pureed
    strawberries
6 to 8 tablespoons plus
    2½ teaspoons sugar
½ teaspoon cassis liqueur
3½ cups (or as needed)
    heavy cream
3 teaspoons vanilla
    extract
⅓ cup amaretto liqueur,
    Frangelico, or Grand
    Marnier
2 tablespoons water
¼ cup confectioner's
    sugar
1 tablespoon cocoa
    powder
Strawberries for garnish

The first time I tasted *zuccotto* was thirty years ago. I was seated at a sidewalk table in a restaurant called Al Campidoglio in Florence. Because I was a guest of a very good friend of the owner, I had been privy to tastes of many house specialties and was already very full. But the sight of this gorgeous, domed tricolored cake garnished with wild strawberries put an end to any ideas I had about not eating dessert. ◆ *Serves 10 to 12*

Preheat the oven to 325°. Butter two 15½ by 10½-inch baking pans, line with baker's parchment or waxed paper, and butter the paper.

For the cake, whisk the eggs, sugar, and salt together in a mixer bowl and set it over barely simmering water. Whisk by hand until the sugar is completely dissolved, then beat with an electric mixer until it forms a ribbon on the batter when the beater is lifted that dissolves in 3 seconds. Sift the flour and nuts over the batter and gently fold until blended.

Pour the batter into the prepared pans and smooth. Bake until the cake is springy and a toothpick inserted into the cake comes out clean, 10 to 15 minutes. Cool the cakes in the pans. (The cakes can be made a day ahead and stored at room temperature.)

For the fillings, melt the chocolate over simmering water in a double boiler. Let cool to room temperature. Stir the strawberries, 2 to 4 tablespoons sugar (depending on the sweetness of the berries), and the cassis together in a bowl and set aside. Put the cream, 4 tablespoons plus 2 teaspoons sugar, and 2 teaspoons vanilla in a mixer bowl and beat until soft peaks form.

For the vanilla cream, spoon slightly more than a third of the whipped cream into a bowl. Add the remaining 1 teaspoon vanilla and ½ teaspoon sugar and beat until stiff peaks form; refrigerate.

For the chocolate cream, spoon half the remaining whipped cream into a bowl, add the cooled chocolate, and fold gently with a whisk until blended. If the mixture is too stiff to spread, loosen it with a little more cream. Set aside at room temperature; do not refrigerate.

For the strawberry cream, fold the strawberry mixture into the remaining whipped cream and beat until stiff peaks form; refrigerate.

To assemble the *zuccotto,* line a 2 ½-quart bowl with plastic wrap. Turn the cakes out of the pans and peel off the parchment paper. Using the bowl as a guide, cut a circle of cake the same size as the top of the bowl; reserve the scraps. Cut the remaining cake crosswise, lengthwise, then diagonally (from corner to corner both ways) in half to make 8 triangles. Line the bowl with the cake triangles with the smooth top side of the cake facing out. Fill any holes with cake scraps. Mix the liqueur and water and brush over the cake. Spoon the vanilla cream into the cake-lined bowl and smooth the top. Spoon the strawberry cream on top of the vanilla and smooth. Top with the chocolate cream and smooth. Brush the smooth side of the cake circle with the liqueur mixture and place it, smooth side up, on the chocolate cream. Press gently to seal. Cover the bowl with plastic wrap and refrigerate overnight to allow the flavors to mellow.

To serve, turn the cake out onto a large serving platter. Mix the confectioner's sugar and cocoa and dust over the cake. Garnish with strawberries and serve chilled.

Chocolate Apricot Torte

A torte for those who love fruit and chocolate combinations. Serve with amaretto crème anglaise, brandy whipped cream, or almond ice cream. ◆ *Serves 8 to 10*

CAKE

10 ounces bittersweet
  chocolate, chopped
¾ cup unsalted butter
8 large eggs, separated
¾ cup plus 2 tablespoons
  sugar
¾ cup fresh ripe or dried
  apricot puree (see
  Note)
¼ cup brandy, rum, or
  amaretto liqueur
½ cup all-purpose flour
  or 3 tablespoons flour
  plus ½ cup ground
  toasted almonds
Pinch salt

CHOCOLATE GLAZE

¾ pound semisweet
  chocolate
½ cup water
½ cup heavy cream
½ cup unsalted butter, at
  room temperature
2 tablespoons brandy or
  amaretto liqueur

½ cup toasted sliced
  almonds for garnish

Preheat the oven to 350°. Butter a 9-inch cake pan with 3-inch sides, line the bottom with baker's parchment, and butter the paper.

For the cake, combine the chocolate and butter in a large mixing bowl and heat over simmering water until melted. Remove from the heat and let cool until just slightly warm.

Whisk the egg yolks and half the sugar together in a mixer bowl and place over simmering water. Stir constantly until warm, 3 to 5 minutes. Remove from the heat and beat until it forms a slowly dissolving ribbon on the batter when the beater is lifted, about 10 minutes.

Stir the apricot puree, liqueur, and flour (and nuts if using) into the slightly warm chocolate mixture. Gently fold in the egg yolk mixture.

In a clean mixer bowl, beat the egg whites, remaining sugar, and the salt to medium-soft peaks. Stir a quarter of the whites into the chocolate mixture to lighten it, then fold in the remaining whites.

Pour the batter into the prepared pan, cover with heavy plastic wrap, and tape down the sides. Place the cake pan in a larger baking pan and add enough hot water so that the cake pan barely floats. Cover all tightly with foil. Bake until a toothpick inserted in the center comes out almost clean with just a few crumbs attached, 40 to 50 minutes.

Remove the pan from the water bath and let the cake cool on a wire rack. Warm the bottom of the pan slightly over very low heat on top of the stove and turn the cooled cake out onto a plate or cardboard circle. Turn it right side up again onto another plate or cardboard circle.

For the glaze, combine the chocolate, water, and cream in the top half of a double boiler and melt over simmering water, stirring occasionally but gently to avoid making air bubbles. Remove from the heat and stir in the butter and liqueur. Let cool until it is the consistency of honey and just thick enough to opaquely coat the back of a spoon.

Trim the sides of the cake to smooth them. Place the cake, still on the cardboard circle, on a rack and ladle the glaze over, tilting the cake to coat the sides. Let the glaze set. For garnish, press the almonds into the glaze around the side of the cake. Place the cake on a serving plate and serve with whipped cream.

NOTE: For dried apricot puree, simmer 1 cup dried apricots with 1½ cups water, ½ cup sugar, and ½ vanilla bean (scrape the seeds into the mixture) until very soft, 20 to 30 minutes. Let cool slightly, remove the bean, and puree.

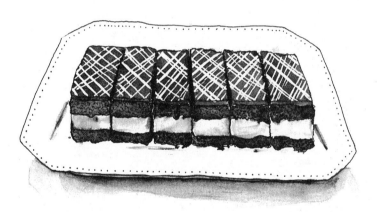

Craig's Date and Walnut Dacquoise

MERINGUES

5 large egg whites
Pinch salt
1/8 teaspoon cream of
    tartar
1 cup sugar
1 cup pitted dates, cut or
    snipped with scissors
    into 1/2-inch dice
3 tablespoons sifted cocoa
    powder
1 cup walnuts, lightly
    toasted, chopped
    medium fine

**CHOCOLATE
BUTTERCREAM**

9 ounces semisweet
    chocolate
1 cup plus 2 tablespoons
    unsalted butter, at
    room temperature
12 large egg yolks
3/4 cup sugar

Confectioner's sugar

I shudder to remember my first attempt at dacquoise. Alas, as a neophyte, I didn't know about baker's parchment and attempted to bake the meringues on waxed paper. The wax melted and I struggled valiantly, cursing all the while, to peel the paper from the meringues without breaking them. I persevered and eventually mastered the dacquoise and other related meringue layer cakes (even using waxed paper, which I still don't recommend). This version is one of the best loved of all of our desserts. It satisfies one's craving for chocolate and delights with its smooth, chewy, and crunchy textures. ◆ *Serves 8 to 10*

Preheat the oven to 350°. For the meringues, beat the egg whites, salt, and cream of tartar in a mixer bowl to soft peaks. Gradually beat in the sugar and continue to beat to stiff peaks. Mix the dates with a few spoonfuls of the beaten whites to separate them, then fold them into the whites with the cocoa and walnuts.

Draw two 9-inch circles on a sheet of baker's parchment and turn the parchment over onto a baking sheet. Spoon the meringue into a pastry bag fitted with a large plain tip and completely fill in each circle with piped meringue. (Or, spread the meringue about 1/2 inch thick over the outlined circles with a spatula.) Bake until set, about 30 minutes. Unlike the traditional dacquoise, these meringues will be soft and chewy rather than dry and crisp. Let the meringues cool on the parchment, then peel off the paper. Store in a cool dry place up to 24 hours.

For the buttercream, melt the chocolate in a double boiler over barely simmering water and let cool to room temperature. Beat the butter in a mixer bowl until light and fluffy; set aside.

In a second mixer bowl, whisk the egg yolks and sugar together. Heat, whisking constantly, over barely simmering water until the mixture is warm and the sugar has dissolved. Beat the egg yolk mixture off the heat until it forms a slowly dissolving ribbon on the batter when the beater is lifted. Gradually mix in the lightened butter and then the chocolate on low speed, then increase the speed and beat until fluffy. Refrigerate until firm, 2 to 3 hours.

To assemble the dacquoise, place one meringue, smooth side up, on a cardboard circle or serving platter. Pipe or spread with half the buttercream. Top with the second meringue round, smooth side up, and press down gently. Pipe or spread the remaining buttercream over the top. Refrigerate 2 hours or overnight. It is easiest to cut the cake while cold and firm, but the taste is better if served at room temperature. Dust with confectioner's sugar and cut with a serrated knife.

Steamed Apricot Pudding

½ *pound dried apricots*
1 *cup water or sweet white wine, such as moscato*
½ *cup unsalted butter*
½ *or* ¾ *cup sugar*
5 *large eggs, separated*

GARNISH

1 *cup heavy cream*
2 *tablespoons sugar*
2 *teaspoons orange flower water (optional)*
Chopped pistachios

Apricots originated in Persia. When dried, their sweet/tart flavor and intense perfume make them the ideal dessert finale of a Middle Eastern dinner. ◆ *Serves 8*

Soak the apricots in the water or wine in a medium sauce-pan at least 2 hours. Simmer over low heat until the apricots are very soft, about 20 minutes, then puree the apricots with the liquid in a blender or food processor. Return the puree to the saucepan and stir in the butter, sugar (use ¾ cup if using water, ½ cup if using wine), and egg yolks. Heat, stirring constantly, over low heat until smooth and creamy and warm to the touch, 5 to 7 minutes. Do not boil. Let cool slightly.

Preheat the oven to 350°. Butter a 1-quart soufflé dish or six 6-ounce custard cups. Beat the egg whites until almost stiff but not dry, then fold them into the cooled apricot mixture. Pour into the prepared dish or cups. Place the dish or cups in a large baking pan and add enough hot water to the pan to come halfway up the sides of the dish or cups. Cover the pan with foil and bake until puffed, about 40 minutes. (Or place the covered pan over low heat on top of the stove and steam the puddings in barely simmering water until done, about 35 minutes.) Remove the dish or cups from the water bath. You may serve immediately or let cool to room temperature.

For the garnish, beat the cream, sugar, and orange flower water if using until soft peaks form. Garnish the pudding with whipped cream and sprinkle with chopped pistachios.

Sopa Dourada

PORTUGUESE-STYLE BREAD PUDDING

SPONGE CAKE

4 large eggs

¾ cup sugar

Pinch salt

¾ cup sifted cake flour

¼ cup finely ground toasted blanched almonds

1 teaspoon finely chopped lemon zest

¼ teaspoon almond extract

Confectioner's sugar

ALMOND PASTE FILLING

1 cup (5½ ounces) blanched almonds

2 tablespoons sugar

¼ cup egg whites (about 2 large)

1 teaspoon fresh lemon juice

½ teaspoon vanilla extract

⅛ teaspoon almond extract

This recipe is a fantasy. Its name means golden soup. Traditionally, the desserts of Portugal are very sweet, often too sweet for our palates. We wanted to make a special bread pudding that would be Portuguese in flavor, fragrant with almond paste, citrus, and cinnamon, yet keep the sugar to a minimum. While we usually prepare bread pudding with toasted bread slices, we thought it would be fun to combine an almond-filled sponge cake roll with the rich egg custard for which the Portuguese are famous.
♦ *Serves 10*

Preheat the oven to 350°. Butter a 15½ by 10½-inch jelly-roll pan, line with baker's parchment, and butter the parchment.

For the cake, whisk the eggs, sugar, and salt together in a mixer bowl. Heat, whisking constantly, over a pot of simmering water until the mixture is warm and the sugar is completely dissolved. Then beat off the heat with an electric mixer until it forms a slowly dissolving ribbon on the batter when the beater is lifted. Sift the flour and nuts over the batter, add the lemon zest and almond extract, and gently fold until blended.

Pour the batter into the prepared pan and smooth the top. Bake until a skewer inserted into the cake comes out clean and the cake is springy to the touch, 10 to 15 minutes. Let cool in the pan on a wire rack 5 minutes. Run a knife around the edge of the cake and turn it out onto a slightly damp towel that has been dusted with confectioner's sugar. Peel off the parchment. Roll up the cake jelly-roll fashion in the towel and let cool.

For the filling, process the nuts and sugar to a paste in a food processor. Add the egg whites, lemon juice, and vanilla and almond extracts and process until blended.

Unroll the sponge cake and spread with the filling. Roll up tightly, like a jelly roll, and cover with plastic. (The cake may be refrigerated up to 2 days.)

CUSTARD

4 cups half-and-half
2 cups heavy cream
3 cinnamon sticks
½ star anise
1 tablespoon grated
*   lemon zest*
7 large eggs
6 large egg yolks
1 cup sugar
1 teaspoon vanilla extract
¼ teaspoon freshly grated
*   nutmeg*

¾ cup golden raisins
½ cup sweet Marsala

For the custard, heat the half-and-half, cream, cinnamon, star anise, and lemon zest in a medium saucepan to barely simmering. Remove from the heat and let steep 2 hours.

Whisk the eggs, egg yolks, sugar, vanilla, and nutmeg together in a mixing bowl. Strain the cream mixture into the bowl and stir to blend. (This mixture can be refrigerated up to 2 days. Let warm to room temperature before using.)

To assemble the bread pudding, warm the raisins in the Marsala in a small saucepan. Let stand about 30 minutes to plump.

Preheat the oven to 300°. Butter a 2-quart Pyrex or ceramic baking dish with 3-inch sides. Sprinkle the raisins over the bottom of the dish. Cut the cake roll into ½-inch slices and arrange the slices on the raisins in a single layer to completely cover the bottom of the dish. Pour the custard mixture over the cake; the cake will float to the top.

Place the dish in a larger baking pan and pour enough hot water into the pan to come three-quarters of the way up the sides of the dish. Bake until the pudding is still a bit jiggly and a knife inserted into the center comes out almost clean, 45 to 55 minutes. Remove the dish from the water bath and let cool 45 minutes. Serve warm with a pitcher of heavy cream.

Honey Mousse

———————————

6 large egg yolks
½ to ¾ cup dark honey
1 cup heavy cream

If you like honey, you will love this truly voluptuous dessert. It is a perfect foil for fresh fruit or a warm fruit compote and is especially nice with raspberries, or figs and raspberries. I do not stabilize this mousse with gelatin because this mixture gives a nicer texture. The freezing helps to maintain the fluffiness. ✦ *Serves 8 to 10*

Beat the egg yolks and honey in a mixer bowl until very thick and very pale, about 10 minutes. Beat the cream to soft peaks and fold into the honey mixture. Pour into 8 to 10 custard cups (depending on size), cover, and freeze 2 to 3 hours or up to 3 days. Let warm at room temperature 15 to 20 minutes before serving to soften the texture.

Chocolate Espresso Pot de Crème

4 cups heavy cream
¼ pound decaffeinated espresso beans (see Note)
3 ounces bittersweet chocolate, chopped
6 large egg yolks
½ to ¾ cup sugar
Pinch salt

For chocolate lovers. Even those who are not avowed chocoholics. ✦ Serves 6

Heat the cream to barely simmering. Add the coffee beans and let steep 2½ hours. Strain the cream into another saucepan and heat to barely simmering (do not let it boil!). Pour the cream over the chocolate in a mixing bowl and stir until smooth. Whisk the egg yolks and sugar together and stir gradually into the chocolate cream. Stir in the salt. Let the mixture cool to room temperature.

Preheat the oven to 300°. Pour the chocolate mixture into six 6-ounce custard cups. Place the custard cups in a large baking pan and add enough hot water to the pan to come halfway up the sides of the cups. Cover the pan with foil and bake until the custards shake like Jell-O but are no longer runny, about 30 minutes. Remove the custards from the pan and let cool to room temperature. Serve or cover and refrigerate until serving time. Serve at room temperature.

NOTE: Regular espresso beans will cause the custard to break.

Coffee-Almond Pot de Crème

5 cups heavy cream
¼ pound decaffeinated coffee beans (see Note, above)
1¾ cups blanched almonds, toasted and ground
9 large egg yolks
1 cup sugar
1½ teaspoons vanilla extract
½ teaspoon salt
½ teaspoon almond extract

It is important not to overbake the custard or you will lose its silken texture. Serve with almond cookies. ✦ Serves 8

Heat the cream to barely simmering. Add the coffee beans and ground almonds and let steep 2½ hours.

Whisk the egg yolks and ½ cup sugar together in a mixing bowl. Pour the cream mixture through a cheesecloth-lined strainer into the yolk mixture. Gently stir in the remaining ingredients (do not whip; you want to avoid making froth).

Preheat the oven to 300°. Pour the cream mixture into eight 6-ounce custard cups. Place these in a large baking pan and add enough hot water to the pan to come halfway up the sides of the cups. Cover the pan with foil and bake until the custards shake like Jello but are no longer runny, 30 to 40 minutes. Remove the custards from the pan and let cool to room temperature. Cover and refrigerate until serving time. Serve at room temperature.

Caramel Pot de Crème

2 cups heavy cream
2 cups milk
1 vanilla bean
1 cup sugar
12 large egg yolks
Caramel Sauce (page 340)

This is the crème de la crème, so to speak. We get more requests for it than for any other dessert in our ever-changing repertoire. Pastry chef Jennifer Millar has created a hard-core group of caramel addicts and made a few converts from chocolate pot de crème along the way.

◆ Serves 8

Preheat the oven to 300°. Pour the cream and milk into a medium saucepan. Cut the vanilla bean open, scrape the seeds into the cream, and add the bean too. Heat to barely simmering and keep warm.

Caramelize the sugar in a heavy saucepan (see Note). Strain the warm cream, then gradually and carefully pour it into the hot caramel, whisking constantly. (Be very careful; the caramel will bubble up.)

Gently, so as not to make bubbles, break up the yolks with a fork in a mixing bowl. Gradually stir in the hot caramel cream and strain again. Ladle or gently pour the mixture into eight 6-ounce custard cups. Place these in a large baking pan and add enough hot water to the pan to come halfway up the sides of the cups. Bake until the custards shake like Jello but are no longer runny, about 40 minutes. Remove the custards from the pan and let cool to room temperature. Cover and refrigerate until shortly before serving time. Serve at room temperature with caramel sauce.

NOTE: To caramelize sugar, place the sugar in a heavy saucepan over medium-high heat. When the sugar starts to melt, stir until all the sugar is dissolved. Heat, stirring occasionally, until the sugar is caramelized and golden brown (not dark brown). Immediately remove from the heat.

Caramel Sauce

1 cup heavy cream
2 cups sugar
Juice of ½ lemon
½ cup unsalted butter

This sauce is great on caramel pot de crème and on ice cream. ◆ *Makes 2 cups*

Heat the cream to barely simmering and keep warm.

Place the sugar and lemon juice in a small heavy saucepan and stir until the sugar is moistened. Caramelize the sugar (see Note, preceding recipe). Gradually pour in the hot cream, stirring constantly. (Be careful; the caramel will bubble up.) Heat to boiling, stirring constantly, then remove from heat. Add the butter and stir until smooth. Pour the mixture into a heatproof bowl. Serve warm. Or cover and refrigerate until serving time, then reheat over a pan of simmering water.

Zabaglione di Moscato de Fior d'Arancio

ORANGE MUSCAT
SABAYON

1 bottle Quady Essensia
   (orange muscat wine),
   about 1⅔ cups)
14 large egg yolks
½ cup sugar
Grated zest of 2 oranges
   (optional)
1 cup heavy cream
   (optional)

In Italy, zabaglione is traditionally prepared with Marsala. The French call it sabayon and make it with white wine. We have made it with a variety of other dessert wines, but our favorite is orange muscat, or Essensia, made by our friend and dessert lover Andy Quady. ◆ *Serves 8*

Whisk all the ingredients except the cream together and strain into a mixing bowl. Set the bowl over a pan of simmering water and whisk constantly until the mixture is light and fluffy and forms a slowly dissolving ribbon on the mixture when the whisk is lifted. Spoon the zabaglione into bowls or goblets and serve warm. Or refrigerate until cold, beat the cream to stiff peaks, and fold into the cooled sabayon. Cover and refrigerate until serving time. Warm or cold, this is excellent with fresh berries or peaches.

Pears Poached in Black Muscat Dessert Wine

4 Bosc or Winter Nellis
    pears
Juice of 1 lemon
½ cup sugar
½ cup water
Zest of 1 lemon, removed
    in strips with a
    vegetable peeler
Zest of 1 orange, removed
    in strips with a
    vegetable peeler
1 cinnamon stick
1 star anise (optional)
1 bottle Quady Elysium
    (black muscat wine,
    about 1½ cups) or red
    or white wine

One of my favorite desserts is a pear poached in wine. Red wine adds a romantic hue, but I find that Andrew Quady's Elysium, a sweet red wine made from the black muscat grape, adds the subtle perfume of roses to the dish. You may, of course, substitute the wine of your choice, but, if you have the opportunity to use this black muscat wine, I think you will enjoy the nuances of flavor the wine imparts to the fruit. Please allow at least five hours for the pears to macerate in the syrup, but for the richest flavor let them sit overnight. ✦ *Serves 8*

Peel and stem the pears, then cut lengthwise in half and remove the seeds with a melon baller. Place the pear halves in a bowl of cold water acidulated with the lemon juice.

Heat the sugar, water, lemon and orange zest, cinnamon stick, star anise if using, and wine in a large saucepan to boiling. Add the pear halves and reduce the heat. Simmer covered until a toothpick easily penetrates the pears, about 30 minutes. Transfer the pears to a bowl with a slotted spoon. Let the poaching liquid cool to room temperature, then pour over the pears. Cover and refrigerate overnight.

Serve the pears with the poaching liquid and with Chocolate, Orange, and Cinnamon Ice Cream (page 351) if you like.

Baked Fig Compote

12 purple figs
½ cup brown sugar
½ cup water

GRAND MARNIER SAUCE

½ cup heavy cream
3 tablespoons
 confectioner's sugar
¼ cup Grand Marnier
½ cup sour cream

½ teaspoon cinnamon
¼ teaspoon ground cloves
Fresh raspberries for
 garnish

We often accompany this compote with Honey Mousse (page 337), but it is also wonderful on its own. ◆ *Serves 4*

Preheat the oven to 350°. Prick each fig with a fork in a few places and place them in a single layer standing on end in a shallow baking dish. Sprinkle with the sugar and pour over the water. Bake, basting often with the liquid, until puffed and tender, 25 to 35 minutes.

Meanwhile, prepare the sauce: Whip the cream to soft peaks. Beat in the sugar and Grand Marnier, then fold in the sour cream.

Dust the hot figs with the spices and serve hot with the pan juices and sauce. Garnish with raspberries.

Stuffed Baked Apples

6 medium Rome Beauty
 apples
½ cup chopped almonds
 or walnuts
½ cup raisins
¼ cup brown sugar
6 tablespoons unsalted
 butter, at room
 temperature
1 tablespoon grated
 orange zest
1 teaspoon cinnamon
¼ teaspoon ground
 ginger or cardamom
¼ cup honey
½ cup fresh orange juice

This dessert is our attempt at a marriage of the Middle East and America. Politics were never as sweet and easy as this. ◆ *Serves 6*

Preheat the oven to 375°. Butter a large baking dish. Core the apples and hollow out the centers to make a good-sized cavity. Pulse the nuts, raisins, sugar, butter, zest, and spices in a food processor until processed to a chunky paste. Divide the paste into 6 parts and roll each one between your hands into a cylinder. Stuff the paste into the apples and place them in the buttered baking dish.

Warm the honey in a small saucepan over low heat until liquefied. Remove from the heat and stir in the orange juice. Baste the apples with a little of the honey mixture.

Bake, basting every 10 minutes with the remaining honey mixture, until a skewer easily penetrates the apples and they feel soft to the touch, 40 to 60 minutes. Serve warm with a pitcher of heavy cream or with vanilla or cinnamon ice cream.

Cameron's Baked Apple in Filo Crust

½ cup water or brandy
½ cup raisins

ALMOND FILLING

10 tablespoons unsalted
    butter, at room
    temperature
6 tablespoons sugar
Pinch salt
2 large eggs, at room
    temperature
⅔ cup almonds, toasted
    and coarsely ground
½ cup finely ground
    amaretti cookies or
    macaroons
2 teaspoons dark rum
1 teaspoon vanilla extract
1 tablespoon chopped
    candied or fresh orange
    zest (optional)

6 Sierra Beauty, Pippin,
    or Granny Smith
    apples, peeled and
    cored from top to
    bottom
9 sheets filo dough
½ cup unsalted butter,
    melted
6 tablespoons sugar

Created for one of our Greek menus, this beautiful preparation makes the apples look as if they are wearing classical drapery. ◆ *Serves 6*

Heat the water or brandy in a small saucepan to simmering. Add the raisins, cover, and let stand about ½ hour.

For the almond filling, beat the butter in a mixer bowl until smooth and creamy. Add ¼ cup sugar and salt and beat until fluffy. Beat in the eggs, then stir in the almonds, cookies, rum, vanilla, and orange zest if using. Refrigerate until cold.

Preheat the oven to 325°. Cut the filo sheets crosswise in half. Cover the filo with plastic wrap or a damp towel to keep it from drying. Brush 1 half-sheet lightly with melted butter. Top with a second sheet, brush with butter, and repeat with a third sheet. Place an apple in the center and push several raisins down to the bottom of the cored cavity to plug it. Fill the cavity to the top with the almond filling and sprinkle the apple lightly with 1 tablespoon sugar. Join the four corners of the filo rectangle at the top of the apple and press to seal. Brush the filo package with melted butter and place on a rack on a baking sheet. Repeat with the remaining apples and filo dough.

Bake 20 minutes. Reduce the heat to 300° and bake until a skewer penetrates the apples easily, 10 to 15 minutes more. Cover with a foil tent if the filo browns too quickly. Serve warm with whipped cream or crème fraîche.

ON MAKING ICE CREAM

Years ago when I was at the peak of my teaching frenzy, I embarked upon an orgy of ice cream making. Using the Kitchen Aid mixer with an ice cream attachment, I attempted to recreate the flavors of French and Italian ice creams. My family and students were willing (an understatement!) guinea pigs. Every cooking class ended with an ice cream evaluation session. With sauce or without? With our homemade preserves and conserves? What combined well? We all broadened our knowledge, our palates, and our hips.

At the height of the cooking class madness of the sixties and seventies, a new rash of ice cream machines appeared at our stores. There was still the old fashioned hand-cranked White Mountain, of course, for those who had family memories of taking turns moving the crank and licking the dasher. Then the electric model made biceps a thing of the past, but we still licked the dasher. Finally more elaborate machines with their own enclosed freezing cabinets appeared on the scene. Pricey but appealing, they made messing with chopped ice and rock salt a thing of the past. As the market became more competitive, less expensive models appeared, and today you can buy fabulous inexpensive plastic ice cream machines that you put in the freezer and crank to almost instant ice cream success. So there is no excuse for not making ice cream today. And if you're worried about bikinis and visible panty line, remember sorbet! But try the recipes, even if only for company dinner or special events. You can't buy them like you can make them!

THE PROVENÇAL ICE CREAM PLATE

For a special menu in celebration of the food of Provence, we came up with a three-ice-cream plate; Lavender Honey, Walnut, and Prune and Armagnac. You don't have to make all three, of course, one at a time is wonderfully satisfying. But, ah, if you have the time, try this trio. It will transport you to the south of France.

Lavender Honey Ice Cream

3 cups heavy cream
1 cup half-and-half
1 sprig thyme or lavender
   (optional)
9 large egg yolks
1 cup lavender honey

♦ *Makes 1 quart*

Heat the cream and half-and-half to boiling in a saucepan. (If using the herb sprig, heat it with the cream mixture to boiling and let steep 1 hour. Remove the sprig, then reheat the cream to boiling.)

Whisk the egg yolks until completely blended. Whisk in about 1 cup of the hot cream, then whisk into the remaining cream. Cook over medium heat, stirring constantly, until thick enough to coat the back of a spoon, 3 to 5 minutes. Do not boil.

Strain the custard into a mixing bowl and place immediately in a larger bowl filled with ice water. Heat the honey over low heat until liquefied, then stir into the custard. Chill the custard well, preferably overnight in the refrigerator. Freeze in an ice cream maker according to the manufacturer's instructions.

Walnut Ice Cream

½ pound plus ½ cup
shelled walnuts
3½ cups heavy cream
1½ cups milk
1 cup sugar
9 large egg yolks

◆ *Makes about 1 quart*

Preheat the oven to 350°. Spread all of the walnuts on a baking sheet and toast until fragrant, 6 to 8 minutes. Coarsely chop in a food processor and set aside ½ cup.

Heat the cream and milk to boiling in a large saucepan. Add all the nuts but the ½ cup and let steep 2 hours. Strain the cream mixture through a cheesecloth-lined strainer or a kitchen towel, pressing the nuts to extract the maximum flavor. Return the cream to the saucepan, add ½ cup sugar, and heat to boiling, stirring to dissolve the sugar.

Whisk the egg yolks and the remaining ½ cup sugar until just combined. Whisk in about 1 cup of the hot cream mixture, then whisk into the remaining cream mixture. Cook over medium heat, stirring constantly, until thick enough to coat the back of a spoon, 3 to 5 minutes. Do not boil.

Strain the custard into a mixing bowl and place immediately in a larger bowl filled with ice water. Chill the custard well, preferably overnight in the refrigerator. Freeze in an ice cream maker according to the manufacturer's instructions. Fold in the reserved ½ cup nuts just before the ice cream finishes freezing.

Prune and Armagnac Ice Cream

♦ *Makes about 1 quart*

1 cup pitted prunes, chopped
½ cup (or as needed) Armagnac
4 cups heavy cream
¾ cup sugar
Pinch salt
9 large egg yolks

Place the prunes in a container with a lid and pour the Armagnac over the prunes. Cover and let macerate at room temperature at least overnight or preferably up to 3 days.

Heat the cream, sugar, and salt in a saucepan over medium heat until the mixture is hot and the sugar dissolved.

Lightly whisk the egg yolks until completely blended. Whisk in about 1 cup of the hot cream mixture, then whisk into the remaining cream mixture. Cook over medium heat, stirring constantly, until thick enough to coat the back of a spoon, 3 to 5 minutes. Do not boil.

Strain the custard into a mixing bowl and place immediately in a larger bowl filled with ice water. Chill the custard well, preferably overnight in the refrigerator. Freeze in an ice cream maker according to manufacturer's instructions. Squeeze the prunes dry and fold into the ice cream when it finishes freezing.

Blood Orange Ice Cream

2 cups blood orange juice
  (about 12 oranges)
4 cups whipping cream
¾ cup sugar
Grated zest of 4 blood
  oranges
9 large egg yolks
1½ teaspoons vanilla
  extract

My first taste of a blood orange was at the covered market across the street from my house in Rome. As a painter I was astounded by their color. As a cook I was delighted by their tart sweet taste. This ice cream has a wonderful pale orange color, less shockingly red than a blood orange sorbet because of the cream. ◆ *Makes 1 quart*

Heat the juice to boiling in a saucepan and boil until reduced to 1 cup.

Mix the cream, sugar, and the zest of 3 oranges in a saucepan and heat to barely simmering, stirring to dissolve the sugar. Remove from the heat and let stand 10 minutes.

Lightly whisk the egg yolks until completely blended. Whisk about 1 cup of the hot cream mixture into the yolks, then whisk into the remaining cream mixture. Cook over medium heat, stirring constantly, until thick enough to coat the back of a spoon, 3 to 5 minutes. Do not boil.

Strain the custard into a mixing bowl and stir in the reduced juice, the vanilla, and remaining orange zest. Place immediately in a larger bowl filled with ice water and chill, stirring occasionally. Refrigerate overnight. Freeze in an ice cream maker according to manufacturer's instructions.

Serve with orange segments if you like or the Blood Orange Caramel (recipe follows).

VARIATION

Try this with tangerine juice, too.

Blood Orange Caramel Sauce

2 cups sugar
¼ cup water
1 cup blood orange juice
Grated zest of ½ blood
   orange if needed

This is gilding the lily. Great on blood orange ice cream and not too bad on vanilla either. ✦ *Makes 2 cups*

Combine the sugar and water in a heavy saucepan and caramelize (see Note, page 339). Pour in the juice off the heat. (Be careful, the caramel may splatter.) The caramel will harden into a mass. Stir over medium heat until the sugar remelts and the sauce is smooth. Chill. If the chilled sauce tastes bland, add the zest. Serve at room temperature or warm it over hot water.

Turkish Coffee Ice Cream

7 cups heavy cream
2½ cups espresso coffee
   beans
1 cup sugar
9 large egg yolks
1 tablespoon rosewater
½ teaspoon ground
   cardamom

I love the ritual of making Turkish coffee. So much so, that I let the coffee boil up an odd number of times—three, five, or seven, as tradition demands. There is less mystery involved in making the ice cream, but it has all the taste of a good rich cup of Turkish coffee. The only drawback is that after eating it, there are no coffee grounds to tell your fortune. ✦ *Makes 1½ quarts*

Heat the cream to boiling in a large saucepan. Remove from the heat and stir in the coffee beans. Let steep 2 to 2½ hours. Strain the cream into another saucepan, add ½ cup sugar, and reheat to boiling, stirring to dissolve the sugar.

Lightly whisk the egg yolks and the remaining ½ cup sugar until blended. Whisk in about 1 cup of the hot cream mixture, then whisk into the remaining cream mixture. Cook over medium heat, stirring constantly, until thick enough to coat the back of a spoon, 3 to 5 minutes. Do not boil.

Strain the custard into a mixing bowl and place immediately in a larger bowl filled with ice water. Stir in the rosewater and cardamom. Chill the custard well. Freeze in an ice cream maker according to the manufacturer's instructions.

Port Ice Cream

This may sound a bit unusual, but it is a nice way to take your port after dinner. We created the ice cream as part of a special Portuguese menu. ◆ *Makes 1 quart*

¾ cup plus 2 tablespoons port, preferably Ficklin or Quady

4 cups heavy cream

¾ cup sugar

Pinch salt

9 large egg yolks

1 teaspoon fresh lemon juice

Boil ¾ cup port until reduced to ¼ cup; let cool to room temperature.

Meanwhile, heat the cream, sugar, and salt in a saucepan over medium heat until barely simmering. Do not boil.

Lightly whisk the egg yolks until blended. Whisk in about 1 cup of the hot cream mixture, then whisk into the remaining cream mixture. Cook over medium heat, stirring constantly, until thick enough to coat the back of a spoon, 3 to 5 minutes. Do not boil.

Strain the custard into a mixing bowl and place in a larger bowl filled with ice water. Stir in the reduced port. Chill the custard well, then stir in the remaining 2 tablespoons port and the lemon juice. Freeze in an ice cream maker according to the manufacturer's instructions. Serve with Walnut Clouds (page 356) and chocolate sauce if you like.

Sambuca and Espresso Chip Ice Cream

A very popular after dinner drink in Rome is *Sambuca con la mosca*, literally Sambuca with the fly, so named because the coffee bean that floats in the liqueur looks like a fly that has fallen into your glass. Actually, those *furbo* (sly) Italians say that if you chew the coffee bean after drinking the liqueur no one will know you've been drinking. This ice cream combines the best of both worlds, the anise taste and the crunch of the coffee beans. However, it does leave a telltale smile on your face. ◆ *Makes 1 quart*

4 cups heavy cream

2 tablespoons medium finely chopped espresso beans

¾ cup sugar

9 large egg yolks

2 tablespoons Sambuca (anise-flavored liqueur)

Heat the cream to boiling in a saucepan. Remove from the heat and stir in the espresso beans and ½ cup sugar. Let steep 1 hour. Strain into an other saucepan, reserving the espresso beans. Reheat the cream to boiling.

Lightly whisk the egg yolks and remaining ½ cup sugar until completely blended. Whisk in about 1 cup of the hot

cream mixture, then whisk into the remaining cream mixture. Cook, stirring constantly, over medium heat until thick enough to coat the back of a spoon, 3 to 5 minutes. Do not boil.

Strain the custard into a mixing bowl and immediately place the bowl in a larger bowl filled with ice water. Stir in the Sambuca. Chill the custard well. Freeze in an ice cream maker according to the manufacturer's instructions. Add the reserved espresso "chips" just before the ice cream finishes freezing.

Chocolate, Orange, and Cinnamon Ice Cream

4 cups heavy cream
Zest of 3 oranges, removed in strips with a vegetable peeler
4 sticks cinnamon
1/2 pound semisweet chocolate
8 large egg yolks
3/4 cup sugar
1 teaspoon vanilla extract

At a winery luncheon during a conference of the American Institute of Wine and Food, despite too many courses and too many wines, everyone had room for this ice cream. At the end of the meal it received a round of applause from the sated dessert maniacs in the crowd. ✦ *Makes 1 quart*

Heat the cream, zest, and cinnamon in a saucepan to boiling. Remove from the heat and let steep 2 hours.

Heat the chocolate in a small heavy pan over low heat until melted. Continue cooking, stirring constantly, until it is "scorched" and thick, about 3 minutes. Transfer to a large mixing bowl.

Strain the cream into another saucepan and reheat to boiling. Whisk the egg yolks and 1/4 cup sugar until combined. Whisk about 1 cup of the hot cream into the yolks, then whisk into the remaining cream. Cook, stirring constantly, over medium heat until thick enough to coat the back of a spoon, 3 to 5 minutes. Do not boil.

Strain the custard into the chocolate and stir until smooth. Strain again. Place in a larger bowl filled with ice water and chill the custard well. Freeze in an ice cream machine according to the manufacturer's instructions.

Granita de Caffe con Panna

ESPRESSO ICE WITH WHIPPED CREAM

GRANITA

3 cups strong hot brewed
  espresso
½ cup (or to taste) sugar

CREAM

1 ½ cups heavy cream
3 tablespoons sugar
2 teaspoons ground
  cinnamon or 3
  tablespoons Frangelico
  (hazelnut liqueur)

This is a dessert for coffee lovers. It is served in Italy during the summer and, like caffeine, may be habit forming. No matter how much you have eaten you will always find room for this dessert. ◆ *Makes 3 cups, enough for 4 servings*

For the *granita,* stir the espresso and sugar until the sugar dissolves. Pour into a shallow metal pan or 2 metal ice cube trays (without dividers). Cover and freeze until ice crystals begin to form, 2 to 3 hours. Whisk with a fork to break up the ice crystals and return to the freezer. Repeat this process every half hour until the *granita* is the consistency of a crunchy slush, 2 to 3 hours.

For the cream, beat all ingredients together until soft peaks form. Serve the *granita* garnished with the whipped cream. (The *granita* must be served the minute it comes out of the freezer. It melts fast!)

Granita de Limone

LEMON ICE

GRANITA

1 cup water
1 cup sugar
Pinch salt
2 cups strained fresh
  lemon juice
2 tablespoons finely
  chopped lemon zest

CREAM (OPTIONAL)

1 cup heavy cream
2 tablespoons
  confectioner's sugar
1 teaspoon grated lemon
  zest
2 teaspoons fresh lemon
  juice

I remember eating this refreshing *granita* on a very hot day in Rome, sitting in a little caffe in the Piazza del Popolo. It made me forget the heat and the noise and made me want another. The lemon-flavored whipped cream is not essential, rather a gilding of the lily. ◆ *Makes 6 cups, enough for 8 servings*

For the *granita,* mix the water, sugar, and salt in a saucepan and heat over medium heat until the sugar is dissolved. Pour into a shallow metal pan or 2 metal ice cube trays (without dividers). Stir in the lemon juice and zest. Freeze until ice crystals begin to form, about 2 hours. Whisk with a fork to break up the crystals and return to the freezer. Repeat this process every half hour until the mixture has the consistency of a crunchy slush, 2 to 3 hours.

For the cream, beat all ingredients together until soft peaks form. Serve the granita garnished with the whipped cream.

Sangria Sorbet

1¼ cups sugar
1½ cups water
1¼ cups strained lemon
   juice
Grated zest of 1 lemon
   (about 2 teaspoons)
1 cup red wine
1 cup white wine
Pinch salt

This recipe evolved during the planning meeting that I regularly have with my pastry department at the start of each new regional menu series. I had, as usual, brought in the fruits of my reading and research: an assortment of recipe titles, names of indigenous ingredients, and descriptions of identifiable flavors and traditional desserts of the region. Our task was to reinterpret these desserts, using our own techniques, while maintaining the authentic flavors of the region. We were talking about sangria, and I had suggested making a sorbet using citrus and red or white wine. But we decided to go all out and use citrus and both red and white wines in a sprightly and refreshing combination. Evan, my son the sommelier, selected the wines, a Spanish *tinto Pesquera* and (okay, so we cheated) an Italian white called Prato de Canzio from Maculan. I think that this is now my favorite sorbet. ◆ *Makes 1 quart*

Heat the sugar and water in a saucepan over medium heat until the sugar is dissolved.

Stir in the remaining ingredients and refrigerate until cold. Freeze in an ice cream maker according to the manufacturer's instructions.

Sorbetto Bellini

PEACH AND
CHAMPAGNE SORBET

1½ pounds ripe peaches
½ cup plus 1 tablespoon
   sugar
½ cup water
3 teaspoons grated lemon
   zest
¾ cup Champagne
2 tablespoons fresh lemon
   juice

Everyone knows that the Bellini is a drink associated with Harry's Bar in Venice. But not everyone knows what a wonderful sorbet it can become. Serve as is or with a few sliced peaches for an ideal summer dessert. ◆ *Makes 3 cups*

Blanch the peaches 2 minutes in a pot of boiling water. Refresh in ice water. Peel and pit the peaches, then mash to a puree with a fork or in a food processor. You should have about 2¾ cups puree. Transfer to a mixing bowl.

Heat the sugar and water to boiling in a saucepan, stirring to dissolve the sugar. Add 2 teaspoons lemon zest and simmer 2 minutes. Let the syrup stand 10 minutes, then strain over the peach puree. Stir in the Champagne, lemon juice, and remaining teaspoon zest. Refrigerate until cold. Freeze in an ice cream maker according to the manufacturer's instructions.

Blackberry Sorbet

5 pints fresh blackberries
  or ollalieberries
1 cup sugar
1 cup water
Pinch salt
1 tablespoon fresh lemon
  juice
2 tablespoons cassis
  liqueur

Cassis is one of the flavors I associate with France. This sorbet can transport you there with its perfume. ◆ *Makes about 1 quart*

Puree the berries in a food processor and strain to remove the seeds. You should have about 4 cups puree.

Heat the sugar, water, and salt in a saucepan over medium heat until the sugar is dissolved. Stir into the berry puree and refrigerate until cold. Stir in the lemon juice and cassis. Freeze in an ice cream maker according to the manufacturer's instructions.

Cantaloupe Sorbet

2 large cantaloupes or
  other melons (about 2
  pounds)
¾ cup plus 1 tablespoon
  sugar
Pinch salt
1 tablespoon kirsch

Do not restrict yourself to cantaloupe for this sorbet. We also make it with Charantais or honeydew melons. The variety of melon is much less important than that it be very ripe and flavorful. Try serving this with a compote of blueberries. ◆ *Makes about 1 quart*

Peel, seed, and puree the melon in a food processor. Strain. You should have about 4 cups puree.

Measure 1 cup melon puree into a small saucepan, stir in the sugar, and heat over medium heat until the sugar is dissolved. Stir into the remaining puree and refrigerate until cold. Stir in the kirsch. Freeze in an ice cream maker according to the manufacturer's instructions.

Biscotti di Mandorle

ALMOND ANISE
COOKIES

½ pound unsalted butter,
  at room temperature

2 cups sugar

5 large eggs, at room
  temperature

5 cups all-purpose flour

2 cups each blanched and
  natural almonds,
  lightly toasted, coarsely
  chopped (see Note)

Juice and grated zest of 1
  lemon

1½ tablespoons anise
  seeds, toasted

1 tablespoon baking
  powder

1½ teaspoons salt

2 tablespoons vanilla
  extract

1 teaspoon almond
  extract

It is an old Italian tradition to eat these cookies with a glass of dessert wine. Every night when I drive home after work, I take a *biscotto* with me (but not the wine!). I don't really mind the crumbs in the car; it is my driving home tradition! ◆ *Makes about 3 dozen*

Preheat the oven to 325°. Beat the butter and sugar in a mixer bowl until light and fluffy, about 3 minutes. Beat in the eggs one at a time. Add the remaining ingredients and mix until blended.

Cut the dough into 4 pieces. Roll each piece into a log about 1½ inches in diameter and the length of your baking sheet. Bake the logs on an ungreased baking sheet until golden brown, about 30 minutes. Let stand until cool to the touch, about 30 minutes.

Reduce the heat to 250°. Cut the logs diagonally into ⅓- to ½-inch slices. Arrange the slices cut sides down on the baking sheet and bake until dried, 8 to 10 minutes. Let cool completely. Store in an airtight container up to 1 week. You may recrisp the cookies in a 250° oven if they soften.

NOTE: You can substitute walnuts for the almonds if you like.

Pine Nut Tile Cookies

1 cup pine nuts
2/3 cup sugar
6 tablespoons all-purpose
  flour
1 tablespoon cornstarch
1/4 teaspoon salt
1 teaspoon vanilla extract
2 large egg whites
1/4 cup unsalted butter,
  melted

These cookies are somewhat fragile and resemble those terra-cotta tiles on roofs in Italy. They are a wonderful accompaniment to ice cream or sorbet. ◆ *Makes about 20*

Preheat the oven to 350°. Line 2 baking sheets with baker's parchment.

Place all the ingredients in a mixer bowl and mix until blended. Drop the batter by heaping tablespoons 3 inches apart on the parchment, then spread each to a very thin circle with the back of a spoon. Bake until lightly browned, 8 to 10 minutes.

With a spatula, carefully remove a warm cookie from the parchment and drape it over a rolling pin to cool in a curved shape. Repeat with the remaining cookies, rewarming them briefly in the oven if they cool and become too brittle to mold. Let the cookies cool completely on the rolling pin. These cookies are best if served the same day they are baked, but they can be stored in an airtight container up to 1 day.

Walnut Clouds

6 tablespoons plus 2
  teaspoons unsalted
  butter, at room
  temperature
1/4 cup granulated sugar
2 teaspoons vanilla
  extract
3/4 teaspoon salt
1 cup walnuts, lightly
  toasted, finely ground
1 cup all-purpose flour
Confectioner's sugar

A rich little cookie to serve with ice cream or a fruit compote. ◆ *Makes about 24*

Preheat the oven to 325°. Line 2 baking sheets with baker's parchment. Beat the butter, granulated sugar, vanilla, and salt in a mixer bowl until light and fluffy. Mix in the nuts, then add the flour and mix until blended.

Spoon the batter into a pastry bag fitted with a large plain tip. Pipe domes of batter, 1 inch in diameter, about 1 inch apart on the parchment. Bake until lightly browned and dry, 8 to 10 minutes. Let cool on a wire rack. Dust with confectioner's sugar when cool.

Almond Tulips

¾ cup unsalted butter, at
   room temperature
1 cup sugar
¾ cup egg whites (about
   6 large)
1 cup all-purpose flour
¼ teaspoon almond
   extract

Use these delicate cookie cups as edible serving dishes for little scoops of ice cream. ◆ *Makes 8 to 10*

Beat the butter and sugar in a mixer bowl until light and fluffy, about 5 minutes. Add the egg whites and mix until barely blended; the batter will look broken. Add the flour and almond extract; mix just until smooth. Refrigerate at least 2 hours.

Preheat the oven to 350°. Line 2 baking sheets with baker's parchment. Drop the batter by heaping tablespoons 3 inches apart on the parchment, then spread each to a very thin circle with the back of a spoon. Bake until golden, about 8 minutes.

With a spatula, carefully remove a warm cookie from the parchment and drape it over an inverted soup or custard cup. Repeat with the remaining cookies, rewarming them in the oven if they cool and become too brittle to mold. Let the cookies cool completely and store in an airtight container up to 1 day, although they are best served the day they are baked.

Grand Marnier Madeleines

3 large eggs
2 large egg yolks
Pinch salt
¾ cup granulated sugar
2 tablespoons Grand
   Marnier
1¼ cups sifted
   all-purpose flour
10 tablespoons clarified
   butter (see Note, page
   26)
Confectioner's sugar

The Grand Marnier adds a delicious perfume to an already fabulous cookie. ◆ *Makes about 48*

Preheat the oven to 350°. Butter and lightly flour 4 standard-sized madeleine molds.

Whisk the eggs and egg yolks together in a mixer bowl over simmering water until warm. Remove from the heat and add the salt. Beat with an electric mixer until the mixture is very thick. Gradually beat in the granulated sugar and continue to beat until the mixture is very thick and very pale yellow. Add the Grand Marnier and beat well. Sift the flour over the batter and gently fold in, then fold in the butter, a little at a time.

Spoon the batter into the molds slightly mounding the tops. Bake until the cookies are golden, about 15 minutes. Gently loosen the sides with a fork and turn out onto wire racks. Dust with confectioner's sugar while still slightly warm.

EVAN'S WINE RECOMMENDATIONS

APPETIZERS

Remember the following factors when pairing wines with starting dishes.

1. Since dishes with vinaigrettes are very difficult to match with wine, it's probably best not to serve one. But if you must, make sure the wine you select is very high in acidity so it stands up to the tartness of the vinaigrette. You might even try using a softer acid for your vinaigrette, such as lemon or lime juice, or perhaps even the wine itself.

2. Keep in mind that this is only the beginning of the meal, so don't select a wine that's too heavy. As with foods, it's best to follow a lighter-to-heavier progression.

3. Don't overlook sparkling wines as good starting wines. They are fairly high in acidity and inherent matching flavors and are lovely openings to any meal. They aren't just for toasts and aperitifs!

Bocconcini   page 19

If you prefer red wine, serve a lighter- to medium-bodied one with some spice: an Italian Dolcetto, a spicy *cru* Beaujolais, or a Barbera. California Gamay or a rustic Pinot Noir (not the breed of Gevrey-Chambertin!) will work, too. Among the white, that will go well are Italian Sauvignon Blanc, Verdicchio, or Vernaccia; a French Sancerre or Pouilly-Fumé; or a more earthy California Sauvignon Blanc.

Baked Goat Cheese in Filo   page 20

White is best here—try a Sauvignon Blanc from France (Sancerre, Pouilly-Fumé, Graves), a bone-dry Chenin Blanc (Savennières), or a zippy Burgundy from Chablis, the Mâconnais (Mâcon-Villages), or the Côte Chalonnaise. A spicy dry Provençal or Loire rosé will work, too.

Tomini Elettrici in Salsa Rossa   page 21

Only red works here because of the nature of the sauce—a simple Pinot Noir such as Mercurey, Rully, and some Californians emphasizing fruitness; a lighter Nebbiolo d'Alba, Barbera, or Dolcetto; even a good Spanish Rioja or an Australian Shiraz with little tannin.

Tomini al Pesto   page 22

White is called for. Try a full-bodied Sauvignon Blanc or a Chardonnay (French Chablis, or one from Friuli or an American in a more austere style); Aligoté from Burgundy or an earthy Sauvignon Blanc-based Graves.

Crostini di Fegatini alla Fiorentina   page 23

Red: a medium Rhône (Gigondas, Saint-Joseph, Côtes-du-Rhône), a Tuscan Rosso di Montalcino or Chianti, or a Barbera, Dolcetto, or Nebbiolo d'Alba from Piedmont; a zippy California Zinfandel or Syrah, rich Spanish reds like a young Rioja, or a southwestern French red such as Minervois or Corbières.

Capriata   page 24

White: full-bodied California Sauvignon Blanc, Australian Sémillon, Loire Valley Sauvignon, medium-bodied Italian whites like Arneis from Piedmont, Vernaccia, or Verdicchio. A dry rosé from Provence or a dry Grignolino from Italy would work.

Fegato alle Uova Sode   page 25

See Crostini di Fegatini alla Fiorentina.

Gorgonzola Brandy Butter   page 25

A soft fruity red would meld well: a simpler Bordeaux or Burgundy, an easy-drinking Australian Shiraz, or a Cabernet Sauvignon from Chile; A *very* rich white like Tokay or Riesling from Alsace (with enough texture to stand up to the butter), or a full-bodied California Chardonnay. Sparkling wines are not a good idea here.

Duck Liver Mousse   page 26

The selection for Crostini di Fegatini alla Fiorentina would be fine here, as would a medium-weight Cabernet Sauvignon from Bordeaux or California.

Suppli al Telefono   page 27

Lighter- to medium-bodied red wines such as Pinot Noir from any country, Chianti or similar Italian reds (such as Rosso di Montalcino). Whites can work, too—a Pinot Bianco or Tocai from northeastern Italy or any other crisp, light, and forward white. Sparkling wines are the perfect accompaniments to fried foods. This one is a marriage made in heaven.

Spuma di Tonno   page 28

A white here is preferable: a zesty French Chablis, a simpler white Burgundy, or a scented and rich Sauvignon Blanc from any country. Or, try medium-rich Italian whites like Verdicchio, Tocai, and Arneis. Although red and rosé wines don't work best here, a good sparkling wine of high acidity and dry spicy flavor would be very nice: nonvintage *cuvées* from Champagne, California, Spain (*cava*), or Italy.

Briouats   page 29

Red wines are first choice—a light Rhône or wine from southwestern France (Minervois or Corbières), a California Zinfandel (not too heavy) or Syrah, or a Rioja or other medium-bodied Spanish wine. If you must have a white, pick a spicy and aromatic Alsatian Gewürtztraminer or a dry Muscat.

Tiropetes   page 30

Whites such as Mâcon-Villages or Montagny from southern Burgundy; lean, austere American Chardonnays; herbal-scented Sauvignon Blancs such as Sancerre or those from New Zealand. A sparkling wine would be very nice too, such as a Loire Valley Saumur or Champagne. Reds and rosés are not successful here.

Shellfish Briouats   page 32

Full-bodied and spicy whites are the best accompaniments: Chardonnay from California, Burgundy, Australia, or the Americas Northwest; Sémillon from France (Graves) or Australia; crisp and earthy Chenin Blanc from the Loire Valley. Although reds are not ideal, a good Provençal rosé or Tavel from the Rhône Valley will work.

Lamb Dolmas   page 33

See Vegetable Dolmas. The red wines are an especially good pairing.

Vegetable Dolmas   page 34

Full-flavored, high-acid dry reds like Pinot Noir; lighter Rhônes; and "claret-style" California Zinfandels. In the whites: Chenin Blanc (Vouvray, Savennières); Riesling from the Pacific Northwest. Rosé and sparkling wines don't work particularly well.

Bresaola   page 35

Red only here; whites just don't work. Try a spicy, uncomplicated Italian like Chianti, Dolcetto, or Barbera; a softer and simpler Cabernet or Merlot from Italy (Veneto or Friuli), France, or California; or a robust and flavorful Zinfandel without too much tannin.

ANTIPASTO AND OTHER MIXED PLATES

Choosing one wine to go with a myriad of different dishes and flavors is hard, for the various tastes can often be matched by more than one selection. When in doubt, have both a red and a white open to give your guests the opportunity to mix and match.

The whites should be light (medium-bodied at the heaviest), with pronounced flavors and crispness and slightly perfumed with elements that will not easily be lost behind the array of tastes. Often the regional character of the dish gives the best clue: If it is Italian, a clean refreshing Pinot Grigio or Sauvignon Blanc from northeastern Italy would be nice. If tapas are featured, the lovely white wines of the Penedès or the inner region of Rueda make splendid accompaniments, and Portuguese dishes are the perfect showcase of the native Vinho Verde. Middle Eastern *mezze* plates work well with California Sauvignon Blanc, which harmonizes beautifully with the bold Arabic flavors.

For reds, simple, light, and fruity examples meld best with the variety of tastes. Again, keep in mind that this is the beginning of the meal, so never serve anything much heavier than a French Burgundian red from Mercurey, Rully, or the Mâconnais; a simple nonclassified red Bordeaux; a Spanish Rioja; Italian Chianti or Nebbiolo d'Alba; or California Gamay, Pinot Noir, or straightforward Cabernet. Again, pay attention to the regional nature of the dish: There is good reason that tapas taste so good with Rioja, and antipasto with Italian reds.

Finally, rosés are nice with these mixed plates, but only if they are dry. Although a white Zinfandel might look lovely with one of these gourmet platters, its sweetness will clash. Provençal rosés from Bandol or the Côtes de Provence, for example, will marry well, as will Tavel from the Rhône, Vin Gris from California, Burgundy, or the Loire, and Italian Grignolino.

MEDITERRANEAN-INSPIRED SALADS

Red wines generally do *not* go with green salads or with vinaigrettes. Whites with high acidity, a nice earthy quality, slightly leafy/green flavors, sharp youthful zest and not too much weight are best—a Sauvignon Blanc from any country, bone-dry Chenin Blanc (remember, in most cases even a little sweetness will taste funny in your mouth), or even a fresh and crisp sparkling wine.

Pear, Celery, Potato, and Watercress page 59

Add to the list in the introduction above a young Kabinett Riesling from Germany, which would pick up on the sweetness of the pear (Mosel only, Rhinegau would be too heavy).

Pear, Provolone, and Arugula page 60

See Pear, Celery, Potato, and Watercress.

Endive, Apple, and Walnut page 61

See the introduction above.

Mushrooms, Gruyère, and Prosciutto page 62

The whites in the introduction would do, but a wine of a bit more weight and substance to stand up to the richness of the meat and the cheese would be ideal. Chardonnays of some substance with an emphasis on an earthy flavor rather than oak would be nice, as would vigorous Italians like Vernaccia, Verdicchio, and some southern varieties. You might try an Australian Sémillon as well.

Black Radish, Carrot, and Fennel with Pecorino Cheese page 63

See the introduction above.

Roast Pepper, Fontina, and Arugula page 64

A generous and fairly full-bodied white goes well here. Both the roasted peppers, which are rich, smoky and almost sweet, and the fullness and texture of the cheese require something along the lines of an American or Australian Chardonnay or Sémillon, a French Burgundy, or perhaps even a Rhône Valley white from Hermitage or Crozes-Hermitage. But a light, fruity red of nominal tannin would also work nicely as the vinaigrette is subdued and the other ingredients call out for a red. A Beaujolais, American Gamay, Loire Valley red such as Chinon or Bourgueil, gentle Grenache wines from any country, or refreshing young Dolcetto from Italy would be lovely.

Panzanella   page 65

See Fattoush.

Fattoush   page 66

Wine is not recommended with this dish, but if you must serve one, make it a very exuberant and herbal white.

Greek Salad   page 67

See the introduction above.

Israeli Avocado Salad   page 68

See the white wine selections for Avocado Catalan.

Grilled Leeks with Walnut Cream Vinaigrette   page 69

Serve whites with high acidity, medium body, and pronounced herbal flavors: Sauvignon Blancs; lean, austere Chardonnays from Chablis, northeastern Italy, or California.

Gazpacho Vinaigrette for Avocado   page 70

No wine will do justice here.

Caponata di Verdure   page 72

See the introduction above.

Avocado Catalan   page 73

The nature major ingredients and the delicacy of the vinaigrette call for a white wine of some substance or a light red—see the suggestions for Roasted Peppers, Fontina, and Arugula. Given this dish's strong flavors, I would probably opt for a lighter Spanish wine like a Rioja, or a simpler but tasty red from the Penedès region.

Scapece   page 74

See Scallop, Orange, and Lemon Salad.

Rice Salad with Grilled Tuna   page 75

Choose a rich, earthy white wine with light herbaceousness: a full-bodied Sauvignon Blanc; Alsatian Riesling; Pinot Gris; Sémillon from Australia; Chardonnay from Italy (Piedmontese or Tuscan), California, or Australia: or dry and spicy rosé.

Grilled Tuna with Charmoula Vinaigrette   page 76

This dish lends itself to many options. For whites, the slightly spicy and hot *charmoula* and the smoky and pungent flavors of the grilled vegetables seem to crave an aromatic, spicy, and slightly off-dry wine: a German Kabinett or Spatlese Riesling, certain American Rieslings and Chenin Blancs, or Chenin Blancs from the Loire. A Gewürztraminer can be lovely, as can a more substantial Chenin Blanc.

A light, fruity red would be acceptable, but the tuna demands a wine with some body: a lighter Rhône (Grenache or Syrah) or a Gamay, such as a Beaujolais.

Grilled Tuna Salad with a Moroccan Salsa   page 78

See the white wine selections for Grilled Tuna with Charmoula Vinaigrette.

Scallop, Orange, and Lemon Salad   page 79

Serve with rich, zesty whites with a little spice: Chardonnay, Alsatian Pinot Gris, Sauvignon Blanc, or Sémillon from California, France, or Australia. Sparkling wines would be appropriate, too.

SOUPS

People are always surprised when I tell them I would rather select a wine to go with a salad than a soup, but I have always found pairing a "liquid" with another "liquid" to be quite challenging. As my mother points out, there are two elements to a good soup: a good stock and flavorful raw materials. When selecting a wine, one must consider a third factor: the thickness of the soup. A pureed soup—be it beans, starchy vegetables (potato and fennel, or butternut squash)—has a thick texture. Such soups are much easier to match than broth-based soups, which force one to pair a wine with a liquid of similar weight.

With both types of soup one needs to make a statement. A thick soup calls for a wine that can cut through the weight of the soup and juxtapose an interesting flavor. High acidity is thus of paramount importance in matching wine with particularly thick or cream-based soups. Fortified wines, such as dry sherry or Madeira, can work very well here too. An example of this pairing would be a full yet youthful and balanced Chardonnay from California or Australia with the Pureed Butternut Squash soup. Both are rich, but the tartness of the Chardonnay's youth allows its flavors to come through together with those of the soup.

Broth-based soups need wine that "speaks" loudly enough to be heard through the similar-weight soup. For example, a medium-bodied but spicy red wine (like a Spanish Rioja or Portuguese Dão) would be the perfect accompaniment to the Portuguese Caldo Verde, which is full of flavor from the sausage, greens, and potatoes and craves something assertive juxtaposed against a broth base of similar weight.

Another texture factor involves those ingredients left whole or added as pieces to a soup: vegetables, shellfish, beans, croutons. The wine should match the flavors and textures of such ingredients. Keep in mind the difference between secondary ingredients, like croutons put in a soup to add crunch, and primary flavor ingredients, like vegetables in a minestrone. I could suggest many wines that would harmonize with the flavors of the vegetables, but I wouldn't worry about finding a "crunchy" wine.

Look at the principal flavors of the soup to decide whether to go with a red or white wine. Hearty, meat-based, rustic "meals-in-a-bowl" peasant soups crave red wines. Many vegetable, shellfish, and other more delicate soups marry better with whites. But there are no right or wrong choices—only what you like.

PASTA AND RICE

If you ask ten people who work in a restaurant what their favorite "easy" or "on the go" meal is, nine will tell you a bowl of pasta and a glass of wine. There are few more soulful combinations in the world than pasta and vino.

Several factors should be kept in mind when matching pasta with wine.

1. Where is the pasta in the meal? Is it the entire meal or a first course? This is an important factor in determining the weight of the wine. Since one builds progressively in a meal, a potent Barolo to accompany your rigatoni when you still have two or three courses to move on to is not a good idea, but if you were having that same pasta as the entire meal for lunch, that same Barolo might be right.

2. There are few better examples of regionalism than in the pairing of pasta and wine. In all of my years of eating and drinking, I have found few selections to go better with most pastas than Italian wines. That is not a definitive statement, and of course one can find many other suitable substitutes, but Italian wine and pasta work wonders together.

Most pasta and noodle or rice dishes are in the category of wholesome, warm, and soulful food. They can be quite refined, but as a general rule they are more easygoing and comforting and do not call for the sophisticated wine matches that main courses may demand. Pasta wants a wine that marries well without calling attention to itself.

Following are a few wine categories with examples. When speaking of the individual dishes I'll refer to these categories. Remember, you don't have to stick to the specific examples, merely try and find something similar.

Light and crisp whites: Pinot Grigio and Chardonnay from Italy's Alto Adige and Friuli; Soave, Frascati, and Verdicchio. Sauvignon Blanc from anywhere in the world.

Light medium to medium-bodied whites: Vernaccia from Tuscany; Chardonnays from Italy, France, or California; Italian white wines from the south (Campania) or the North (Veneto); earthy whites from Spain, like those of Catalonia and Rueda.

Light-bodied, nontannic reds: Dolcetto, Valpolicella, Bardolino, and Merlot from Italy; Gamay from California; lighter southern French wines from Provence or the Rhône; and simple and tasty reds from Spain (Rioja and La Mancha are good regions for these types) and Portugal (Colares).

Medium-bodied, flavorful reds: Chianti, Barbera, Nebbiolo d'Alba, Rosso di Montalcino from Italy are classics and among the best pasta wines; more recent efforts in Italian Merlot and Cabernet Sauvignon are very nice too; Rioja from Spain, Shiraz from Australia, medium-strength reds of France's Provence, Rhône, and Midi; American Zinfandel (though not too heavy), Barbera, and Pinot Noir.

Big, robust reds: Barolo and Barbaresco, Brunello and Vino Nobile di Montepulciano from Italy; California Pinot Noir, Syrah, and Zinfandel; rustic Bordeaux and Australian Shiraz; meatier French reds from the Rhône and southern France.

Türteln   page 114

A medium, rich, full-bodied white with earthy qualities, such as Vernaccia, goes well. Reds of the Chianti-like style would also work well.

Cialzons di Timau   page 115

Rich, spicy, aromatic white wines are called for here: perhaps a Tocai from Friuli. An off-dry white like a Riesling or Chenin Blanc would be nice too. If you prefer a red, select a light nontannic example, such as a northern Italian Merlot.

Cassunziei Ampezzani   page 116

Version 1—See Türteln; the white need not be quite as rich. Version 2—A rich, medium-body white is called for here. Version 3—Toasty and earthy whites (perhaps from Spain) or light reds and even sparkling wines would be nice here.

Ravioli alla Potentina   page 117

See Ravioli di Melanzane. One could also have a heavier red, such as Barolo or Barbaresco.

Culingiones di Patate   page 118

See Türteln.

Ravioli Caprese   page 119

Light and nontannic reds or medium-body flavorful reds go well. Valpolicella is a popular choice.

Zembi d'Arzillo   page 120

A medium-bodied red would work well too, especially one stressing fruitier flavors, such as Merlot. A rich white wine, such as a California Chardonnay, would pick up on the flavors and sweetness of the fish.

Ravioli Verdi al Salmone   page 121

This dish calls for rich, full-flavored whites with a minimal emphasis on wood (the flavor from aging in oak barrels). Wines stressing greener and more herbal flavors, such as a Sauvignon Blanc, would be good matches. Full-flavored rosé wines (Vin Gris, Tavel, or a dry blush type) would match well, as would a spicy, light Pinot Noir.

Ravioli di Melanzane   page 122

A medium-body red, such as Barbera, is called for here.

Ricotta-Goat Cheese Filling page 123

A medium-bodied white with the tartness of high acidity will match up with the goat cheese: a Pinot Grigio with bite is one choice.

Ricotta-Gorgonzola Filling page 123

Light- to medium-bodied reds, such as Bardolino, go well here.

Leeks and Cheese Filling page 123

This needs a full-flavored white like Chardonnay or a light- to medium-bodied red like Dolcetto.

Pasta à la Barigoule page 124

Earthy, full-flavored whites and lighter, nontannic reds are called for: Vernaccia is one good choice. Rosé would not work well.

Fettuccine alla Turque page 125

Light- to medium-bodied whites stressing citrus and floral flavors—youthful, with a touch of "greenness"—are best: perhaps a northern Italian Chardonnay.

Fettuccine alla Genovese page 126

An off-dry white wine would be the best marriage. Those of high acidity work best: German Riesling, Chenin Blanc, and some Gewürtztraminer.

Fettuccine with Goat Cheese and Swiss Chard page 127

Earthy and full flavored whites—high acidity a must. Vernaccia from Tuscany or a similar white is called for.

Strascinate page 128

Light, nontannic reds only: a Rhône wine is one idea.

Pizzoccheri page 129

Earthy whites, such as Vernaccia, or soft and nontannic youthful reds are best. Don't overlook the reds from the Valtellina: Sassella, Grumello, and Inferno.

Fusilli alla Napoletana   page 130

See Rigatoni alla Norma

Bigoli co l'Anara   page 131

Rich, full-bodied reds are needed: Valpolicella is from the region of this recipe and works very well.

Rigatoni alla Norma   page 132

Medium-bodied reds like Chianti.

Rigatoni with Fennel Sausage and Peppers   page 133

See Rigatoni alla Norma. Rich, robust reds will also go well here.

Rigatoni with Little Herbed Meatballs   page 134

See Rigatoni alla Norma

Spaghetti with Tuna, Three Ways   pages 135–137

Spicy and full-bodied whites, such as Sicilian Corvo, or light and youthful reds, such as Bardolino.

Pasta alla Cataplana   page 138

Medium-bodied reds or full and hearty reds if you're working with a particularly spicy and coarse sausage; thus, you can choose from Valpolicella to Barbera.

Pasta in Zimino   page 139

An off-dry white with some zest works here: Riesling or Chenin Blanc. If you add anchovies, add an earthy type of medium-bodied white: Vernaccia. If you add tomatoes, add a light red or hearty rosés: Chianti or Rosso di Salento.

Spaghetti with Scallops, Roasted Red Peppers, and Pine Nuts   page 140

Rich almost unctuous whites, such as chardonnay, and light but exuberant reds, such as Dolcetto.

Linguine with Squid and Clams   page 141

Full-bodied whites like Sauvignon Blanc, or spicy reds of minimal tannin: Pinot Noir would be ideal here.

Fettuccine al Barese   page 142

See Linguine with Squid and Clams

Fettuccine à la Grecque   page 143

See Linguine with Squid and Clams

Borlenghi ai Quattro Formaggi   page 145

Medium-bodied reds are called for. You can choose a wine from the region of the dish, such as Sangiovese di Romagna.

Gnocchi, Ristorante Archimede   page 146

Light and delicate reds of little tannin and, if possible, more complex flavor: an Italian Merlot would work well. Light whites too can be used, but keep in mind balancing them off the acidity of the tomatoes.

Crochette di Riso   page 152

Light- to medium-bodied reds, such as Nebbiolo, toasty medium-bodied whites, such as Tocai, and, of course, since they match so well with fried foods, sparkling wines can all be used.

Risotto alla Paesana   page 156

Medium-bodied reds like Chianti are best here.

Seafood Risotto with Spinach and Peas   page 157

Medium- to full-bodied whites go well here. A crisp northern Italian Pinot Grigio would be an excellent choice.

Seafood Risotto with Tomatoes and Gremolata   page 158

See Seafood Risotto with Spinach and Peas.

Risotto alla Primavera   page 159

The wine selection depends on the presence or absence of tomatoes. With tomatoes, lighter and fruity reds like Merlot. No tomatoes, light to medium-bodied whites like Chenin Blanc.

Paella   page 160

Only medium-bodied reds work here, with a stress on regionalism (Spanish Rioja or southern French Côtes-du-Rhône). Pinot Noir is a great match with paella.

FISH AND SHELLFISH

No category of cooking seems to have adapted and changed as much recently as seafood. In her introduction to fish and shellfish, Joyce suggests that perhaps the biggest revelation for all of us is that eating fish is no longer what it once was. Many people grew up dreading "fish on Fridays," but many of us now head right to the fish section of restaurant menus or make special trips to the fish market when cooking at home, both part of our new devotion to fresh products. The advent of fresh seafood on the menu and the dining table has also opened up the thinking on wine as its mate. The centuries-old adage that one has red wine with meat and white with fish is now longer valid.

Another old adage—"a fish is a fish is a fish"—is just not true. There are many types of fish: sweet filet type, such as sole, trout, and turbot; meatier fish, such as sword, tuna, and shark; "flakier" fish like cod and snapper; and then there are those that resemble shellfish, such as angler. Several others (in addition to meatier fishes) are, like salmon, very "red wine" fish.

Each of these categories calls for a different wine style. Sweet fillet fishes are best with light, crisp, and delicate wines that highlight and show off the fish's inherent sweetness: German Kabinett Riesling, exuberant and delicate Loire Valley Chenin Blanc, simpler but flavorful French Burgundies like Saint-Romain, Mâcon-Villages, and Montagny. Meatier fish require full-bodied whites: Chardonnay from California or Australia and some of the new big Italian examples; French white Burgundy; Australian Sémillon; and many of the bigger Sauvignon Blancs from the Loire Valley. The almost meatlike texture of these fish can often demand (especially if the preparation asks) a medium-bodied and flavorful red wine with little or no tannin: Pinot Noir from France, California, and Oregon; Beaujolais or other Gamay wines; Dolcetto; Bourgueil and Chinon from the Loire; and simple Bordeaux reds (or other Cabernet Sauvignon wines).

Flaking fish (such as cod and snapper) seem to demand a wine somewhere in between, and (as we will see in the recipes) the preparation, rather than the fish itself, dictates the accompanying wine. Shellfishlike fish (angler and monk) should be treated as shellfish and can handle the same full-bodied whites that one would have alongside a lobster: rich and full-flavored Chardonnays and other semiunctuous whites. Salmon calls for either red (again, lighter less-tannic styles) or a rich and oily white, depending on the preparation and your preferences.

With shellfish, full and elegant, luscious and complex are almost always the keys. Such wines almost always work, be it the most simple preparation (with the exception of the fail-safe raw oysters with Chablis or Muscadet) or the most complex. Pay close attention to the preparation, and if a red is required opt for a wine that is flavorful and round, yet not tannic or too vigorous.

The preparation of the dish is of the utmost importance. Is it hot or cold? Complex or simple? With many accompanying flavors and textures or *au natural?* Grilled, sauteed, or merely steamed? This is where your personal preferences and experimentation will assist you in creating your own nautical harmony. Remember, the simpler the preparation the better the opportunity to give a dish some flair with a more complex, but not competing, wine. The more complex the entree, the better the opportunity to let the wine play innocent bystander.

Trote Ripiene Grigliate all'Iseana   page 167

This dish calls for medium-rich and flavorful whites with good acidity and light smokiness (particularly if the fish is grilled). A Washington State Riesling or German Kabinett Riesling, a Chenin Blanc of a drier style, a simple and earthy Chardonnay, and some clean and fresh Italian whites, like Soave or Pinot Grigio, would go well. Light-bodied reds, such as Gamay, Dolcetto, and Pinot Noir offer other possibilities. Clean and refreshing rosés, such as those from Bandol in Provence, would be nice mates too.

Trota allo Zenzero   page 168

See Trote Ripiene Grigliate all'Iseana. To the whites you can add aromatic Alsatian whites like Riesling and dry Muscat. Similar reds will work fine.

Salmon Wrapped in Grape Leaves   page 169

Reds don't work well here, but if one insists the wine should be light and fruity. Whites are best, particularly those that are slightly off-dry, like Chenin Blanc and Riesling from California or rich and fruity Chardonnays from America, Australia, and New Zealand.

Salmone al Giuliese   page 170

Light- to medium-bodied reds with an herbal emphasis, like Chinon and Bourgueil from the Loire Valley; herbal and scented Pinot Noir from France, California, and Oregon; and simple non-pedigree Bordeaux make good reds here. For whites, choose an earthy and lean Chardonnay, a Sauvignon Blanc from the Loire or Graves, or a Muscadet.

Salmonete Grelhado com Maionese Setubalense   page 171

A rich and full-bodied white, textured and spicy, is called for. Rhône whites would be lovely here—Hermitage or Crozes-Hermitage—Alsatian Rieslings or Pinot Gris, and rich and round Chardonnays. Light and peppery red wines with soft tannins—Pinot Noir, Rioja, Portuguese reds from Colares and Bairrada—would go well. A more powerful and robust rosé wine like a full-bodied Vin Gris from Burgundy, Provence, or the Loire Valley is another choice.

Portuguese-Style Salmon with Curry, Lemon, and Cream   page 172

Such aromatic and exotic whites as Alsatian Riesling, Muscat, and Pinot Gris work well here. Condrieu, white Hermitage, and Australian Sémillon are other choices. Soft and easy drinking reds present yet another choice: Beaujolais *nouveau* or *primeur* (sold shortly after the grape harvest) also go well.

Salmon with Red Onions and Red Wine   page 173

As the name implies, red only here. Many medium-bodied Italian reds would fit nicely here: Chianti or Rosso di Montalcino; Pinot Noir would also be good. One helpful hint is that it's always a safe bet to serve the same wine that you use in the preparation of the dish (in this case the *confit*). Rosés of a vigorous style could work here too.

Baked Fish with Preserved Lemons and Onion Confit   page 174

Dry Alsatian wines are a good choice: Riesling, Muscat, Pinot Gris. Chenin Blanc from the Loire, either dry (Savennières) or off-dry (Vouvray), also work. Off-dry rosés, like Rosé d'Anjou, offer another choice.

Moroccan Charmoula for Fish   page 175

See Baked Fish with Preserved Lemons and Onion Confit. Reds like meaty Pinot Noirs also work well.

Swordfish à la Turque   page 176

Off-dry whites of some substance are called for here: Chenin Blanc or German or American Riesling. Certain full-bodied whites, such as Chardonnay, are powerful enough to penetrate the flavors and have some persistence. Soft and easy-drinking reds of light peppery and spicy flavors, such as certain Zinfandels, might also work (be careful, for it's easy to clash with the lemon).

Pescespada Ripieno alla Siciliana   page 177

Medium-rich green and youthful whites are best here: Sauvignon Blanc from France (Loire or Graves); Verdicchio, Vernaccia, and Arneis from Italy; austere Chardonnays from around the world. Other possibilities include soft and supple reds with some light tannins—medium-weight Italian reds, Pinot Noirs, Beaujolais, soft Rhône reds (Saint-Joseph, Crozes-Hermitage), or Rioja.

Espadarte Grelhado a Lisboeta   page 178

See Grilled Swordfish on Tuna with Sun-Dried Tomatoes, Olives, and Lemon. Emphasis should be placed on more "regional" Portuguese and Spanish reds: Colares from Portugal, Valdepeñas from Spain.

Grilled Swordfish or Tuna with Sun-Dried Tomatoes   page 179

Mainly lighter- to medium-bodied red wines are needed here. Something of a more Italian flavor is perhaps best: Barbaresco, Barbera, Nebbiolo d'Alba, or Chianti. Pinot Noirs, Zinfandels, and lighter-style Bordeaux wines are also agreeable. White is tough here, but if you must, choose a full-bodied and complex white with slight smoky flavor: Pouilly-Fumé might be best.

Tonno alla Griglia con Pepe Ammaccato   page 180

I prefer this dish with a red as opposed to a white and, given the pepper, would choose a full and relatively powerful red wine: Rhône reds, Bandol, Barolo, or Taurasi. An off-dry white might pick up on the sweetness of the tuna and counterbalance the heat of the pepper: Riesling, Chenin Blanc, or an American Gewürztraminer.

Tonno in Gradela   page 181

This dish needs a rich and fairly full-bodied white with a light herbal undertone: Sauvignon Blanc, Mâcon-Villages, Montagny, Rully; Italian whites from Friuli (Tocai, Ribolla) or whites from the Veneto (specifically from Breganze).

Bolinhos de Santola   page 182

Best here are off-dry whites like German or American Riesling or Chenin Blanc (Vouvray). Reds can work here in a lighter style (emphasizing fruit; *nouveau* are best) if the heat in the dish is played down: try Beaujolais.

Merluzzo all'Istriana   page 184

See Tonno in Gradela.

Polpettine di Pesce all'Ebrea   page 185

See Tonno in Gradela. Lighter and simpler reds, such as Bardolino, and light but flavorful rosés, such as those of Provence, are also welcome.

Teglia di Branzino e Granchio   page 186

Light and flavorful red wine is ideal here: Pinot Noir, softer Bordeaux, Provençal reds, Chianti, Barbera, Rosso di Montalcino, Rioja and Penedès, rosé wines like Tavel or those of Provence, Bardolino.

Tiella di Cozze   page 187

This classic dish demands a full-bodied white: Meursault, Chassagne-Montrachet, buttery California or Australian Chardonnay, white Rhônes.

La Triestina   page 188

This is a red only dish: Soft Rhône and Provençal reds from France, American Pinot Noirs of a meatier style, medium-bodied Zinfandel and Syrah from California, Barbaresco, Rosso di Montalcino, Australian Shiraz or Shiraz/Cabernet blends.

Fish Couscous with Charmoula   page 190

See Moroccan Charmoula for Fish

Rape con Grelos y Almejas   page 192

This calls for a full-bodied white wine, particularly those stressing herbal flavors, such as Pouilly-Fumé and Sancerre. Easy drinking and supple reds from the Côte Chalonnaise in Burgundy, Pinot Noirs from the United States, and Cabernet Franc–based wines from Chinon and Bourgueil. Medium-body rosés will also go well.

Ameijoas na Cataplana   page 194

Medium-bodied red wines are great here, and those with a regional flair are best: Portuguese Dão, Bairrada, Colares; Spanish Rioja, Penedès; also Pinot Noirs and softer Midi and Provençal reds from France.

Fritto Misto al Mare   page 195

Sparking wine goes good here (Champagne from France, Italian sparkling Franciacorta, American dry sparkling wine, and cava from Spain), but my own personal preference with this dish is a glass of pilsner beer!!

POULTRY

Poultry is unarguably the most flexible wine-and-food category. While red meat is usually best with red wines and fish and shellfish—although I am not completely convinced—best with whites, poultry really goes best with both. Few chicken, squab, or duck dishes cannot be matched with a selection of both red and white wines.

Chicken is the best-selling "bird" at our restaurant. Because it is in such demand, we have found many ways to serve it. The flavor of chicken is quite delicate, with an inherent sweetness, so can be easily overpowered by a wine—white or red—that is too strong. As in the case with red meat, one must pay close attention to the way the chicken is cooked and how it is seasoned and served. The simplest and most classic roast chicken with minimal seasoning (salt and pepper, garlic, and perhaps a few wedges of lemon tucked in the cavity) really wants a lighter wine, white or red, to accompany it: soft red Bordeaux; a scented but not too intricate Burgundy, like a Santenay, Monthélie; or red Mâcon—all of which are light in body, flavor, and tannin. As for whites, a German Riesling would be lovely, as would a medium-bodied fresh and delicate Chardonnay from anywhere in the world. If the preparation of the chicken is off the grill, a wine to foil the flavor of the grill (which can often be stronger than the chicken) is called upon. And as chicken is very neutral in flavor, more often than not one needs to pay closer attention to the other flavor factors: marinades, accompanying vegetables, herbs, spices, and the like.

Duck is quite different. Not only is its flavor a bit coarser and gamier than that of chicken, but its textures are completely opposite. Duck is a very fatty bird and must be paired with wines that have some body and richness, without being flabby. Even in the leanest form, a duck breast that has been removed from it's "cover" of fat is still a rich meat. Like chicken, duck can go with both red and white wines. Unlike chicken, because of it's stronger flavor, it requires wines that are a bit more muscular and earthy. Here too, it pays to scrutinize the manner in which the duck is being prepared and served. I personally find for reds that Pinot Noirs are almost "sure hits" every time, with the nature of the dish dictating the level of intensity and structure of the wine. For white wines, I like wines with rich texture: Chardonnays from Australia, France, and California; Pinot Gris and Riesling from Alsace; the rich and full-bodied white wines of the Rhône (white Hermitage and Condrieu); and finally wines of high acidity as a foil to the duck's richness, such as Savennières and Chablis.

Squab is in a category by itself. Although a bird, its flavors are very meaty and more pungent than either duck or chicken. I almost always lean toward red wine with squab and treat it as a "meat," although very vigorous white wines can marry well. It too, like duck, is a wonderful marriage with Pinot Noir or similar medium-bodied wines of soft tannic structure and spicy flavors. Softer Rhône wines can be very nice as well as California Zinfandel and Italian reds like Chianti, Nebbiolo d'Alba, and Barbera. Sturdy wines can be paired if the nature of the dish calls for it—a very spicy marinade, a heavy char from the grill, or a powerful accompanying sauce.

Cornish hens, turkey, and quail, like chicken, are best with lighter, more supple wines that will not mask their already delicate flavors. Game birds like pheasant, goose, and partridge should be regarded along the lines of duck or squab, depending on how long they have been hung (if they are wild) or if they are farm raised.

With as many wine options as types of poultry, one should have no problem in discovering combinations that will work well.

Grilled Chicken in an Algerian Marinade   page 201

Try a medium-bodied red wine, spicy and fruity, but with soft tannins: Côtes-du-Rhône, Gigondas, and Côtes du Ventoux from France's Rhône; Côtes de Provence, Corbières and Minervois also from France's south would be nice. A simple but satisfying Pinot Noir, like a Mercurey, Santenay, or even a young Volnay would be splendid, as would examples from Oregon or California. Slightly off-dry whites with exuberance and aroma, like Riesling from Germany, Vouvray from France, and either Chenin Blanc or Riesling from California or off-dry rosé wines like Rose d'Anjou are good choices too.

Catalan-Style Grilled Chicken   page 202

See Grilled Chicken in an Algerian Marinade. This calls for a more "ethnic orientation": Spanish reds from the Penedès or young crianza Rioja; Portuguese Colares and Periquita. Off-dry whites and even an off-dry but not too sweet Muscat wine would be lovely. Off-dry rosé types would be nice here too.

Grilled Chicken in a Moroccan Marinade   page 203

See Grilled Chicken in an Algerian Marinade, page 201. Play up on the exotic spicing a little more: Pinot Noirs are excellent reds here, having similar flavors as the marinade, and rich Alsatian whites (Pinot Gris, Gewürztraminer).

Grilled Chicken with Piri-Piri Hot Sauce   page 204

Full-bodied reds that can stand up to hot African spicing are needed: full-bodied Rhône wines from France (Hermitage, Côte Rôtie), California Syrah and Zinfandel, Italian Brunello. A nice foil here is a fruity, refreshing red served with a slight chill! Beaujolais, California Gamay, Dolcetto, and even some Loire Valley Chinon.

Pollo al Pumate e Mirto   page 206

This dish is so Italian by nature it really seems silly to recommend anything but Italian wines. Medium- to full-bodied wines are needed: young Chianti, Rosso di Montalcino, Vino Nobile di Montepulciano, and spicy young Barbera d'Alba. Suitable substitutes from other countries would be Australian Shiraz, California Pinot Noir, French Burgundy, and Spanish Rioja. White wines can work here too if full bodied and earthy: Greco di Tufo from Campania (Italy), Sancerre and Pouilly-Fumé from France, and herbal California Chardonnays.

Koto Psito   page 207

White wines of full body and slightly herbal flavors are best: rich Sauvignon Blancs from California, France's Graves, or New Zealand; full and sturdy styles of Chardonnay that stress earth and complex fruit. Light reds can work here too.

Puddighinos a Pienu   page 208

Medium, forceful reds of a more "country-wine" flavor. Southern Italian Taurasi or Aglianico del Vulture have harmonious flavors that go well with this dish. Gamy, meaty Pinot Noir from France, Oregon, or California; Barbaresco or Nebbiolo d'Alba; and of course a full flavored and firm Chianti—all would work here.

Moroccan-Style Roast Chicken with Couscous   page 209

Soft reds are best here, with an emphasis on ethnic style (what they would drink in Morocco: rich, soft, fruity, and spicy) like Rhônes, Barbera from Italy, California Gamay or Syrah. Grenache-based wines and off-dry whites can work here too, as can full-bodied Chardonnays.

Roast Chicken Stuffed with Ricotta and Pesto   page 210

See Koto Psito. Aside from full-bodied, herbal whites, medium-bodied reds, like Chianti, Rosso di Montalcino, and Nebbiolo d'Alba from Italy, Shiraz from Australia, Merlot from California, and soft Bordeaux reds go well. Dry, fresh rosés like Burgundy's Vin Gris or Rosé de Loire. Grignolino offers another possibility.

Fricassee of Chicken with "Forty Cloves" of Garlic   page 211

Complex and full white wines are needed: white Burgundy—Meursault, Chassagne-Montrachet—California Chardonnay, Australian Sémillon, and Rhône Valley whites. Medium-bodied and fragrant reds all go well: Burgundy (Clos Saint-Denis, Chambolle-Musigny), Morgon and Juliénas from Beaujolais, and Châteauneuf-du-Pape from the Rhône. Italian Merlot from Friuli is yet another choice.

Sautéed Chicken with Moroccan Hot and Sweet Tomato Sauce   page 213

See Grilled Chicken in an Algerian Marinade. Similar wines but for different reasons: the off-dry white picks up on the sweet while offering a foil for the heat, and lighter fruity reds are a nice "stage" for the dish. Off-dry rosés, for similar reasons to the whites, also work: Rosé d'Anjou is an example.

Pollo alla Potentina   page 214

Spicy and earthy red wines work best here: from Italy, robust and muscular wines from Piedmont (Barolo, Barbaresco), Taurasi, Rosso di Montalcino, or a gusty young Barbera; Rhône wines like Cornas; and good spicy California Zinfandel.

Pollo con Carciofi   page 215

This dish is a sommelier's nightmare: artichokes kill wine, making almost all wines taste bitter. If one must have wine, a white wine of very tart acidity and earthiness is the best choice: Chablis from France, young Pinot Grigio or Tocai from Friuli in Italy, and zesty young Sauvignon Blanc from California.

Pollo con Pumate   page 216

Classic medium-bodied Italian reds fit right in here. Chianti Classico, Rosso di Montalcino, Vino Nobile di Montepulciano, Nebbiolo d'alba, Merlot from the Veneto and Friuli provide the first choices. Round, harmonious reds from the Mediterranean—Rioja in Spain, Dão in Portugal—complete the picture.

Kotopitta   page 217

Medium-bodied, rich, and herbaceous whites: Sancerre, California and Australian Sauvignon Blanc, Provençal whites of Bandol. In my experience, reds and rosés just don't work well here.

Bastilla   page 218

Off-dry, aromatic white wines are best: Moscato d'Asti (not sparkling); Chenin Blanc, Gewürztraminer, and Riesling from California; German Riesling; Gewürztraminer and Muscat Vendage Tardive from Alsace.

Petti di Pollo Trifolati   page 220

See Pollo con Pumate. This recipe also pairs with medium-bodied, earthy whites like Vernaccia from Italy and Pouilly-Fumé from the Loire Valley.

Catalan-Style Grilled Quail Stuffed with Figs   page 221

A personal favorite, this dish works best with soft and fruity red wines, such as Rioja and those of Valdepeñas, California Gamay, simple Merlot, and light Zinfandel. French *cru* Beaujolais (Fleurie, Saint-Amour, and Brouilly), and soft southwestern French wines like Corbières and Minervois. Full and fruity white wines like white Rioja, Sémillon from Australia, and Chardonnay from America also go well here.

Moroccan Fried Squab with Saffron and Ginger   page 222

See Grilled Chicken with *Piri Piri* Hot Sauce

Roast Duck with Honey, Lavender, and Thyme   page 224

Rich and textured aromatic white wines: Rhône whites (Condrieu, white Hermitage), Alsatian Pinot Gris, California and Australian Chardonnays. Delicate and scented reds of soft tannin are also good: Pinot Noirs from most anywhere that stress the fruit: Volnay, Monthélie, California and Oregon Pinot Noir.

Pato con Peras   page 226

See Roast Duck with Honey, Lavender, and Thyme, page 224.

Anitra con le Lenticchie page 227

Full-bodied, robust red wines are a must here. Italian Barolo and Barbaresco, Brunello di Montalcino, and young Tuscan blends of Cabernet Sauvignon and Sangiovese (Grifi, Tignanello) are good choices. Red Bordeaux, Cahors, Côte Rôtie, and Hermitage from France or California Cabernet Sauvignon and full-bodied Syrah would also marry well.

Anitra in Porchetta page 228

See Pollo con Pumate page 216. Medium- to full-bodied red wines are needed. Emphasis on regional wines leads to Italian wines. Similar wines from France, Spain, or America would be adequate substitutes. Again, pay attention to the rich nature of the duck and don't select a wine that can't stand up to it.

Duck with Port, Prunes, and Pearl Onions page 229

Medium- to full-bodied red wines stressing richness of fruit will marry well with the port sauce. Rhône reds and those of southwestern France (wines of Languedoc, Aude, and Gard), Zinfandel from California, dry Port wines, Spanish wines from the Ribera del Duero (Vega Sicilia, Pesquera) are all good choices.

Roast Duck with Red Wine, Orange, and Sage Sauce page 230

Pay attention to the red wine you use in the sauce and pick a similar wine to serve with the dish. Reds that work well here are Rhône wines, Zinfandel, Shiraz from Australia, and other wines that stress interesting earth components and generous fruit.

Grilled Quail Stuffed with Honeyed Onions page 231

Off-dry white wines are excellent here, like Riesling from Washington State or the Mosel in Germany, Vouvray and Saumur from France, and clean, exuberant Moscato from Italy. Lighter, fruity reds work well here: Beaujolais, Dolcetto, and less tannic styles of young California Zinfandel or Pinot Noir.

MEATS

I enjoy being called over to a table to consult on the wine selection for a meal. Although many people "build" a progression of wines in their meal, most select a bottle to accompany their entrees, which are usually meat dishes. One night a guest pulled me over to the table and asked about a "good bottle" to go with his steak. After much discussion, and against my strongest pleas, the selection was made: a bottle of Sauternes (a French sweet dessert wine). While I profess to be liberal when harmonizing wine and food, when it comes to the pairing of meat and wine, I suppose that I'm a member of the conservative right wing.

If I look back on my "top 10" favorite food and wine marriages, I can safely say that the majority of them were some sort of combination of meat and wine. This "pairing" is the most often discussed and is at the roots of food and wine matching.

Just as all fish is not the same, all meat is not identical. There are beef, lamb, pork, veal, offal (sweetbreads, liver, kidneys, tripe) and game (including venison and boar). There are also various styles of preparation: is it sauteed, grilled, roasted, boiled, or deep fried? Has the meat been "treated": marinated or smoked? Is the preparation simple, like a roast or a grilled steak, or is it part of a complex and flavorful tajine or ragout? One could make a chart to map out all of these factors, but it need not be that complicated.

First, let's examine meat. As illustrated above, there are many types of meat. All have the factor in common that they are meat, but that is where the resemblance stops. There are two basic types of meat: red and white (much like wine in that sense, as you'll see). Red meats are those that have a red flesh and include beef, lamb, liver, and game. They are strong in flavor and more robust and demand wines that are firm. The classic reds are best here: red Bordeaux, red Burgundy, California Cabernet Sauvignon, Merlot, and Pinot Noir, Italian Barolo and Brunello di Montalcino.

White meats are those whose flesh is "white" and include veal, pork, sweetbreads, rabbit, and the like (though many people could arguably put rabbit in the poultry category). The flavors here are sweeter, more delicate, and not as forward. One has to have flexibility, for a classic or more robust red (depending, of course, on the preparation) can easily dominate these types of meat. Often a light- to medium-bodied red or even a white wine is the best choice.

Two common treatments of meat involve marinades and smoking. Marinating a meat in a wine serves a dual purpose: tenderizing the meat and adding flavor. The key here is to never select a wine that is less flavorful than the wine of the marinade. Let's say, for illustration, that you marinated a pork loin in a light red like a Beaujolais or Dolcetto to add some fruitiness to the preparation. One would not want to serve a full-bodied Cabernet Sauvignon with that dish, as the flavor of the wine in the marinade would get lost. Pick a wine that is similar in style and body, or better still serve the same wine that you marinated the pork in as the table wine with dinner: the two will pick up on each other nicely. This is also true of cooking with wine and serving the same or a similar wine with the dish. Marinades by nature are strong and add flavors to the meat. Make sure the wine you select can hold its own against the marinade.

The flavors imparted during the smoking of meat can be quite intense. Match these dishes with a wine of equal intensity. Very smoky meats require robust and powerful wines. Light and more subtle smoking demands less vigorous wines that will allow the smoke to be tasted. Thus, while a smoked sausage may crave a spicy and tough Rhône red like a Cornas, a smoked pork loin may find happiness alongside a full-bodied Chardonnay or Pinot Noir.

The type of meat gives one a clue as to what wine to have as an accompaniment, and the method of cooking and type of dish hold the rest of the answer. The rule of thumb to follow with meat and wine is the simpler the preparation of the meat, the better the backdrop or stage it provides to show off the wine and vice versa. No better "sure bet" exists than matching an elegant aged bottle of Bordeaux, full of complexity, nuance, and intricacy, with a simple but well-aged roast of beef. An equally stunning match could be the marriage of a simple but solid bottle of Australian Shiraz alongside a vibrant and assertive ragout of lamb, vegetables, and spices served over couscous.

Grilling meat always makes even the most delicate of white meats demand something full bodied and firm. A veal chop may ask for a rich and full white wine when sauteed with a tarragon and mustard cream sauce, but the same veal chop needs a medium-bodied Bordeaux when taken off the grill and served with a dab of tarragon and mustard butter. Classic red meats do not seem to change as much in personality, although one needs to adjust the vigor of the wine upward if the meat has been grilled over mesquite or charcoal.

Finally, the temperature at which the meat is being served has an effect on the type of wine selected. Often, especially when the weather warms up, we serve cold meat dishes: a cold marinated leg of lamb or a tender spiced filet of beef as a main course. Here, the wine needs to be very harmonious. I always am a fan of lighter and fruitier wines, be they white or red, as opposed to searching for that perfect marriage that one builds up to when the meat dish is the center of the meal.

Ossobuco alla Reggiana   page 235

See Rolle di Vitello. Try even stronger wines, such as Barbaresco, Vino Nobile di Montepulciano, or Taurasi. Herbal white wines also work: Sauvignon Blanc, Pinot Blanc, and Pinot Gris from America; Mâcon-Villages, Saint-Véran, and Sancerre from France; Italian Vernaccia and Greco di Tufo.

Rolle di Vitello   page 236

Medium-bodied red wines, with soft tannins, are best here. Italian wines are nice "ethnically": Chianti or Rosso di Montalcino, Venetian and Friulian Merlot, and Piedmontese reds like Barbera and Nebbiolo d'Alba. French counterparts such as Côtes-du-Rhône or Côtes de Provence, and easy-drinking reds from the Loire—Chinon and Bourgueil—also meld well. American Merlot, Pinot Noir, and Gamay and muscular white wines like Vernaccia, Greco di Tufo, and Arneis from Italy, Chardonnays from around the world with an emphasis on herbal flavors are other choices. Rosés too, if highly flavored, can work here.

Costata di Vitello al Sugo di Porcini   page 238

This dish wants rich, full-flavored reds of some complexity: Barolo, Brunello, and Barbaresco or Tuscan blended wines (Cabernet and Sangiovese); youthful Bordeaux, California Syrah, Cabernet Sauvignon, and Merlot; Australian Cabernet Sauvignon and Cabernet/Shiraz blends; and rich Spanish reds from the Ribera del Duero: Pesquera, Vega Sicilia.

Grilled Stuffed Loin Veal Chops   page 239

See Rolle di Vitello. White only if the wine is smoky and powerful with earthy flavors: Pouilly-Fumé, Rully, and Montagny from Burgundy.

Costoletta del Curato   page 240

Full-bodied, vigorous, and muscular white wines: Sauvignon Blanc from Graves in France, Sancerre, and Pouilly-Fumé, Vernaccia, American and Australian Chardonnay, simple yet distinctive white Burgundy (Mâcon-Villages, Rully, Montagny, Saint-Véran). Softer reds, like Dolcetto, Barbera, Gattinara, and Merlot, match well, as do firm and flavorful rosés. But why not match this dish with a bottle of young Orvieto—the wine from its birthplace!

Sautéed Baby Veal Chops with Herbed Bread Crumbs   page 241

See Costoletta del Curato. Here, one should use whites with a little more breed: Meursault or Chassagne-Montrachet, for example.

Spiedini di Vitello alla Campagna page 242

See Ossobuco all Reggiana, page 235. Reds seem to work best here in a medium- to full-bodied style.

Scaloppine di Vitello con Peperoncini page 243

Soft and fruity reds of minimal tannin are best to pick up on the sweetness of the peppers and pinenuts; try a Merlot from France, Italy, or California. *Cru* Beaujolais of a more intense flavor (Morgon and Moulin-à-Vent) or Tuscan wines like Chianti or Rosso di Montalcino are also good choices.

Veal Scaloppine with Eggplant and Tomatoes page 244

A veal version of Rigatoni alla Norma, page 132. Italian wines are just the right choice: Spanna, Gattinara, Nebbiolo d'Alba, or Chianti. For non-Italian wines, Provençal reds like Bandol and Palette go well, as do some of the fruity and refreshing Côtes-du-Rhône and Côtes du Ventoux wines. Spanish Rioja and Portuguese Minho red wines and those of Bairrada are other choices.

Grilled Rib-Eye Steak with Porcini Butter page 245

This calls for a classic "big" red wine: Barolo, Barbaresco, Brunello, or Tuscan blends from Italy; Bordeaux and hearty red Burgundy (Vosne-Romanée, Clos de la Roche); California Cabernet Sauvignon and Merlot.

Grilled Flank Steak on a Bed of Peppers and Onions page 246

This preparation requires full-bodied reds with an emphasis on fruit: Pomerol and Saint-Emilion from Bordeaux; Moulin-a-Vent and Morgon from Beaujolais; Hermitage and Chateauneuf-du-Pape from the Rhône; Barbera and Dolcetto or young Nebbiolo-based wines (Nebbiolo d'Alba, Barolo). Beer is lovely with this dish: a cool frothy mug of a pilsner beer, such as Pilsner Urquell.

Bistecca al Diavolo page 247

Firm and robust red wines are called for here: Barolo, Brunello, Barbaresco, and Tuscan Cabernet blends; hearty Rhône wines like Côte Rôtie and Cornas; American Cabernet Sauvignon and Syrah. Red wines here need to emphasize spice and zip.

Bife Acebollado page 248

A medium- to full-bodied red wine with some regional flavor is needed: Spanish Rioja and wines from Penedès and the Valdepeñas; Dão, Bairrada, and Minho reds from Portugal; simple Burgundian reds from the Côte Chalonnaise (Givry, Rully); easy-drinking reds from Bordeaux and California (from California, both Pinot Noir and Cabernet Sauvignon)

Gulyas Triestina page 249

See Bife Acebellado. You can put emphasis on "local" wines: Venetian Merlot, Friulian Merlot, Pinot Noir from the Alto Adige.

Stracotto di Manzo "Peposo" page 250

See Bistecca al Diavolo

Farsu Magru page 251

See Bistecca al Diavolo

Bollito Misto ai Cinque Salse page 252

This is a very versatile dish. Medium-bodied red wines such as Italian Merlot and Chianti or rich and full whites (Sauvignon Blanc or Chardonnay). Don't forget beer. Beer is very nice here, in styles ranging from a frothy and refreshing lager (Moretti and Peroni are two Italian recommendations) to a medium-bodied ale.

Izmir Koftesi with Hunkar Begendi page 254

This could prove difficult if the eggplant puree is too bitter, so flavorful and round red wines are best: Australian Shiraz, Rhône Valley Saint-Joseph, Crozes-Hermitage, and Gigondas, California Zinfandel, Petite Sirah, and Italian Dolcetto or Barbera.

Kefta page 255

Beer is a very apropos choice; for wine, go with muscular and fruity reds: Côtes-du-Rhône, Nebbiolo d'Alba, Australian Shiraz, California Zinfandel.

Foie M'Chermel page 256

A fairly robust red would be nice here. From France, a Rhône such as Gigondas or Cornas, red Burgundy from Mercurey, Rully, or Givry, and southern French wines like those of Corbières and Minervois. California Pinot Noir, Zinfandel, and Syrah; Australian Shiraz; or Italian Barbera and Barolo are other choices.

Sautéed Calves Liver with Onions, Pancetta, and Hazelnuts
page 257

This is a case for rich and supple reds. Classic red Burgundy, flavorful reds from the Medoc, Italian Barbaresco and Brunello di Montalcino, American Pinot Noir of some substance. One needs wines of firm texture here.

Fegato all'Abruzzese page 258

This classic Italian dish demands a classic Italian wine: Montepulciano d'Abruzzo, Chianti Classico, Amarone, Valpolicella, and Bardolino.

Sautéed Calves Liver with Mustard Sauce page 259

See Sauteed Calves Liver with Onions, Pancetta, and Hazelnuts. When doing this recipe with duck or chicken livers, the wines need be no heavier than medium body (so one would eliminate Brunello and Barbaresco).

Costolette d'Agnello Scottadito page 260

See Bistecca al Diavolo

Costolette d'Agnello al Modo di Camoscio page 261

See Grilled Rib-Eye Steak with Porcini Butter

Grilled Lamb Chops with Lemon-Thyme Butter and White Bean Ragout page 262

This dish cries for a regional French wines from the south, hearty but refined: Bandol or Palette from Provence, Hermitage from the Rhône, a good sturdy red from Bordeaux or a straightforward and flavorful Madiran or Bergerac from the southwest. California Cabernets or Merlot, Italian Barbaresco, and Australian Cabernet Sauvignon are also good.

Costoletas de Carneiro Escondidinho page 265

A tasty and fruity red wine with soft tannin and good depth of flavor is best here: wines like a Portuguese Dão or Bairrada (or dry red port wine), Spanish reds from the Ribera del Duero, Rhône reds with high percentages of Grenache (Gigondas, Côtes-du-Rhône, Lirac.), Italian Dolcetto and Barbera, American Gamay and soft youthful Zinfandel and Syrah.

Fritto Misto   page 266

This is a very diverse dish due to the simple seasoning and the "neutral" mode of cooking. Beer is just wonderful here. For wines, soft and fruity red wines (Dolcetto, Barbera, Gattmara, Merlot) or full-bodied whites (Sauvignon Blanc, Graves, Sancerve, Pouilly-Fumé). Clean and spicy rosé wines, such as Sancerre rosé and Bandol rosé, are lovely.

Leg of Lamb Avgolemono with Asparagus   page 269

This dish cries out for a complex, deep red wine: Bordeaux from the heart of the Medoc (St.-Julien and Pauillac); California Cabernet Sauvignon and Merlot; Hermitage and Côte Rôtie from the Rhône; and great firm red Burgundy (Gevrey-Chambertin, Nuits-Saint-Georges). Due to the eggs, high acidity (younger as opposed to older wines) is a must.

Qodban   page 270

See Roast Leg of Lamb with a Moroccan "Mechoui" Marinade

Roast Leg of Lamb with a Moroccan "Mechoui" Marinade
page 271

A big, intense, spicy red wine is called for: Italian Barolo; hearty Rhône reds like Gigondas, Cornas and Côte Rôtie; California Zinfandel, exuberant Cabernet Sauvignon, and Merlot; Australian Shiraz.

Souvlaki   page 272

Much depends on whether you grill this over fire or use the broiler, which imparts less flavor. The more grill, the bigger the wine: Generally, medium-bodied red wines with slightly herbal flavors are best: Chinon, some red Graves and Margaux wines from Bordeaux, California Cabernets from the Alexander Valley, Pinot Noirs from Oregon and California.

Chanfana   page 273

See Costoletas di Carneiro Escondidinho

Talas Borek   page 274

See Izmir Koftesi

Agnello al Calderotto   page 275

A serious Italian red wine is called for here: Barolo, Barbaresco, Vino Nobile di Montepuleiano, or Brunello. You could also use a more rustic red from another country: Côte Rôtie, Hermitage, or Chateauneuf-du-Pape in the Rhone, a powerful and meaty red Burgundy (Pommard, Nuits-Saint-Georges, Chambertin); California Cabernet and Pinot Noir.

Spezzatino d'Agnello con Gremolata   page 276

This dish has so many different flavors exploding in your mouth that a wine's role here is only one of a backdrop. A simple red such as a Dolcetto, Valpolicella, or Spanna from Italy; a Côtes-du-Rhône or Beaujolais from France; a pleasant and uncomplicated Shiraz from Australia is needed.

Moroccan Lamb Tagine with Lemon and Olives   page 277

See Roast Leg of Lamb with a Moroccan "Mechoui" Marinade. Beer works nicely here too.

Mishmishaya   page 278

See Izmir Koftesi and Hunkar Begendi. Beer would not work here, but a full white wine, with a very aromatic quality or a slight sweetness would be very good. Gewürtztraminer, Muscat, and Riesling Vendage Tardive wines from Alsace work well with this dish, as do many California Gewürtztraminers and Rieslings. Red is still my first choice, but these combinations are fun.

Roast Pork Loin with Tarragon and Mustard Sauce   page 279

Whites are the most logical choice and should have high acidity, rich full flavors, and an emphasis on herbal tones: Sancerre, Pouilly-Fumé, Corton-Charlemagne, white Graves, and Meursault. From California, a ripe and aromatic Chardonnay or herbal Sauvignon Blanc would work. Australian Sémillon of a less fruity nature would be a nice accompaniment. Soft, easy-drinking reds with an herbal emphasis: Cabernet Franc wines of California, or France's Loire Valley . . . Bourgueil, Chinon, and Saumur-Champigny. A herbaceous Pinot Noir from anywhere in the world will work.

Lomo di Cerdo Almendrado   page 280

Supple medium-bodied red wines of "local" flavor are needed: Spanish Rioja, wines of the Penedès, La Mancha, and Valdepeñas; Portuguese Periquita, Bucelas, and Carcavelos; Merlot or Pinot Noir in a fruitier style from Oregon or California; simple reds from Bordeaux and Italian Chianti-like wines. Whites would marry well here, and those of full texture work best: Pinot Gris from Alsace, Sauvignon Blancs in a richer and creamier style from the Graves in France and California; Verdicchio from Italy and Sémillon from Australia. Rosés such as Bandol rosé or Tavel would harmonize nicely.

Pork Loin Marinated in Red Wine   page 281

Pay close attention to the wine you use in the marinade and select a "bigger" wine to drink with the pork dish. In the marinade, soft fruity red wines are the best choice for adding another flavor dimension to the pork while enhancing it's inherent sweetness. Serve with it, a nontannic fruity red with a little more stuffing: Rhône reds from the south (Gigondas, Chateauneuf-du-Pape, Côtes du Rhône, Vacqueyras); Barbera and young Chianti from Italy; Australian Shiraz; and firm and flavorful California Zinfandel.

Costata di Maiale Ubriaco   page 282

See Pork Loin Marinated in Red Wine Select a wine with a little "local color": something from Tuscany, like a good Chianti.

Costoletta di Maiale al Rosmarino   page 283

White wine is my choice here, although reds work equally well. For whites, full-flavored wine, herbal and slightly off dry: German Spätlese Riesling, Washington State Riesling, California Riesling or Gewürztraminer, Savennières or other Chenin Blanc wines form the Loire valley. For reds, softer and fruitier styles with flavors echoing the cinnamon: Pinot Noir, *cru* Beaujolais, and softer Rhône wines from France; Oregon and California Pinot Noirs, Dolcetto and easy-drinking Barbera from Italy. Rosé wines, both off dry (Rose d'Anjou) and dry (Tavel and Provencale), would work nicely with this preparation.

Pork Scaloppine alla Zaragozana   page 284

See Lomo di Cerdo Almendrado, page 280. Also good would be a spicy and balanced rosé: a Provençal rosé from Bandol, a Tavel, or a Vin Gris of Pinot Noir from either Burgundy or Sancerre.

Middle Eastern Pork Brochettes with Pomegranate and Honey   page 285

See Costoletta di Maiale al Rosmarino Put the emphasis on red wines; no rosé here.

Lomo di Porco com Pimentos Doces   page 286

See Lomo di Cerdo Almendrado.

Polpette con Pecorino   page 287

Here are needed rich earthy white wines with pungent, strong flavor. Vernaccia, Greco di Tufo, Verdicchio, and Tocai Friulano from Italy; from France, some of the earthier southern French whites of Provence and the Midi; Pinot Gris from both Oregon and Alsace in France; and soft reds such as Grignolino, Valpolicella, Spanna, and Montepulciano d'Abruzzi.

Sicilian Meatball Ragout with Artichokes and Peas   page 288

This wants big and intense Italian reds, rich and mouth-filling: Barolo, Vino Nobile di Montepulciano, Taurasi. From France, red Burgundy of a fruitier style (Volnay, Savigny-les-Beaune); Provençal and Rhône reds of some substance, honest reds like Madiran, Bergerac, and Minervois. In California, Barbera, Zinfandel, and Syrah would be harmonious. Softer Cabernet Sauvignon from Chile would marry well.

Merguez   page 290

See Qodban, page 270. A good rich ale is nice here too.

Umbrian Pork Sausage   page 291

See Costeletta di Maiale al Rosmarino. Soft to medium reds and off-dry and aromatic whites.

Lucanica   page 293

See Sicilian Meatball Ragout.

Fennel Sausage   page 294

This dish is similar to Lucanica but "more classic" (French), so try Rhône reds from Cornas, Chateauneuf-du-Pape, and Côte Rôtie, spicy young Bordeaux, Spanish Rioja, and California Zinfandel and Petite Sirah.

Linguisa   page 295

This has a Portuguese accent so try a Dão, Bairrada, Periquita red.

Loukanika   page 296

See Sicilian Meatball Ragout. Since these are not as spicy and piquant, the wines need not be as coarse.

Chorizo   page 297

See Sicilian Meatball Ragout. Select wines with more "local color": Spanish and southwestern France (Rioja, Valdepeñas).

Mixed Grills

See the wine selections given for each dish.

DESSERTS

The matching of desserts and dessert wines has long been overlooked. There are many possible reasons for this: First, we are often so full at the end of the meal that no one cares to think about such things and, anyway, people are not paying attention; Second, many people are health and calorie conscious and bow out before we can even tempt them with the possibility; and finally, time frequently does not allow it.

Intimidation has also played a major role in this area of food and wine harmony. It is often hard enough to master the basic "red-with-meat-and-white-with-fish" lessons much less worry about pairing the right Sauternes with a pear dessert or the right sugar and acid levels in a Riesling to marry with a sorbet of minimal sweetness.

My experiences have showed me that people are beginning to "play around" a bit, paying attention to this course in the context of the meal. The fact that the dessert and dessert wine class I teach here at the restaurant fills up before most of the others leads me to believe that there is no shortage of sweet-toothed diners out and about.

In the sweet world of gastronomic harmony there are a couple of rigid guidelines.

1. *Sugar concentration and levels.* This rule of thumb will simplify your life and remove the shroud of secrecy: The level of sugar/sweetness in the wine must be *greater* than that of the dessert or the wine will taste sour in comparison.

2. *Acidity level and balance.* Acidity in dessert wines is as important as it is in dry wines. It is paramount that the dessert wine have a good level of acidity and balance so that it does not taste dull and flabby and die on the palate. A balance of acid/tartness in a dessert wine also keeps the wine from being overly syrupy and cloying. A wine can in fact be fairly sweet, but if the acid is high it keeps the wine in balance. Naturally sweet wines that are affected by the "noble rot" *Botrytis cinerea*—Sauternes and Loire Valley sweet wines in France, German QmP wines (Auslese through Trockenbeerenauslese)—have a natural inherent acidity balance that is created by the mold.

There are many categories of dessert wines available:

1. *Sparkling.* We certainly have all had a sweet Asti Spumante at least once in our lives. But there are many others. In Champagne in France, there are two levels of what I would describe as dessert level sweetness: *Sec* and *Demi-Sec*. These have levels of sweetness that can actually be paired with a dessert. A third style, *Doux*, now very rare, is the sweetest of the three. Dry sparkling wines are often seen as accompaniments to dessert (weddings and special events), but they don't work very well. Try a bottle of Dom Perignon with wedding cake if you need illustration! If you insist on having a dry sparkling wine, have it prior to or after the dessert. Sparkling wines of some sweetness are also made in California, Italy, and other parts of France.

2. *Fortified wines.* These wines are fortified with the addition of brandy. Ports, sherries, and Madeiras fit into this category. While port is perhaps most thought of as a cheese course "dessert" wine or to have with a bowl of walnuts, it, as well as cream sherries and sweeter Bual and Malmsey Madeiras, can match nicely with desserts.

3. *Still dessert wines.* This wide category includes everything from Sauternes to Late Harvest Riesling, Trockenbeerenauslese to Beaumes-de-Venise. Many different sorts are made in many different countries, each with it's own unique flavors. Here are some of the more celebrated examples:

France: Sauternes, Coteaux du Layon (Chaume, Quarts de Chaume), Beaumes-de-Venise, Muscat de Frontignan, Banyuls (actually a fortified wine), late-harvested Alsatian wines (*Sélection de Grains Nobles*)

Italy: Vin Santo, Recioto della Valpolicella, Recioto di Soave, Marsala (actually a fortified wine)

California: Late-harvested Sauvignon Blanc, Sémillon, Riesling, Muscats (Black and Orange included), Chardonnay, Zinfandel, and California Ports.

Germany: Auslese, Beerenauslese, Trockenbeerenauslese, Eiswein

Hungary: Tokay Aszú and Tokay Essencia.

Australia: "Stickies" made of late-harvested Sémillon, Muscat, and Sauvignon Blanc; Muscat and "other" ports.

The pairing of these wines with desserts is very subjective, but certain dessert wines have some basic flavors that are associated with them. Pear is the central flavor of Sauternes along with hints of honey, vanilla, and flowers. Lychee and apricot (exotic apricot) are the chief flavors of most Muscat wines (including Beaumes-de-Venise) along with lightly floral and nectarlike overtones. Rieslings have pronounced flavors of apricots if in a Rhine style and nectarines if in a Mosel. Dessert ("cream") sherries are usually nutty and laced with nuances of vanilla, butter, and spice, and Madeiras are similar with just a hint of lemon and zest.

Finally, you may do too much and complicate things by trying to find the right wine to go with a dessert. Perhaps more than at any other part of the meal, this is a situation in which both the wine and the food have flavors that are best relished by themselves, and they can clash when they have to "compete for your attention." Give them both a chance, but remember to have the sweeter one second or allow yourself some time in between.

acorda, 97
agliata, 197
agnello al calderotto, 275
aioli, 193, 252
    orange and black pepper,
        171
    red pepper, 183
    saffron and walnut, 197
Algerian vegetable *tagine,*
    313
almond(s):
    anise cookies, 355
    Catalan-style duck with
        pears and, 226–227
    -coffee *pot de crème,* 338
    crunchies, 280
    -lemon pie, 322–323
    and onion soup, Catalan,
        93
    tulips, 357
ameijoas na cataplana, 194
anchovy garlic vinaigrette,
    64
anise vinaigrette, beets with,
    45
anitra con le lenticchie, 227
anitra in porchetta, 228
appetizers, 17–18
    baked goat cheese in filo,
        20

borek, 31
chicken liver croutons,
    23
chicken liver pâté, Italian
    style, 25
duck liver mousse, 26
filo pastries with shrimp
    or crabmeat, 32
fresh tuna pâté, 28
goat cheese in pesto
    vinaigrette, 22
goat cheese in spicy
    tomato vinaigrette,
    21
Greek cheese-filled filo
    pastries, 30–31
grilled bread with white
    bean puree and
    wilted greens, 24
grilled garlic bread,
    23
lamb dolmas, 33
marinated fresh
    mozzarella, 19
Roman rice croquettes,
    27
spiced beef filet, 35
spiced potato-filled filo
    pastries, 29
vegetable dolmas, 34

apple(s):
    Cameron's baked, in filo
        crust, 343
    endive, and walnut salad,
        61
    stuffed baked, 342
    and walnut pie, rustic,
        324
apricot(s):
    Middle Eastern lamb
        ragout with, 278
    pudding, steamed, 335
    torte, chocolate, 332–333
Armagnac and prune ice
    cream, 347
artichoke(s):
    chicken with, 215
    pasta with, 124
    pasta with lemon, cream
        and, 125
    and pea soup, 98
    Sicilian meatball ragout
        with peas and, 288
    with tomato vinaigrette,
        48
    Turkish, 47
arugula, pear, and
    provolone salad, 60
arugula, roasted pepper,
    and fontina salad, 64

asparagus, leg of lamb *avgolemono* with, 269
avocado:
    Catalan, 73
    gazpacho vinaigrette for, 70–71
    salad, Israeli, 68

baba ghanouj, 42
baked:
    cod with onions and mint, 184
    fig compote, 342
    fish with preserved lemons and onion confit, 174–175
    goat cheese in filo, 20
    salmon with capers and toasted bread crumbs, 170
balsamic vinaigrette, 62
basic homemade pasta, 110–114
    see also pasta
basic vinaigrette, 65
bastilla, 218
basting butter, for poultry, 207, 209, 210
béchamel sauce, 311
beef:
    braised, chicken, sausage, and vegetables with five sauces, 252–253
    dilled Turkish meatballs with eggplant puree, 254
    filet, spiced, 35
    grilled flank steak on a bed of roasted peppers, 246
    grilled rib-eye steak with porcini butter, 245
    grilled steak with a spicy tomato sauce, 247
    Middle Eastern "hamburger," 255
    Portuguese steaks with onions and tomatoes, 248
    ragout from Trieste, 249
    Sicilian braised rolled steak, 251

    stew, peppery Tuscan, 250
beef stock, 104
beet raviolis from the Veneto, three, 116
beets with anise vinaigrette, 45
bife acebollado, 248
bigoli co l'anara, 131
biscotti di mandorle, 355
bistecca al diavolo, 247
bittersweet chocolate glaze, 325
black bean salad with eggs and prosciutto, 52
blackberry sorbet, 354
black pepper pasta, 113
black pepper vinaigrette, 79
black radish, carrot and fennel salad with pecorino cheese, 63
blood orange caramel sauce, 349
blood orange ice cream, 348
bocconcini, 19
bolinhos de santola, 182
bollito misto al cinque salse, 252–253
bonissima, la, 325
borek, 31
borlenghi ai quattro formaggi, 145
braised:
    beef, chicken, sausage, and vegetables with five sauces, 252–253
    lentils with pancetta and aromatic vegetables, 151
    stuffed leg of veal, 236
    veal shanks, 235
brandy butter, Gorgonzola, 25
bread:
    crumbs, toasted, 73
    and garlic soup with egg, Portuguese, 97
    pudding, Portuguese-style, 336–337
    salad, Italian, 65

    salad, toasted Lebanese pita, 66
bresaola, 35
brine, 286
briouats, 29
briouats, shellfish, 32
broccoli soup with white beans, 101
brochettes:
    Greek lamb, 272
    Moroccan lamb, 270
    with pomegranate and honey, pork, 285
    Roman-style veal, 242
bruschetta, 23
buckwheat pasta, 112
    with greens and potatoes, 129
buckwheat ravioli filled with greens, ricotta, and cumin, 114
butter:
    basting, 207, 209, 210
    Gorgonzola brandy, 25
    lemon-cilantro, 264
    lemon-sage, 242
    lemon-thyme, 262
    spiced red wine, 176
    tapenade, 28
buttercream, chocolate, 334–335
butternut squash soup, 85

cake:
    cheese-, Italian, 327
    for chocolate apricot torte, 332–333
    nut sponge, 330–331
    sponge, for Portuguese-style bread pudding, 336–337
    sponge, layered, filled with ricotta, chocolate, and orange, 328
Calabrese pork and lamb sausage, 293
caldo de pimenton, 83
caldo verde, 99

calves liver with Moroccan
spiced onions, 256
see also liver
canja, 91
cantaloupe sorbet, 354
*caponata de verdure alle
sarde*, 314
caponata di verdure, 72
capriata, 24
caramel *pot de crème*, 339
caramel sauce, 340
blood orange, 349
carrot(s):
black radish and fennel
salad with pecorino
cheese, 63
Moroccan, 315
salad, Moroccan, 45
salad with mint, 53
soup with egg and lemon,
Portuguese, 92
cassata alla siciliana, 328
cassunziei ampessani, 116
Catalan:
baked eggplant with
honey and tomatoes,
312
onion and almond soup,
93
-style duck with pears
and almonds,
226–227
-style grilled chicken, 202
-style grilled quail stuffed
with figs, 221
cauliflower:
with red pepper
vinaigrette, 49
salad, celery, cucumber,
spinach, curly endive
and, 72
cayenne, peppers with
cilantro and, 53
celery:
pear, potato, and
watercress salad, 59
root and fennel soup, 96
salad, cauliflower,
cucumber, spinach,
curly endive and, 72
Champagne vinaigrette, 60
chanfana, 273

charmoula, Moroccan, 175
fish couscous with,
190–191
charmoula vinaigrette, 76–77
cheese, *see specific types of
cheese*
cheese and leeks filling for
ravioli, 123
cheesecake, Italian, 327
chicken:
with artichokes, 215
braised beef, sausage, and
vegetables with five
sauces, 252–253
fricassee, with "forty
cloves" of garlic,
211–212
liver croutons, 23
liver pâté, Italian style, 25
pie with a filo crust,
Greek, 217
or pigeon and almonds,
Moroccan filo pie
with, 218–219
sautéed, breasts with
porcini mushrooms,
220
sautéed, with Moroccan
hot and sweet
tomato sauce, 213
soup with rice,
Portuguese, 91
stock, 103
with sun-dried tomatoes,
216
with tomato sauce, hot
pepper, and
pancetta, 214
chicken, grilled:
in an Algerian marinade,
201
Catalan-style, 202
in a Moroccan marinade,
203
with *piri-piri* hot sauce,
204
Sardinian-style, 206
Turkish-style grilled
chicken with yogurt
and cumin, 205
chicken, roasted:
Greek-style, 207

Moroccan-style, stuffed
with couscous, 209
Sardinian-style, with
stuffing, 208
stuffed with ricotta and
pesto, 210
chick-pea soup with greens
and pasta, 100
chocolate:
buttercream, 334–335
espresso *pot de crème*, 338
filling, cream, strawberry
and, 330–331
glaze, 332–333
ice cream, orange,
cinnamon and, 351
layered spongecake filled
with ricotta, orange
and, 328
sherry torte, 329
chops, *see* lamb chops; pork
chops; veal chops
chorizo, 297
cialzons di timau, 115
cilantro, peppers with
cayenne and, 53
cilantro-lemon butter, 264
cinnamon, chocolate, and
orange ice cream,
351
cinnamon onions, 283
citrus vinaigrette, 63
clam(s):
linguine with squid and,
141
pasta with sausage and,
138
with sausage, Portuguese
steamed, 194
and tomato sauce,
sole-filled ravioli
with, 120
cod, baked, with onions
and mint, 184
coffee-almond *pot de crème*,
338
coffee ice cream, Turkish,
349
cold Spanish tomato soup,
94
cookies, *see* desserts
cornmeal pastry, 319–320

cornmeal tart with fruit,
Italian, 319–320
costata di maiale ubriaco,
282
*costata di vitello al sugo di
porcini*, 238
*costoletas di carneiro
escondidinho*, 265
costoletta del curato, 240
*costoletta di maiale al
rosmarino*, 283
*costolette d'agnello al modo de
camoscio*, 261
costolette d'agnello scottadito,
260
court bouillon, 48
couscous, 163
fish, with *charmoula*,
190–191
Moroccan-style roast
chicken stuffed with,
209
crab cakes with mint and
cilantro, Portuguese,
182
crabmeat, gratin of sea bass
and, 186
crabmeat or shrimp, filo
pastries with, 32
Craig's date and walnut
dacquoise, 334–335
Craig's *tarta de Sevilla*,
322–323
crêpes, rosemary, filled with
four cheeses, 145
crocchette di riso, 152
croquettes:
potato, 306
rice, 152
Roman rice, 27
salmon, Jewish style,
185
crostata di ricotta, 327
crostini de melanzane arroste,
41
*crostini di fegatini alla
fiorentina*, 23
croutons, chicken liver, 23
croutons, Italian eggplant,
41
cucumber, cauliflower,
celery, spinach, and

curly endive salad,
72
cucumber salad with yogurt,
mint, and raisins, 46
culingiones di patate, 118
curry, Portuguese-style
salmon with cream
and, 172
custard, 337

date and walnut *dacquoise*,
Craig's, 334–335
dessert fillings:
almond, 343
almond paste, 336
apple, 324
cream, chocolate, and
strawberry, 330–331
for Italian cheesecake,
327
lemon, 322–323
ricotta, 328
for Venetian rice
pudding tart, 326
walnut, 325
desserts, 317–318
almond anise cookies,
355
almond tulips, 357
baked fig compote, 342
blackberry sorbet, 354
Cameron's baked apple
in filo crust, 343
cantaloupe sorbet, 354
caramel *pot de crème*,
339
chocolate apricot torte,
332–333
chocolate espresso *pot de
crème*, 338
chocolate sherry torte,
329
coffee-almond *pot de
crème*, 338
Craig's date and walnut
dacquoise, 334–335
custard, 337
espresso ice with whipped
cream, 352
Florentine pumpkin-
shaped pudding,
330–331

Grand Marnier
madeleines, 357
honey mousse, 337
Italian cheesecake, 327
Italian cornmeal tart with
fruit, 319–320
layered spongecake filled
with ricotta,
chocolate, and
orange, 328
lemon-almond pie,
322–323
lemon ice, 352
meringues, 334–335
peach and Champagne
sorbet, 353
pears poached in black
muscat dessert wine,
341
pine nut tile cookies,
356
plum tart, 321
Portuguese-style bread
pudding, 336–337
rustic apple and walnut
pie, 324
sangria sorbet, 353
steamed apricot pudding,
335
stuffed baked apples, 342
Venetian rice pudding
tart, 326
walnut clouds, 356
walnut-honey tart, 325
see also ice cream
dessert toppings and sauces:
bittersweet chocolate
glaze, 325
blood orange caramel,
349
caramel, 340
chocolate buttercream,
334–335
chocolate glaze, 332–
333
Grand Marnier, 342
icing, 328
orange muscat sabayon,
340
dilled Turkish meatballs
with eggplant puree,
254

dolmas:
  lamb, 33
  vegetable, 34
dressing, salad, *see*
  vinaigrette
dressing, tahini, 255
dried tomatoes and tuna,
  spaghetti with, 136
duck:
  Catalan-style, with pears
    and almonds,
    226–227
  with lentils, 227
  with port, prunes, and
    pearl onions, 229
  roast, in the manner of
    suckling pig, 228
  roast, with honey,
    lavender, and thyme,
    224
  roast, with red wine,
    orange, and sage
    sauce, 230
duck liver mousse, 26
duck stock, 225

egg(s):
  black bean salad with
    prosciutto and, 52
  fettuccine with pancetta,
    cream and, 128
  Portuguese bread and
    garlic soup with, 97
  Portuguese carrot soup
    with lemon and, 92
eggplant:
  Catalan baked, with
    honey and tomatoes,
    312
  croutons, Italian, 41
  -filled ravioli, 122
  pasta from Catania,
    Sicilian, 132
  puree, dilled Turkish
    meatballs with, 254
  puree with tahini, Middle
    Eastern, 42
  salad, Moroccan, 43
  salad with onions and
    peppers, Spanish, 44
  sandwiches, Turkish
    deep-fried, 309

soup, roasted, 84
veal scaloppine with
  tomatoes and, 244
zucchini, and tomato
  gratin, 310
endive, apple, and walnut
  salad, 61
endive, curly, cauliflower,
  celery, cucumber,
  and spinach salad,
  72
escalivada, 44
espadarte grelhado a lisboeta,
  178
espresso:
  chip and Sambuca ice
    cream, 350
  ice with whipped cream,
    352
  pot de crème, chocolate,
    338

fagioli all'uccelletto, 150
farsu magru, 251
fattoush, 66
fegato all'abruzzese, 258
fegato alle uova sode, 25
fennel and celery root soup,
  96
fennel sausage, 294
fettuccine:
  with artichokes, lemon,
    and cream, 125
  with goat cheese and
    Swiss chard, 127
  with pancetta, eggs, and
    cream, 128
  with shrimp and garlic,
    142
  see also pasta
fettuccine:
  al barese, 142
  alla genovese, 126
  strascinate, 128
  alla turque, 125
fig compote, baked, 342
figs, Catalan-style grilled
  quail stuffed with,
  221
filet, spiced beef, 35
filo:
  baked goat cheese in, 20

crust, baked apple in,
  343
crust, Greek chicken pie
  with, 217
crust, Middle Eastern
  lamb ragout with,
  274–275
pastries, Greek
  cheese-filled, 30–31
pastries, spiced
  potato-filled, 29
pastries with shrimp or
  crabmeat, 32
pie with pigeon or
  chicken and
  almonds, Moroccan,
  218–219
fish:
  baked, with preserved
    lemons, 174–175
  couscous with *charmoula,*
    190–191
  fumet, 105
  ragout, Spanish, 192
  see also specific types of fish
Florentine pumpkin-shaped
  pudding, 330–331
foie m'chermel, 256
fontina, roasted pepper,
  and arugula salad,
  64
French salad, 51
fresh tuna pâté, 28
fricassee of chicken with
  "forty cloves" of
  garlic, 211–212
fritto misto, 266–267
fritto misto al mare, 195
fusilli alla napoletana, 130

garlic:
  bread, grilled, 23
  and bread soup with egg,
    Portuguese, 97
  fettuccine with shrimp
    and, 142
  sausage, 292
  spring, and potato soup,
    87
  vinaigrette, 65
  vinaigrette, anchovy, 64
  vinaigrette, oregano, 67

gazpacho, 94
gazpacho vinaigrette for
    avocado, 70–71
ginger and shallot butter,
    trout with, 168
*gnocchi, Ristorante
    Archimede*, 146–147
goat cheese:
    baked, in filo, 20
    in pesto vinaigrette, 22
    in spicy tomato
        vinaigrette, 21
Gorgonzola:
    brandy butter, 25
    cream vinaigrette, 59
    -ricotta filling for ravioli,
        123
Grand Marnier madeleines,
    357
Grand Marnier sauce, 342
granita de caffè con panna,
    352
granita de limone, 352
grape leaves:
    lamb, 33
    salmon wrapped in, 169
    vegetable, 34
gratin of mussels, onions,
    and potatoes, 187
gratin of sea bass and
    crabmeat, 186
Greek:
    cheese-filled filo pastries,
        30–31
    lamb brochettes, 272
    pork sausage, 296
    salad, 67
    -style roast chicken, 207
gremolata, 276
gremolata, seafood risotto
    with tomatoes and,
    158
grilled:
    bread with white bean
        puree and wilted
        greens, 24
    chicken in a Moroccan
        marinade, 203
    chicken in an Algerian
        marinade, 201
    chicken with *piri-piri* hot
        sauce, 204

flank steak on a bed of
    roasted peppers, 246
garlic bread, 23
lamb chops with
    lemon-thyme butter
    and white bean
    ragout, 262
lamb chops with port
    and mustard cream
    vinaigrette, 69
leeks with walnut cream
    vinaigrette, 69
pork chop in a red wine
    and spice marinade,
    282
quail stuffed with
    honeyed onions, 231
radicchio, 307
rib-eye steak with porcini
    butter, 245
salmon with orange and
    black pepper *aioli,*
    171
steak with a spicy tomato
    sauce, 247
stuffed loin veal chops, 239
stuffed trout from Lake
    Iseo, 167
swordfish, Lisbon style,
    178
swordfish or tuna with
    sun-dried tomatoes,
    179
veal chops with wild
    mushroom sauce,
    238
vegetable ratatouille, 308
grilled tuna:
    with *charmoula*
        vinaigrette, 76–77
    with cracked pepper, 180
    rice salad with, 75
    salad with a Moroccan
        salsa, 78
    with spaghetti, 135
Gruyère, mushrooms, and
    prosciutto salad, 62
gulyas triestina, 249

"hamburger," Middle
    Eastern, 255
harissa, 191

hazelnut(s):
    and mushroom soup, 89
    sautéed liver with onions,
        pancetta, and, 257
    vinaigrette, 61
honey:
    Catalan baked eggplant
        with tomatoes and,
        312
    lavender ice cream, 345
    mousse, 337
    pork brochettes with
        pomegranate and,
        285
    -walnut tart, 325
horseradish cream, 35, 252
hot peppers, chicken with
    tomato sauce,
    pancetta and, 214
hot pepper vinaigrette, 75
hunkar begendi, 311

ice cream:
    blood orange, 348
    chocolate, orange, and
        cinnamon, 351
    lavender honey, 345
    making of, 344
    port, 350
    prune and Armagnac,
        347
    Sambuca and espresso
        chip, 350
    Turkish coffee, 349
    walnut, 346
icing, 328
Israeli avocado salad, 68
Italian:
    bread salad, 65
    cheesecake, 327
    cornmeal tart with fruit,
        319–320
    eggplant croutons, 41
    mushroom soup with
        vermouth and
        tomato, 88
    salad, 51
    seafood salad, 74
    -style chicken liver pâté,
        25
izmir koftesi with *hunkar
    begendi,* 254

Jewish-style salmon
croquettes, 185

kefta, 255
kotopitta, 217
koto psito, 207

lamb:
brochettes, Greek, 272
brochettes, Moroccan,
270
dolmas, 33
leg of, *avgolemono* with
asparagus, 269
Middle Eastern, ragout
with a filo crust,
274–275
Middle Eastern, ragout
with apricots, 278
ragout, Portuguese, 273
ragout with *gremolata*,
276
ragout with tomatoes,
greens, and cheese,
pugliese, 275
roast leg of, with a
Moroccan
"mechoui"
marinade, 271
sausage, Calabrese pork
and, 293
sausage, Moroccan, 290
stock, 268
tagine with lemon and
olives, Moroccan,
277
lamb chops:
grilled, with lemon-thyme
butter and white
bean ragout, 262
grilled, with port and
mustard cream, 265
mixed fry of rice
croquettes,
vegetables and,
266–267
Portuguese-style stuffed,
264
lavender honey ice cream,
345
layered spongecake filled
with ricotta,

chocolate, and
orange, 328
Lebanese toasted pita bread
salad, 66
leeks, grilled, with walnut
cream vinaigrette, 69
leeks and cheese filling for
ravioli, 123
leg of lamb *avgolemono* with
asparagus, 269
lemon(s):
-almond pie, 322–323
-cilantro butter, 264
cream vinaigrette, 62
ice, 352
pasta with artichokes,
cream and, 125
Portuguese carrot soup
with egg and, 92
preserved, 174, 277
-sage butter, 242
scallop, and orange salad,
79
-thyme butter, 262
*lenticchie con pancetta e
verdure*, 151
lentil(s):
braised, with pancetta
and aromatic
vegetables, 151
duck with, 227
salad, 50
linguine with squid and
clams, 141
linguisa, 295
liver:
calves, with Moroccan
spiced onions, 256
chicken, croutons, 23
duck, mousse, 26
pâté, chicken, Italian
style, 25
sautéed, with mustard
sauce, 259
sautéed, with onions,
pancetta, and
hazelnuts, 257
sautéed calves, with
onions, orange zest,
and pistachios, 258
lomo de cerdo almendrado,
280

*lomo de porco com pimientos
doces*, 286
loukanika, 296
lucanica, 293

marinated olives, 174
marinated sautéed tuna in a
fennel and bread
crumb crust, 181
marmalade, onion, 295
meatball(s):
with eggplant puree,
dilled Turkish, 254
little herbed, rigatoni
with, 134
ragout with artichokes
and peas, Sicilian,
288
Sicilian, 287
melissima, la, or *torta di mele
e noce*, 324
merguez, 290
merluzzo all'istriana, 184
Middle Eastern:
eggplant puree with
tahini, 42
"hamburger," 255
lamb ragout with a filo
crust, 274–275
lamb ragout with
apricots, 278
or Persian-style rice, 153
salad, 51
mint:
baked cod with onions
and, 184
carrot salad with, 53
cucumber salad with
yogurt, raisins and,
46
and mustard sauce, 263
vinaigrette, 53
mishmishaya, 278
mixed fry of fish or
shellfish, 195
mixed fry of lamb chops,
rice croquettes, and
vegetables, 266–267
mixed grills, 298–299
mixed plates, 37–40
Moroccan:
carrots, 315

Moroccan (cont'd)
    carrot salad, 45
    charmoula, 175
    eggplant salad, 43
    filo pie with pigeon or
        chicken and
        almonds, 218–219
    fried squab with saffron
        and ginger, 222–223
    lamb brochettes, 270
    lamb sausage, 290
    lamb tagine with lemon
        and olives, 277
    -style roast chicken
        stuffed with
        couscous, 209
mousse, duck liver, 26
mousse, honey, 337
mozzarella, marinated fresh,
    19
mozzarella-stuffed ravioli
    with tomato sauce,
    119
mushroom(s):
    Gruyère, and prosciutto
        salad, 62
    and hazelnut soup, 89
    porcini, sautéed chicken
        breasts with, 220
    sauce, grilled veal chops
        with wild, 238
    with sherry vinaigrette, 49
    soup with vermouth and
        tomato, Italian, 88
mussels, gratin of onions,
    potatoes and, 187
mustard:
    cream, grilled lamb chops
        with port and, 265
    herb sauce, veal chops
        with, 240
    and mint sauce, 263
    sauce, sautéed liver with,
        259

nut sponge cake, 330–331

onion:
    and almond soup,
        Catalan, 93
    confit, 174–175
    marmalade, 295

orange:
    and black pepper aioli,
        grilled salmon with,
        171
    ice cream, chocolate,
        cinnamon and, 351
    layered spongecake filled
        with ricotta,
        chocolate and, 328
    muscat sabayon, 340
    roast duck with red wine
        sage sauce and, 230
    salad, scallop, lemon and,
        79
    zest, sautéed calves liver
        with onions,
        pistachios and,
        258
oregano garlic vinaigrette,
    67
ossobuco alla reggiana, 235

paella, 160–161
pancakes, potato, 305
pancetta, chicken with
    tomato sauce, hot
    pepper and, 214
pancetta, sautéed liver with
    onions, hazelnuts
    and, 257
pan de jerez, 329
panzanella, 65
passato di zucca, 85
pasta, 107–109
    with artichokes, 124
    with artichokes, lemon,
        and cream, 125
    basic homemade,
        110–114
    black pepper, 113
    buckwheat, 112
    buckwheat pasta with
        greens and potatoes,
        129
    chick-pea soup with
        greens and, 100
    linguine with squid and
        clams, 141
    potato gnocchilike
        clouds, 146–147
    red (beet), 113
    red pepper, 113

rigatoni with fennel
    sausage and peppers,
    133
rigatoni with little herbed
    meatballs, 134
rosemary, 113
rosemary crêpes filled
    with four cheeses,
    145
saffron, 113
with sausage and clams,
    138
with seafood and greens,
    139
Sicilian eggplant, from
    Catania, 132
sole-filled ravioli with
    tomato and clam
    sauce, 120
spinach, 114
Venetian whole-wheat
    pasta with duck
    sauce, 131
whole-wheat, 113
see also fettuccine; ravioli;
    spaghetti
pasta:
    à la barigoule, 124
    alla cataplana, 138
    fusilli alla napoletana, 130
    in zimino, 139
pastry:
    cornmeal, 319–320
    pie, 322
    see also filo
patlican boregi, 309
pato con peras, 226–227
pea and artichoke soup, 98
peach and Champagne
    sorbet, 353
pear(s):
    Catalan-style duck with
        almonds and,
        226–227
    poached, 226
    poached in black muscat
        dessert wine, 341
    salad, celery, potato,
        watercress and, 59
    salad, provolone, arugula
        and, 60
peasant's risotto, 156

pepper(s):
  with cayenne and cilantro, 53
  hot, chicken with tomato sauce, pancetta and, 214
  rigatoni with fennel sausage and, 133
  roasted, salad, fontina, arugula and, 64
  roasted red, spaghetti with scallops, pine nuts and, 140
  Spanish eggplant salad with onions and, 44
peppery Tuscan beef stew, 250
pescespada ripieno alla siciliana, 177
pesto, 22
pesto, roast chicken stuffed with ricotta and, 210
petti di pollo trifolati, 220
pie:
  Greek chicken, with a filo crust, 217
  lemon-almond, 322–323
  Moroccan filo, with pigeon or chicken and almond, 218–219
  rustic apple and walnut, 324
pigeon or chicken and almonds, Moroccan filo pie with, 218–219
pine nuts, spaghetti with scallops, roasted red peppers and, 140
pine nut tile cookies, 356
piri-piri butter (hot sauce), 204
pistachios, sautéed calves liver with onions, orange zest and, 258
pita bread salad, Lebanese toasted, 66
pizzaiola sauce, 143
pizzoccheri, 129
plum tart, 321

poached pears, 226
  in black muscat dessert wine, 341
poaching liquid, 320
polenta, 162
pollo:
  con carciofi, 215
  alla potentina, 214
  con pumate, 216
  al pumate e mirto, 206
polpette con pecorino, 287
polpettine di pesce all'ebrea, 185
pomegranate, pork brochettes with honey and, 285
pork:
  brochettes with pomegranate and honey, 285
  Calabrese, and lamb sausage, 293
  fennel sausage, 294
  garlic sausage, 292
  loin marinated in red wine, 281
  loin with almonds, garlic, and parsley, 280
  loin with mustard sauce, roast, 279
  Portuguese-style scaloppine with roasted peppers, 286
  Portuguese-style spicy sausage, 295
  ragu, ricotta-filled ravioli with, 117
  sausage, Greek, 296
  sausage, Umbrian, 291
  scaloppine alla zaragozana, 284
  Sicilian meatballs, 287
  spicy Spanish sausage, 297
pork chop(s):
  grilled, in a red wine and spice marinade, 282
  grilled, on a bed of cinnamon onions, Venetian-style, 283
port, shallot, and tarragon sauce, 268

port ice cream, 350
Portuguese:
  bread and garlic, 97
  carrot soup with egg and lemon, 92
  chicken soup with rice, 91
  crab cakes with mint and cilantro, 182
  lamb ragout, 273
  soup with potato, sausage, and greens, 99
  steaks with onion and tomato, 248
  steamed clams with sausage, 194
  -style bread pudding, 336–337
  -style pork scaloppine with roasted peppers, 286
  -style salmon with curry and cream, 172
  -style spicy sausage, 295
  -style stuffed lamb chops, 264
potato(es):
  buckwheat pasta with greens and, 129
  croquettes, 306
  -filled filo pastries, spiced, 29
  gnocchilike clouds, 146–147
  gratin, 304
  pancakes, 305
  ravioli filled with ricotta and, 115
  roasted, 302
  salad, pear, celery, watercress and, 59
  strudel, 303
potato soup:
  of many disguises, 86
  Portuguese, with sausage and greens, 99
  spring garlic and, 87
preserved lemons, 174, 277
prosciutto, black bean salad with eggs and, 52

prosciutto, mushrooms, and Gruyère salad, 62

provolone, pear, and arugula salad, 60

prune and Armagnac ice cream, 347

prunes, duck with port, pearl onions and, 229

puddighinos a pienu, 208

pudding:
bread, Portuguese-style, 336–337
Florentine pumpkin-shaped, 330–331
steamed apricot, 335
tart, Venetian rice, 326

pugliese lamb ragout with tomatoes, greens, and cheese, 275

puree, Middle Eastern eggplant, with tahini, 42

qodban, 270

quail, grilled, stuffed with figs, Catalan-style, 221

quail, grilled, stuffed with honeyed onions, 231

radicchio, grilled, 307

radish, black, carrot and fennel salad with pecorino cheese, 63

ragout:
beef, *à la* Trieste, 249
lamb, with *gremolata,* 276
Middle Eastern lamb, with a filo crust, 274–275
Middle Eastern lamb, with apricots, 278
pork, with ricotta-filled ravioli, 117
Portuguese lamb, 273
pugliese lamb, with tomatoes, greens, and cheese, 275
shellfish, from Trieste, 188

Sicilian meatball, with artichokes and peas, 288

Spanish fish, 192

white bean, 150

white bean, grilled lamb chops with lemon-thyme butter and, 262

raisins, cucumber salad with yogurt, mint and, 46

rape con grelos y almejas, 192

ratatouille, grilled vegetable, 308

ravioli:
buckwheat, filled with greens, ricotta, and cumin, 114
eggplant-filled, 122
filled with potato and ricotta, 115
mozzarella-stuffed, with tomato sauce, 119
ricotta-filled, with pork ragu, 117
Sardinian, 118
sole-filled, with tomato and clam sauce, 120
spinach, filled with salmon, 121
three beet, from the Veneto, 116
see also pasta

ravioli:
caprese, 119
di melanzane, 122
alla potentina, 117
verdi al salmone, 121

ravioli, making of, 112

red (beet) pasta, 113

red pepper:
aioli, 183
pasta, 113
soup, 83
vinaigrette, cauliflower with, 49

rice:
with chicken soup, Portuguese, 91
croquettes, 152
croquettes, mixed fry of lamb chops,

vegetables and, 266–267
croquettes, Roman, 27
Middle Eastern or Persian-style, 153
pudding tart, Venetian, 326
salad with grilled tuna, 75
Square One, 152
see also risotto

ricotta:
buckwheat ravioli filled with greens, cumin and, 114
chocolate, and orange, layered spongecake filled with, 328
-filled ravioli with pork ragu, 117
-goat cheese filling for ravioli, 123
-Gorgonzola filling for ravioli, 123
ravioli filled with potato and, 115
roast chicken stuffed with pesto and, 210

rigatoni alla Norma, 132

rigatoni with fennel sausage and peppers, 133

rigatoni with little herbed meatballs, 134

risotto, 154–155
peasant's, 156
seafood, with spinach and peas, 157
seafood, with tomatoes and *gremolata,* 158
see also rice

risotto:
alla paesana, 156
alla primavera, 159

roast(ed):
chicken stuffed with ricotta and pesto, 210
duck in the manner of suckling pig, 228
duck with honey, lavender, and thyme, 224

duck with red wine, orange, and sage sauce, 230
eggplant soup, 84
leg of lamb with a Moroccan "mechoui" marinade, 271
pork loin with almonds, garlic, and parsley, 280
pork loin with mustard sauce, 279
potatoes, 302
rolle di vitello, 236
Roman rice croquettes, 27
Roman-style veal brochettes, 242
romescu, 193
rosemary crêpes filled with four cheeses, 145
rosemary pasta, 113
rustic apple and walnut pie, 324

sabayon, orange muscat, 340
saffron and walnut *aioli*, 197
saffron pasta, 113
sage-lemon butter, 242
sage sauce, roast duck with red wine, orange and, 230
salad:
　black bean, with eggs and prosciutto, 52
　carrot, with mint, 53
　cucumber, with yogurt, mint, and raisins, 46
　French, 51
　Italian, 51
　lentil, 50
　Middle Eastern, 51
　Moroccan carrot, 45
　Moroccan eggplant, 43
　Spanish eggplant, with onions and peppers, 44
　white bean, 50
　zucchini, with walnuts and dill, 46

salad, Mediterranean, 55–58
　black radish, carrot, and fennel, with pecorino cheese, 63
　cauliflower, celery, cucumber, spinach, and curly endive, 72
　endive, apple, and walnut, 61
　Greek, 67
　grilled leeks with walnut cream vinaigrette, 69
　Israeli avocado, 68
　Italian bread, 65
　Lebanese toasted pita bread, 66
　mushroom, Gruyère, and prosciutto, 62
　pear, celery, potato, and watercress, 59
　pear, provolone, and arugula, 60
　roasted pepper, fontina, and arugula, 64
salad, Portuguese:
　black bean, with eggs and prosciutto, 52
　carrot, with mint, 53
　peppers with Cayenne and cilantro, 53
salad, seafood:
　grilled tuna, with a Moroccan salsa, 78
　grilled tuna with *charmoula* vinaigrette, 76–77
　Italian, 74
　rice, with grilled tuna, 75
　scallop, orange, and lemon, 79
salad dressing, *see* vinaigrette
salmon:
　baked, with capers and toasted bread crumbs, 170
　croquettes, Jewish style, 185
　with curry and cream, Portuguese-style, 172

grilled, with orange and black pepper *aioli*, 171
　with red onions and red wine, 173
　spinach ravioli filled with, 121
　wrapped in grape leaves, 169
salmone al giuliese, 170
salmonete grelhado com maionese setubalense, 171
salsa rossa, 252
salsa verde, 252, 253
Sambuca and espresso chip ice cream, 350
sandwiches, Turkish deep-fried eggplant, 309
sangria sorbet, 353
Sardinian:
　ravioli, 118
　-style grilled chicken, 206
　-style roast chicken with stuffing, 208
　vegetable sauté, 314
sauce(s):
　aioli, 193, 252
　béchamel, 311
　for Catalan-style duck with pears and almonds, 227
　horseradish cream, 35, 252
　for leg of lamb *avgolemono* with asparagus, 269
　mint and mustard, 263
　Moroccan *charmoula*, 175
　for Moroccan fried squab with saffron and ginger, 222–223
　orange and black pepper *aioli*, 171
　pesto, 22
　piri-piri butter, 204
　pizzaiola, 143
　port, shallot, and tarragon, 268
　red pepper *aioli*, 183

sauce(s) (cont'd)
  red wine, orange, and
    sage sauce, for roast
    duck, 230
  romescu, 193
  saffron and walnut *aioli,*
    197
  salsa rossa, 252
  salsa verde, 252, 253
  Sephardic *zemino,* 178
  sherry cream, 280
  for spinach ravioli filled
    with salmon, 121
  Square One hot mustard,
    240, 252
  tarator, 196
  tomato, 118
  triestina, 189
  see also butter; dessert
    toppings and sauces;
    vinaigrette
sausage, 289
  braised beef, chicken,
    and vegetables with
    five sauces, 252–253
  fennel, 294
  fennel, rigatoni with
    peppers and, 133
  garlic, 292
  Greek pork, 296
  lamb, Calabrese pork
    and, 293
  Moroccan lamb, 290
  pasta with clams and, 138
  Portuguese soup with
    potato, greens and,
    99
  with Portuguese steamed
    clams, 194
  Portuguese-style spicy,
    295
  spicy Spanish, 297
  Umbrian pork, 291
sautéed:
  baby veal chops with
    herbed bread
    crumbs, 241
  calves liver with onions,
    orange zest, and
    pistachios, 258
  cherry tomatoes with
    fresh herbs, 306

chicken breasts with
    porcini mushrooms,
    220
chicken with Moroccan
    hot and sweet
    tomato sauce, 213
liver with mustard sauce,
    259
liver with onions,
    pancetta, and
    hazelnuts, 257
veal with roasted red
    peppers, 243
scallop, orange, and lemon
    salad, 79
scallops, spaghetti with
    roasted red peppers,
    pine nuts and, 140
scaloppine:
  pork, alla zaragozana,
    284
  Portuguese-style pork,
    with roasted red
    peppers, 286
  veal, with eggplant and
    tomatoes, 244
*scaloppine di vitello con
    peperoncini,* 243
scapece, 74
sea bass, gratin of crabmeat
    and, 186
seafood:
  pasta with greens and,
    139
  risotto with spinach and
    peas, 157
  risotto with tomatoes and
    gremolata, 158
  salads, *see* salad, seafood
sesame vinaigrette, beets
    with, 45
shallot and ginger butter,
    trout with, 168
shellfish stock, 105
sherry:
  cream sauce, 280
  torte, chocolate, 329
  vinaigrette, mushrooms
    with, 49
shish kabob, 272
shrimp, fettuccine with
    garlic and, 142

shrimp or crabmeat, filo
    pastries with, 32
Sicilian:
  braised rolled steak, 251
  eggplant pasta from
    Catania, 132
  meatball ragout with
    artichokes and peas,
    288
  meatballs, 287
  -style stuffed swordfish,
    177
sole-filled ravioli with
    tomato and clam
    sauce, 120
sopa de cenouras, 92
sopa dourada, 336–337
sorbet:
  blackberry, 354
  cantaloupe, 354
  peach and Champagne,
    353
  sangria, 353
sorbetto bellini, 353
soup(s), 81–82
  artichoke and pea, 98
  broccoli, with white
    beans, 101
  butternut squash, 85
  Catalan onion and
    almond, 93
  celery root and fennel, 96
  chick-pea, with greens
    and pasta, 100
  cold Spanish tomato
    soup, 94
  fish *fumet,* 105
  Italian mushroom, with
    vermouth and
    tomato, 88
  mushroom and hazelnut,
    89
  Portuguese, with potato,
    sausage, and greens,
    99
  Portuguese bread and
    garlic soup with egg,
    97
  Portuguese carrot, with
    egg and lemon, 92
  Portuguese chicken, with
    rice, 91

potato, of many disguises, 86
red pepper, 83
roasted eggplant, 84
shellfish *acorda*, 102
spinach, 90
spring garlic and potato, 87
tomato, 95
see also stock
souvlaki, 272
spaghetti:
  with grilled tuna, 135
  with scallops, roasted red peppers, and pine nuts, 140
  with tuna, lemon, and olives, 137
  with tuna and dried tomatoes, 136
  see also pasta
spaghetti alla puttanesca, 144
Spanish eggplant salad with onions and peppers, 44
Spanish fish ragout, 192
spezzatino d'agnello con gremolata, 276
spiced beef filet, 35
spiced potato-filled filo pastries, 29
spiced red wine butter, 176
spicy Spanish sausage, 297
spiedini di vitello alla campagna, 242
spinach:
  cauliflower, celery, cucumber, and curly endive salad, 72
  pasta, 114
  ravioli filled with salmon, 121
  soup, 90
spring garlic and potato soup, 87
spuma di tonno, 28
Square One hot mustard, 240, 252
Square One rice, 152
squash soup, butternut, 85

squid, linguine with clams and, 141
steak, *see* beef
steamed apricot pudding, 335
stew, peppery Tuscan beef, 250
stock(s), 103
  beef, 104
  chicken, 103
  duck, 225
  fish *fumet*, 105
  lamb, 268
  shellfish, 105
  veal, 237
stracotto di manzo "peposo," 250
strascinate, 128
strawberry, cream, and chocolate filling, 330–331
strudel, potato, 303
stuffed baked apples, 342
stuffing, chicken, 207, 209, 210
sun-dried tomatoes, chicken with, 216
sun-dried tomatoes, grilled swordfish or tuna with, 179
suppli al telèfono, 27
Swiss chard *tagine*, 315
swordfish:
  grilled, Lisbon style, 178
  Sicilian-style stuffed, 177
  or tuna, grilled, with sun-dried tomatoes, 179
  à la turque, 176

tahini, Middle Eastern eggplant puree with, 42
tahini dressing, 255
talas borek, 274–275
tapenade and *tapenade* butter, 28
tarator sauce, 196
tarts, *see* desserts
tavuk izgara, 205
teglia di branzino e granchio, 186

three beet raviolis from the Veneto, 116
thyme-lemon butter, 262
tiella di cozze, 187
tiropetes, 30
toasted bread crumbs, 73
toasted cumin vinaigrette, 68
toasted pita bread salad, Lebanese, 66
tomato(es):
  Catalan baked eggplant with honey and, 312
  cherry, sautéed with fresh herbs, 306
  gratin, eggplant, zucchini and, 310
  Italian mushroom soup with vermouth and, 88
  seafood risotto with *gremolata* and, 158
  sun-dried, chicken with, 216
  sun-dried, grilled swordfish or tuna with, 179
tomato sauce, 118
  chicken with hot pepper, pancetta, and 214
  Moroccan hot and sweet, sautéed chicken with, 213
  mozzarella-stuffed ravioli with, 119
  sole-filled ravioli with clam and, 120
  spicy, grilled steak with, 247
tomato soup, 95
  cold Spanish, 94
tomato vinaigrette:
  with artichokes, 48
  goat cheese in spicy, 21
  sweet and sour, 48
tomini elettrici in salsa rossa, 21
tomino al pesto, 22
tonno all griglia con pepe ammaccato, 180
tonno in gradela, 181

torta di granturco e frutta,
319–320
torta turchesca, 326
triestina, la, 188
triestina sauce, 189
trota allo zenzero, 168
*trote ripiene grigliate
all'Iseana,* 167
trout, grilled stuffed, from
Lake Iseo, 167
trout with ginger and
shallot butter, 168
tuna:
marinated sautéed, in a
fennel and bread
crumb crust, 181
pâté, fresh, 28
with spaghetti and dried
tomatoes, 136
or swordfish, grilled, with
sun-dried tomatoes,
179
see also grilled tuna
Turkish:
artichokes, 47
coffee ice cream, 349
deep-fried eggplant
sandwiches, 309
-style grilled chicken with
yogurt and cumin,
205
turteln, 114

Umbrian pork sausage, 291

veal:
braised stuffed leg of,
236
brochettes, Roman-style,
242
sautéed, with roasted red
peppers, 243
scaloppine with eggplant
and tomatoes, 244
shanks, braised, 235
stock, 237
veal chops:
grilled, with wild
mushroom sauce,
238
grilled stuffed loin, 239

with a mustard herb
sauce, 240
sautéed baby, with
herbed bread
crumbs, 241
vegetable dolmas, 34
vegetable sautée, Sardinian
314
Venetian:
rice pudding tart, 326
-style grilled pork chops
on a bed of
cinnamon onions,
283
whole-wheat pasta with
duck sauce, 131
vinaigrette:
anchovy garlic, 64
anise, beets with, 45
balsamic, 62
basic, 65
black pepper, 79
Champagne, 60
charmoula, 76–77
citrus, 63
garlic, 65
gazpacho, for avocado,
70–71
Gorgonzola cream, 59
hazelnut, 61
hot pepper, 75
lemon cream, 62
mint, 53
oregano garlic, 67
pesto, goat cheese in, 22
red pepper, cauliflower
with, 49
sesame, beets with, 45
sherry, mushrooms with,
49
spicy tomato, goat cheese
in, 21
toasted cumin, 68
tomato, 48
walnut, 61
walnut cream, 69

walnut(s):
and apple pie, rustic, 324
clouds, 356
cream vinaigrette, 69

cream vinaigrette, grilled
leeks with, 69
and date *dacquoise,*
Craig's, 334–335
endive and apple salad,
61
-honey tart, 325
ice cream, 346
and saffron *aioli,* 197
vinaigrette, 61
watercress, pear, celery,
and potato salad,
59
zucchini salad with dill
and, 46
white bean:
with broccoli soup, 101
puree, grilled bread with
wilted greens and,
24
ragout, 150
ragout, grilled lamb
chops with
lemon-thyme butter
and, 262
salad, 50
whole-wheat pasta, 113
with duck sauce,
Venetian, 131
wine recommendations,
359–395

yogurt, cucumber salad with
mint, raisins and, 46
yogurt, Turkish-style grilled
chicken with cumin
and, 205

*zabaglione di moscato de fior
d'arancio,* 340
zembi d'arzillo, 120
zucchini, eggplant, and
tomato gratin, 310
zucchini salad with walnuts
and dill, 46
zuccotto, 330–331
zuppa di broccoli e fagioli,
101
zuppa di ceci e verdure, 100
*zuppa di sedano rape e
finocchio,* 96